Reassessing 1970s Britain

Manchester University Press

Reassessing 1970s Britain

Edited by Lawrence Black,
Hugh Pemberton and Pat Thane

Manchester University Press

Published by Manchester University Press
Altrincham Street, Manchester M1 7JA, UK
www.manchesteruniversitypress.co.uk

British Library Cataloguing-in-Publication Data is available

Library of Congress Cataloging-in-Publication Data is available

ISBN 978 0 7190 9979 3 *paperback*

First published by Manchester University Press in hardback 2013

This edition first published 2016

The publisher has no responsibility for the persistence or accuracy of URLs for any external or third-party internet websites referred to in this book, and does not guarantee that any content on such websites is, or will remain, accurate or appropriate.

Printed by Lightning Source

Contents

Figures and tables

Figures

Tables

Contributors

James E. Alt is Frank G. Thomson Professor of Government at Harvard University, where he was founding Director of the Center for Basic Research in the Social Sciences (now the Institute for Quantitative Social Science). He was a Guggenheim Fellow and is a member of the American Academy of Arts and Sciences. He is the author, co-author or editor of several books and numerous articles in the field of comparative political economy, most recently emphasising fiscal policy and political institutions.

Lawrence Black, alone among the contributors to this book, was born in the 1970s. He is Professor of Modern British History at the University of York. His latest book is *Redefining British Politics: Culture, Consumerism and Participation, 1954–70* (Palgrave Macmillan, 2010) and he is now working on a study of shopping in the USA and UK since 1899.

Dean Blackburn is a PhD student in the Department of Historical Studies at the University of Bristol. He is currently completing a doctoral thesis entitled 'Penguin Specials and the centre-left, 1937–86' and has recently published in *Parliamentary Affairs*.

Sir Samuel Brittan is a columnist at the *Financial Times*. He started work at the paper as a journalist and returned to it after working first at the *Observer* (1961–64) and then as adviser to the government at the

Department of Economic Affairs (1965). In addition to his journalism, he is the author of a number of influential books and journal articles on political economy. He has held a number of honorary posts in universities, both British and American. The recipient of several prizes for his journalism, he became a *Chevalier de la Légion d'Honneur* in 1993.

Stuart Holland was adviser on European affairs to Harold Wilson in the 1960s, special adviser to the Minister of Overseas Development 1974–75, and in the 1970s and 1980s served on several Labour Party sub-committees as well as on its National Executive Committee. The author of a number of influential books and papers on economic policy, his ideas became the basis of the Labour Party's industrial strategy in the 1970s and early 1980s. In the 1980s, he was Labour Member of Parliament for Vauxhall and a shadow minister. He has published widely and is Professor of Economics at the University of Coimbra, Portugal.

Peter Mayer is President and Publisher of the Overlook Press in New York and Managing Director of Gerald Duckworth Publishers, Ltd, in London. In 1978, at which time he was President of Pocket Books, Simon & Schuster, in New York, he was appointed Chief Executive Officer of Penguin Books International by its owner, Pearson Ltd. He ran Penguin from London and New York until 1996.

Roger Middleton is Professor of the History of Political Economy and Head of the School of Humanities at the University of Bristol. An economic historian, he has written in the areas of modern British economic history and the history of economics and economic policy. His most recent book is *Inside the Department of Economic Affairs: Samuel Brittan, the Diary of an 'Irregular', 1964–6* (Oxford University Press, 2012). He is currently working as general editor of the British Historical Statistics Project to produce a new print and online edition of B. R. Mitchell's *British Historical Statistics* (Cambridge University Press, 1988).

Bill Osgerby is Professor of Media, Culture and Communications at London Metropolitan University. He has published widely in the areas of twentieth-century British and American cultural history. His books include *Youth in Britain Since 1945* (Blackwell, 1998), *Playboys in Paradise: Youth, Masculinity and Leisure-Style in Modern America* (Berg/New York University Press, 2001), *Youth Media* (Routledge, 2004) and a co-edited anthology, *Action TV: Tough-Guys, Smooth Operators and Foxy Chicks* (Routledge, 2001).

Hugh Pemberton is Senior Lecturer in Modern History at the University of Bristol. He is the author of *Policy Learning and British Governance* *in the 1960s* (Palgrave Macmillan, 2004) and of other publications on postwar British economic and social policy. He is currently working on a new book on the history of the 1974–79 Labour governments.

Lynne Segal is Anniversary Professor of Psychology and Gender Studies in the Department of Psychosocial Studies at Birkbeck College, University of London. Her books include: *Is the Future Female? Troubled Thoughts on Contemporary Feminism* (Peter Bedrick Books, 1988); *Slow Motion: Changing Masculinities, Changing Men* (Rutgers University Press, 1990); *Straight Sex: The Politics of Pleasure* (University of California Press, 1994); *Why Feminism? Gender, Psychology and Politics* (Polity Press, 1999); and *Making Trouble: Life and Politics* (Serpent's Tail, 2007). She is currently writing a book on ageing.

Pat Thane is Research Professor in Contemporary History, King's College London, and Fellow of the British Academy. Her publications include: *The Foundations of the Welfare State* (Longman, 1982, 2nd edition 1996); *Old Age in England: Past Experiences, Present Issues* (Oxford University Press, 2000); *Women and Ageing in British Society Since 1500*, co-edited with Lynn Botelho (Longman, 2001); *The Long History of Old Age* (ed.) (Thames & Hudson, Getty Museum, Los Angeles, 2005); *Britain's Pensions Crisis: History and Policy*, co-edited with Hugh Pemberton and Noel Whiteside (British Academy/Oxford University Press, 2006); *Unequal Britain. Equalities in Britain Since 1945* (ed.) (Continuum, 2010); *Women and Citizenship in Britain and Ireland in the Twentieth Century: What Difference Did the Vote Make?* co-edited with Esther Breitenbach (Continuum, 2010); and *Happy Families? History and Family Policy* (British Academy, 2010). She is a convenor of History and Policy (www.historyandpolicy.org).

Jim Tomlinson is Bonar Professor of Modern History at the University of Dundee, and has published widely on the historical political economy of modern Britain, including *The Politics of Decline: Understanding Post-war Britain* (Longman, 2000). His most recent publications are *The Decline of Jute: Managing Industrial Change* (Pickering & Chatto, 2011) (with Carlo Morelli and Valerie Wright) and *Jute No More: Transforming Dundee* (Dundee University Press, 2011) (co-edited with Chris Whatley).

Mark Wickham-Jones is Professor of Political Science at the University of Bristol. He has written extensively about Stuart Holland and about Labour's economic strategy more generally during the 1970s and 1980s. More recently, he has published widely on the history and on the current politics of the British Labour Party.

Acknowledgements

The editors thank the British Academy for hosting the symposium from which this volume sprang, all the contributors for their hard work and patience, and a Manchester University Press anonymous reader for particularly useful comments and suggestions. We also thank others who contributed to our thinking, and to that of our contributors, particularly in discussions at the British Academy and Centre for Contemporary British History, University of London.

Abbreviations

A&HCI	Arts & Humanities Citation Index
BNOC	British National Oil Corporation
CCCS	Centre for Contemporary Cultural Studies
ECD	'The economic contradictions of democracy' (Samuel Brittan)
ECDR	'The economic contradictions of democracy revisited' (Samuel Brittan)
EEC	European Economic Community
ENI	Ente Nazionale Idrocarburi (the Italian state hydrocarbons corporation)
GDP	gross domestic product
GLC	Greater London Council
HBBS	'How British is the British sickness?' (Samuel Brittan)
IEA	Institute of Economic Affairs
IMF	International Monetary Fund
IRI	Instituto per la Ricostruzione Industriale (the Italian Industrial Reconstruction Institute)
LPA	Labour Party Archive
NDC	National Deviancy Conference
NEB	National Enterprise Board
NEC	National Executive Committee (Labour Party)
NWAF	National Women's Aid Federation
OECD	Organisation for Economic Co-operation and Development
OPEC	Organization of the Petroleum Exporting Countries

OPEC1	The first OPEC oil price increase, 1973
OWAAD	Organisation of Women of Asian and African Descent
PA	Penguin Archive
PED	*The Politics of Economic Decline* (James Alt)
PLP	Parliamentary Labour Party
PoP	Publish or Perish
SDP	Social Democratic Party
SSCI	Social Science Citation Index
WLM	Women's Liberation Movement
WoS	Web of Science

1

Introduction. The benighted decade? Reassessing the 1970s

Lawrence Black and Hugh Pemberton

In 2008, when we first conceived the project out of which this book has sprung, we did so because we were surprised at the lack of attention being paid to the 1970s by contemporary historians. We felt strongly that a better understanding of the 1970s, a decade in British history which we felt was widely misrepresented and bedevilled by characterisations that were both lazy and (often subconsciously) highly politicised, was essential to understanding the trajectory of British political, economic, social and cultural change since the end of the Second World War. Since then, the decade has been much in the imagination. With the collapse of Lehman Brothers on 15 September 2008, Britain (and the rest of the world) entered a new phase in which we have had to grapple with the fall-out from the worst financial crisis since 1929. In Britain's case, a deep recession and anaemic recovery, a weak pound, rapidly increasing public borrowing and rising unemployment have both invoked and reinforced memories of the seventies. Three years on from Lehman Brothers' demise, for example, at the time we were finalising this book, the British media were replete with references to the likelihood of a new 'winter of discontent' that could equal or exceed in scope that of 1978–79. As described in the media, the situation was uncannily reminiscent of that earlier dispute, with public sector workers, experiencing continued reductions in real wages and benefits, being called out on strike by their unions in what was billed as likely to be the most wide-scale stoppage since the general strike of 1926.[1] In other words, a situation of crisis akin to the 1970s, a crisis in which the state is seen as at once over-mighty and ineffectual, is apparently back, and with a vengeance.

One problem is that the historical parallels made with the 1970s are often far from exact. We can see evidence of this in the small example just cited: in 1979, there were 13 million trade union members (55.4 per cent of all British workers), but since then membership has more than halved, to 6.5 million (26.6 per cent of the workforce).[2] During the winter of 1978–79 the unions were in dispute with a Labour government, not a coalition of the Conservatives and the Liberals; and their objection then was to a government incomes policy embodying controls over the incomes of every worker in the land, a policy intended to reduce inflation, rather than an attempt by government to reduce public borrowing and the size and power of the state by, *inter alia*, cutting the public sector wage bill. But the problem is bigger than this, for, we would argue, a very particular vision of the 1970s is to be found in current coverage. In turn, this misrepresentation of the events of the 1970s makes it more difficult for us to understand those events, and thus is a barrier to understanding the broader sweep of postwar British history, not to mention the true relevance of the 1970s to the present.

In this introductory chapter we proceed as follows. First, we discuss in more detail the contemporary vision of the 1970s as a dismal and benighted decade in contemporary British history. We then suggest that there are alternative readings of these years, as ones of severe, even existential, 'crisis', before considering the argument that in our present received wisdom about the 1970s there may be a species of 'false memory syndrome' at work. In doing so, we do not argue that the decade was one of sweetness and light. We do, however, suggest that we need to be aware that in the 1970s media and political characterisations of 'crisis' may have embodied an element of 'moral panic' (though a better term might perhaps be 'social panic'); that where crises existed they may be more complex than acknowledged in public discourse both then and now; and that the characterisation of the decade as one in which Britain experienced a convulsive crisis (economic, political, social and cultural) as the failures of the postwar settlement were laid bare and out of which a new order emerged itself potentially embodies an important (but often unacknowledged) set of politicised assumptions. Having outlined this argument we go on to examine the assertion that the decade of the 1970s marked an intellectual crisis in political economy that broke open the policy process and created a much broader 'marketplace for ideas' in Britain, and we suggest that this conceptualisation of the decade can also profitably be used in a more general reconceptualisation of Britain in the 1970s.

Ultimately, therefore, our focus is on ideas: on aspects of the vigorous intellectual ferment that characterised the decade (though we recognise

the danger of simplistic decadal periodisation). Whether the 1970s constituted a 'real' crisis is less our concern than recognising and examining
the widespread perception of crisis at the time, and its effects. In subsequent chapters, we pair the progenitors of some of these ideas with a
contemporary historian, with each returning to the idea(s) in question
and reassessing them with the benefit of hindsight. (The only exception
to this pattern is that, unfortunately, as a result of ill-health, Stanley
Cohen was unable to complete his chapter revisiting the 'moral panic'
concept). We do not pretend that our survey of ideas is anywhere near
complete. Nor are we the first historians to revisit the ideas that were
so important in the 1970s – there has, for example, been much recent
attention to the rise of the New Right.[3] We would, however, argue that
in its pairing of primary and secondary reappraisals of some of the key
ideas of the seventies it represents a novel contribution to a much-needed
reassessment of this most significant decade in postwar British history.

We recognise, of course, that 'decaditis' is an abiding irritant for many
readers.[4] Joe Moran, for example, has complained about a narrative
'tendency to package decades as entities', a process which he protested
has 'very little to do with history'.[5] We naturally agree that events rarely
coalesce into neat decadal slices. However, notwithstanding the arbitrari-
ness of such 'decadology', there is equally no doubt that 'the 1970s' has
become adjectival and popular shorthand for certain political, economic
and cultural characteristics as much as for the chronological period
1970–79. This book is interested in exploring what the 1970s means
as an adjective, not just as a period of time. Thus, for example, we fully
accept that the events of the 1970s had both long-term roots and long-
term effects, and these facts inevitably inform the analysis. We are also
happy to accept that subdivision of the decade will often be appropriate and some of the ensuing chapters reflect this. In some instances,
of course, the decadal periodisation does actually have some purchase:
the fact that it is bracketed at one end by a general election in which
the Heath government entered office with (ultimately disappointed)
ambitions to implement some quite significant breaks with the postwar
settlement and ends with a general election that ushered in the ten-year
Thatcher premiership gives it a certain political logic at least.

The benighted decade

The contemporary memory of Britain in the 1970s is of a dismal, benighted decade. Certainly, they were not easy years. In 1973, to many
Britons, the country's entry into the 'common market' of the European
Economic Community seemed emblematic of its declining importance
in the world. During the winter of 1973–74, to deal with the twin

pressures of the oil price rise implemented by the Organization of the Petroleum Exporting Countries (OPEC) and a miners' strike, energy was rationed via power cuts, shop windows fell dark by government order, candles (which had been removed from the Retail Price Index in 1956 and thus apparently consigned to history) sold out and the working week was curtailed to three days, to save power. In 1975, inflation hit 26.9 per cent, a level not seen since the Napoleonic Wars. Unemployment doubled between 1975 and 1977 – reaching a level five times higher than in the 1950s, and one not seen since the 1930s. In 1976, with public spending apparently out of control, the government was forced to go 'cap in hand' (one of numerous declinist colloquialisms that became rife in the 1970s) to the International Monetary Fund (IMF) to secure a $3.9 billion loan (then the largest loan ever made by that institution). The decade saw racial conflict and the Irish 'troubles' entrenched themselves in domestic politics as republican terrorism came to the mainland with devastating explosions and assassinations across the country. There were as many elections and more strikes in the 1970s as in the troubled decade after the First World War. Strikes seemed endemic and talk of industrial decay, work-to-rules, go-slows, demarcation, flying and secondary pickets became common parlance in a decade that was the heyday of the industrial correspondent (a species now virtually extinct).[6] So too, in assorted moral panics, did muggers, scroungers, streakers, strikers, punks and hooligans.

In short, Britain seemed to be becoming, if not already to have become, ungovernable – another keyword associated with the decade and the subject of a considerable political science literature – with an apparent hollowing out of governmental capability and public authority.[7] With nationalism advancing, not just in Northern Ireland, but in Scotland and Wales, the very future of the United Kingdom could be called into doubt.[8] All this easily elided into apocalyptic talk of crisis. In 1973, as the three-day week approached, the *Daily Mirror* was reduced to wondering, 'Is everybody going mad?'[9] By early 1979, even before the public sector strikes of that winter had begun, the *Sun* was warning that '3 MILLION FACE THE DOLE QUEUE' (somewhat ironically in the light of developments in the early 1980s) and the *Daily Express* was asking 'Is ANYONE running Britain?'[10]

It was not just in the newspapers that a whiff of crisis was in the air. The titles of influential contemporary studies flavoured the times: *Is Britain Dying?, Britain Against Itself* (two American studies), *The Break-Up of Britain, Policing the Crisis,* even *Derelict Britain.*[11] This was the decade when popular experience seemed to match the long-standing declinist opinion of experts and elites that Britain was 'on the slide' and the purpose of government should be to manage its decline to best effect. In his compelling popular history of the decade, broadcaster and MP

Philip Whitehead noted that 'pessimism was the pattern' in 'a decade of gloom and fitful despair'.[12] Another early spot judgement, by journalist Christopher Booker, noted how the 'bankruptcy ... of culture' in the 1970s 'intruded more inescapably and prominently than ever before'.[13] Some of the prized assumptions and lifestyles of postwar affluent Britain seemed at peril in the 1970s: petrol shortages hit at the car; bread short-ages recalled wartime rationing; televisions went dark as TV closed down early (at 10.30 p.m.) to encourage people to go to bed and save energy, or because of power cuts or technicians' strikes.[14] To ordinary Britons, decline seemed now to be all too apparent and experienced at home, not in some distant dusty desert.

Culturally, the seventies seemed to pale by comparison with the decade's immediate successor and with its predecessor – epitomised by 1971's highest-grossing (verb used advisedly) film in the UK being not the exotic Bond thriller *Diamonds Are Forever* but, in the pointedly parochial sub-*Carry On* genre, *On the Buses*. Its legacy, for one of the creators of the *League of Gentleman*, was a memory of 'watching Reg Varney chuck a fag end into a piss-drenched lavatory bowl and the toilet exploding' in *Holiday on the Buses*.[15] When the Clash discharged '1977' they complained:

> In 1977 I hope I go to heaven / cos I been too long on the dole / and I can't get work at all / ... no elvis, beatles or rolling stones / ... knives in West 11 / ... sten guns in Knightsbridge / ... you're on the never-never / you think it can't go on forever / ... sod the jubilee / ... the toilet don't work / ... here come the police.

Another 1971 hit film, *The Day of the Jackal*, was thinly veiled Europhobia, but Europhiles were no less impressed by the symptoms of British decline. Margaret Drabble's novel *The Ice Age* (1977) nodded towards a more individualist (Thatcherite) future, but painted a drab picture of the binds of England's economic travails in the 1970s. More recently, Jonathan Coe's 2001 novel *The Rotters' Club*, dramatised by the BBC in 2005, offers a similarly crisis-stricken view of the decade, punctuated by nostalgic, youthful escapism. Set in Birmingham, it broaches racial and industrial discord, features the pub bombings by the Provisional Irish Republican Army (IRA) in November 1974 and manages a side-swipe at the legendary poor quality of British cars at the time – 'Why don't you buy a decent car for once? A foreign one', suggests Doug Trotter to his father (a Longbridge shop steward) as the gearbox of his Austin Maxi breaks.

Alternative readings of the decade

Key representations of the 1970s could be, and often were subsequently, readily wrapped in declinist rhetoric. But might it be that this declinist verbiage was more than wrapping? Did it actually help to define the decade through such classic 1970s motifs as punk, hooligans, strikers and incompetent politicians? It is tempting to add 'heritage' to this list, the idea of British culture mesmerised and inhibited by its decline as it wallowed in nostalgia for past glories (to be seen in the rise of Laura Ashley for example, or the persistent popularity of war comics) while yearning for a former greatness now 'gone to the dogs'. The vibrancy, variety and volume of sociology, criminology and cultural studies poured out on this terrain in the seventies were tribute to how culture had become a keyword and storm-centre of debate since the 1960s. They established that subcultures were not just fads, bad behaviour or upshots of decline, though were rather less certain about precisely what they symbolised. Stanley Cohen, reflecting on the moral panics about youth culture during the 1970s and the procedures of semiotic-structuralist analysis lavished on them, wondered whether they were quite the 'rituals of resistance' alleged.[16] What we contend is not only that too much interpretive weight is placed on quite a partial range of evidence, but also that its weighting is too lopsided, too laden with value judgements. Instead, we suggest that the actions of those who were often seen as troublemakers of the 1970s can be read in different ways – in a wider context, and their actions as creative, democratic, demotic acts. As with a revisionist shift from 'decline' to 'declinism' as the prism through which to view the country's political economy, we suggest that negative accounts of the 1970s contain snippets and kernels of a different story.

Beginning with punks, the ur-text of 1970s cultural studies, Dick Hebdige's *Subculture* explained how 'punks were not only directly *responding* to increasing joblessness ... they were *dramatizing* what had come to be called "Britain's decline"' and had 'appropriated the rhetoric of crisis which filled the airwaves and editorials throughout the period and translated it into tangible (and visible) terms'.[17] Critics of punk – spitting mad in the regional and national media and considerably outnumbering fans – and the 'establishment' could not have agreed more that punk was as much an agent of 'decline' as a product of it.[18] No less than Thatcherites, the likes of Malcolm McLaren and Julie Burchill pitched themselves against consensus, liberals and hippies, but shared the latter's distaste for establishment and their lack of deference to authority. As much as punk can be read as creative, demotic or as a marker for the future, however, it is also worth recalling that in 1977 no punk band other than the Sex Pistols had a top-ten single; more generally, other musical forms like northern soul, reggae and disco merit more attention.[19] Echols' recent study, for example, locates US disco as a site for women and black performers and gay liberation, and as a legacy of sixties hedonism, besides mere escapism, and Schulman renders it, through events like 1979's 'disco demolition', as a key sociological and cultural divider.[20]

Hooliganism was rather (unreasonably) assumed to be a new invention and a peculiarly English disease. Its elimination was a cause taken up by the more authoritarian political right. Like punk, it provided a popular source of media outrage and a rich vein of sociological research. It was variously analysed in terms of declining behavioural standards, notably among young males, the roles of policing and the media, the fracturing of working-class social cohesion, alienation and suburbanisation, race, de-industrialisation, audience–player composition and relations, commercialisation, stadia, and masculine emotional culture and fashion. It was held to be fed by alienation, nationalism and anti-Europeanism – a symptom of a catastrophic breakdown in behavioural standards and means of control. But it was neither uniquely English nor specific to the seventies – indeed, the panic about hooligans discloses at least as much about the power of the media and about the framework of declinism as about hooliganism and the 1970s.[21] Sport itself remained subject to less scholarly interest, but was also a source of anxiety and the malaise of the 1970s.

When it comes to strikers, there was a certain affection for 'Wolfie' Smith (of BBC television's sit-com *Citizen Smith*, 1977–80) and the Tooting Popular Front (one episode of which was cancelled because of strike action in December 1978) – Wolfie being a sort of young left-wing variant of the right-wing loudmouth television character Alf Garnett. But 'Red Robbo', alias Derek Robinson, a shop steward of the Amalgamated Engineering Union (AEU) at Longbridge, was widely portrayed by the media as an emblem of all that was wrong with the unions. Robbo was responsible for more than 500 stoppages between 1977 and 1979 which, British Leyland management estimated, cost the plant production of 113,000 engines. Less the amiable misguided Fred Kite (of the Boulting Brothers' film *I'm Alright Jack*, 1959), Robbo was portrayed by the media as a sinister bogeyman – a role Arthur Scargill of the National Union of Mineworkers would play in the 1980s.[22] Yet, 'You won't get me I'm part of the union' was a (number 2) hit for the Strawbs in 1973.[23] The prominence of the trade unions in the seventies helped reinstate the political salience of class, hitherto blurred by affluence and permissiveness and increasingly rivalled by categories like race, and it remained epicentral in the 1980s. Trade unions were thus ripe for political and media pillorying. However, even as their public popularity fell, trade union membership grew (peaking in 1979). We should also acknowledge that more days were lost through sickness and accidents than strikes – 98 per cent of establishments had no dispute.[24] Colin Hay argues that the 1978–79 'winter of discontent' was portrayed by the media and New Right as an over-exertion of power by trade unions versus civilised society, and thereby constituted a crisis so serious as to call into question the viability of the British state. In fact, far from being a story of excessively powerful trade union barons, it is possible to argue that the real issue was an ideological and power vacuum at the heart of the union leadership (which, as George Woodcock, a former general secretary of the Trades Union Congress, acknowledged in 1972, actually had no sanctions over members and, even if it had, had no power to enforce them).[25] Yet the narrative of over-mighty 'union barons' was deployed thereafter both by the media and successively by Thatcher and Blair and, as a result, it has bled into the national psyche.[26]

Closely linked with the growing perceptions that unions were 'out of control' was the perceived failure of politicians to govern the country effectively. The Heath government's pushing through of the Industrial Relations Act 1971, seeking to reform the unions where Labour had failed in 1969 with 'In place of strife', touched off a wave of industrial action that saw days lost to strikes per annum rise to nearly 24 million in 1972 (around ten times the level of the mid-1960s). It was the political impact of the unions that was perhaps more important, however. The unions were widely perceived to have brought down governments in 1970 and particularly in 1974 and 1979, and were given little political credit for the sacrifices made by union members, particularly in the public sector, to see off hyper-inflation via the acceptance of reductions in real wages.

More generally, as much of the political science literature of the decade made clear, expectations of the capability of government had by the seventies risen to an extent that any government would have found it hard to meet them, let alone governments confronted by such severe economic challenges, both international and domestic. Recession, rising unemployment and inflation were thus laid firmly at the door of government, and by extension of the putative Keynesian social democratic 'consensus' model of policy-making, within which policy had apparently been made for the previous quarter of a century. Ultimately, therefore, any failure was necessarily the fault of incompetent and pusillanimous politicians. Ironically, however, there was much to be gained by politicians by playing up this 'political failure'. For the right, it opened up many promising lines of attack, not just on Labour but on the postwar compromises with social democratic means, if not ends, that Conservatives had felt impelled to make since 1945; likewise, for the left, it created the prospect of solving the 'crisis' through equally radical but very different policies, most notably via the Alternative Economic Strategy.[27]

The hegemony of memory?

This outline of alternative readings serves mainly to emphasise how powerful is the prevailing myth of seventies Britain. The hegemonic memories and popular representations of the seventies have become a by-word for all that was worst about postwar Britain. The reasons why these memories and representations have persisted for so long are complex. We would highlight four reasons in particular.

First, the decade's economic difficulties came as a considerable shock to contemporaries after a quarter of a century of continuous economic growth and rising affluence. As we have noted elsewhere, though there was much agonising about Britain's economic performance relative to other countries during what came to be dubbed the 'golden age', from the late 1940s to the early 1970s, it was the shock of recession after 1973 that led contemporaries to see those years in such positive terms, and the years that followed in such a negative way.[28] In assessing that shock we need to historicise it, to imagine its impact without the benefit of hindsight. And as a recent major international history has contended, the decade was characterised by a severe shock to a whole series of conventional wisdoms and hegemonic perspectives – not only economic, and not only Western, let alone purely British.[29] While unemployment in the 1970s was nowhere near as bad as would be experienced in the 1980s, a million unemployed easily conjured up memories of the thirties for those who had lived through them (which meant anybody aged forty or more). The apparent failure of the Keynesian 'consensus' politics of the 'golden age' was experienced as and should be seen in terms of this shock.

Second, developments in the seventies were portrayed at the time by the British media, not least by newspapers, in a way that served to create an impression of a country uniquely challenged by the difficult economic conditions in the world economy in these years. There was little recognition that other countries were facing similar challenges. We have noted above that Hay, for example, has highlighted the politicised nature of media coverage and the conflation of disparate problems into a veritable crisis of the British state.[30] He is not the only one to have argued that we need to recognise that though Britain did face real problems in the 1970s, as Moran puts it, 'much of the crisis talk now seems overstated'. The economic crisis did not threaten the survival of the nation and the media played an important 'amplifying' role in creating the sense that it did.[31]

Third, if journalists writing 'the first draft of history' were responsible for a particular, and sometimes pretty partial, view of Britain in the seventies, the second draft of history was in large part written by social scientists in the 1970s and 1980s.[32] On the whole, their verdicts were overwhelmingly negative, shot through with assumptions about relative decline, concerned with the poor quality of British governance and fears of state 'overstretch' or 'overload'. There is a dissonance here between elite and popular experience, but also a surprising unawareness of developments elsewhere in the world, and a profound pessimism about the future.

Fourth, and finally, we would emphasise the way in which the politics of the ensuing thirty years saw both Thatcher and Blair hardwire such negative memories and representations of the decade into the national and popular consciousness. The former in particular sought from the start to craft an image of herself as a stalwart warrior against the apparent failings of 'the postwar consensus', over-mighty trade unions and the dead hand of a state grown too large as a result of the failure of previous Conservative governments to 'reverse the socialist ratchet'.[33] Thatcher's 1985 Conservative conference speech depicted 'the Labour Britain of 1979' as 'a Britain in which union leaders held their members and our country to ransom' and 'a Britain that was known as the sick man of Europe'.[34] As late as 1992, the Conservatives were still deploying 'Labour's terrible winter of discontent' in their party election broadcasts.[35] The fact that the events of that winter had become an emblem for all that was wrong with Britain, and with the Labour Party, in the 1970s explains why the architects of New Labour sought consciously to forge an identity at the heart of which was a contrast with the Labour Party of the 1970s. A month before his 1997 election victory, for example, Blair promised in *The Times* that there would be 'no return to the 1970s' and the party was acknowledged by the *Sun* to have undertaken the 'bold and courageous decision to drag itself out if its 1970s mindset'.[36] The quintessential image of failure in both these visions and narratives, an image burnished by the right-wing press both at the time and in succeeding years, is the 'winter of discontent'.[37]

Nor has the decade enjoyed the best of reputations among contemporary historians. For economic historians it marks the end of the postwar boom. For political historians it is when the postwar consensus fractured, governance failed and ideological polarisation ensued. For social and cultural historians the bright lights of the 1960s cast a long shadow. For example, social historian Arthur Marwick's tour of the decade ('the time of troubles', 1973–82) was a downbeat panorama of the nation, reminiscent of the 1930s: 'a deepening depression in the old heavy industries'; 'the derelict coal mining villages of Northumberland and Durham set[ting] a new benchmark for dilapidation and deprivation'; Teesiders 'living in an atmosphere often made foul by the chemical works'; Lancashire, Liverpool and Blackpool (built on cotton, docks and tourism respectively) dying; Yorkshire 'an industrial museum'; the South-East's prosperity circling rather than including London.[38] Even the discovery of North Sea oil in 1971 (on tap from 1975 and in full flow from 1978, when production topped a million barrels a day) did not really assuage the sense of decline, for as well as holding out the prospect of easier times ahead, it fuelled Scottish nationalism and anxieties about the 'break-up' of Britain.

The result is that a particular memory of the 1970s has endured even among those too young to remember it. By contrast with the optimism of 1945 and the 1960s, as Weight's *Patriots* has it, the 1978–79 'winter of discontent' (the Shakespearean sobriquet reworked by Callaghan adviser David Lipsey and turned by the media into everyday currency) 'entered British folklore and became a direct counterpoint to the Finest Hour, creating a legend of resistance to enemies within just as the war had done the same for enemies without'.[39] Britain's fortunes helped revive the phrase 'the sick man of Europe' (popularised in Peter Calvocoressi's 1978 study), one which resonated powerfully in Britons' imaginations. Under pressure from Irish, Welsh and Scottish nationalists it seemed more like the disunited Kingdom. There was scant chance of sociologists writing a piece about the 1977 Silver Jubilee to match Ed Shils and Michael Young's seminal sociological celebration of the comparative cohesion of British society, 'The meaning of the coronation' (1953).[40]

Most recent perspectives have reinforced the decade's pejorative image. There is, for example, a sense and recurring use of the 1970s as a harsher, more visceral experience than the utopias of the 1960s or consumerist 1980s and what is often portrayed as the politically enervated/ socially liberal, benign (or banal to critics of 'Cool Britannia') Blair boom. This perspective was firmly apparent in BBC TV's hit retro science fiction drama *Life on Mars* (2006–07). Or contrast the affable tone of Nick Hornby's novel *Fever Pitch* (1992) with the North Bank Arsenal fans who were the subject of a 1978 study of working-class youth, *Knuckle Sandwich*.[41] Some nostalgia can be detected in these for unpleasant but certain realities; some nostalgia for a more collectivist and less individualistic society. It can also be detected in Mark Garnett's history (which starts in 1975) of Britons' drift *From Anger to Apathy*.[42] And such understandings of the seventies are far from confined to Britain. For example, in May 2009, when Times Square was closed to traffic and New Yorkers lounged on a pedestrianised Broadway, the city's newspaper reported: 'some worried that it would sap the square of its chaotic energy ... apparently nostalgic for the seediness of the 1970s'.[43]

In the wake of the 2007–08 financial crisis and ensuing recession, there was, in the undergrowth of economics and political commentary, a sense that things were back to normal, that Britain must again face up to hard economic realities, that the long boom since 1992 had been an exceptional break with a seemingly inexorable long-term decline. The media drew ready parallels with the 1970s. Columnists reprised the ethos of 'make do and mend' (an echo of the Second World War, in that the original 1943 pamphlet *Make Do and Mend* was reissued during the three-day week and bread shortages of the 1970s) and cooking, sewing, evening classes, knitting and DIY all experienced reported revivals, as did allotment gardening (reawakening memories of the BBC 1970s hit comedy *The Good Life* and the middle-class fad for self-sufficiency).[44] Commentators saw in Brown's failure to call the expected election in the autumn of 2007 uncanny echoes of Callaghan's unexpected decision not to go to the country in 1978 and the way in which Labour was then brought low by the 'winter of discontent' (although, as Hay has pointed out, commentators glossed over the fact that a clear-cut ideological divergence between the major political parties in the late 1970s was actually lacking). By September 2009, 'union barons' were reported to be in talks with the Prime Minister at Chequers over the latter-day equivalent of 'beer and sandwiches' (beer and chicken balti), with the unions apparently issuing a blunt warning that wage freezes would be unacceptable, in negotiations in which they 'h[e]ld the whip hand'.[45] In the run-up to the 2010 general election, a British Airways industrial dispute prompted much talk of a 'spring of discontent', in which 'echoes of 1979 – national bankruptcy and strikes – are growing increasingly loud'.[46] There were echoes, too, of the negative view of the relationship between trade unionism and the Labour Party in the 1970s, with the reporting of UNITE (a descendant of the Transport and General Workers' Union) parachuting in preferred Labour candidates and 'tak[ing] control of a weakened Labour Party'.[47]

The prospect was, as Moran imagined it from 2039, that the fate of the 'noughties' would be that of the 1970s (and earlier the 1930s). It would be set up as a period whose policies were best avoided. This would be achieved via a process of selective memory, myth-making and nostalgia for a pre-lapsarian 'golden age' that would see the 'blame' ascribed not to bankers and markets but to excessive spending by a bloated state. As with the 1970s, therefore, the 2000s would be reduced by such 'decadology' to a 'cautionary tale'.[48] But the 'memory' embodied within that tale might be a particularly partial reading of events.

A 'social panic'?

In our preceding discussion, we proposed four factors in particular that we see as having contributed to the construction of a particular memory of the 1970s. Three of these relate to the construction of perceptions in the decade itself, the fourth to the subsequent perpetuation and even deepening of a particularly gloomy reading of the decade. In conjunction, we would suggest that our first three factors coalesced when the very real economic problems of the 1970s were amplified by the media (which we define broadly to encompass print and broadcast journalism as well as book publishing), by academics and, inevitably perhaps, by politicians.

In this process, we detect elements of what Cohen has termed a 'moral panic' – appropriately, a concept first developed in the 1970s. When Cohen popularised the term in 1972 in his seminal book *Folk Devils and Moral Panics*, he noted that, periodically, societies could become consumed by concern when a 'condition, episode, person or group of persons emerges to become defined as a threat to societal values and interests; its nature is presented in a stylised and stereotypical fashion by the mass media'.[49] Though Cohen developed the concept in cultural terms, focusing on the panic about mods and rockers in the 1960s, and while one can plainly detect similar instances of genuinely 'moral' panic in the 1970s such as that over punks (discussed by Bill Osgerby in chapter 10) or mugging,[50] we suggest that the concept has a broader relevance to those investigating the events of this decade. We see the utility of widening the focus to include political economy panics as well as those of a socio-cultural nature.

We recognise that the concept of moral panic is far from unproblematic. Waddington, for example, sees it as 'a polemical rather than an analytical concept', in that it implies that 'official and media concern is … without substance or justification', and notes that people may panic in a fire but this does not mean there is no fire in the building.[51] The point, however, is not that there is no fire but that, as Goode and Ben-Yehuda point out, the response to it may be disproportionate, and that an assessment of disproportionality is perfectly possible.[52] In the context of the 1970s, it might be argued that the sense of crisis at the time was disproportionate and this theme runs through many of the contributions in this volume.

In disaggregating the concept of moral panic, Goode and Ben-Yehuda identify five key elements: a heightened level of concern about a group or problem affecting the rest of society; hostility towards the source of the problem; a consensus that the threat is real; a disproportionate level of concern; and a degree of volatility, in that the panic erupts and then vanishes, almost without trace.[53] We recognise the last of these, but we do not believe that it is an essential element: in other words, we believe that moral panics can sometimes have lasting effects, and we believe this applies to many of the panics we detect in the 1970s. The disproportionate sense of crisis, for instance, has remained indelibly associated with the decade. However, we would argue that the term 'social panic' might be more appropriate, given the succession of perceived severe threats to the established order that characterise that decade.[54]

It seems to us that a common thread running through the preceding discussion, and through the more general and pervasive characterisation of the 1970s as a decade of profound, even existential, crisis in Britain is the role of the media and of politicians. Thompson has noted that, whereas the American tradition tended to focus on interest groups and social movements, early British studies of moral panics (such as Hall *et al.*'s *Policing the Crisis*) tended to focus on a crisis of capitalism and a consequent increase in social authoritarianism. In doing so, Thompson suggests that their most significant theoretical contribution was to highlight a '"signification spiral" – a way of publicly signifying issues and problems which is intrinsically escalating'.[55] In this process, however, he argues that the role of the mass media has been persistently underestimated. Others have also highlighted the way in which a highly politicised media contrived to raise public concerns in ways that benefited the Conservatives at the 1979 general election.[56] Thompson highlights the way in which, by the early 1980s, a centralised and 'incestuous' media, politicians and others with vested interests had 'played on the fears of those who [felt] anxious about mounting risks' (for example, the loss of authority of traditional elites, post-colonial anxiety, the growing diversity of British society) and in the process created 'a discursive formation that articulated together a combination of neo-liberal individualism and neo-conservative nostalgia for a moral golden age – an imagined national community unified by common values'.[57]

A marketplace for ideas?

The point here is that, if reactions to the 'crisis' may have been overdone, and if we are right that false memories persist of what exactly the crises consisted of, then our present understanding of those crises (or non-crises) may be wanting. We have little doubt that Britain in the 1970s did undergo a convulsive moment: this is why we see the decade as so important to an understanding of the trajectory of postwar British history. But, once we have analysed and stripped away the 'social panic' dimension of that convulsion, we need better to understand its real nature. Here we think Peter Hall's 'marketplace for ideas' can be helpful.

Hall argues that the economic challenges of the 1970s exposed important shortcomings in the prevailing 'Keynesian' model of economic policy. The result was that the Treasury struggled to cope and, as a result, became increasingly discredited. This in turn led to 'an extraordinary intensification in debate about economic issues in the media and financial circles. As the Treasury lost influence, what we might call the outside "marketplace in economic ideas" expanded dramatically in the 1975–79 period.'[58] Thus policy failure served not just to discredit policy-makers but to encourage actors outside the policy elite to advance alternative ideas about how to conduct policy. These ideas were then taken up by politicians and a political battle ensued about which idea (or set of ideas) should be adopted. Ideas, interests and institutions were thus all at work in a process that would lead ultimately to a paradigm shift with the institutionalisation of a new idea at the heart of economic policy-making.

In short, Hall's focus is on the way in which the discrediting of the prevailing policy paradigm broke open the policy process and then led to a political battle of ideas between a Labour government seeking to amend, and thereby save, the Keynesian policy-making model and those on the right advocating 'monetarist' solutions. But one could just as easily apply the concept of the marketplace for ideas to the quest on the left of British politics for an 'alternative economic strategy'. Equally, one could widen the field of vision from political economy, for it seems to us that one of the significant features of the 1970s is the breadth of the 'battle of ideas', a battle fought in the media (see Brittan and Middleton in chapters 4 and 5 of this volume on its political economy dimension), in publishing (see Peter Mayer and Dean Blackburn in chapters 11 and 12), in the much expanded higher-education sector and, of course, in the political arena.

Rewriting the history of the 1970s

The very persistence of a powerful 'folk wisdom' about Britain in the 1970s, and the weakness with which that reading of the decade has been challenged, may be one factor that helps explain why the seventies have so far been comparatively ill-served by historians (as is also the case for the USA). Coverage of 'the sixties' is exhaustive, but thereafter the literature is thin until the 1979 general election, after which there are numerous studies (Richard Vinen's among the newest) that detail Thatcherism.[59] Even New Labour is more regularly taught and rigorously served by the academic literature. Other disciplines (notably political science, through the likes of Hay) and journalists (most recently Andy Beckett and Francis Wheen) have seemed keener to delve into the seventies.[60] Yet this 'much disparaged decade', as Rodney Lowe has noted in urging more attention be paid to it by contemporary British historians, was the key division in existing narratives of postwar Britain, the fulcrum around which the postwar period moved in virtually all the sub-fields of history, and a generational rupture between those who had grown up in the 1930s (an era of market failure and demands for state intervention) and the postwar generation born into affluence (which fed a much lower tolerance for the shortcomings of the state).[61] Thus the decade is fundamental to our understanding of the whole postwar period.

For those who have not missed the 1970s, or who never experienced that decade, it has been mostly, as the title of Beckett's recent study has it, been depicted as the decade 'when the lights went out'. But there are other perspectives on offer. In a recent cultural history, for instance, Howard Sounes, who largely blots out economic problems, sees it as a 'brilliant' decade. Alwyn Turner's account is more detailed, also picking up on the vibrancy and uses of popular culture in the 1970s, but its title, *Crisis? What Crisis?* hints at how it too simply inverts conventional narratives. Yet, as we have noted elsewhere, too often such popular accounts struggle convincingly to integrate economic, political, social and cultural factors or to think beyond conventional wisdoms.[62] This is historians' (far from easy) task now.

Contemporary historians must ask themselves, 'Were the seventies so different, so bad?' In answering this question, the trick will be to integrate the decade's political economy with sociological and cultural perspectives. Some familiar trends from the 1960s and earlier were recognisable. Sexual liberation continued (Alex Comfort's *The Joy of Sex*, first published in 1972, was a bestseller, as was David Reuben's *Everything You Always Wanted To Know About Sex: But Were Afraid To Ask*). Trends associated with affluence continued: domestification, central heating, freezers and home telephones became more common in British homes. The number of Britons taking holidays abroad continued to increase in what was the heyday of the 'package' holiday. Scientific and technical progress in medicine (*in vitro* fertilisation, CAT scanning) and in leisure (video-recorders, the Sony Walkman) continued apace.[63] It was a decade in which British advertising went through a particularly creative period.[64] There were also continuing advances on issues raised during the sixties. Radical theatre (culture *as* politics) reached its creative and institutional apogee in the 1970s. Nationalism, while often decried, was a democratic cause for many. There were notable and important legislative measures in the social arena: the Sex Discrimination Act 1975 created the Equal Opportunities Commission, the 1970 Equal Pay Act came into force in 1975, the Domestic Violence and Matrimonial Proceedings Act 1976 protected victims much more effectively than had the common law hitherto; the Race Relations Act 1976 set up the Commission for Racial Equality, to succeed the toothless Race Relations Board; and consumer rights were strengthened by the creation of the National Consumer Council in 1975.[65] And developments like feminism are surely rather more significant than just a delayed blooming of 1960s liberation. It was the 1970s that saw feminism and women's activism more generally boom, both intellectually and more popularly, through the likes of Germaine Greer's *The Female Eunuch* (1970), Virago Press and *Cosmopolitan* magazine.[66]

Some popular myths can also easily be burst. Bernard Donoughue's diaries have recently reminded us that the Callaghan-led government had considerable achievements to its credit, not least bringing down inflation and restarting growth.[67] Tiratsoo has effectively argued that the country's political and economic travails were a function of global trends, with which the much-maligned Labour governments made a reasonable job of grappling. Strikes, fabled as the British 'disease', turn out to have been more virulent in, for instance, Italy and the USA (as in the 1960s). Moreover, strikes might not be about over-mighty, militant-controlled unions or economic decline but, as in the case of the Grunwick dispute in 1977, about the rights of ethnic minority immigrant women workers. The notion of the idle, strike-prone British worker has thus, to a degree, been culturally constructed. Nor, as Tiratsoo notes, were deficiencies in British management exactly hard to locate.[68] As with the 'winter of discontent', this does not make the more general industrial relations problems any less real, but does raise vital questions about their nature.

Alternative ways of thinking about the seventies might be that industry was being relocated as the axis of understanding society *or* that Britain was transitioning into the first post-industrial nation. This latter transition was as problematic as was dealing with the country's post-coloniality. *Small Is Beautiful* (1973), a critique of growth economics and surprise bestseller by Ernst Schumacher (a former adviser to the National Coal Board), suggested that the decade was also another important staging post in a shift towards post-materialism (like 'moral panics', one of the decade's more enduring concepts), a shift in part the product of the promise of 1960s affluence and cultural politics but then exacerbated rather than expunged by economic slowdown. Given all the talk of industrial difficulties, it is little wonder an organised green politics emerged in the form of the Ecology Party or that ruralism appealed – *The Country Diary of an Edwardian Lady*, for example, was the bestselling book in Jubilee year and spent three years in the bestseller lists.[69] These were boom years for the heritage industry – Hewison noted in 1987 that half of Britain's museums were founded after 1971 – which, like punk and other subcultures, rapidly shed its declinist associations to take on democratic, participatory, creative, fashionable and modern connotations.[70]

Chapter overviews

In the chapters that follow, our contributors begin to address some of these issues. As stated already, our focus is on ideas and the format we have adopted is to ask a number of those who played an important role in the generation and dissemination of some of the many new 'products' that were on offer in the vibrant marketplace for ideas that can be found in the 1970s to review that work with the benefit of hindsight. Each contributor is paired with a contemporary historian, who is tasked with reassessing not just the work in question but its significance to our understanding of the 1970s.

We begin with James Alt, who, in chapter 2, returns to his book *The Politics of Economic Decline*.[71] Alt considers the present economic crisis an opportune moment to reflect on (and learn from and draw parallels to and differences with) the 1970s and its pervasive sense of decline. He argues, using detailed economic data and statistics on public opinion and voting, that there were serious and real long-term structural difficulties in the British economy that came to a head in the 1970s, but he also revisits his predictions for the political and social consequences of economic decline. In chapter 3, Jim Tomlinson offers a close reading of Alt's work, acknowledging that it was both important and influential, but seeking to locate it within a 'declinist' analysis. For Tomlinson, the book is embedded in contemporary assumptions about Britain's 'decline' from which historians of the 1970s should now seek to maintain some critical distance. We need, in short, to build on Alt's work by allying it with an approach which gives greater weight to the political and rhetorical framing of Britain's economic problems in the 1970s.

In chapter 4, we return to one of our primary sources, in this case Sir Samuel Brittan, who was then, as now, a journalist on the *Financial Times* and a highly influential proponent in the 1970s not just of the idea that radical changes to British economic policy were desirable but that they were actually essential. Brittan played a key role in translating economic theory into language understandable by mere mortals and disseminating it through his journalism, but he also published for an academic audience and here he revisits an influential article, 'The economic contradictions of democracy', he wrote for the *British Journal of Political Science*, a work which he subsequently developed as a book.[72] In this work, he identified two threats to liberal democracy: the then excessively high level of expectations of what governments could and should achieve; and the deleterious effects produced by 'the pursuit of self-interest by rival coercive groups' such as trade unions (though Brittan is at pains to say that his main concern at the time was personal freedom rather than democracy or economic performance). Brittan's key publications in the 1970s are then considered by Roger Middleton in chapter 5. In the process, Middleton highlights not just the analysis developed by Brittan but its influence. Using novel bibliometric techniques, he is able to chart the extraordinary impact that Brittan, operating outside the academy, had on academic thought.

Turning from the political right to the left, chapter 6 sees Stuart Holland, author of *The Socialist Challenge*[73] and the principal architect of Labour's Alternative Economic Strategy in the seventies, revisit the marketplace for ideas that he sought so effectively to supply. He agrees that the shortcomings of the prevailing Keynesian model of economic policy-making created opportunities for those on the left who desired a more dirigiste approach to policy, not least as the means by which the excessive power of multinational corporations might be curbed. Holland aimed to provide what he terms the 'missing middle' in Keynesian thought. In chapter 7, Mark Wickham-Jones emphasises just how radical were many of Holland's proposals in *The Socialist Challenge* and how important they were seen to be at a time of acute economic and intellectual crisis, and of profound political uncertainty. He evaluates Holland's impact on Labour's policy programme and considers what inspired his work.

We return to a revisiting of the 1970s by a primary source with Lynne Segal's re-exploration of the Women's Liberation Movement, in chapter 8. Segal was co-author of *Beyond the Fragments*,[74] a book that powerfully criticised the left for failing to integrate the experiences and insights of the women's movement in the seventies. For feminist activists, Segal suggests, the decade was very far from the dismal era that the majority of historians and other commentators suppose. In chapter 9, Pat Thane takes a different approach, contextualising both women's activism and the 1970s in a longer perspective across the twentieth century as a whole.

In chapter 10, we depart from the paired chapter approach, Stanley Cohen's ill-health having precluded him completing his contribution. Instead, Bill Osgerby returns to Cohen's seminal work *Folk Devils and Moral Panics*.[75] The origins of the 'moral panic' concept and its impact on academic thought on cultural studies in the 1970s (and subsequently) are explored in detail.

Chapter 11 sees a shift away from a focus on the creation and perception of ideas in the 1970s to a focus on their dissemination. Peter Mayer, who became managing director of Penguin Books in 1978, reflects on Penguin's non-fiction publishing in the 'long 1970s' after the death of the firm's founder, Allen Lane, in 1970. He highlights the way in which Penguin moved to the left editorially in these years and argues that this represented a considerable problem because that shift led the firm away from its readers: in short, Penguin was supplying a particular type of product in the marketplace for ideas for which there was insufficient demand from the public. Commentary on Mayer's chapter is provided in chapter 12 by Dean Blackburn, who provides background on Penguin's development up to the 1970s, outlines the development of its editorial direction and considers its place in the wider publishing marketplace.

Notes

1 Examples include: 'Winter of strikes to cripple UK', *Daily Star*, 15 September 2011, p. 1; 'Strike chaos to cripple Britain', *Daily Express*, 15 September 2011,

p. 1 (accompanied by a photograph of rubbish piling up in London's Leicester Square in early 1979); M. Ellis, 'Unions fight for public pensions', *Daily Mirror*, 25 October 2011, p. 6; 'Biggest strike in history', *The Times*, 11 October 2011, p. 37.

2 J. Achur, *Trade Union Membership, 2010* (London: Department for Business, Innovation and Skills, 2010), p. 3.

3 Most notably B. Jackson, 'At the origins of neo-liberalism: the free economy and the strong state, 1930–1947', *Historical Journal*, 53:1 (2010), pp. 129–51; B. Jackson and R. Saunders (eds), *Making Thatcher's Britain: Essays on the History of Thatcherism* (Cambridge: Cambridge University Press, 2012); B. Harrison, *Finding a Role? The United Kingdom 1970–1990* (Oxford: Oxford University Press, 2010); S. Katwala, 'In Maggie's shadow', *Public Policy Research*, 16:1, pp. 3–13; K. Hickson, 'Conservativism and the poor: Conservative Party attitudes to poverty and inequality since the 1970s', *British Politics*, 4:3 (2009), pp. 341–62; R. Backhouse, 'Economists and the rise of neo-liberalism', *Renewal*, 17:4 (2009), pp. 17–25.

4 The term was first coined by Ferdinand Mount in his review of Peter Hennessy's 2006 book *Having It So Good: Britain in the Fifties*: F. Mount, 'The doctrine of unripe time', *London Review of Books*, 28:22 (16 November 2006), pp. 28–30.

5 J. Moran, 'Decoding the decade', *Guardian*, 13 November 2009, at www.guardian.co.uk/commentisfree/2009/nov/13/1, accessed 25 October 2011.

6 N. Jones, *The Lost Tribe: Whatever Happened to Fleet Street's Industrial Correspondents* (London: Nicholas Jones, 2011).

7 On 'ungovernability' and 'overload' see for example: J. Douglas, 'The overloaded crown', *British Journal of Political Science*, 6:4 (1976), pp. 483–505; A. King, 'Overload: problems of governing in the 1970s', *Political Studies*, 23:2–3 (1975), pp. 284–96; R. Rose, 'Ungovernability: is there fire behind the smoke?', *Political Studies*, 27:3 (1979), pp. 351–70.

8 'Disunited kingdom?', *Economist*, 24 August 1974, pp. 14–15; 'Can we survive as a nation?', *Sunday Express*, 5 December 1976, p. 7; 'Warning on danger to unity of UK', *The Times*, 40 June 1978, p. 16.

9 *Daily Mirror*, 5 December 1973, p. 1.

10 *Sun*, 15 January 1979, and *Daily Express*, 8 February 1979, cited in J. Thomas, *Popular Newspapers, the Labour Party and British Politics* (London: Routledge, 2005), pp. 79–80.

11 I. Kramnick, *Is Britain Dying? Perspectives on the Current Crisis* (Ithaca, NY: Cornell University Press, 1979); S. H. Beer, *Britain Against Itself: The Political Contradictions of Collectivism* (London: Faber, 1982); T. Nairn, *The Break-Up of Britain: Crisis and Neo-nationalism* (London: New Left Books, 1977); S. Hall, C. Critcher, T. Jefferson, J. Clarke and B. Roberts, *Policing the Crisis: Mugging, the State and Law and Order* (London: Macmillan, 1978); J. Barr, *Derelict Britain* (Harmondsworth: Penguin, 1969).

12 P. Whitehead, *The Writing on the Wall* (London: Michael Joseph, 1986), p. xiii.

13 C. Booker, *The Seventies: Portrait of a Decade* (Harmondsworth: Penguin, 1980), p. 261.

14 One such strike at ITV, for instance, delivered an unexpectedly high audience for the BBC's acclaimed version of Mike Leigh's satire on middle-class taste and anxieties, *Abigail's Party*, which was broadcast in November 1977.

15 'The big league', *Guardian*, 20 May 2005, p. 10.

16 S. Cohen, 'Symbols of trouble: introduction to the new edition', in S. Cohen, *Folk Devils and Moral Panics: The Creation of the Mods and Rockers* (Oxford: Martin Robertson, 1980), pp. i–xxxiv; for an historical overview see A. Wills,

'Delinquency, masculinity and citizenship in Britain 1950–70', *Past and Present*, 187 (2005), pp. 157–85.

17 D. Hebdige, *Subculture: The Meaning of Style* (London: Methuen, 1979), p. 87.

18 See R. Sabin (ed.), *Punk Rock, So What? The Cultural Legacy of Punk* (London: Routledge, 1999).

19 See 'Pop report', UK Chart History, 1977, at www.popreport.co.uk, accessed 2 November 2011.

20 A. Echols, *Hot Stuff: Disco and the Re-making of American Culture* (New York: Norton, 2010); B. J. Schulman, *The Seventies* (New York: Free Press, 2001), pp. 72–5, 144–5.

21 See J. Kerr, *Understanding Soccer Hooliganism* (Buckingham: Open University Press, 1994); G. Pearson, *Hooligan: A History of Respectable Fears* (Basingstoke: Macmillan, 1983).

22 T. Claydon, 'Images of disorder: car workers' militancy and the representation of industrial relations in Britain, 1950–79', in D. Thoms, L. Holden and T. Claydon (eds), *The Motor Car and Popular Culture in the 20th Century* (Aldershot: Ashgate, 1998), pp. 227–43.

23 By the 2000s it had been repackaged and sanitised for Norwich Union advertisements.

24 See the testimonies in L. Black and H. Pemberton, 'The winter of discontent in British politics', *Political Quarterly*, 80:4 (2009), pp. 553–61; N. Tiratsoo, '"You've never had it so bad"?', in N. Tiratsoo (ed.), *From Blitz to Blair: A New History of Britain Since 1939* (London: Phoenix, 1998), pp. 173–90.

25 R. Taylor, '"What are we here for?" George Woodcock and trade union reform', in J. Mcilroy *et al.* (eds), *British Trade Unions and Industrial Politics, 1945–79: Vol. 2* (Aldershot: Ashgate, 1999), p. 187.

26 A not dissimilar process has been detected in the vilification of the 'loony left' during the 1980s, with the spectre of the seventies deployed by Labour modernisers, Thatcherites and the tabloids against unions, town hall radicals and the left. See C. Hay, 'Narrating crisis: the discursive construction of the "winter of discontent"', *Sociology*, 30:2 (1996), pp. 253–77; J. Curran, I. Gaber and J. Petley, *Culture Wars* (Edinburgh: Edinburgh University Press, 2005).

27 On the Alternative Economic Strategy see D. Dutton, *British Politics Since 1945: The Rise, Fall and Rebirth of Consensus* (Oxford: Blackwell, 2nd edition, 1997); M. Wickham-Jones, *Economic Strategy and the Labour Party* (Basingstoke: Macmillan, 1996); N. W. Thompson, *Political Economy and the Labour Party: The Economics of Democratic Socialism, 1884–2005* (London: Routledge, 2nd edition, 2006). See also chapters 6 and 7 of the present volume.

28 L. Black and H. Pemberton (eds), *An Affluent Society: Britain's 'Golden Age' Revisited* (Aldershot: Ashgate, 2004), pp. 5–7.

29 N. Ferguson, C. Maier, E. Manela and D. Sargent (eds), *The Shock of the Global: The 1970s in Perspective* (Cambridge, MA: Belknap, 2010).

30 C. Hay, 'Narrating crisis'; C. Hay, 'The winter of discontent thirty years on', *Political Quarterly*, 80:4 (2009), pp. 545–52; C. Hay, 'Chronicles of a death foretold: the winter of discontent and construction of the crisis of British Keynesianism', *Parliamentary Affairs*, 63:3 (2010), pp. 446–70.

31 J. Moran, '"Stand up and be counted": Hughie Green, the 1970s and popular memory', *History Workshop Journal*, 70:1 (2010), pp. 172–98.

32 One might cite A. King, *Why Is Britain Becoming Harder to Govern?* (London: BBC Books, 1976); S. H. Beer, *Britain Against Itself: The Political Contradictions of Collectivism* (London: Faber, 1982); R. Clutterbuck, *Britain in Agony: The Growth of Political Violence* (London: Faber, 1978); W. Beckerman (ed.), *Slow Growth in Britain* (Oxford: Clarendon Press, 1979); S. Pollard, *The Wasting of*

the British Economy: British Economic Policy 1945 to the Present (London: Croom Helm, 1982); R. Bacon and W. Eltis, *Britain's Economic Problem: Too Few Producers* (Basingstoke: Macmillan, 1976); A. Glyn and J. Harrison, *The British Economic Disaster* (London: Pluto Press, 1980); J. Seabrook, *What Went Wrong: Why Hasn't Having More Made People Happier?* (New York: Pantheon, 1978); J. Eatwell, *Whatever Happened to Britain* (London: Duckworth, 1982). The list widens if one includes non-academic but well informed commentators such as S. Brittan, *The Economic Consequences of Democracy* (London: Temple Smith, 1977), on which see chapters by Brittan and Middleton in this volume.

33 M. Thatcher, *The Downing Street Years* (London: HarperCollins, 1993), esp. p. 7.

34 See the transcript of the 11 October 1985 speech in the Thatcher Archive, at www.margaretthatcher.org/document/106145, accessed 26 October 2011.

35 See transcript of the Conservative Party election broadcast, 3 April 1992, at www.politicsresources.net/area/uk/pebs/con92.htm, accessed 25 October 2011.

36 N. Tiratsoo, '"You've never had it so bad"?', p. 186; T. Blair, 'We won't go back to the 1970s', *The Times*, 31 March 1997; Thomas, *Popular Newspapers*, p. 130.

37 See Hay, 'Narrating crisis'; and J. Thomas, '"Bound in by history": the winter of discontent in British politics, 1979–2004', *Media, Culture and Society*, 29:2 (2007), pp. 263–83.

38 A. Marwick, *British Society Since 1945* (Harmondsworth: Penguin, 2003), pp. 154–61.

39 R. Weight, *Patriots: British National Identity Since 1940* (London: Macmillan, 2002), pp. 564–6. The elision is encapsulated by a 9 February 1979 cartoon in the *Daily Telegraph*, by David Garland, which showed a statue of Field-Marshall Montgomery amidst Leicester Square's reeking piles of garbage.

40 P. Calvocoressi, *The British Experience 1945–75* (Harmondsworth: Penguin, 1978); E. Shils and M. Young, 'The meaning of the coronation', *Sociological Review*, 1:2 (1953), pp. 63–81.

41 N. Hornby, *Fever Pitch* (London: Gollancz, 1992); D. Robins and P. Cohen, *Knuckle Sandwich: Growing Up in the Working-Class City* (Harmondsworth: Penguin, 1978).

42 M. Garnett, *From Anger to Apathy: Politics, Society and Popular Culture in Britain Since 1975* (London: Jonathan Cape, 2008).

43 *New York Times*, 26 May 2009.

44 C. Hay, 'Chronicles of a death foretold'. See also articles by: Hay, 'The winter of discontent thirty years on'; Black and Pemberton, 'The winter of discontent'; 'From the high life to the good life: cutting one's cloth is back in fashion', *Observer*, 25 January 2009; Ministry of Information, *Make Do and Mend* (London: Ministry of Information, 1943, reissued London: Imperial War Museum, 2007).

45 H. Craig, 'Beer and sandwiches at Chequers!', Sky News, 10 September 2009, http://blogs.news.sky.com/boultonandco/Post:3fa72cb3-a31b-4260-b4e2-64d36d2c36ff, accessed 25 October 2011; 'Gordon Brown forced to listen as union barons finally come in from the cold', *Observer*, 13 September 2009, p. 3.

46 'A spring of discontent', *Daily Telegraph*, 26 March 2010, p. 29.

47 'The union challenge to our democracy', *Daily Mail*, 31 March 2010, at www.dailymail.co.uk/debate/article-1260773, accessed 25 October 2011.

48 Moran, 'Decoding the decade'.

49 Cohen, *Folk Devils and Moral Panics*, p. 1. The term 'moral panic' had actually been coined earlier, by J. Young, in his chapter on 'The role of the police as amplifiers of deviancy, negotiators of reality and translators of fantasy', in S. Cohen (ed.), *Images of Deviance* (Harmondsworth: Penguin, 1971), pp. 27–61.

50 Hall *et al.*, *Policing the Crisis*.

51 P. A. G. Waddington, 'Mugging as a moral panic: a question of proportion', *British Journal of Sociology*, 37:2 (1986), p. 258.

52 E. Goode and N. Ben-Yehuda, *Moral Panics: The Social Construction of Deviance* (Oxford: Blackwell, 1994), pp. 75–7.

53 *Ibid.*, pp. 33–41.

54 J. Rowbotham and K. Stevenson, *Behaving Badly: Social Panic and Moral Outrage – Victorian and Modern Parallels* (Aldershot: Ashgate, 2003), pp. 7–8.

55 K. Thompson, *Moral Panics* (London: Routledge, 1998), pp. 16–17.

56 Hay, 'Narrating crisis'; Moran, 'Stand up and be counted'; J. Tomlinson, *The Politics of Decline: Understanding Post-war Britain* (London: Longman, 2000).

57 Thompson, *Moral Panics*, pp. 27–50, 141–2.

58 P. A. Hall, 'Policy paradigms, social learning and the state: the case of economic policy making in Britain', *Comparative Politics*, 25:3 (1993), p. 286.

59 R. Vinen, *Thatcher's Britain: The Politics and Social Upheaval of the Thatcher Era* (London: Simon & Schuster, 2009).

60 A. Beckett, *When the Lights Went Out* (London: Faber, 2009); F. Wheen, *Strange Days Indeed: The Golden Age of Paranoia* (London: Fourth Estate, 2009).

61 R. Lowe, 'Life begins in the seventies?', *Journal of Contemporary History*, 42:1 (2007), pp. 162–3.

62 Beckett, *When the Lights Went Out*; H. Sounes, *Seventies: The Sights, Sounds and Ideas of a Brilliant Decade* (London: Simon & Schuster, 2006); A. W. Turner, *Crisis? What Crisis? Britain in the 1970s* (London: Aurum, 2008); H. Pemberton, 'Strange days indeed: British politics in the 1970s', *Contemporary British History*, 23:4 (2009), pp. 583–95; L. Black, 'An enlightening decade? New histories of 1970s Britain', *International Labor and Working-Class History*, 81:2 (2012).

63 Weight, *Patriots*; N. Ferguson, 'Crisis? What crisis?', in N. Ferguson *et al.* (eds), *The Shock of the Global*, pp. 20–21. Though if affluence did not make people happier (as powerfully argued by Offer and others) then perhaps we should be wary of assuming that harder economic conditions necessarily reduced well-being. Several recent and contemporary commentators have noted evidence that Britons' well-being peaked in 1976 and that they were then among the most contented in the world. See New Economics Foundation, 'Chasing progress: beyond measuring economic growth', March 2004, at www.neweconomics.org/publications/chasing-progress, accessed 2 November 2011; R. Dahrendof, 'Is Britain really that sick?', *Wall Street Journal*, 18 August 1977; A. Offer, *The Challenge of Affluence: Self-control and Well-being in the United States and Britain Since 1950* (Oxford: Oxford University Press, 2006); R. Layard, *Happiness: Lessons From a New Science* (London: Penguin Press, 2005); A. Oswald, 'Happiness and economic performance', *Economic Journal*, 107:445 (1997), pp. 1815–31.

64 Of *Campaign*'s 100 best advertisements of the century, twenty (the most) came from the 1970 and, despite pressure on advertising budgets, the business held up 'surprisingly well'. V. Fletcher, *Powers of Persuasion: The Inside Story of British Advertising* (Oxford: Oxford University Press, 2008), pp. 96–8.

65 P. Thane (ed.), *Unequal Britain: Inequalities in Britain Since 1945* (London: Continuum, 2010).

66 For a vibrant memoir, see L. Segal, *Making Trouble: Life and Politics* (London: Serpent's Tail, 2007).

67 B. Donoughue, *Downing Street Diary, Vol. 2: With Callaghan in No. 10* (London: Jonathan Cape, 2008).

68 Tiratsoo, '"You've never had it so bad"?'

69 J. Sutherland, *Reading the Decades: Fifty Years of the Nation's Bestselling Books* (London: BBC, 2002), pp. 86–9, 94–5; on post-materialism, see R. Inglehart, *The Silent Revolution* (Princeton, NJ: Princeton University Press, 1977).

70 R. Hewison, *The Heritage Industry: Britain in a Climate of Decline* (London: Methuen, 1987). See P. Wright, *On Living in an Old Country* (Oxford: Oxford University Press, 2009) for an overview of heritage debates.
71 J. E. Alt, *The Politics of Economic Decline: Economic Management and Political Behaviour in Britain Since 1964* (Cambridge: Cambridge University Press, 1979).
72 S. Brittan, 'The economic contradictions of democracy', *British Journal of Political Science*, 5:2 (1975), pp. 129–59 (the quotation is from p. 150); Brittan, *The Economic Consequences of Democracy*.
73 S. Holland, *The Socialist Challenge* (London: Quartet, 1975).
74 S. Rowbotham, L. Segal and H. Wainwright, *Beyond the Fragments: Feminism and the Making of Socialism* (London: Merlin Press, 1979).
75 Cohen, *Folk Devils and Moral Panics*.

2

The politics of economic decline in the 1970s

James E. Alt

I came to Britain as a graduate student in 1968, to the then very new University of Essex. Eleven years later I left again for the USA, ironically and coincidentally buying my ticket on 3 May 1979, the day Margaret Thatcher was elected. In between I was fortunate to be able to learn from Anthony King and especially the late Brian Barry, then in a phase of enthusiasm for political science evident in his *Sociologists, Economists, and Democracy*[1] and editing the *British Journal of Political Science. The Politics of Economic Decline* (hereafter *PED*),[2] which Rudolf Klein once rightly remarked 'does not make for easy reading',[3] was written in the interstices of collaborations on voting behaviour with Ivor Crewe and Bo Särlvik at the British Election Study, which was based at Essex. The book describes how the economy interacts with voter and government behaviour and political institutions to shape electoral accountability.[4] Similar questions continued to motivate and frame my subsequent research at Washington University and then at Harvard. My emphasis has clearly shifted away from surveys of individuals and towards the analysis of institutions, but the theme persists whether I was writing about government behaviour, budget transparency or political corruption.

The book had two proximate origins. On the one hand, I thought that on the interaction of economic phenomena, popular understanding of those phenomena and voting as described in Butler and Stokes' path-breaking *Political Change in Britain*[5] there was simply much more to be said about explanatory variables than 'valence' and 'ignorance'. On the other hand, relative to the apocalyptic literature, I thought that rather less should be said about 'ungovernability'. Unlike prophets of gloom and doom, I believed that Britain's political institutions would survive because they, like the citizens I wrote about, would adapt to even prolonged and severe economic stress, while the political parties, though maybe not as attractive to voters as before, would continue to compete. Not as exciting a view, fair enough, but not too far off the mark as it turned out.

The editors of this volume posed the question of how far the negative tone of the phrase 'politics of economic decline' still 'feels' right as a description of the 1970s. It still feels exactly right to me, though as I stress below there are things I would do differently if I were writing today. But I chose the word 'decline' to get at the idea of people adjusting to a process continuing slowly over a substantial period, as opposed to a crisis or collapse. Was the decline real or 'constructed', the product of 'negative imaginings'? That is a more nuanced question: there was real decline and also some alarmism, as I implied above. While I thought (and still think) that the British public and their institutions came off pretty well in *PED*, maybe the decade looks worse to some in retrospect than I thought it was then.

I next summarise the argument of the book and talk about what change the 1970s brought to the role of economic affairs in the politics of the welfare state. Having discussed what was real about the decade, I turn to the question of what was constructed, how, and why. I then consider some comparisons with other times and places. With the return of economic dislocation in recent years, this is a good time to look back at the 1970s by looking at *PED* and its subject.

What the 1970s and the book were about

Oddly, what now seems to me politically to be the most consequential event of the decade, Britain joining the then European Economic Community (EEC), at the time appeared much less significant. It is hardly mentioned in *PED*. It is not given explicit treatment in this volume. It did internally divide both major parties and by the 1980s it was clear that these divisions were enduring and consequential. But at the time it seemed more like just joining another trade agreement, with some added posturing or renegotiation that solved a political problem in the Labour Party for a while.

Even without attention to Europe, I believe the 1970s were a watershed decade. During those years, for want of a better expression, many familiar features of the previous thirty to fifty years went into reverse, or at least became exhausted. The features that disappeared prominently included a 'consensus' about relying on government to provide a planned economy, welfare state and some public ownership, with domination of political competition by two major parties. Most simply, I believe that what happened in Britain's political economy in the 1970s was that something went wrong. The real meaning of 'economic decline' was that the consensus, broadly similar economic management policies pursued by both parties, was no longer 'producing the goods' in the sense of financing and engendering popular support for policies that made up the fabric of the welfare state. This development opened up a lot of space for new ideas in policy circles (by the time Nixon said we were all Keynesians, we weren't). These new ideas had important consequences for mass political behaviour: that was the subject of *PED*.

The 'politics' of this economic decline in the 1970s had a number of features. To reiterate, I chose the word 'decline' to suggest gradual and ongoing: I did not believe there was much of a sense of panic or of economic crisis. Of course, there were several headline-grabbing events, like the miners' strike and three-day week or the 'winter of discontent', which were connected to the economy as part of the failure of bipartisan incomes policies to deal with inflation. Perhaps there was a crisis atmosphere around the loan from the International Monetary Fund (IMF) in 1976 but, if so, it passed quickly. But I never had the feeling of writing in the midst of a panic. Rather, I saw people groping with the novelty of the situation and searching for new understandings in a new era.

Hence a leading theme of *PED* was that people were making more sense of this complex issue than you might otherwise expect, as Rudolf Klein rightly described in his *New Society* review.[6] Ralf Dahrendorf focused on another idea, the conclusion that people had ceased to expect government to deliver the goods.[7] I did indeed want to bring that side out too, but my goal was to look more closely at popular support for the policies that made up the welfare state. What I had in mind was this. There is a well known way to think about the consequences of self-interest for political demands. Suppose one orders individuals' propensity to think and vote left on policy to vary according to their level of income. That approach finds the origins of redistributive policy in the fact that social transfers from rich to poor win majority support, essentially because there are more (poorer) recipients than rich (taxpayers).[8] But I wanted to examine another side of this relationship, to look more closely at how threats to affluence diminish altruism among those paying for policy benefits that they do not receive. Vernon Bogdanor precisely described the argument when he analysed the Conservative Party's resounding victory in the 1983 general election:

> The recession diminishes altruism and so undermines popular support for the Welfare State.... In 1983 the voters did not believe politicians ... who told them that unemployment could be lowered by alternative economic policies.[9]

Hard times change what people want and do so in ways that broadly do not advantage left policies: this was (and is) the main contribution of *PED* to how we should view the 1970s. How people translated the economy into personal terms, how far they accurately perceived trade-offs in economic policy and the overall decline of partisan fervour in policy preferences was the infrastructure for the basic argument. I believed data could shed some light on all of these related issues.

For me, the starting point was that lying behind Bogdanor's observation that 'recession diminishes altruism and so undermines popular support for the Welfare State' is the straightforward idea that people will be as generous as they feel they can afford to be. How generous is affected by economic change, and in particular by whether the overall economy is good or bad. The way it works is that when the economy is bad, it becomes a *more* important problem. Consequently, because the economy becomes more important, people see social policies as a *less* central issue, not more. We can watch this process evolve (the change is as true today as it was then) by viewing the trade-off between the relative prominence of 'the economy' and 'social policy' or 'services' among what people see as the most important political problems of the day. *PED* included this information for the decade ending in 1978 and figure 2.1 here updates and extends it. It shows the first fundamental

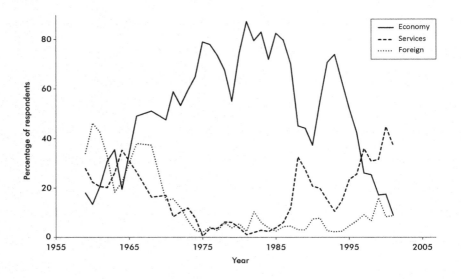

2.1 Most important problems/issues, 1959–2001

Source: J. Alt, *The Politics of Economic Decline: Economic Management and Political Behaviour in Britain Since 1964* (Cambridge: Cambridge University Press, 1979), p. 49.

feature of the political context of the 1970s and after: a long-running public focus on the economy as the most important problem facing the country.[10] Social policy is briefly the more important issue in 1964–65, but from 1966 on the economy is the more important problem, usually by a lot, for about thirty years.

The first thing to notice about the 1970s is that the proportion finding the economy most important doubles from about 40 per cent to 80 per cent. That is a huge change to observe in an opinion series. The issues are still in the same relative places as Britain emerges from recession in 1983–84; after the shock of 1992 the attention to the economy surges again. Only after 1996 or 1997 does the economy improve and people feel more secure economically. As figure 2.1 shows, at that point for some years the economy ceases to be a significant problem and social services become not just 'a' but 'the' problem. Subsequently (but outside the timespan of the figure) crime and terrorism-related issues and the Iraq War eclipse social services as a concern. By early 2009, however, the economic crisis reasserted itself: among the most important issues seen as facing Britain then, the economy came up four times as often as social policy.[11] So, as a first takeaway point, the 1970s were transformative for a basic understanding of what politics was about. I felt the decade ushered in an era of economic centrality in popular thinking about politics and political issues, more than many other analysts believed. The change was durable as well as big: the policy priority attached to the economy was no short-term thing.

The rest of my reasoning about the 1970s was also straightforward. It was not just that people became more aware of the economy; in the 1970s there was genuine economic trouble. Growth rates fell, unemployment rose and prices rose fast. That, broadly speaking, had to make people more uncertain and even edgy about protecting their standard of living, which is what reduces generosity. Economic concerns could be magnified if people were used to economic improvement and it disappeared: slow growth feels less good after faster growth than if one has never had growth in the first place.[12] Finally, this took place, as the subtitle of *PED* reminds us, in an era of active economic management, so you could expect people not just to feel the consequences of economic decline but also to see policy failure on the part of government. This in turn interacted with centrality, the fact that the economy was a public obsession for much of the time. Because voters were observing, updating and thinking more about economic affairs, the effects of economic decline and policy failure were magnified.

In fact voters saw something remarkable: a notable failure in short order of both parties to deal with the economy using a more or less similar set of remedies founded on managing prices through negotiated incomes policies. That vision (multiple 'similar' failures in short order) is not necessarily something we would expect to see in every case, but it was important here. I showed (not in *PED* but soon after[13]) that the mass perception of policy failure, which means not believing one's normally preferred party was better able than the other to handle what one felt was the most important problem facing the country, was sufficient to explain the weakening of party attachments in the electorate at the time. That in turn explains the disbelief Dahrendorf and Bogdanor mentioned. All those things were what I saw and wanted to write about.

Decline, economic decline, economics and politics

In the following chapter in this volume, Jim Tomlinson places *PED* in a 'declinist' literature dating back to the late 1950s. He therefore finds it unsurprising that *PED* took decline as given. I am happy to meet him half way on this. Decline is indeed an old subject, just as Britain is an old country. There was the end of Empire, a devalued pound and probably some domestic shortfall of modern physical capital, so some kind of decline of national power did seem evident. Nevertheless, that decline was not often framed in economic terms, even though economic decline may seem like a well established theme now. As late as the early 1970s, however, it was novel. Evidence of this is not easy to come by but, for example, when you search Harvard's online library catalogue (an admittedly imperfect, informal source) for books with 'keywords anywhere' including *all* of 'Britain', 'economic' and 'decline' only *one* book comes up between the end of the Second World War and 1970. Then there are five before mine in the 1970s, but *eighty-one more* since then, at an average of three a year, with bursts of energy (predictably) in recession-following years like 1982 and 1994. So it seems that the negative, 'economic declinist' view of the 1970s certainly did take hold in the 1980s and 1990s, but as a contemporaneous account it was less common. In any case, I recall no feeling at all of mining a well known literature while I was writing *PED*.

General perceptions of decline as connected to problems of economic management began to emerge only in the late 1960s and early 1970s; naturally, the idea of connecting economic decline and politically feasible solutions came later still. Nevertheless, that was *not* because people in general failed to connect politics and economic policy. Trade protection in the 1930s was a political economic policy issue, just as reconstruction and the planned economy after the 1940s were political matters. After 1964 everyone, including the media and the politicians themselves, came to agree that economic policy was a significant part of competitive party politics. It is worth noticing that today no one could write seriously about voting behaviour without acknowledging the potential relevance of the economy as well as government performance. That is because the conventional wisdom and the literature really changed in this respect after the 1970s: *PED*, just a tiny bit ahead of the curve, was part of that change.

Real or constructed?

It is true that the surge in what I called 'economic centrality' in the minds of voters was not a normal response to an economic shock. Maybe people would have felt the same way in any recession but probably not as much or for as long as they did in the 1970s. Other studies of opinion change suggest smaller and shorter-term mass responses to this kind of event.[14] The economy might rise to be top concern for a few months or even a couple of years, but it would fade when things started to get better. The long-running policy priority we see in figure 2.1 does not happen in every recession. The longer, larger obsession with economics was an *immersion*: an unusual prolonged period of exposure to difficult economic conditions and arguments about whether 'doing something' was within the competence of the political system. The 1970s offer an unprecedented opportunity to see what immersion in economics meant for politics. However, the durability of this economic centrality deserves explaining. A question with which to start is, would the immersion have been the same if politicians and media had not encouraged people to feel this way?

That is, is the view of the 1970s as a period of economic decline 'constructed' rather than founded in fact, as Jim Tomlinson suggests? 'Declinist' arguments, he believes, were constructed at the time through a mixture of parties' competitive posturing, with important contributions from the media and intellectuals. This construction tied the undeniable short-term shocks to a contestable assumption that they were part of a long-run decline, using questionable 'expert' analogies with earlier situations. I certainly agree that the centrality of the issue to the mass public, while not constructed by any individual's specific design, would surely not have come about without the process Jim describes. However, I would turn his argument on its head: I think the attention paid to the economy by politicians and media is the distinctive political consequence of the mass obsession with economic dislocation at the time.[15]

Naturally, we cannot examine the counterfactual of what the popular response to the economy in the 1970s would have been with less media attention. But we can look at how much economic trouble there actually was and when. Tomlinson wants us to see the 'real economy' that lies behind arguments about decline. Stylising for brevity, he wants the problem to be a short-term surge of inflation, but not obviously part of a

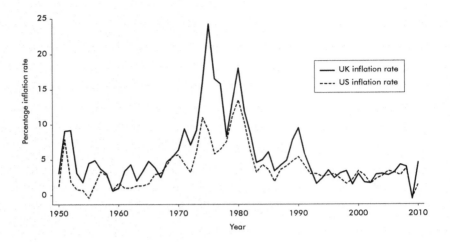

2.2 UK and US rates of inflation, 1950–2010

Source: US inflation data downloaded from www.usinflationcalculator.com/inflation/historical-inflation-rates. Rates of inflation are calculated using the current Consumer Price Index published monthly by the Bureau of Labor Statistics (BLS). UK inflation data based on Retail Price Index downloaded from www.ons.gov.uk/ons/datasets-and-tables/data-selector.html?dataset=mm23.

broader, genuine, longer-term decline. Indeed, inflation *was* the headline story of the 1970s. Whether you consult figure 2.2 (taken from *PED* but again extended) or Middleton's[16] study for a longer-period view, Britain was among the worst inflation performers among the big countries, which was the comparison people tended to make. As figure 2.2 shows, the British inflation rate was approximately 'the US rate plus two percentage points' from 1960 to 1973 as well as after 1980, and 'plus a lot more' in between. Indeed, while the surge in relative inflation lasted only a few years, the inflation rate itself was still in double figures in 1979, though down by 60 per cent from the highs of 1974–75. But just as important as the surge in the 1970s is the ongoing, creeping weakness against the USA. The long-term 'decline' is relevant because creeping relative inflation is one of many factors reflected in a weakening dollar exchange rate of sterling, which was a headline number at several points in time.[17] In any case, I am not convinced that the problem of relatively high inflation in Britain's economic decline was entirely a short-term surge magnified by reporting excess.

It is difficult for politicians to create smoke if there is not some real fuel burning. Even if there was some 'constructed centrality' of decline that continued on beyond the 1970s, there were certainly some genuine longer-term problems in the real economy lying beneath the surface. These include lagging growth of real incomes and rising unemployment. On the former, Livingston was strident:

> The problem of obtaining faster growth in the British economy is one of the most important facing any government.... The rate of growth has been ... probably for most of the twentieth century, far less than most [comparable] industrial nations.... One result of this has been that ... [b]y the early 1970s ... Britain had a lower standard of living than every country but one [Ireland] north of the Alps and west of the Pyrenees.[18]

More general (at least you don't need a map to make the relevant comparisons) is Middleton's evidence.[19] He shows that Britain's real growth over 1950–73 was well below not just that of the USA, but also of the European Union countries, the G-7 and the OECD-17. Of course, things did not fall apart completely after 1973. There *was* some real economic growth even through the late 1970s, though at half the rate that prevailed from 1960 to 1973. Nevertheless, the period 1960–73 was itself indeed slightly *better* than the preceding decade, though in fact it was also rapidly growing *worse* relative to plans.[20] Perhaps the disappointment of missing overly ambitious targets should be part of the story of constructed decline. However, in comparison with this drop in the rate of real growth, unemployment unambiguously increased over an even longer period. Unemployment was just over 1 per cent in 1965; it had nearly doubled by around 1970. The number of registered unemployed (frequently a headline number) then increased by 50 per cent between 1970 and 1975, and by a further 60 per cent between 1975 and 1980, before peaking at 3 million (about 13 per cent of the labour force) by 1983.[21] No international comparisons were needed to make people aware of this. The bottom line is this: even if absolute performance was not bad in every respect and relative performance was not weak for every indicator with every comparison group, 'decline' is not a misnomer for developments over what looks more like fifteen to twenty than five years. There may be other factors to take into account, but they do not alter the fact that British economic performance worsened over a longer period than just a few years in the mid-1970s.[22] Voters saw this and responded to it, with significant political consequences. That was the real political economy behind any 'declinist' construction of events, however more negatively it came to be reinterpreted later.

As a result of these real, observable, negative outcomes, the two major parties promoted solutions that involved either fixing economic dislocation or blaming it on others. That is not exactly 'construction', though it is indeed what parties try to do: to shape and frame issues in ways that they hope or believe will be politically advantageous to them. For example, Labour chose to make the balance of payments its standard of performance evaluation in 1970, even though very few people understood it, knew what it was, or spontaneously mentioned it as something important. Consequently, politicians sometimes created the headlines that undid them, but that is just part of competitive party politics. At other times, as with growth, some targets of policy were too ambitious. That did contribute to a perception of decline, no doubt, but would voters have felt more positive if targets were as unambitious as the actual performance was poor?

The main point is that both parties tried to manage prices through incomes policies, and neither succeeded. Indeed, since governments had only some leverage in the public sector and little in the private sector, this approach simply guaranteed continuing conflict over the distribution of incomes (intensifying when things got worse). People became more frustrated with politics in general for apparently having little to offer on what was seen as the most important issue of the day, but they did not panic over this; that is, indeed, broadly what my analysis showed. If there was heightened concern, it was in minds closer to where policy was made. That (along with other communications channels) could have affected, indeed did affect, what people made of it all. That had some important and irreversible effects on partisan elections in the 1970s.

Further consequences of the politics of economic decline

As I look over *PED* now, I see one thing that jumps off the page more clearly than when I wrote the book. This is how the public perceived the dominant inflation control policy, shown in a chart in *PED* and reproduced here as figure 2.3. This was a complicated analysis, but it had a simple and consequential intuition that I wish I had brought out better. My analysis of people's rankings of alternative policies suggested a 'dimension' of inflation control policy possibilities in the minds of the 1970s electorate. How did people think inflation should be controlled? They differed, from those supporting more taxation (on the left) to allowing unemployment to rise (on the right) as alternative means of reducing demand and relieving pressure on prices. At the same time they differed significantly along party lines, but mostly between these two end-of-dimension policies that were not really on the political or governmental 'agenda' in the 1970s.

Instead, the largest part of the 1974 electorate clustered in the middle. For example, in the sample of 1,349 voters on which figure 2.3 is based, there was a group of 402 who preferred wage controls (indicated by W) to spending cuts (S) to allowing unemployment to rise (U), with tax increases last (T): they are indicated by the ordering $WSUT$ just to the right of centre of the figure. The average Conservative

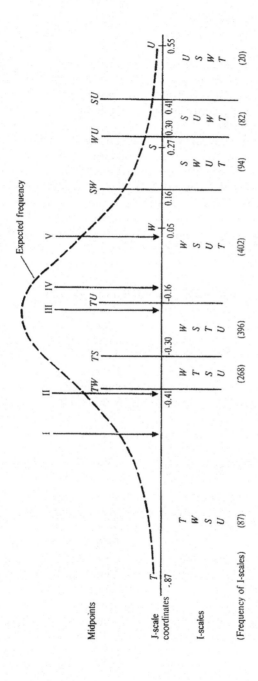

2.3 Thatcher's inflation control policy jump

Source: Alt, *Politics of Economic Decline*, p. 215 (figure 11.3). The dominant *J*-scale, its *I*-scales and the positions of various groups. Group I: Britain governed relatively well, same/more social services, great deal of interest, prices not very important (scale value = −0.430, n = 26). Group II: Britain governed relatively well, same/more social services, some further education (scale value = −0.302, n = 11). Group III: Average Labour voter (scale value = −0.196, n = 543). Group IV: Average Conservative voter (scale value = −0.098, n = 439). Group V. Britain not governed well, cut back social services, middle class, private sector, expect economy will get worse (scale value = −0.026, n = 76).

voter (located as IV) had these preferences. Just to the left are a group of 396 with preferences ordered *WSTU* (the same top two but more unemployment last); the average Labour voter (group III) is here. Sixty per cent of the electorate who could be located on this scale were in these two groups, and one observes just how narrow was the gap at this time between the average Conservative voter and the average Labour voter. Another 20 per cent could be found just further to the left: they also most preferred wage controls first but felt more taxes were better than spending cuts (*WTSU*).

What figure 2.3 makes clear is how far Thatcher jumped away from the centrist opinion. Imagine a group of electors who believed in 1974 that Britain was not governed well and expected the economy to get worse, and who typically were middle class, worked in the private sector and believed social services should be cut. That is group V in the figure: Thatcher leapt right over them. Her preferred ordering of policies (revealed *ex post* by what she did in office) was: first reduce social spending (*S*), next allow unemployment (*U*) to rise, and treat both increased taxation (*T*) and controls over wages (*W*) as out of bounds.[23] Far out on the right of the figure is a group whose preferences were *SUWT*: probably she would have been one of them. But that was a group that contained only eighty-two respondents, 5 per cent of the electorate in the figure, so her move has to be seen more as grasping an opportunity to persuade than as a grab for available votes. The British electoral system certainly empowers politicians with this sort of non-centrist policy preferences to implement them once elected.[24]

I would really like to know if empowering *SUWT*, the acronym for her preference order, made many friends in the electorate, but to what extent it did is a question for another day. I'm guessing not too many, since there is no obvious widespread belief in policy 'success' and resurgence of partisanship in the 1980s. But that this sort of policy gamble could 'work' at all well electorally in 1979 seems to require that voters be feeling ungenerous towards others, which is the consequence of economic failure for altruism that was at the core of the book's message.

I bring this up for two reasons. One is to speculate that the politics of economic decline had further consequences that I did not foresee when I wrote the book. I did observe in *PED* how economic decline had continued to increase hostility to foreign immigrants, even though Britain was a long way from the point where significant numbers actually believed that repatriation was a solution to the country's and their own economic ills. 'Were the sort of anti-permissiveness and racism bred by economic deterioration to come to be seen as a cure for economic problems, the story could be quite different', I wrote then.[25] That might have happened in the early 1980s: I lack data to say anything on this, but I am quite prepared to speculate that another legacy of the politics of economic decline was that economic decline and narrowed altruism set the stage for the success of Thatcher's subsequent racial policies. What the editors describe as 'opening up a marketplace for ideas' certainly had consequences beyond economics.

On the second reason, there is evidence that this sort of protectionism and the politics of fear that I wrote about in *PED* are happening today, in similar ways, in the USA. A decade or so ago, two-thirds of Americans in polls chose the USA as 'the leading economic power in the world today' and only one in ten chose China; two years ago a small plurality chose China.[26] That is perceived decline again. Asked 'Do you think the recent economic expansion in countries like China and India has been generally good ... or bad for the US economy', four times as many picked 'bad' as 'good', the negative inference. 'I would be willing to pay higher taxes so that everyone can have health insurance': about fifty–fifty now, but in better times, in the 1990s, the last time the issue loomed this large, a two-to-one majority was willing to pay for universal coverage. That's the narrowing of generosity.[27]

Politicians swing towards blame shifting when there is little for which they can claim credit. If people can be persuaded to connect some outgroup with the source of their economic woes, this becomes a powerful electoral lever to exploit. Recognition that other countries are doing better can be channelled into creating fear and threat perception, and ultimately support for what I would call 'inward-looking' policies like immigration controls or trade protection. In the end, that is because in hard times, or even more when good times are followed by hard times, support for 'generous' social policies and the political parties that espouse them will not go up. Instead, people will be as generous as they feel they can afford to be. And that is, then and now, the key to the politics of economic decline as I see it, and therefore also to political-economic developments in the 1970s.

Summary

Recently, Colin Hay, in writing about the winter of discontent, has observed that:[28]

> The story of the 1970s is really one of the attempted rise and management of a condition of ... rising inflation and rising unemployment [and] the exhaustion, first, of the Conservatives' and then of Labour's capacity to use [incomes policies] to manage inflationary pressures.

That is how I see it too, though I would throw in falling growth rates and point out that 'rising inflation and rising unemployment' actually begin several years before 1970. Regardless of how interpretation and reinterpretation of these rises shaped future views of the decade, the voters I studied were reacting to real economic change. The way they reacted – in the process learning more about ways in which changes in the broader economy affected them personally, losing faith in the abilities of both parties and conventional remedies to improve conditions, and turning away from socially 'generous' policies as economic decline and uncertainty increased – was not the product of a constructed idea of 'decline'. Indeed, they were at least as likely to be the foundation on which such construction would succeed electorally.

To return finally to one of the editors' questions, despite the fact that so much of what I wrote about seems like the consequences of normal political behaviour, why has the decade of the 1970s had an enduringly negative image? I have a simple answer where political economy is concerned. Even without any exaggeration, the decade *was* one of negatives: both economic, as conditions worsened, and political, as the comfortable policy and institutional remedies of the past failed. Psychologists' experiments suggest that when people recall how painful an experience like surgery was, they attach a lot of weight to two factors: how it was at its worst (economically, at the worst the 1970s were very bad); and how it ended (not well, as Hay reminds us).[29] So perhaps the enduring negative image of the 1970s also reflects no more than the ordinary processing by human beings of a painful experience.

Notes

1 B. Barry, *Sociologists, Economists, and Democracy* (London: Collier-Macmillan, 1970).
2 J. Alt, *The Politics of Economic Decline: Economic Management and Political Behaviour in Britain Since 1964* (Cambridge: Cambridge University Press, 1979, reissued 2009).
3 R. Klein, 'What we vote for', *New Society*, 8 November 1979, p. 332.
4 *PED* was reviewed quite widely, in France, Germany and Italy as well as the USA and Britain, and in sociology and economics as well as political science, where it got attention in 'policy debate' sources like *New Society* and *Political Quarterly*, as well as heavier journals.
5 D. Butler and D. Stokes, *Political Change in Britain: The Evolution of Electoral Choice* (London: Macmillan, 2nd edition, 1974).
6 Klein, 'What we vote for'.
7 R. Dahrendorf, *On Britain* (London: BBC, 1982), ch. 15.
8 A. H. Meltzer and S. F. Richard, 'A rational theory of the size of government', *Journal of Political Economy*, 89 (1981), pp. 914–27.
9 V. Bogdanor, 'The meaning of Mrs. Thatcher's victory', *Encounter*, September–October 1983, pp. 14–18, at p. 17.
10 There are moments when other issues like strikes take precedence, but these are brief. Figure 2.1 merges data on most important 'problems' (Gallup) and 'issues' (IPSOS–Mori). 'Economy' includes also references to 'unemployment', 'inflation' and 'the pound'. 'Social' includes 'health', 'education' and 'housing'.

More recent data were supplied by Chris Wlezian and Will Jennings. See W. Jennings and C. Wlezian, 'Distinguishing between most important problems and issues?', *Public Opinion Quarterly*, 75:3 (2011), pp. 545–55; and H. D. Clarke, D. Sanders, M. C. Stewart and P. F. Whiteley, *Performance Politics and the British Voter* (New York: Cambridge University Press, 2009).

11 The most recent observations are based on IPSOS–Mori data viewed at www. ipsos-mori.com/researchpublications/researcharchive/poll.aspx?oItemID= 56&view=wide, accessed 24 January 2012.

12 That would be an example of the Kahneman–Tversky 'endowment effect': that people place a higher value on something when they have actually had it than when they only see it in prospect. See D. Kahneman, J. L. Knetsch and R. Thaler, 'Experimental tests of the endowment effect and the Coase theorem', *Journal of Political Economy*, 98 (1990), pp. 1325–48.

13 J. Alt, 'Dealignment and the dynamics of partisanship in Britain', in P. Beck, R. Dalton and S. Flanagan (eds), *Electoral Change in Advanced Industrial Societies* (Princeton, NJ: Princeton University Press, 1984), pp. 298–339.

14 See for instance T. Smith, 'Is there real opinion change?', *International Journal of Public Opinion Research*, 6:2 (1994), pp. 187–203.

15 In the same spirit, where Tomlinson emphasises inflation 'as a force of social and political disruption', I see the roots of disruptiveness in the uncertainty and conflict over income distribution described above.

16 R. Middleton, *The British Economy Since 1945: Engaging with the Debate* (New York: St Martin's Press, 2000), table 2.4.

17 The exchange rate is itself affected by many other factors, including relative interest rates, trade flows, natural resource discoveries and exploitation, to say nothing of relative cost factors. I am not trying to describe a causal effect, just making a comment.

18 J. M. Livingston, *The British Economy in Theory and Practice* (Basingstoke: Macmillan, 1974), p. 79. He must have meant 'west of the Alps and north of the Pyrenees' for this to have meaning.

19 Middleton, *The British Economy*, table 2.4.

20 L. Black and H. Pemberton, *An Affluent Society? Britain's Post-war 'Golden Age' Revisited* (Aldershot: Ashgate, 2004), figure 8.1. Other related economic problems also became acute in the 1970s. For example, if we compare the late 1970s to 1960–73, the average public sector borrowing requirement as a fraction of gross domestic product quadrupled.

21 Data downloaded from http://stats.oecd.org/Index.aspx?DatasetCode=MEI LABOUR, accessed 24 January 2012. See also J. Denman and P. McDonald, 'Unemployment statistics from 1881 to the present day', *Labour Market Trends*, 104:1 (January 1996), pp. 5–18.

22 Looking at some of Tomlinson's other points, I am happy to believe that the balance of payments was not in as much trouble in the 1960s as many then thought. Moreover, if government itself was a source of the payments problem because a 'big country' illusion led it to overspend overseas, that is also fine. Was this heightened by the way statistics were collected and published? I don't know. If Britain's comparatively slower growth was due to an unfavourable distribution of factors of production, voters and maybe even politicians and planners do not seem to have known this at the time.

23 In some ways her policies resembled recommendations of the never-implemented Selsdon resolution of a few years earlier. For better or worse, we are certainly seeing 'taxes out of bounds' again today in the USA.

24 For example, top rates of income taxation over the last quarter century in Britain reflect a series of 'non-median' policy choices by successive governments. See

J. Alt, I. Preston and L. Sibieta, 'The political economy of tax policy', in Institute for Fiscal Studies, *Dimensions of Tax Design: The Mirrlees Review* (Oxford: Oxford University Press, 2009), pp. 1204–79.

25 Alt, *Politics of Economic Decline*, p. 272.

26 Data come from a variety of public opinion poll results viewed at www. pollingreport.com.

27 When the question 'Do you see foreign trade more as an opportunity for economic growth through increased US exports or a threat to the economy from foreign imports?' was asked recently, 'threat' narrowly won, exactly as after the previous recession in early 1992, and quite unlike the end of the long 1990s boom, when a remarkable three-to-two majority chose 'growth'.

28 C. Hay, 'Chronicles of a death foretold: the winter of discontent and construction of the crisis of British Keynesianism', *Parliamentary Affairs*, 63:3 (2010), pp. 446–70, esp. pp. 460–1.

29 D. A. Redelmeier and D. Kahneman, 'Patients' memories of painful medical treatments: real-time and retrospective evaluations of two minimally invasive procedures', *Pain*, 66:1 (1996), pp. 3–8.

3

The politics of declinism

Jim Tomlinson

James Alt's book *The Politics of Economic Decline* (hereafter *PED*) was a major contribution to the academic literature on the relationship between the British economy and political behaviour in the 1970s, deploying a sophisticated conceptual and statistical apparatus which went far beyond what had previously been attempted in such innovative works as Butler and Stokes' *Political Change in Britain*.[1] From the point of view of British academia it represented an attempt to import a largely American rational-choice framework into the study of British politics, akin to other attempts to 'reform' British academic disciplines in the name of positivistic social science (compare, for example, the contemporaneous upsurge in cliometrics in economic history). In British political science, such importation has perhaps had more impact than in most other social science disciplines (except, notably, economics), though overall it remains a marginal force. While the methodological approach of Alt's book never conquered academic political analysis in Britain, its substantive discussions remain important and influential, in part reflected in the book's reissue in 2009, on the thirtieth anniversary of its first publication. However, this chapter will argue that, while its distinctive approach generates many important insights, with hindsight the book can be seen as embedded in certain contemporary assumptions from which historians of the 1970s should now seek to maintain some critical distance.

Alt's key arguments

At the most general level, the question asked by *PED* is one character-istic of political science at this time – can existing political institutions survive? Above all this meant: can the two-party system survive current economic problems? Alt's answer was clear: while economic decline, he argues, has undermined enthusiasm for the major political parties (Conservative and Labour), he expects that they will continue to alternate in government, and there is no reason to anticipate a break-down in political order. This conclusion marks a contrast with much political literature produced in the 1970s, by politicians, academics and journalists, which commonly adopted a much more pessimistic and in some cases apocalyptic tone.[2] Alt's sophisticated empirical methodol-ogy provided a very effective insulation against the 'moral panic' which affected many of the British intelligentsia and commentators (as well as politicians) in this period, arguably one the most striking features of the 1970s, and something returned to below.

While the arguments of *PED* are complex, the central focus is on the 'behaviour of the public as it is affected by, and reacts to, economic change' (p. vii), with 'behaviour' largely concerned with support for the two main political parties. The economic change focused upon is the 'decline' of the British economy, and the period studied is largely between 1964 and 1974, with a limited but very interesting discussion of the 1975–76 period. The book, it should be noted, pre-dates the idea of 'Thatcherism' as a political force; indeed, her name nowhere appears in the text. Although qualified by highly detailed methodological and statistical discussion, a number of clear conclusions about this behaviour are drawn from a wide range of empirical sources, but especially from major surveys of opinion carried out at the time of the general elections of 1974. First, economic issues had become more important to electors since the 1960s, and inflation had by the early 1970s become the most significant of those issues. Second, electors had broadly accurate expec-tations about economic performance, basing these on 'communications' from a range of sources, rather than their own past experience (though in the early 1970s expectations of inflation were commonly significantly exaggerated, as Alt states on pp. 65–73). Third, in understanding both the general impact of economic issues and inflation specifically, 'one should pay closest attention to those things which are the closest to the electorate, and which have the most immediate impact upon them' (p. 21). Alt sees a trend towards the 'personalisation' of economic issues, by which he means increased significance given by electors to price and tax changes that directly affected them, rather than more 'abstract' issues such as the balance of payments (pp. 49–51). This personalisation he links to a reduction in the generosity of approach of the electorate to economic issues as the economy 'declined'. This shift in turn related to key arguments about changes in expectations. He suggested that the average 2 per cent growth of British real incomes in the 1950s and 1960s had become built into popular expectations by the late 1960s, and so the slowing expansion of the economy thereafter was registered by electors as an important 'failure'. (And thus delivering 'only' this degree of prosperity did not benefit incumbent governments, as Alt states on p. 94.) Popular adjustment to this failure tended to undermine support for more 'generous' policies, among which he includes a lessening of support for reducing unemployment (as well as welfare spending). Thus, he suggests (p. 261), affluence favoured electoral support for the Labour Party as it made people feel well-off enough to continue to stand behind that party's 'altruistic' agenda; 'decline' ultimately favoured the Conservatives by reducing that sense of altruism. The key analytical assumption here is that, faced with the political possibility of prioritising cutting inflation or unemployment, reducing unemployment is the altruistic option because it affects only a limited section of the electorate, while inflation affects all. Finally, while decline therefore had some differential impact on support for the two main political parties, there was overall a decreasing belief that they could do much to change economic performance, and this was part of the reason for a reduction in overall political partisanship (pp. 131, 200). However, as stressed above, the book argued that this disillusion was not so serious as to be fatal to the continuation of the two-party system.

Inflation and its effects

In commenting on *PED* and its perspective on the 1970s, this chapter will focus on two main issues. Both relate to the idea of 'decline'. The first concerns the relationship between decline and the specific issue of inflation; the second concerns the whole idea of decline as a way of characterising the British economy in this period.

PED is predicated on a diagnosis of economic failure across the board in the period 1964–74; chapter 2 'provides a picture of economic deterioration and the failure of economic management in Britain between 1964 and 1974' (p. 24). The various components of this claimed decline are returned to below, but the one which is most important in the specific arguments of the book is the acceleration of the inflation rate in the 1970s. Indeed, it would not be unfair to say that much of the book could be called 'the politics of inflation', so central is that issue to most of the text. This tendency to conflate economic 'decline' with the acceleration of inflation is defended by Alt on the basis that inflation is both symptom and cause of other economic ills, and because 'it has come to be seen as the central economic problem' (p. 158).

PED spends a chapter (chapter 4) discussing evidence on contemporary expectations about inflation. This is useful in emphasising that popular understanding of inflation is not irrational, as suggested by economists' use of terms such as 'money illusion'.[3] But before focusing on the basis of the electorate's beliefs about the scale of future inflation, there would seem to be an important prior question: why should an elector worry about inflation at all? Why and how did it come to be seen as such an important problem? On this matter Alt's discussion is much less extensive. Part of the difficulty is that the evidence suggests that the implications of inflation for changes in real income were much misunderstood at the time, with the great majority in 1974 seemingly believing that real incomes had fallen, when they had actually increased considerably (pp. 95–6). Thus people may have had realistic expectations about future inflation, while quite misjudging the significance of this for their personal economic well-being.

In the discussion of 'Self-interest, unemployment and inflation' (pp. 187–92) *PED* notes the redistributive effects of inflation (from profits to earned incomes), but beyond that the book says little on its effects or how these were portrayed in the 1970s. I want to suggest that, from an historian's point of view, this is to miss a crucial aspect of both the economics and the politics of the decade.

Intriguingly, *PED* begins with a quote which provides a useful starting point for discussing precisely this issue. It comes from the MP Raymond Fletcher in a 1972 book by Robbins about inflation: 'Inflation, as we all know, is socially disruptive. It transforms an ordered society into an undisciplined mob. This is what happened in Germany in the 1920 and in many countries in Europe after the 1939–45 war.'[4] This notion of the effects of inflation, as a force of social and political disruption, was a crucial feature of political argument in the 1970s, and to understand its genesis, deployment and effects is one of the key tasks of the historian of that period. Only a few suggestions on each of these can be made here.

The origin of such views lies in part in responses to historic hyper-inflation, especially that in Germany and parts of Eastern and Central Europe in the early 1920s, the key reference here being Keynes' suggestion that Lenin had 'declared that the best way to destroy the capitalist system is to debauch the currency'.[5] Ironically, one of the key figures in applying such analysis to the Britain of the 1970s was Keynes' sharpest critic, Friedrich Hayek. Hayek's theories emphasised the economic damage done by inflation's impact on relative prices, but more broadly he emphasised the social and political harms that inflation could wreak.[6] The political tone of some of his 1970s writing (not untypical of the times) is caught in his allegation in the mid-1970s that 'the present inflation has been deliberately brought about by governments on the advice of economists. The British Labour Party planned it that way as early as 1957.'[7]

As is well known, Margaret Thatcher regarded Hayek as a key intellectual influence on her own thinking, and her speeches and writings drew strongly upon his apocalyptic analysis of the effects of inflation.[8] However, it should be noted that, as always, the relationship between economists' arguments and their use by politicians was not straightforward. While politicians like Thatcher drew upon the work of 'monetarist' economists such as Hayek (and Milton Friedman) in emphasising the harms done by inflation, they commonly rejected the monetarist view that wage bargaining was wholly irrelevant to inflation, because they wanted to deploy that alleged link to support their attack on the trade unions. This important tension in Conservative policy-making, between economic theory and *realpolitik*, was central to the party's internal debates after Thatcher's accession to the party leadership in 1975.[9] As Alt rightly suggests (p. 220), the decision of the Conservative Party to treat counter-inflation policy as a question of industrial relations introduced 'different dimensions into popular appraisal of economic policy'. In retrospect one might put the point much more strongly; this treatment became central to the successful politics of 'Thatcherism'.

The deployment of apocalyptic notions about the effects of inflation was widespread in the 1970s, beginning well before inflation reached its peak in 1975/76. One striking example is *The Times'* commentaries at the time of the military coup in Chile, which supported this action (which left c.50,000 dead and perhaps a million people in exile) on the grounds that the Chilean rate of inflation was intolerable.[10] Thatcher was also, of course, a strong supporter of Pinochet, the leader of the coup.[11] Similar notions were at work in, for example, the *Banker*'s claim in March 1974, in a commentary headed 'The last chance', that unless inflation were dealt with the last opportunity would have been lost 'for the parliamentary system to cope with Britain's economic problems'.[12] The following year *The Economist* claimed 'Britannia's dream of apocalypse is horribly close to coming true'. There was much more in the same vein in these influential publications.[13]

As Richard Johnson has suggested, the early/mid-1970s saw 'The great fear' take hold as 'important sections of the middle classes did lose confidence. For the first time parts of the Establishment began seriously to consider alternatives to our present form of parliamentary democracy.'[14] Perhaps the 'sections' most evidently showing this loss were parts of the intelligentsia and the 'serious' press. It should be noted that, while it was generally those on the right who were making the running, such views spread across the political spectrum. Thus, for example, the *Guardian* journalist Peter Jenkins, a consistent member of the 'radical centre', published some of the most extreme versions of this 'loss of confidence' with his repeated suggestions that Britain was sliding towards 'Third World Status'.[15]

What were the effects on Britain more generally of this 'panic' among much of the 'serious' press and the chattering classes? As Alt (p. 266) rightly stresses, across the mass of the population 'the reaction to the rapid inflation of 1974 and 1975 was very calm, and far indeed from the doom-laden predictions some journalists made in 1974 of chaos and the breakdown of democracy in Britain'. This is borne out by other data, such as the findings published in the *Gallup Political Index*, which shows a strong popular concern about inflation, a declining belief in the capacity of political parties to manage the economy, but no evidence of a fundamental loss of faith in British government institutions.[16] Though not published at the time, similar conclusions were drawn from survey and focus group work carried out by the Labour government's Counter-Inflation Publicity Unit, as evidence in the National Archives suggests.[17] Alt accounts for this lack of panic largely as a result of the acceleration in inflation being expected, part of a 'revolution of declining expectations' that made people believe governments could do little about the problem, leading to 'not a politics of protest, but a politics of quiet disillusion' (p. 270). Curiously, given his emphasis on the continuing if declining significance of unemployment to popular opinion, he mentions only in passing that the response to the inflation was muted by the fact that the accompanying unemployment was rising but still quite low (peaking at 6 per cent in 1976). More generally, it may be suggested that the muted response was based on the hugely important fact that the 'real' economy did not suffer a sustained collapse in the 1970s – the dip in output was relatively small and growth soon resumed. Christopher Dow measures 1973–75 as the least severe of the five major recessions of the twentieth century.[18] In addition, the rise in unemployment relative to the fall in output was notably smaller in the 1970s recession (in this respect it has similarities to the 2008/09 downturn, which also saw a robust 'Keynesian' response). This, of course, registered in the economic statistics as a stagnation in the growth of productivity, and this stagnation is commonly used as a measure of the decade's economic failures. But in terms of economic welfare, sustaining employment should be seen as marking an important success for policy in the 1970s, given the immense and sustained harms done by unemployment, which go far beyond any temporary loss of income.[19]

Alongside the limited impact on output and especially employment, the kind of major arbitrary redistributions of income said to be the likely consequence of inflation by the 'apocalypse now' school did not actually occur in the 1970s. The main redistribution during the mid-1970s (when inflation was high) was through the failure of building society interest rates to keep pace with the inflation rate, leading to a redistribution of incomes from savers to mortgagees.[20] This shift is not to be dismissed as insignificant. It was retrogressive in its consequences, as many building society savers were relatively elderly and their savings were not usually very large, while mortgagees on the other hand were typically better-off. Nevertheless, in the context of the economy as whole, the redistribution was limited (and was later partly offset by the introduction of index-linked savings products). In other regards, older people were protected by the fact that the state pension rose in line with earnings rather than prices (until this policy was ended in 1981).[21]

Among the great mass of wage and salary earners, the impact of all the inflationary excitement of the 1970s was limited, with some small narrowing of vertical pay differentials during the flat-rate incomes policy period, reversed later in the decade. The main sustained alteration in differentials was between parts of the public sector and the private sector, because of the much greater effectiveness of incomes policies on many low-paid public sector workers.[22] It was these workers who were squeezed most in the 1970s; it was they, of course, who were also at the forefront of the 'winter of discontent' in 1978/79, as the government's 5 per cent pay policy threatened to squeeze their real incomes further. So, again, inflation had important impacts on popular welfare in the 1970s, but without ever showing signs of generating the kinds of responses imagined in the nightmares of some of the 'opinion formers' and ideologues noted above.

Finally, inflation was associated with a shift of income from profits to wages and salaries. Undoubtedly this was reinforced by the mid-1970s inflation, especially because of the absence of indexation of taxation on profits, but how far it was mainly the consequence of inflation remains doubtful. There had been a trend towards a reduction in the profit share since at least the 1960s and the recession of 1973/74, like most recessions, exacerbated the shift, so it is difficult to separate out the effects of inflation.[23]

If the mass of the population seem to have been immune from the panic about inflation among some journalists and politicians in the mid-1970s, this does not mean that panic did not matter. An important channel of influence for such views, especially as expressed in the financial press, was by their impact on financial markets, which in turn could potentially powerfully shape government policy because of the need for governments to sustain financial confidence at a time when they were heavy borrowers.[24] How far such pressures shaped policy in the 1970s is therefore another key issue in assessing the political impact of inflation.

Importantly, such pressures do *not* seem to have been decisive in the initial policy shift under Labour, when in his budget of April 1975 Denis Healey made clear that reducing inflation would be given priority over sustaining employment. This shift in macroeconomic priorities, accompanied by the Social Contract to try to limit the unemployment effects of deflationary policies, was crucial in reversing the inflationary trend, though of course its effects were felt only with a considerable lag. Despite this policy shift, re-establishing financial confidence proved a hard struggle for the Labour government, and it was only after the trauma of the loan negotiations with the International Monetary Fund in 1976 that the government received a financial 'seal of approval'.[25] The intriguing question is: why did it take those traumas to restore financial confidence when policy had already clearly shifted in a deflationary direction? Perhaps part of the answer is the panic in sections of the financial press, and the impact of that panic on financial markets over-riding, at least for a period, the evidence of changes in actual policy? In any event, this episode drove it home to Labour leaders that maintaining the confidence of the financial markets was a key requirement if scope for managing the national economy was to be retained.

The problems of 'decline'

As noted above, while much of *PED* concentrates on inflation, the pre-supposition of the book is that the inflationary problem was just one symptom of an overall 'decline' in the British economy dated back to 1964. It is unsurprising that a book written in the mid-1970s should take such decline as given. Since they were invented in the late 1950s/early 1960s, 'declinist' accounts of the postwar British economy have been extremely pervasive, and the 1970s saw a notable growth of publications premised on such notions.[26] However, while still strongly embedded in popular and political discourse, declinist accounts have been subject to considerable challenge since the 1990s. This challenge has come from a number of vantage points. Historians of science and technology have undermined the caricature of Britain as a welfare state, neglectful of its technological capacity.[27] Political historians have stressed how far notions of 'decline' were the product of political strategy.[28] Economic historians have emphasised how well the British economy performed in this period compared with other periods.[29]

Challenges to declinism have arisen in part from different perspectives on the data usually employed to show British 'decline'. *PED* refers to the standard four indicators of economic performance – growth, unemployment, inflation and the balance of payments (table 3.1) – and these can be used to indicate some of the crucial data issues involved.

One generic trope of declinist accounts is what might be called the use of the 'Promiscuous Other', where Britain's performance is compared with a shifting set of other countries, comparators arbitrarily

Table 3.1 British economic performance, 1951–73, 1979–97

	1951–73	1979–97
Growth (% real gross domestic product)	3.0	2.1
Unemployment (%, national definition)	2.1	9.2
Inflation (%, Retail Price Index)	4.4	5.8
Balance of payments (current account % of gross domestic product)	+0.4	–1.2

Sources: figures for growth, unemployment, inflation from R. Middleton, *The British Economy Since 1945* (Basingstoke: Macmillan, 2000), pp. 28, 149; current account calculated from *Economic Trends Annual Supplement 2006* (London: HMSO, 2006), p. 111.

chosen to show British performance in a bad light. *PED* (pp. 27–33) is guilty of this to a degree – thus, while British economic growth is compared with that of a broad range of exclusively European countries, the low-inflation cases of the USA and Canada are brought in when inflation rates are compared, whereas in dealing with unemployment, while the American method of calculating this figure is used, the strikingly lower rates of unemployment in Britain compared with the USA is not noted in the text. On the balance of payments, no international comparison is attempted, except to note that France and the USA also devalued their currency in this period.

Let us look at these four standard performance criteria in more detail. At the core of most declinism is adverse comparison of British growth rates. On this measure of performance *PED* is most unequivocal, rightly noting that the British growth rate of gross domestic product (GDP) stretching back to the 1950s was lower than that achieved in almost all Western European countries, though the fact that it was faster than in the USA is *not* noted (p. 27). The work of Crafts has explained this pattern during the 'golden age' down to 1973 largely in terms of catch-up and convergence, whereby among the rich Western countries of 1950 subsequent growth rates can largely be explained as inverse to absolute levels at that date. Hence a very rich country like Britain in 1950 converged slowly on the even richer USA, while the bulk of poorer countries grew faster and caught up with Britain.[30] Crafts, it should be emphasised, does not think this explains all the divergence in growth rates, and he still thinks Britain suffers from significant deficiencies, but his work suggests a large part of British 'decline' resulted not from any failure in performance, but from the different historical trajectory of the British economy. As the 'first industrial nation', Britain shifted a large part of its workforce out of agriculture in the nineteenth century, yielding 'one-off' productivity benefits that most of Western Europe did not enjoy until after 1950. In that later period, Britain had no possibility or repeating this growth-boosting structural change.

Table 3.2 Comparative economic performance, 1950–73

	France	West Germany	Italy	UK
Growth in gross domestic product (% p.a.)	5.0	6.0	5.6	3.0
Unemployment (standardised %)	2.0	2.5	5.5	2.8
Consumer prices (% increase p.a.)	5.0	2.7	3.9	4.6
Current account (% gross domestic product, 1960–73)	0.9	+0.9	–1.0	0.1

Source: OECD Historical Statistics (Paris: OECD, 1996).

Comparisons of Britain's inflation rate before 1974 also do not bear out the idea of a sustained poor performance compared with other developed countries. Alt claims that 'throughout the last 15 to 20 years, Britain's inflation rate has persistently been amongst the highest in the Western World' (p. 29). However, Middleton's data show the British rate as below the mean of all countries in the Organisation for Economic Co-operation and Development (OECD), for all the dates covered within that time period, 1960, 1964, 1968 and 1973.[31] Similarly, table 3.2 shows the British rate significantly above only that of West Germany among the West European 'big four'. On unemployment the comparative position is less favourable, with Britain's (standardised) percentage above the OECD mean in all the years from 1964, though it should be noted that the maximum figure is 3.1 per cent, in both 1968 and 1973, a very low level by any standard except that of the 'golden age'.[32]

The British balance-of-payments position is more difficult to summarise because it is not at all clear what, if anything, should be the measure of performance on this indicator. If one takes the commonly used current account balance, the UK had a small (0.1 per cent of GDP) average surplus in 1960–73 (table 3.2) and a slightly larger surplus in 1951–73 (table 3.1). This is perhaps the most striking contrast to declinist notions of Britain's economic performance, given the seemingly permanent state of alarm about the payments situation in these years. But this alarm largely reflected not a 'declinist' failure of competitiveness in British exports, as commonly alleged, but a failure to meet ambitious targets for a current account surplus to fund overseas investment, military spending and development aid. The problem was one of 'overstretch' rather than competitive failure.[33] If one focuses upon the commercial balance, excluding government transactions, the story is even more striking: the private sector was earning a very large current surplus throughout the 1950s and 1960s.[34]

With the benefit of hindsight it seems clear that the 1950s and 1960s were the 'golden age' of economic performance, with all four of the main indicators performing better than in the decades after 1979 (table 3.1).

Table 3.3 Major economic indicators, 1974–79

	France	West Germany	Italy	UK
Output growth (% p.a.)	3.1	2.7	2.3	2.0
Unemployment (%, national definition)	4.5	3.6	6.6	4.5
Inflation (% gross domestic product deflator)	10.4	4.3	16.9	16.3
Current balance (% gross domestic product)	−0.6	+1.0	−0.2	−1.3

Source: M. Artis and D. Cobham, *Labour's Economic Policies 1974–79* (Manchester: Manchester University Press, 1991), p. 267.

However, between these two periods there was the 1970s interregnum, in which British economic performance clearly deteriorated and was undoubtedly poor (table 3.3), though even here it is clear that the characteristic British problems of the mid-1970s were shared to a significant degree with comparable Western European economies.

The purpose of deconstructing narratives of decline is to historicise them – to make clear that while there are continuities in their characteristic forms, they are also the contingent products of specific conjunctures. Within those conjunctures a wide range of forces may come into play – the production of particular kinds of economic statistics, for example, or the prevalence of particular national cultural norms. But undoubtedly a key element in most of these conjunctures is politics, and it is on the politics of declinism in the 1970s that I want to conclude.

As already indicated, declinism was not invented in the 1970s, but it was in that decade and the early years of the next that it was probably most prevalent and most politically significant. While the declinism of the late 1950s and early 1960s was invented on the political centre left, in part to attack the Conservative government of 1951–64, it was taken up by many on the right in the 1970s and was at the centre of Thatcher's politics. As David Cannadine has argued, Thatcher followed Joseph Chamberlain in constructing a 'politics of decline', in which she based her claim to power on having the unique ability to reverse the country's decline.[35] Central to this narrative was the argument that the problems of the mid-1970s were not short term, but the culmination of a long-term decline, deeply embedded in British society and in its political economy. A distinctly right-wing declinism was thus deployed to make the case for a radical change in policy direction, while also being used to defend the short-term consequences of this change once implemented after 1979. Hence the argument that declinism helps to explain how Thatcher constructed a coherent rhetoric in her bid for power, and also how her government survived the slump of the early 1980s; it enabled the Conservatives in the early 1980s to portray mass unemployment as the inescapable price to be paid for correcting many years of deep-seated 'decline' rather than the consequence of the government's short-run management of the economy.

James Alt's book was concerned with some of the key issues of the 1970s – inflation, 'decline' and public understandings of and reactions to these terms. Historians of that decade now need to pursue similar issues, but with a more distanced view, which focuses upon how these terms were *constructed*, how they were then deployed in a highly politicised fashion, and what the political consequences of their deployment were. On inflation, we need an analysis of how an acceleration in price rises was turned from a contingent consequence of international monetary instability and then the consequence of the first of the increases in the price of oil implemented by the Organization of the Petroleum Exporting Countries (OPEC1) into the underpinnings for the 'great fear', and how this fear was deployed to mobilise a coalition to attack the postwar settlement. On decline, we need to examine how this notion was transformed from an underpinning for a broadly social democratic politics in the 1960s into the basis for a New Right attack on the postwar settlement in the mid-1970s. In both areas we need to take on board Alt's stress on the importance of popular expectations which that settlement had encouraged about rapidly rising material living standards as the norm, against which any slowdown would be registered as failure. Despite evidence that those rising living standards were beginning to yield little benefit in terms of other measures of economic welfare,[36] the 'golden age' had seen the mass of the population increasingly trapped on a 'hedonic treadmill' which meant that any slowdown in the economy would be traumatic. Perhaps this helps to explain the overheated politics of the 1970s?

The problem of 'Keynesianism'

These questions suggest an approach to the 1970s which differs substantially from that most commonly derived from political science and recently put to work by some historians, which focuses upon an allegedly crucial battle between 'economic ideas' in understanding economic policy development in this decade. The key author here is Peter Hall.[37] The overarching theme of his work is to see the 1970s as bringing about a decisive victory of one set of economic ideas, 'monetarism', over another, labelled 'Keynesianism'.

As an historical narrative, this has one obvious flaw. With hindsight we now know that Keynesianism was not decisively defeated in the 1970s, as it was clearly deployed in many countries as an initial response to the 2008/09 recession.[38] Thus the 'death of Keynesianism' was much exaggerated.[39] To understand how this exaggeration arose, and what it tells us about the problems of focusing on the 'marketplace for ideas' as central to the 1970s, we need to look in some detail at the structure of Hall's arguments. The key themes are summarised in one article, though this both draws on previous work and has been re-deployed in later accounts.[40]

Hall's schema combines a critique of excessively 'state-centred' approaches to policy-making with a notion of 'normal science' and 'paradigm shifts' derived from the work of Thomas Kuhn. This combination yields an argument in which policy changes are divided into a hierarchy of 'orders'. Least significant are changes in 'instrument settings' such as interest rates or tax rates. Second-order changes are where new instruments of policy are introduced, but the aims of policy remain unaltered. These changes are 'normal policy-making' by analogy with Kuhn's 'normal science', do not shift the fundamental assumptions of policy and come about largely as a result of debates *within* the state apparatus. Third-order changes are where the hierarchy of goals behind policy changes (along with first- and second-order changes) and involve radical changes in the overarching terms of policy discourse. The analogy is here with Kuhn's 'paradigm shift', where 'change is likely to involve the accumulation of anomalies, experimentation with new forms of policy, and policy failures that precipitate a shift in the locus of authority over policy and initiate a wider contest between competing paradigms'.[41] This is how Hall characterises the shift from Keynesianism to monetarism in the 1970s and 1980s, and crucially he asserts that this kind of change is influenced by societal forces outside the state and shifts in the locus of authority in economic policy-making. This shift, he argues, was accompanied by a dramatic expansion in the 'marketplace for economic ideas', especially in the 1975–79 period. Ultimately monetarism triumphed because the Conservatives adopted it as a means to resolve Britain's economic problems which was politically congenial to them, and then the party went on to win the 1979 election and hence was able to implement those monetarist policies.[42]

What is one to make of this approach? First, it has to be noted that, while widely used, and despite its congenially sociological approach to changes in scientific understanding, Kuhn's notion of paradigms is deeply ambiguous. One author has identified twenty-one different meanings attached to the word in Kuhn's key text, which in turn can be grouped into three quite distinct groups: one metaphysical, one socio-logical and one which defines paradigms as constructs.[43]

This ambiguity, I would argue, is carried over into Hall's use of the term. This is most evident in his discussion of Keynesianism. On the one hand, his meta-analysis of the whole postwar period uses the terminology of the 'Keynesian era' and the 'Keynesian welfare state', the latter the key underpinning for the whole 'socioeconomic policy regimes' of the years from 1945 down to the 1970s.[44] On the other hand, when looking in detail at the alleged shift from Keynesianism to monetarism in Britain in the 1970s, Keynesianism becomes a much more specific doctrine about the instability of capitalism and the means to correct those instabilities.[45] This ambiguity raises serious issues about the helpfulness of the language of 'paradigms'. Was there a fundamental policy shift in the 1970s, and one which can be adequately encapsulated in the notion of a transition from a Keynesian to a monetarist 'paradigm'?

Most narratives of postwar Britain and the rest of the capitalist world take it as given that fundamental changes took place in the 1970s. So before discussing how these changes are to be understood, it is worth pausing to at least qualify what are often exaggerated notions of how much changed. Focusing on the British case, and with the benefit of hindsight, we can suggest that the crisis of the 1970s was less fundamental than is often suggested. The recession of the 1970s was a mild one in Britain's 'real economy' and, as noted above, its unemployment consequences muted – though, of course, as the first significant recession since 1945 it was responded to by contemporaries in a more excitable way than now, with the benefit of hindsight, seems appropriate. While the financial system came under pressure in the 1970s, these pressures were mild indeed compared with what was to occur in the 2000s. The crisis was largely driven by two issues – inflation and fiscal deficits. It was the concurrence of these two problems which defined most of the economic debate of the 1970s, though, as already noted, the politics of the period led to both of these being treated as symptoms of an allegedly deeper malaise.

Hall's account recognises the crucial importance of inflation to economic policy-making in the 1970s, seeing the key 'third-order' shift as when 'inflation replaced unemployment as the preeminent concern of policymakers'. Inflation was also crucial to the damaging 'internal anomalies' in the Keynesian paradigm, because that paradigm could not cope with the simultaneous occurrence of inflation and unemployment.[46] This anomaly was, according to Hall, one of the key problems which undermined Keynesianism as a doctrine, opening up the 'marketplace for ideas' and the eventual triumph of monetarism.

But this alleged anomaly is being asked to do too much work here. Keynesians in the 1970s has a perfectly good explanation for the simultaneous occurrence of inflation and unemployment. While, of course, textbook Keynesian models suggested a 'knife-edge' framework, in which as aggregate demand expanded the economy moved from unemployment and stable prices to full employment and inflation, Keynesian economists had long recognised that external shocks, such as the Korean War commodity boom or OPEC1, could impart externally generated inflationary pressures on the economy which had nothing to do with the state of domestic demand.[47] Hall is right to suggest that the polemics of the time suggested 'stagflation' was fundamentally damaging to Keynesian economic analysis, but this characterisation was not an objective judgement on the 'paradigm'.

Conversely, Hall glosses over the tensions in 1970s-style monetarism as a policy package when he suggests that it 'provided a coherent challenge to the policies of the Labour government'.[48] First, as he himself notes, the basic monetarist proposition that the key to defeating inflation and stabilising the economy was to control the growth of the money supply did not lead to a clear policy prescription.[49] Friedman's idea of monetary base control was rejected by the Conservative government after 1979, in favour of a focus on controlling public borrowing (the public sector borrowing requirement, PSBR), which Friedman sarcastically referred to as akin to 'attempting to control the supply of steel by controlling the demand for cars'.[50] It seems clear that on coming into power in 1979 the Conservatives had very little in the way of a clear policy prescription for controlling monetary growth and, indeed, their early years were dominated by the extraordinary appreciation of the exchange rate as a result of 'tight money' (sharp deceleration of monetary growth) and expectations unleashed by their policy rhetoric, an appreciation which seems to have been almost entirely unexpected by the new government.[51] A key problem for Thatcherite Conservatives was that while they willed the end of tight money, they baulked at the means – high interest rates – especially because of their impact on the housing market and thus on home-owning voters. As the Chancellor of the Exchequer, Nigel Lawson, lamented, Thatcher's commitment to the 'property-owning democracy' made her loath to see interest rates rise in the way 'proper monetarism' required.[52]

Monetarism also raised problems for Conservatives because of its implications for policy towards trade unions. Hall rightly notes that 'the monetarist idea that the "natural rate" of unemployment could be decreased only by reducing the power of the trade unions also fit[ted] well with the Conservatives' growing antipathy toward the unions'.[53] But this is only part of the story. The long-standing antipathy of Conservatives to trade unions had been strongly reinforced in the postwar period by the claim that they were responsible for Britain's persistent inflation, a stance reinforced by the acceleration of inflation in the 1970s. So the monetarist claim that inflation was 'always and everywhere a monetary phenomenon', and therefore could not be caused by unions, was problematic for Conservative politics, and led to anguished debates in top Conservative circles about how monetarist doctrine and political predisposition were to be reconciled.[54]

The key point here is that the notion of a 'marketplace for ideas' as applied to the 1970s exaggerates the policy coherence of monetarism, and in doing so puts too much emphasis on the intellectual power of its challenge to existing policies. It might also be said that, while, as suggested above, Hall in some respects overstates the challenges to Keynesian theories posed by the simultaneous occurrence of inflation and unemployment, it is true to say that, like 'monetarism', Keynesianism was a rather loose-coupled and sometimes contradictory package of ideas once it moved from the textbooks to diagnosis and policy prescriptions. There is a good case to be made for fundamentally rethinking this whole monetarism/Keynesianism dichotomy as a way of understanding the evolution of British economic policy.[55]

One of the most curious elements in Hall's discussion of the events of the 1970s is when he says: 'Little noticed but especially important in the 1975–79 period was the pressure that the financial markets, notably for government debt and foreign exchange, placed on the Government', which he sees as having driven 'many of the ad hoc adjustments towards monetarism made by the 1974–79 Labour government'.[56] But in fact this was far from 'little noticed', either at the time or subsequently; more importantly, it is much more central both to the specific story of the 1970s and to the broader discussion of 'the Keynesian paradigm' than Hall allows.[57]

As suggested earlier in this chapter, we should put the politics of inflation (in its widest sense) at the centre of our discussion of economics and politics in the 1970s. At one level Hall does this by linking his 'third-order' change to a shift in policy priority from unemployment to inflation. But he fails to tell us why this displacement took place, in part because he wholly neglects to analyse how unemployment and inflation were *constructed* as political problems. This is one of the key problems of the 'social learning' approach to policy-making: it tends to treat social and economic problems as givens, rather than as constructs.

A key part of the politics of inflation in the 1970s was the way in which price changes became a key indicator of 'credibility' for financial markets, and it was through this mechanism, I would argue, that 'Keynesian' policies of public borrowing were constrained in the 1970s. Yes, there was a 'marketplace for ideas' in the 1970s, but this was much less important than the financial markets, where the construction of credibility became the key determinant of the room for manoeuvre of national economic management.

This specific point about the 1970s is tied to a broader argument about the Keynesian 'paradigm'. Like all borrowers, governments pursuing fiscal expansion are subject to the views of lenders. Those views are not given. In the 1970s, lenders to governments were mainly concerned with inflation, alongside the perennial concern with debt sustainability.[58] The levels of inflation that characterised Britain in the 1970s therefore greatly constrained Keynesian policies. In the crisis of 2008/09, strikingly, Britain was able to borrow readily, without any threat of a crisis (despite the mendacious claims of the Coalition government to the contrary). Keynesianism was possible, in contrast to the 1970s, because there was no inflation threat to spook the markets and Britain's debt levels were clearly sustainable. This analysis obviously puts much less weight on the availability of coherent policy 'paradigms' as the key to policy-making than Hall's approach. In the argument made here, the role of economic ideas is not discarded, but they are seen as much more malleable, and as providing much less in the way of coherent world views, than Hall suggests. Keynesianism is seen more in the context of institutional constraints and political calculation than of a 'marketplace for ideas'.

Conclusion

James Alt rightly identified as key issues of the 1970s both inflation and popular understanding of that phenomenon, albeit it might be said that he confused the issues by conflating inflation and 'decline'. He brought a robustly empirical approach to bear (and one might note here the contrasting lack of empirical data in Hall's analysis of the 1970s). Our understanding of this decade can build on Alt's work if it is allied to a more constructivist approach to economic 'problems', where the political and rhetorical framing of the economy is given much greater weight.[59] Alongside understanding the construction of that framing, we need to understand much better how framing is responded to both by the populace in general and by key actors, not least those in financial markets.

Notes

1 J. Alt, *The Politics of Economic Decline: Economic Management and Political Behaviour in Britain Since 1964* (Cambridge: Cambridge University Press, 1979, reissued 2009); D. Butler and D. Stokes, *Political Change in Britain* (London: Macmillan, 1969).
2 S. Brittan, 'The economic contradictions of democracy', *British Journal of Political Science*, 5:2 (1975), pp. 129–59; S. Brittan, *The Economic Consequences of Democracy* (London: Temple Smith, 1977); S. Haseler, *The Death of British Democracy* (London: Elek, 1976); P. Hutber (ed.), *What's Wrong With Britain?* (London: Sphere, 1978); P. Jay, *Employment, Inflation and Politics* (London: Institute of Economic Affairs, 1976).
3 The most extensive discussions of popular understandings of inflation in this period are by Hilde Behrend: see her *Problems of Labour and Inflation* (London: Croom Helm, 1984).

4 L. Robbins, *Inflation, Economy and Society* (London: Institute of Economic Affairs, 1972), p. 69, cited in *PED*, p. 3.

5 J. M. Keynes, *The Economic Consequences of the Peace* (London: Macmillan, 1919), p. 143; also R. White and K. Schaler, 'Who said "debase the currency": Keynes or Lenin?', *Journal of Economic Perspectives*, 23:2 (2009), pp. 213–22.

6 J. Tomlinson, *Hayek and the Market* (London: Pluto, 1990), pp. 68–80.

7 F. Hayek, *New Studies in Philosophy, Politics, Economics and the History of Ideas* (London: Routledge & Kegan Paul, 1978), p. 216. The year 1957 saw the publication of Labour Party proposals in *National Superannuation* (earnings-related pensions), which necessarily had some inflation projections to assess the future impact of the proposals; these projections were, of course, forecasts, not *advocacy* of any future rate of price increase.

8 House of Commons, *Hansard*, 10 March 1981, vol. 1000, col. 756.

9 J. Tomlinson, 'Thatcher, inflation and the "decline" of the British economy', in B. Jackson and R. Saunders (eds), *Making Thatcher's Britain: Essays on the History of Thatcherism* (Cambridge: Cambridge University Press, 2012).

10 *The Times*, 13 September 1973, p. 17, and 28 September 1973, p. 19.

11 A. Beckett, *Pinochet in Piccadilly* (London: Faber & Faber, 2002).

12 *Banker*, March 1974, p. 205.

13 *The Economist*, 17 May 1975, p. 9; J. Tomlinson, *The Politics of Decline* (Harlow: Longman Pearson, 2001), pp. 85–90.

14 R. Johnson, *The Politics of Recession* (London: Macmillan, 1985), p. 131.

15 P. Jenkins, 'The map for Britain's journey into the third world', *Guardian*, 27 September 1978, reprinted in P. Jenkins, *Anatomy of Decline*, edited by B. Brivati and R. Cockett (London: Indigo, 1996).

16 *Gallup Political Index*, nos 174–97 (London: Gallup, 1975–76).

17 Some of this evidence is discussed in J. Tomlinson, 'Popular understanding of the economy. British government and inflation in the 1970: the Counter-Inflation Publicity Unit', Economic History Conference, University of Cambridge, March 2011.

18 C. Dow, *Major Recessions* (Oxford: Oxford University Press, 2000), pp. 24–7.

19 D. Blanchflower and J. Oswald, 'Well-being over time in Britain and the USA', *Journal of Public Economics*, 88:7–8 (2004), pp. 1359–86.

20 J. Foster, 'The redistributive effects of inflation on building society shares and deposits, 1961–74', *Bulletin of Economic Research*, 28:1 (1976), pp. 68–75.

21 W. Smith, *Inflation and Elderly People* (London: Age Concern, 1983).

22 J. Fallick and R. Elliott (eds), *Incomes Policies, Inflation and Relative Pay* (London: Allen & Unwin, 1981).

23 C. Cohen, *The Welfare Effects of Inflation – The British Case* (Paris: Société Universitaire Européene de Recherche Financières, 1980); A. Glyn, *British Workers, Capitalism and the Profit Squeeze* (Harmondsworth: Penguin, 1972).

24 W. Keegan and R. Pennant-Rea, *Who Runs the Economy?* (London: Temple Smith, 1979), chs 4–6; W. Parsons, *The Power of the Financial Press* (Aldershot: Elgar, 1989), ch. 6.

25 S. Ludlam, 'The gnomes of Washington: four myths of the 1976 IMF crisis', *Political Studies*, 11:4 (1992), pp. 713–27; K. Burk and A. Cairncross, *Goodbye Great Britain: The 1976 IMF Crisis* (New Haven, CT: Yale University Press, 1992).

26 Tomlinson, *The Politics of Decline*, chs 2 and 6.

27 D. Edgerton, *Warfare State: Britain, 1920–70* (Cambridge: Cambridge University Press, 2006); D. Edgerton, *Science, Technology and the British Industrial 'Decline' 1870–1970* (Cambridge: Cambridge University Press, 1996).

28 D. Cannadine, 'Apocalypse when? British politicians and British "decline" in

the twentieth century', in P. Clarke and C. Trebilcock (eds), *Understanding Decline: Perceptions and Realities of Britain's Economic Performance* (Cambridge: Cambridge University Press), pp. 263–9.

29 J. Tomlinson, 'Inventing "decline": the falling behind of the British economy in the post-war years', *Economic History Review*, 49:4 (1996), pp. 734–60.

30 N. Crafts, 'The golden age of economic growth in Western Europe, 1950–1973', *Economic History Review*, 48:3 (1995), pp. 429–47.

31 R. Middleton, *Government Versus the Market* (Cheltenham: Elgar, 1996), p. 441.

32 *Ibid.*

33 J. Tomlinson, 'Balanced accounts? The British balance of payments "problem" 1951–1973', *English Historical Review*, 104:509 (2009), pp. 863–84.

34 W. Manser, *Britain in Balance: The Myth of Failure* (Harmondsworth: Penguin, 1971); R. Middleton, 'Struggling with the impossible: sterling, the balance of payments and British economic policy', in A. Arnon and W. Young (eds), *The Open Economy Macro-model: Past, Present and Future* (Boston, MA: Kluwer, 2002), pp. 103–54.

35 Cannadine, 'Apocalypse when?'

36 R. Layard, *Happiness: Lessons from a New Science* (London: Penguin, 2005); A. Offer, *The Challenge of Affluence: Self-control and Well-being in the United States and Britain Since 1950* (Oxford: Oxford University Press, 2006).

37 P. A. Hall, *Governing the Economy: The Politics of State Intervention in Britain and France* (Cambridge: Polity, 1986); P. A. Hall, *The Political Power of Economic Ideas: Keynesianism Across Nations* (Princeton, NJ: Princeton University Press, 1989).

38 This was not just an emergency measure; in Britain, New Labour's key economic analysts had always seen the need to develop a policy framework in which Keynesian policies of 'coarse tuning' would be sustainable, though they certainly did not foresee the scale of the crisis unleashed by the banking collapse. B. Clift and J. Tomlinson, 'Credible Keynesianism? New Labour's macroeconomic policy and the political economy of coarse tuning', *British Journal of Political Science*, 37:1 (2007), pp. 47–69.

39 J. Tomlinson, 'Tale of a death exaggerated: how Keynesian policies survived the 1970s', *Contemporary British History*, 21:4 (2007), pp. 429–48.

40 The key paper is P. A. Hall, 'Policy paradigms, social learning, and the state: the case of economic policy-making in Britain', *Comparative Politics*, 25:3 (1993), pp. 275–96. For a recent account which deploys the same schema see P. A. Hall, 'The political origins of our economic discontents: contemporary adjustment problems in historical perspective', at http://empac.ucsd.edu/assets/006/11485.pdf, accessed 15 July 2011.

41 Hall, 'Policy paradigms', p. 280.

42 *Ibid.*, pp. 284–87.

43 The key text is T. S. Kuhn, *The Structure of Scientific Revolutions* (Chicago, IL: Chicago University Press, 1962). See also M. Masterman, 'The nature of a paradigm', in I. Lakatos and A. Musgrave (eds), *Criticism and the Growth of Knowledge* (Cambridge: Cambridge University Press, 1970), pp. 59–89.

44 Hall, 'The political origins', pp. 1–5.

45 Hall, 'Policy paradigms', p. 284.

46 *Ibid.*, pp. 284–5.

47 N. Kaldor, *The Scourge of Monetarism* (Oxford: Oxford University Press, 1982), pp. 108–9; J. Trevithick, *Inflation: A Guide to the Crisis in Economics* (Harmondsworth: Penguin, 1980), pp. 101–9.

48 Hall, 'Policy paradigms', p. 286.

49 *Ibid.*, pp. 282–3.

50 M. Friedman, 'Memorandum', in House of Commons Treasury and Civil
    Service Committee, *Memoranda on Monetary Policy*, HC 720 (London: HMSO,
    1980), pp. 55–61.
51 J. Tomlinson, 'Mrs Thatcher's economic adventurism', *British Politics*, 2:1
    (2007), pp. 3–19.
52 N. Lawson, *The View From Number 11* (London: Bantam, 1992), pp. 629–30.
53 Hall, 'Policy paradigms', p. 286.
54 Tomlinson, 'Thatcher, inflation and the "decline" of the British economy'.
55 On one aspect of this see B. Clift and J. Tomlinson, 'When rules started to rule:
    the IMF, neo-liberal ideas and economic policy change in Britain', *Review of
    International Political Economy*, forthcoming.
56 Hall, 'Policy paradigms', p. 288.
57 Much of 1976 was taken up by the 'IMF crisis', which was all about the attempt
    to resolve the downward pressure on the pound from adverse views of British
    economic policy held by debt holders. For an early, journalistic discussion see
    Keegan and Pennant-Rea, *Who Runs the Economy?*
58 L. Mosley, *Global Capital and National Governments* (Cambridge: Cambridge
    University Press, 2003).
59 For a recent example of such an approach, see C. Hay, 'Chronicles of a death
    foretold: the winter of discontent and construction of the crisis of British
    Keynesianism', *Parliamentary Affairs*, 63:3 (2010), pp. 446–70.

4

A time for confession

Samuel Brittan

It has been said that old men should be explorers. They should, however, also be confessors. Since Roger Middleton has flattered me in chapter 5 in this volume by his immensely detailed, thorough and fair-minded critique of my 1975 paper 'The economic contradictions of democracy'[1] in the context of my other work, the least I can do is to be more explicit than I have hitherto been about the circumstances in which it came to be written – not the national economic context which Middleton has covered in his chapter, but the personal one. A famous political economist once wrote that the editor of papers he wrote in the 1920s was a greater authority on what he thought then than he was himself. I am not quite at that stage, but I should get something down while my long-term memory is still there.

But I must make two clarifications. First, though Middleton highlights 'The economic contradictions of democracy' as a work of 'declinism', I was not consciously contributing to the 'declinist literature'. I could not have been, as I had never even heard of it when I wrote the paper. Indeed, when I did learn about the phenomenon in the 1990s I was amazed how long it persisted. At a time when governments of both political persuasions were lauding the superiority of UK performance, I came across university courses going ahead full tilt on British decline as if nothing had happened to the statistics of comparative performance. It may be that since the credit crunch we have entered a new period in which declinism may be relevant again. I would not claim to know. In any case, who am I to grumble? Declinism gave my paper a currency it might not otherwise have had.

Secondly, my paper was not meant to be just about the UK. I drew many of examples from the UK, as this was the country where I was living and which I knew best. But I was concerned primarily with pressures and stresses endemic to liberal democracy and left it to the reader to decide how far they had gone in other countries.

At the British Academy conference at which Roger Middleton first set out his analysis of 'The economic contradictions of democracy' I was comforted by the 'bibliometric' confirmation of my supposition that this essay was my best-known work among 'academic students of politics'. But I noted then that this was a very narrow reference group: a small minority inside that minority of the public that takes political and economic issues seriously. Academic political scientists have had a reasonable deal from journalists and politicians. Their psephological researches have been minutely studied and there has always been a keen market for biographies and recent political history. But that part of 'political science' concerned with the study of the impact of ideas on the political culture had certainly not taken root outside a narrow circle, certainly when I wrote in the 1970s and possibly not even today.

This brings me to Peter Jay and the gross understatement of his role in the 1970s in generating the pessimistic warnings of the time, something which is alluded to by Middleton in chapter 5. Jay came to political ideas as a philosopher; and indeed he at one time embarked on a specialist study of John Stuart Mill. But he had no particular desire to engage in the 'political science' literature of the 1970s. His natural outlet for his speculations on political economy was the ongoing economic debate in the broadsheet media and in publications of organisations like the Institute of Economic Affairs. Moreover, he was a prolific and well known broadcaster reaching a wide public. So his time and perhaps taste for 'political science' were inevitably limited. His role in the wider, but still far from popular, debate is hinted at in note 75 of Middleton's chapter when he reveals that Jay scored more hits than I did in the Economist Historical Archive.

The common intellectual influence on both of us was Milton Friedman's assertion that there was a 'natural' rate of unemployment, on which the government could not improve by 'demand management', that is, by stimulating public or private spending. This is the doctrine which emerged in Prime Minister Callaghan's famous or notorious speech to the 1976 annual Labour conference to which Jay contributed. The label 'natural' was indeed unfortunate, although its technical origin in the economic literature was fairly innocent. It later became sanitised as the 'non-accelerating inflation rate of unemployment' (NAIRU) and is nowadays often further sanitised by reference to the closely related 'output gap'. But whatever it was called, we both agreed it was far too high. Jay famously conjectured that it was in the 'low millions'. We even both agreed that the root of the problem was union monopoly power, although Jay preferred to talk of 'collective bargaining'.

We differed as to remedies. Jay regarded a head-on attack on union power as impractical in a democracy and advocated instead a systemic shift to employee ownership of major enterprises, which would have to compete against each other. I was never entirely convinced and was more prepared to contemplate a Thatcherite wearing down of union power. I had neither love for, nor guilt feelings towards, the unions. As Middleton has discovered, my background was much more radical than generally realised. Rightly or wrongly, I once supported those Labour MPs who advocated a 'socialist foreign policy', which should have been called a radical liberal one, on the lines of A. J. P. Taylor's 'dissenters'. The main obstacle to Labour moving in that direction, in opposition as well as in government, was the union bloc vote, at that time controlled by the Labour right. Later, when I became a 'growth man' in the 1960s, union wage push seemed to be the main obstacle to a move for rapid growth. Thus, when my analysis shifted in the 1970s to union power as the root of high unemployment, I was not breaking new political ground.

The one thing that annoys me in the so-called political science literature is the insinuation that the diagnosis of excessive union power came from a right-wing political motivation. If those so insinuating would only demean themselves by looking at a supply-and-demand diagram of the kind that used to appear in elementary economic textbooks they will see that monopolies operate by restricting demand and raising price. In the union case it was by maintaining uncompetitively high wages for 'insiders' at work at the expense of others remaining unemployed. Why did some economic writers focus on unions rather than, for instance, business monopolies? Simply because they were quantitatively more important. The great bulk of domestic costs are, and certainly were, labour costs. Even those that seemed not to be, such as materials and components, were effectively labour costs at one remove. Employer monopolies operated on the margin between these costs and final price. But if you want a less abstract demonstration, Denis Healey, Labour Chancellor in the 1970s, recently said that a great advantage that Gordon Brown had over him was that Brown did not have the unions to contend with.

Nonetheless, while I was prepared to endorse a Thatcherite analysis of union power, and of the way in which it should be reduced, I was never part of the Thatcher entourage, as Middleton has conceded in his chapter. I was (and I hope remain) a personal friend of Nigel Lawson; but that is an entirely different matter. Nor – looking in the other direction – was there anything dirigiste about my first book on the Treasury.[2] If anything, it was a plea for a non-dirigiste radicalism, arguing not that the government should try to plan industry but that it should let the pound float.

One should also remember that the union power (or insider–outsider) diagnosis was at the time also attacked from the neo-classical side – or, if you must be political, from the right wing. At the height of union power there was always a substantial non-unionised sector. Why could not the victims of union power price themselves into work there? Was not the root of the matter the wage floor provided by social security payments? Let me admit that what we should have said was that union collective bargaining provided those priced out of work with the unattractive choice between the dole and very-low-wage employment. I do not, however, think that this concession would have made the policy argument very different.

But I now come to the embarrassing part. The subject of semi-monopoly brings me back to the Jay–Brittan relationship. It is a commonplace of anti-trust economics that sellers will not naturally compete unless forced to do so. For much of the 1970s Jay was principal economics writer on *The Times*, as I was on the *Financial Times*. In truth, our relationship was not as competitive as our employers would no doubt have liked it to have been and most of the time we amiably exchanged insights and even information. But even if that could be said to have been 'most of the time', speaking for myself, there was 10–20 per cent of the relationship that remained competitive.

Jay received a lot of attention for his thesis of the incompatibility of collective bargaining, full employment and democracy. Attention centred not so much on his suggested worker cooperative cure but on his prediction of unemployment reaching and staying in the 'low millions', and that democracy 'had itself by the tail and is eating itself up fast'. His warning was of course one of many such warnings in vogue at the time. The political atmosphere was febrile and there was semi-serious talk of a coup by retired press barons and military men.

I felt I had to join this race to be heard. Hence my conjecture about liberal representative democracy in my paper 'The economic consequences of democracy'. I did not, I am afraid, take it all that seriously, as I more or less admitted in my *Political Quarterly* paper in which I revisited that article.[3] But I need to be more explicit. My view was and is that we have no crystal balls for predicting the future. I used this conjecture to put forward other ideas, of which I was far more confident.

Many of them, helpfully listed again in Middleton's chapter, came straight from Joseph Schumpeter's *Capitalism, Socialism and Democracy*.[4] My main differences from Jay were that my political conjecture appeared a bit harder and I combined the union–unemployment dilemma with a second, related thesis on the excessive expectations liable to be generated by democracy. This became known in political science circles proper as the 'overload' theory, especially associated with Anthony King.[5] I still believe it to be true, although punctuated by occasional periods of irrationally low expectations about the potentiality of government, such as can be seen in the present day and perhaps also in the mid-1980s.

Schumpeter himself believed that socialism could be compatible with democracy. It was about democracy itself that he gave his warnings. Very, very briefly, the conditions required for it to work included: a limited range for political decisions – hence the importance of bodies such as an independent central bank and a well trained permanent civil service, and useful myths such as the gold standard and the balanced-budget rule; tolerance and democratic self-control involving broad agreement on the structure of society and the existence of a non-collectivised sphere so that personal prospects do not entirely depend on who is in office in the capital or town hall; and the survival of semi-feudal beliefs, which gave a perhaps mistaken aura of legitimacy to the social and economic hierarchy. It must be added that although *Capitalism, Socialism and Democracy*, first published in 1942 in the USA, has outsold by far his other, more technical writings and continues to sell well to this day, it was not highly valued by Schumpeter himself, who thought of it as some kind of pot-boiler. Indeed, I saw the book as a series of warnings given over breakfast by a conservative Central European uncle – I could not take too seriously his insistence that he had become an American and should be called by everyone Joe.

Why did I write my paper 'The economic contradictions of democracy' for the *British Journal of Political Science*? I have always been basically more interested in political ideas than in very technical economics and the opportunity to write for an academic political journal provided by contacts made in a sabbatical at Nuffield College was too good to miss. Moreover, this was the heyday of economic imperialism. By this I do not mean one country conquering another, but the belief that the methods of economics could clarify a great deal about political behaviour. I should add, by the way, that in addition to Anthony King I was also helped in getting through the academic hoops by the late Brian Barry, who may not have agreed with me at all but was very helpful in giving my paper the appropriate academic dress.

I have a further confession to make. My original intention was to write an economic paper on the concept of involuntary unemployment. But this was getting nowhere fast, as the late Harry Johnson warned me after seeing an early draft. This was the time when academic economics had just embarked on its mathematical kick and there was no chance that I could get an article on this or any other subject accepted by a reputable journal (even if I had found a mathematical collaborator, we might not have easily agreed on substance). To this day, I have far more contacts from graduate students in subjects like modern history or politics, who want to question me on economic history and ideas, and who fear that if they went to economists proper they would have their heads bitten off.

One question left open by all versions of the Jay–Brittan thesis is why the rate of unemployment compatible with stable and low inflation was so much lower in the first two or three decades after the Second World War than it afterwards became. Analysts of a purely political orientation tend to give a lot of credit to the habit of cooperating with national policy goals which remained with union leaders as a legacy of the Second World War, but which disappeared with a new, more aggressive generation of union chiefs, who were determined to use every ounce of monopoly behaviour and more. There is something in this; but I would attach at least as much importance to the persistence of 'money illusion' – that is, the habit of thinking in money terms despite the existence of creeping inflation. It took several shocks such as the impact of the 1967 devaluation and the first oil price explosion after 1973 for the illusion to be finally shattered and for wage setters to take full account of expected inflation. Explanations in terms of persistent money illusion are within the spirit of Friedman's doctrine of long and variable lags, though they would be anathema to the neo-classical, rational-expectations school. But after recent events since 2008, we should not lose too much sleep over that school's objections.

Three and a half decades after my pessimistic conjecture about its future, liberal democracy is still here, recognisably the same as it was in the mid-1970s, with all its faults and virtues. So my conjecture must be regarded as well and truly falsified; and I do not wish to cheat by pushing its fulfilment further ahead. Man does not live by bread alone and other, not strictly economic influences undoubtedly play a role. But if you are searching for an economic element, I would give pride of place to the weakening of union power. This probably applies less to other European countries, where unions retain more of their numerical strength and role in the virtual constitution but have instead modified their aspirations.

The period from the mid-1990s to about 2007 witnessed an erratic but definite slow decline in unemployment, while inflation remained low and stable. Some of the credit must surely be given to the delayed action effect of the legislation of the Thatcher governments, which you can call 'union bashing' or removing some of their legal privileges, according to taste, and which the succeeding Labour government decided rather quietly not to repeal after 1997. Also involved was Thatcher's sheer bloody-mindedness in facing down union power in a series of confrontations, of which the victory over the Scargill miners' strike in 1984–85 was only the most notable. Another big influence was the secular decline of manufacturing – which, outside the public sector, was the main stronghold of unionism. Difficult to quantify was the slow drip effect of various supply-side measures to improve the working of the labour market, such as top-up credits for low-paid workers and improvements in the government's job placement centres. Still another and growing influence – at least until the present recession – was competition from emerging economies in supplying cheap products to Western countries, which were as effective a brake on inflation at a given level of unemployment as anything that Western governments did.

Postscript

We have entered a new phase with the credit crunch which began in 2007 and which then developed into a full recession in 2008 on a scale not seen since the early 1930s. This was not due to union monopoly or any other interest group but the failure of the financial mechanism in a way not experienced in the UK since the early days of the First World War, in 1914. We can at a pinch cite excessive expectations as a factor behind the ludicrous rise in property prices before the bust. But these expectations did not impinge directly on government and appeared to be realised for a time only because of absurdly permissive financial institutions.

At the time of writing, in mid-2011, I have no idea whether we are in the beginnings of a genuine economic recovery or simply experiencing a pause before the next leg of a deep recession. There is clearly a danger of effective demand being deficient for quite a long time. The cure for this is the famous helicopter drop of money associated with Friedman or burying pounds in the ground as suggested by Keynes in a moment of desperation. Unfortunately, the body politic is not sophisticated enough for such simple measures and the authorities have had to resort to complicated devices with names like quantitative easing and government-sponsored business recovery schemes.

If I were to pick a domestic threat to liberal democracy today, it would be the slash-and-burn policies towards the public sector that have been adopted, and which politicians and political commentators vie with each other in demanding. I am enough of a libertarian to wish to see some shift away from collective spending towards the individual variety. But panic cuts in public spending due to an imaginary budgetary crisis are not the way to achieve this.

In the language of my 1975 paper, the problem now is not excessive expectations of what government can achieve but the poverty of aspirations. Behind it all is an intellectual failure to realise that a national budget is not the same as that of a family or firm. In fact, it is just when the private sector is drawing in its horns that the need is for a national budget to be in large enough deficit for as long as it takes to do the trick. The main problem is that the threat of deficient demand is global while economic policy is still national. The problem is eased but not solved by the existence of floating exchange rates.

There is another possible source of tension which even the most sane monetary and fiscal policy will be hard put to defuse. One reason why central banks were slow to reverse policies in 2008 despite gathering recessionary forces was a temporary flare-up in inflation. (The European Central Bank increased its policy rate as late as July 2008 and was the first major central bank to raise rates after the recession had begun.) This was not due to domestic overheating in Western countries. Not only oil, but other commodity prices doubled or trebled in a short space of time.

These events may be a portent of speed limits to growth due not to excess demand or inflated expectations in the West but to neo-Malthusian physical constraints. Whether these are indeed physical, reflecting increasing difficulties in increasing supplies of essential materials, or the machinations of people like the rulers of Russia and Iran, does not affect the possibility of a tourniquet being applied to Western economies, however moderately and prudently their affairs are conducted. I am not going to make any conjectures this time, but simply point to sources of danger to which governments and think-tanks should be devoting some consideration.

A final word

Finally, and at the risk of a non-sequitur, I am particularly grateful to Roger Middleton for realising that my main concern has been personal freedom rather than either democracy or economic performance. But I want to offer a word of caution about the 'economic freedom' indices noted by Middleton at one point in his chapter. They may have some limited value on a narrow front; but I have deliberately avoided them in my work. I value economic freedom only as one aspect of personal freedom; and I cannot take seriously listings in which Singapore ranks above Denmark or the Netherlands. The contrast is stark when these economic freedom indices are compared with broader indices published, for instance, by Freedom House.

Notes

1 S. Brittan, 'The economic contradictions of democracy', *British Journal of Political Science*, 5:2 (1975), pp. 129–59.

2 S. Brittan, *The Treasury Under the Tories, 1951–1964* (Harmondsworth: Penguin, 1964).

3 S. Brittan, '"The economic contradictions of democracy" revisited', *Political Quarterly*, 60:2 (1989), pp. 190–203.

4 J. A. Schumpeter, *Capitalism, Socialism and Democracy* (London: Allen & Unwin, 1943, and many subsequent editions).

5 A. King, 'Overload: problems of governing in the 1970s', *Political Studies*, 23:2–3 (1975), pp. 284–96.

5

Brittan on Britain: decline, declinism and the 'traumas of the 1970s'

Roger Middleton[1]

> The British disease pertains not to a particular country, but to a stage in political and economic development.[2]

Reflecting on the changing economic role of government at the beginning of the new millennium, Samuel Brittan, doyen of British economic journalists, described the Britain of the 1970s in terms of a series of 'traumas': some the longer-term consequence of the policy mistakes of the 1960s and others errors of the 1970s, of which some were initiated by external shocks but others were wholly 'unnecessary'.[3] Some thirty-five years earlier, in 1978, in a major essay, 'How British is the British sickness?' (hereafter HBBS), Brittan had characterised the decade in terms of an 'orgy of pessimism and self-doubt among British leaders' about national decline,[4] a pessimism to which he contributed in another major essay in 1975, 'The economic contradictions of democracy' (hereafter ECD) – one of the most cited contributions to the declinist canon of the decade – in which he had warned that, without remedial action, liberal democracy was 'likely to pass away within the lifetime of people now adult'.[5]

It had been argued by Peter Jenkins, a hard-core declinist,[6] that the 'notion of Britain in decline had become a commonplace ... among a dispirited intelligentsia' by the mid-1970s,[7] but certainly in the intervening period a literature, significant in scale but above all influence, arose on declinism.[8] Indeed, declinism was, at least during the 1980s and 1990s, not just the dominant motif of the contemporary British historiography but a key driver for the creation of contemporary history itself as a sub-field. The hard-core variant of declinism has been likened to 'inverted Whiggism',[9] one combining the classic ingredients of the genre of the so-called 'British disease' in terms of 'what went wrong': of timing (when the fatal mistakes were made); of opportunities foregone; and of villainy, stupidity and culpability by trade unions, management and above all by politicians.[10] Brittan never subscribed to anything resembling this version of declinism. The softer variants of the genre, where – with appropriate allowance for iconoclasm – we would position Brittan, are informed by scientific evaluation of the empirical evidence viewed within an appropriate analytical framework, but even so there is an explicit concern that the postwar British economy underperformed before the Thatcher government addressed the most pressing aspects of the British, if not disease then at least, condition.[11]

The purpose of this chapter is not to reopen the mainstream declinism debate, empirically or conceptually, but rather to examine *perceptions* of the *risk* of decline by one public intellectual, Samuel Brittan, who has been widely viewed as influential in preparing the political and policy ground for the diagnosis of decline and its remedy that the Thatcher governments pursued. Our subject is thus highly germane to the current stage of the declinism debate, which rightly is about perceptions. Additionally, it has a much broader purpose: that of an exercise in micro intellectual history (a close study of one author and the two essays already identified, ECD and HBBS) to explore the construction of a crisis and its remedy through the lens of economic ideas at a time when the marketplace for such ideas was particularly contestable, in the process examining why that market was then so contestable. With the intellectual origins of the New Right in Britain now becoming a focus for scholarly attention,[12] this paper uses micro intellectual history, first, to contribute to some greater precision on the genesis of the New Right in Britain and of its influence on the Thatcher governments and beyond; second, to rebalance that literature, hitherto too focused on think-tanks and leading politicians, to include the central role of elite journalists and with a demonstration that, *pace* one characterisation,[13] they were not all academics *manqué*; and third, to make a contribution towards rectifying one aspect of the acknowledged methodological underdevelopment of contemporary history by showing that with modern bibliometric tools it is possible to say something usefully quantitative about the impact of particular authors and their works.

We proceed as follows: the following section examines closely Brittan's two essays, while the third section introduces Brittan's significance as an economic commentator and demonstrates that, while undoubtedly an important resource for the New Right, he was very far from being a member of the New Right. The fourth section explores why the market for economic ideas was unusually contestable in the 1970s and how this worked to Brittan's advantage. This integrates Hall's conception of the marketplace for ideas and also introduces the Brittan–Jay nexus. The fifth section reports some quantitative indicators on Brittan's significance as a political economist and the impact of the two essays. Having thus demonstrated that Brittan was no mere academic *manqué*, the sixth section surveys Brittan's place in the declinist historiography, while the seventh examines why the two papers (ECD in particular) were so significant as academic declinism, by contextualising them in terms of the broader declinist literature, and especially that which sought to marry anxieties about the health of British politics to anxieties about the market economy. Some conclusions are then drawn.

Brittan on Britain: ECD and HBBS

Brittan's two essays here under review were both written while he was enjoying sabbatical leave from the *Financial Times*: ECD while at Nuffield College, Oxford, during 1973–74; and HBBS when a visiting professor at the University of Chicago Law School in 1978, the latter a locale for many New Right economists. The former essay was published in a relatively new political science journal which was at the forefront of the then professionalisation path that transformed British political studies into something now resembling internationalised political science, while HBBS was the seventh Henry Simons lecture, part of a series which included contributions by Milton Friedman and other Nobel laureate economists. Both ECD and HBBS examined the economics of politics, though the former more so than the latter, which contains much topical empirical matter on Britain's economic performance in comparative context. Of the two essays, ECD is better known and is more dramatic because of its predictions about the fate of liberal democracy. It is also the more cited, being Brittan's most significant publication of all time in terms of academic citations, though HBBS is his second – after ECD – most significant journal article of that decade (see the section 'Beyond the qualitative', below).

Although Brittan is seen as a key figure in the declinist historiography of Britain, both papers were about stresses endemic to contemporary Western liberal democracy, not just those in Britain. Nonetheless, the British context matters and was significantly but subtly different when the two papers were written. ECD was initiated just after the Yom Kippur War and amid the implosion of the Heath government; its objective, as he later rationalised it in an essay which revisited ECD (hereafter ECDR),[14] was to confront the then dominant view that Britain's economic problem was that of a country beset by an oil-price-induced supply-side shock (what we now call OPEC1), for this distracted attention from significant longer-term forces ('certain strains in liberal democracy') which 'could do great damage unless countervailing forces appeared or policies or attitudes were changed' (ECDR, p. 191). By contrast, HBBS was written after the 1975–76 crisis that engulfed the Wilson–Callaghan government appeared to have passed and Brittan was more optimistic that the problem of stagflation would be temporary, resulting as it did from 'mistakes in economic management of a kind unlikely to be repeated in so blatant a form' (HBBS, p. 268). This optimism was born of a judgement that 'the British authorities have now had irrefutable evidence that budget deficits financed by excess monetary creation lead to an inflationary crisis rather than the much desired real growth' (HBBS, p. 261), but of course the other objective of HBBS was to explore the suggested explanations for long-run relative economic decline, which typically were 'not sufficiently distinguished' from these shorter-term forces in the developing discourse of Britain's economic problem in the 1970s (HBBS, p. 245). Indeed, HBBS constitutes a devastating critique of the simplistic 'causes' in the developing declinist narrative that very soon would find full expression in the works of the key right-wing declinists, Wiener and Barnett, and thence the first Thatcher government.[15] ECD dated from the year of the miners' strike, 'when union power broke one government and demoralised the whole governing order' (HBBS, p. 264), whereas HBBS, although written less than four years later, was conceived in the short interval between the Callaghan government being seen to have surmounted the difficulties of 1975–76 but not yet having been confronted by what came to be known as the 'winter of discontent'. This rapid ebb and flow of events, of expectations and changing perceptions of risks and opportunities counsels grave caution about a generalised conception of declinism; it also reinforces our contention that Brittan is a representative agent only of himself.

While both ECD and HBBS are quite different in content and structure, and addressed to different audiences and delivered in different countries, they nonetheless have much in common. They share what we might call a common political economy framework, entailing deep engagement with the writings of key political economists, including Bagehot, Dicey, Schumpeter, Hayek, Downs, Nozick and Rawls in ECD; and Dicey, Marshall, Friedman, Maddison and Olson in HBBS. Both also involve close analysis of the minutiae of contemporary events and, in the case of HBBS, very recent economic data. This would be a rare combination for an academic, rarer still for one outside academe, though Andrew Shonfield comes to mind as someone with similar ambitions and capabilities. The two essays are also directly linked, with the closing sentences of HBBS (p. 268) making the connection to ECD's central message: 'The British disease pertains not to a particular country, but to a stage in political and economic development. The disease is that of collective action by special interest groups preventing a reasonably full use being made of our economic resources.' Here we come to the heart of ECD and thence of Brittan's contribution to understanding the 1970s and beyond through to the present day.

In ECD Brittan identified two endemic threats to liberal democracy: 'the generation of excessive expectations' and 'the disruptive effects of the pursuit of group self-interest in the market place' (ECD, p. 129). Importantly, most of his essay 'was devoted not to crying woe but to explaining the checks, balances and limitations which had kept the competitive outbidding at bay and thus enabled limited, constitutional democracy to survive' (ECDR, p. 195). Brittan offered no headline solutions in ECD ('Liberal democracy will not be saved by detailed policy programmes which will soon be overtaken by events' – ECD, p. 159), merely hints for alleviating the strains on liberal democracy.[16] Detailed policy prescriptions were similarly absent from HBBS, though his analysis now incorporated the proto catch-up and convergence framework of Maddison,[17] which made more sense of decline as a relative rather than an absolute phenomenon for Britain, with in-built 'self-correcting forces' (HBBS, pp. 246, 267–8), and what would become in the early 1980s the much-discussed Olson thesis of institutional sclerosis.[18] Common to both papers was detailed attention to the deleterious effects of trade unions, the principal 'group self-interest' threatening liberal democracy.

Brittan: doyen of economic journalists

The names of Peter Jay and, above all, Samuel Brittan occur frequently in the roll call of those who were instrumental in 'thinking the unthinkable' in the 1970s and thereby overturning the Keynesian consensus on big government.[19] For Arthur Seldon, who, together with Ralph Harris, was the driving force of the Institute of Economic Affairs (IEA),[20] Brittan was 'the doyen of the editor-scholars'.[21] Another friend, indeed former colleague at the *Financial Times*,[22] Nigel Lawson, was in no doubt that upon joining the *Financial Times* Brittan 'soon became (and remains) the leading British commentator on the passing economic scene, and the issues which lie behind it, contributing more to our understanding than at least 90 per cent of academic economists and acquiring in the process a unique international reputation'.[23] For Cockett, unofficial historian of the IEA, 'Most Conservative and Labour MPs learnt more about economic liberalism from the journalism of Samuel Brittan and Peter Jay than they did from their own Party "research" organisations or from the universities'.[24] That two of Brittan's pamphlets were on Keith Joseph's famous reading list alongside such canons of political economy as Adam Smith's *The Wealth of Nations* and *The Theory of Moral Sentiments* is about as good evidence as the historian can expect of his subject being at least read by those right at the very heart of Thatcherism.[25]

Unsurprisingly, Brittan's significance as a key economic commentator and opinion former is emphasised as much by those who at the time and since opposed the neo-liberal agenda.[26] Yet Brittan is often misrepresented and frequently misunderstood. Some have dubbed Brittan a New Right theorist,[27] 'right wing',[28] a 'renowned conservative economist' and a 'former student' of Friedman.[29] These are simplistic judgements based upon surface readings of his more accessible writings, typically his journalism; they also derive from erroneous assumptions about the philosophical underpinnings of his policy positions as he reacted against the Keynesian consensus during the 1970s. As we shall see, there is nothing conservative about Samuel Brittan, or indeed Conservative, save being the elder brother of Leon Brittan, who served in Thatcher's cabinet between 1981 and 1986, and plying a trade that required networking with political and other elites. As Marquand put it pithily, Brittan was 'no tory and still less a nationalist'.[30] The misrepresentation of Brittan is symptomatic of much weak scholarship on British political economy in the 1970s and 1980s, in which too often an imprecision in delimiting the New Right results in a failure to capture the complexity of individual and group positions.

We begin by situating Brittan among the five 'overlapping movements' of academics, journalists and others of Cowling's prosopography of the New Right.[31] The identification of Brittan as a New Right theorist, or at least as a fellow traveller, is widespread, and it is not difficult to see why: he was publishing with the IEA from 1971; he was one of the lecturers to the Selsdon Group (established in 1973);[32] he was known to be assisting Joseph with speeches, including the notorious September 1974 Preston speech, which, *inter alia*, is a milestone in rethinking Conservative macroeconomic policy on its journey towards monetarism;[33] and, with the election of Thatcher as party leader, Brittan became part of an informal group of economists and financiers who met with her and shadow cabinet members in the four years of preparation for government.[34] Brittan, of course, was in the vanguard of economic journalists whose second thoughts on Keynesianism led eventually to the monetarist experiment of the first Thatcher government.[35] However, the conflation of monetarism with the New Right is one of the most egregious of errors in the current neo-liberal historiography of Britain. For the sake of economic accuracy, it is essential to remind the non-economist reader that Brittan was no orthodox monetarist: he took from Friedman the natural rate analysis but not the Friedmanite monetary transmission mechanism, a vital difference.[36]

More fundamentally, neo-liberal triumphalism needs to distinguish between participation and partisanship. It is one thing to argue that Brittan made an indirect contribution to the emerging economic policy programme of the Conservatives before the 1979 general election, and quite another to claim, as some have done, that he was part of 'Thatcher's entourage'.[37] Moreover, and again invoking economic criteria, Brittan would fail many of the tests of true 'Thatcherism', not least that he viewed the 1981 budget as 'badly judged'.[38] That budget, at minimum a watershed in postwar economic policy, was the subject of collective derision by 364 economists, but for many 'true disciples' it was Thatcher's Stalingrad.[39] In short, Brittan was a resource for the New Right; he was not a member of the New Right. To have otherwise does neither him nor the New Right justice. Brittan was (and remains) no (either large or small c) conservative, but an economic and social liberal, one to whom it was 'saddening ... that the sound idea of shifting the responsibility for decisions from the State to the individual should be discredited by the glib and superficial nature in which it has been applied'.[40] Indeed the New Right, more broadly neo-liberalism in practice, posed an especial problem for Brittan, as what transpired in Britain was an unintended synthesis of liberalism and authoritarianism.[41] Brittan's views about personal freedom were long-standing and well known, as was his antipathy to much that comprised orthodox social conservatism.[42] Abhorring nationalism, Brittan was 'by family origin and personal leaning ... a European and could never be anything else',[43] and was independent of any political party, an 'iconoclastic libertarian, as concerned with moral and ethical questions as with formal economic arguments'.[44] He has himself observed: 'I have never been a Tory. I have never liked the Conservatives very much. So I was not dancing in the street at the prospect of a Thatcher government. There was something paradoxical about using authoritarian means to bring in a liberal order.'[45]

The market for economic ideas and Brittan's comparative advantage

Brittan's standing as a leading economic journalist was well established by the late 1960s.[46] What distinguished him and made him especially effective as a 'self-appointed educator of the influential classes'[47] was that the market for economic ideas was more highly contested than normal during the 1970s. Indeed, contestability is central to Hall's conception of the policy shift of that decade, upon which his focus was macroeconomics (from Keynesianism to monetarism) and not the rise of neo-liberalism *per se*.[48] For Hall, a distinguishing characteristic of the

1970s paradigm shift in Britain was that 'Social scientists were unable to reach a definitive conclusion regarding the superiority of one of these economic paradigms over the other' and therefore 'Politicians became seriously involved in the debate over their validity'.[49] Thus, 'it was not civil servants or policy experts engaged by the Government, but politicians and the media, who played the preeminent role in this process of policy change', with, in particular, the 'monetarist assault' led by influential journalists, of whom he names William Rees-Mogg, editor of *The Times*, and Brittan. Importantly, for Hall, and our analysis would support this, the 'process of policy change did not primarily take place within the confines of the State itself ... [but] began with a shift in the locus of authority away from the Treasury toward a growing marketplace of economic ideas outside the State'.[50]

Hall's conception of the process of policy change chimes with a contemporary analysis by Peter Jay in 1972 (by then at *The Times* as economics editor) which he did not cite. In a BBC radio broadcast and an accompanying essay, Jay argued that academic economists had entered a phase of 'offer[ing] diminishing returns to policy-makers' and this provided the opportunity for accomplished economic journalists to exploit their position as the true inheritors of the eighteenth- and nineteenth-century political economy tradition, which 'is essentially a literary tradition orientated to the illumination and solution of real problems'.[51] Economic journalism, Jay argued, was a postwar innovation pioneered by Brittan and one other *Financial Times* journalist: Shonfield, the author of one of the key canons of the first wave of British postwar declinism.[52]

Brittan bridged the divide between the different types of economic knowledge favoured by the policy community, academic-theoretical but above all practical (here embracing two of Peden's categories in his taxonomy of useful economic knowledge).[53] There were few of his contemporaries who could match his felicity of expression, his adroitness with translating technical economic issues for everyman, his eye for the main story and his enormous intellectual appetite, both for new ideas and for recovering those, especially from continental European (principally Austrian) economics, which he felt had a new relevance for current times. There were also few contemporaries who could match his prodigious output: to the staple of *Financial Times* reportage and commentary there was added a steady stream of contributions to the then widely read bank reviews, the important role of which is still under-appreciated;[54] to think-tanks, not least the IEA, and often as an opportunity to provide a more approachable version of his major books;[55] to international periodicals (*Encounter*, *Fortune*, *Washington Quarterly*);[56] to economic journals, not least the *Economic Journal*, then very much the organ of British academic economics; and to literary journalism. Nor should one underestimate the growing appeal of the maverick, in this case typically in the vanguard, and often very uncomfortably so, and particularly during the final years of the Bretton Woods fixed exchange regime, when Brittan was well ahead of academic economists, let alone the British policy community, in thinking the unthinkable about the virtues of flexible exchange rates.[57] Undoubtedly, declinism also helped as the currency of comfortable nostrums became strongly devalued in face of a growing perception of economic and political crisis.

These were considerable attributes, but what gave Brittan his special advantage was his personal network (in terms of both quantity and quality). This was forged during his first period on the *Financial Times* and then developed at the *Observer*, when he researched what became his first book.[58] This consolidated his reputation as a premier economic journalist, not least for the methodological innovation that it was based in part upon official and somewhat unofficial interviews with civil servants and politicians.[59] The publication of this book coincided with his taking up a post as a temporary civil servant in George Brown's ill-fated Department of Economic Affairs, a period Brittan considered 'important mainly for the contacts I made and the subsequent beliefs of people that I was writing about Whitehall from experience',[60] but which, in the longer run, contributed to his growing scepticism about big government and Keynesian-style demand management, at least as practised in Britain since the 1950s. Thus, upon his return to the *Financial Times* in early 1966, Brittan was possessed of a rare, perhaps unrivalled, network of contacts in academe, finance and politics, which ensured that those outside of Whitehall–Westminster had to be attentive to his writings.

The Jay–Brittan nexus, which involved both competition and co-operation, probably worked more to the advantage of Brittan. Certainly, Brittan admits to competition with Jay, and vice versa, with each seeking to differentiate their product with the inevitable consequence of having to be a little bolder and certainly a little louder in the crowded market-place for ideas, though characteristically both are very generous to each other in print and in person.[61] Additionally, Jay often publicised Brittan's work; for example, it was he who, on the front page of *The Times*, first brought to attention Brittan's ECD paper[62] and often reviewed his works, as for example in the glowing assessments of subsequent editions of his Treasury book.[63] Brittan considers that orthodox accounts of the 1970s understate Jay's role in generating the pessimistic warnings of the time. We are grateful for that perspective, but we speculate that one reason why this might be the case is that Jay's literary output was far less (and, as we shall see, attracted less academic attention) than that of Brittan, as he was also developing a broadcasting career. In particular, we identify his London Weekend Television Sunday news analysis programme and speculate that, through its 'mission to explain', it did much, *inter alia*, to prepare the ground for the assault on the Keynesian consensus. With John Birt as founding editor, and Jay as principal presenter for the first five years (1972–77), *Weekend World* was both an experiment in 'analytical' as against 'adversarial' journalism and, with respect to economics, a challenge to prevailing broadcasting logic by 'employ[ing] the word rather than the image in telling the tale of modern politics and society'.[64] While Jay has expressed some scepticism about Parsons' assessment of his supposed influence, he does not deal with the specific issue of the relative influence of television as against print journalism in shaping opinion.[65] To obtain a fuller picture of declinism in the 1970s requires that this research be undertaken and that historians be attentive to the medium as well as to the message.

Beyond the qualitative: contemporary history and bibliometrics

Brittan's own assessment (ECDR, p. 190) was that ECD 'attracted almost no attention among economists, but was frequently cited by academic students of politics and was reprinted in various forms'.[66] (Brittan made no self-assessment of the influence of HBBS but when reprinting the essay in a later collection he reworked the original article somewhat, brought the data up to date and added a significant new footnote, that Wiener 'miss[ed] the nature of the problem' about class, dismissing the volume as a 'cult book in management education circles'[67]). A search of the ISI Web of Science (WoS) Social Science Citation Index (SSCI) and Arts & Humanities Citation Index (A&HCI) databases for ECD confirms the distribution of citations as between the two disciplines,[68] but he is altogether too modest about their quantity. ECD is Brittan's most cited publication (seventy citations on WoS)[69] and HBBS his third equal most cited (nine citations) by this indicator. This needs to be normalised against a modal citation per paper in the social sciences (including political science) of zero,[70] such that, as Giles and Garand concluded after an extensive quantitative exercise: 'Publications in most academic journals in political science are stones that fall into the pool of disciplinary discourse without causing a ripple. They are lines on a resume without resonance.'[71]

Citation data for Brittan are given in table 5.1; this highlights the two essays upon which we focus, but additionally we should note the significance of Brittan's Treasury book, ranked (using a different methodology, about to be discussed) second and ninth by total citations, though, when aggregated, still some distance short of total citations for ECD. Citation exercises of this sort have well known limitations, even when the source

Table 5.1 Samuel Brittan's key writings by numbers of citations[a]

Publish or Perish ranking	Publication title	Published	Type	Publisher/journal	Citations	
					Web of Science	Google Scholar
1	'The economic contradictions of democracy'	1975	Academic paper	British Journal of Political Science	70	304
2	Steering the Economy	1969	Book	Secker & Warburg		164
3	The Economic Consequences of Democracy[b]	1977	Essay collection	Temple Smith		157
4	Capitalism With a Human Face	1996	Book	Edward Elgar		81
5	The Role and Limits of Government	1983	Essay collection	Temple Smith		73
6	'The politics and economics of privatisation'	1984	Academic paper	Political Quarterly	14	63
7	Capitalism and the Permissive Society	1973	Book	Macmillan		62
8	A Restatement of Economic Liberalism	1973; 1988	Essay collection	Macmillan		54
9	The Treasury Under the Tories, 1951–64	1964	Book	Penguin		47
10	The Delusion of Incomes Policy (with P. Lilley)	1977	Book	Temple Smith		47
11	'How British is the British sickness?'	1978	Academic paper	Journal of Law and Economics	9	41
12	'Inflation and democracy', in F. Hirsh and J. H. Goldthorpe (eds), The Political Economy of Inflation	1978	Chapter	Martin Robertson		32
13	Left or Right	1968	Book	Macmillan		31
14	How to End the Monetarist Controversy	1981	Pamphlet	IEA		30
15	'Privatisation: a comment on Kay and Thompson'	1986	Academic paper	Economic Journal	9	28
16	Participation Without Politics	1975	Pamphlet	IEA		27
17	Is There an Economic Consensus?	1973	Book	Macmillan		24
18	Second Thoughts on Full Employment Policy	1975	Pamphlet	Centre for Policy Studies		22
19	Beyond the Welfare State (with S. Webb)	1990	Book	David Hume Institute		22
20	'Can democracy manage an economy', in R. Skidelsky (ed.), The End of the Keynesian Era	1977	Chapter	Macmillan		17

[a] Books, pamphlets and journal articles, not newspaper journalism.
[b] Ch. 23 'The politics of excessive expectations' was the precursor of the British Journal of Political Science's version of 'The economic contradictions of democracy'.
Sources: Web of Science and Publish or Perish, accessed 15 July 2011.

is a paper in the natural sciences (where the journal rules supreme as the dominant publishing outlet), but for ECD and HBBS we would expect their visibility in the literature to be as much, if not more, in books and current affairs magazines, neither category of which is enumerated by WoS, which also suffers from its restricted range of journals enumerated.[72] Nonetheless, citation analyses have become a commonplace of the sociology of science, one tool among many for exploring the basis of professional reputation, and they ought not to be dismissed out of hand by contemporary historians. Economists, for example, have been in the forefront of applying this methodology. Examination of the data available on the WoS citations of ECD and HBBS reveal: their spatial breadth (albeit within the English-speaking world); that ECD and HBBS captured attention among academics based in elite institutions and journals; that, for ECD, citations extended beyond political science into all of the other social sciences (detecting penetration from one discipline into another is where bibliometrics can be particularly helpful); and that even ten years after its publication ECD was still being cited with some frequency.

In relation to Giles and Garand's conclusions, Brittan's citations in quantity and quality position him among the front rank for academics. ECD is a significant paper; its author even more significant. Tony King, admittedly a friend and collaborator, was nonetheless not devoid of objectivity when he observed in 1989 that, even after a decade or more of the professionalisation of British political studies into political science, 'most of Britain's best political scientists (Peter Jenkins, Sam Brittan, Peter Riddell) are, for some reason, journalists'.[73] The reference group ought also to be extended to economists, for while ECD does not feature in EconLit, Brittan as an economist certainly does have an impact and more than as an economic journalist, being, for example, in the first edition of *Who's Who in Economics* (subsequent editions used citation analysis as the sole currency of esteem).[74] If the comparator group be economic journalists, Jay received not a single citation in either database, though he was much more prominent in *The Economist* than Brittan, as one might have expected since Jay was from the early 1970s onwards building a parallel career as a broadcaster as well as an author and commentator.[75] Moreover, as figure 5.1 shows, Brittan has a sustained citations presence in the academic literature, building in the 1970s, peaking in the 1980s, but enduring right up to the present. This is the citation profile of a highly successful academic social scientist, having an output which, in quantity and quality (as measured by citations), exceeded the median British political scientist by a very considerable margin.

Traditional bibliometric sources have more recently been supplemented by new tools that begin to exploit the internet and the plethora

(a) Brittan's publications recorded on Web of Science by year, 1960–2011

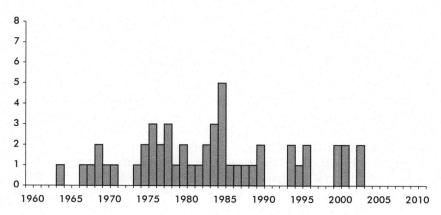

(b) Citations of Brittan recorded on Web of Science by year, 1960–2011

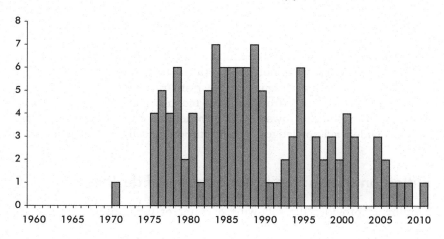

5.1 Samuel Brittan's publications and citations. (a) Web of Science recorded publications by year, 1960–2011; (b) Web of Science recorded citations by year, 1960–2011.

Source: Search for Brittan S* on Web of Science, accessed 21 July 2011.

of resources that it has generated. Foremost, there is Google Scholar, which captures books and journals that have an internet footprint. No doubt this is already used widely but informally. It does, however, have potential for much more systematic exploitation.[76] Some very casual empiricism yields 304 citations for ECD (with 101 'related items') and 41 citations for HBBS,[77] that is, for ECD over four times the number of WoS citations (similarly for HBBS). Again, taking Jay as a comparator, Brittan's ECD has been cited over ten times more than Jay's most cited publication, and nearly seventeen times more than for his most cited contribution to the declinist literature. However, even newer citations tools, for example Publish or Perish (PoP),[78] show the relative standing of Brittan in relation to other contemporary authors. Much further bibliometric analysis is possible, in particular now that WoS can generate citation maps, but here we limit ourselves to reporting Brittan's *h*-index. This index is now routine, if highly contentious, in science,[79] being designed to measure both the scientific productivity and the apparent scientific impact of a scientist in terms of citations.[80] With an *h*-index of 21 (Jay, 7), Brittan stands head and shoulders above his contemporaries, including almost all of those with full-time academic posts. These quantitative measures of influence are, of course, wholly inadequate for our task in anything other than a supporting role, but they were worth a detour to signal that in certain cases, for certain authors and public figures, something quantitative can be done and the contemporary historian is not limited to the traditional craft of making sense of the subject's presence in the primary and secondary sources without much assistance from modern technologies. This is offered as a modest contribution towards the sub-field of contemporary history, which is widely acknowledged to be methodologically underdeveloped.

Brittan on Britain: the historiography of declinism

Tomlinson provides the following account of the context and significance of both ECD and HBBS:[81]

A characteristic of the 1970s' panic was that while the immediate stimulus was ... economic issues such as inflation and public borrowing..., it was the alleged political implications of economic development that underpinned much of the extreme scaremongering. This linkage is very evident in the writings of that characteristic figure of the period, the economic journalist turned political pundit. Peter Jay is one obvious example of this, with his column in *The Times* being an initial source of monetarist ideology in Britain, but this being coupled with attempts to make 'profound' statements about the British polity. A similar trajectory may be seen in the work of Samuel Brittan, the *Financial Times* journalist, with his publications on 'The economic contradictions of democracy' and 'The British sickness'. Both these authors were also part of the groups involved with the right-wing think-tanks, at this time the most important being the Institute of Economic Affairs..., but it was as journalists that they probably had the most impact, with the think-tanks being relatively minor players, despite retrospective claims to their significance.

But it was not just the academics *manqués* who contributed to this climate. Respected political scientists speculated in the same vein about whether the British polity could survive the pressures of 'decline', arriving at strikingly pessimistic conclusions. Books about British politics routinely used 'decline' in their titles, even if the meaning of the term was a vague amalgam of long-term growth failings and high inflation and unemployment.

Tomlinson's depiction of Jay and Britain as academics *manqués* would not be shared by all who have analysed the declinism of the 1970s, even if – as I do – they concur broadly with his assessment of the meaning and significance of declinism. In any case, so far as Brittan is concerned, our citation analysis has shown him to be more of an academic than most academic political scientists. Indeed, Brittan's ECD paper has more citations in WoS and Google Scholar (respectively 70 and 304) than the contemporaneous and, according to its author, complementary paper by King on overload[82] (respectively 45 and 266), which is another staple of the declinist literature, as well as being King's most cited paper (although his *h*-index is higher, at 26). Moreover, from what we know of political scientists' publication rates at this time,[83] Brittan's output was exceptional also in terms of quantity.

Examining the historiography more closely, we find that Brittan's work is taken seriously as academic declinism by most who have written on the 1970s and 1980s,[84] including importantly English and Kenny, whose interview with Brittan was part of their 'rethinking of British decline' which 'features some of the intellectual figures whose ideas and theories in relation to decline have played a critical role in the development of debates in this field'.[85] For English and Kenny, Brittan had become one of a number of 'public intellectuals' who 'have all "borne witness" to the division and destruction wrought upon the nation by mistaken and self-interested policies and institutional configurations'.[86] Public intellectual is a highly contestable concept in Britain,[87] but English and Kenny are undoubtedly right in trying to be more systematic about both declinism (with the shift of attention to perceptions of decline) and the contribution of leading commentators such as Brittan.[88]

Johnson has observed that most of the declinist literature was 'part of the problem, not part of the solution'.[89] This forms a potential benchmark for Brittan's ECD and other papers contributing to the declinism of the 1970s and the 1980s, although for obvious reasons the ECD paper cannot be judged alone but must be seen as part of his broader corpus. The following is not exhaustive, but forms a starting point, in that such an evaluation must include Brittan's role in educating political elites and public opinion: first, to be more discriminating in distinguishing between longer-term relative economic decline and the shorter-term problem of stagflation, along with the political connections between them (upon which his HBBS is particularly important); and second, to understand that in postwar Britain a presumption had taken root in policy-making circles and much of the commentariat that, in practice, market failure exceeded government failure.[90] In all of this, Brittan was one voice among many but, as we have seen, his was an especially effective voice. However, he was also highly critical of certain foundations of what would become the declinist canon. For example, he has not been one of the commentators who has fretted about the balance of payments or the value of sterling as symbolic of economic decline. He has also been a vocal critic of the idea of competitiveness, which became important in the 1990s as declinism evolved into a new stage of anxiety associated with globalisation.[91]

Brittan was (and remains), however, highly typical of much of the 'right' of the declinist literature in his strictures about the role of organised labour in longer-term economic underperformance and shorter-term political crises. In ECD, organised labour is the central 'group self-interest through coercive means in the market place' that is identified for its disruptive effects (ECD, p. 142). More broadly, labour market reform does become a central part of his vision for an economically liberal Britain, and in his retrospectives on the Thatcher–Major years he has been more positive about this (and about privatisation) than any other aspects of economic policy reform.[92] Of course, and as I have shown elsewhere,[93] ECD did not give equal attention to market power in product markets. Nor did it engage with any of the then contemporary critiques of multinational companies and other big businesses' pricing policies and their contribution to inflation and threat to government autonomy. Additionally, while Brittan was well aware that Britain was no more strike prone than comparator economies (HBBS, p. 263), given that issues of distributive justice featured strongly in ECD, he was vulnerable to the following:[94]

> At the level of analysis, issue can be taken with Brittan's isolation of the unions (and ignoring of business) as a quasi-political threat. If we agree that group self-interest in the marketplace, along with the democratic process of political competition, does push expectations and demands systematically upwards, it remains hard to separate out particular groups as primarily responsible. In a political culture which is materialistic and individualistic, and with an economy which is struggling, it is not at all

surprising that the question of what they get, and what others get, is crucial to most people. Obviously, the treadmill effect can be devastating. But one result is that the issue of distribution is not ignored and cannot be outlawed.

ECD and HBBS as academic declinism

Having demonstrated that Brittan was no mere academic *manqué*, and that ECD and HBBS are significant publications by robust academic standards, we can now explore further their context and contemporary significance. We have already discussed the foundations of Brittan's comparative advantage as an economic journalist and identified what was distinctive about his academic writing. We now move towards a conclusion by considering why his declinist writings of the 1970s, ECD in particular,[95] might have been so significant.

The answer lies in the manner in which Brittan was part of a small group developing a political science of Britain's economic problem which was contemporaneous with economists such as Friedman and Bacon and Eltis, who were developing economic diagnoses which focused especially on public sector growth, so-called excess bias and the Leviathan state.[96] Of the former discipline, ECD was the first of a trio of papers published in 1975 which developed the 'ungovernability' discourse, with the others being King's much cited overload paper, described by its author as 'complementary in many ways' to ECD, and the now less well known Tom Wilson on adversary politics (181 citations in Google Scholar),[97] a variant of the overload thesis.[98] These married anxieties about the health of British politics to worries about the market economy, but Brittan's paper was arguably the most novel and effective and not just because of the boldness of its prediction and the felicity of its expression.

Ungovernability and the concept of overload made an academic appearance simultaneously in Britain and the USA. Brittan's thinking was thus moving in parallel with a number of other writers (not least Jay and King). In particular, ECD and Jay's two contributions of 1976–77[99] were grounded in the generality of an incipient crisis of liberal democracy, which had reached a more extreme form in Britain, where it had become a problem of social democracy. In ECD (p. 130) Brittan proposed a formula which linked the twin problems of excessive expectations and the pursuit of group self-interest in terms of the 'excessive burden ... placed on the "sharing out" function of government'. In a later commentary, Beetham called these the 'mediating factors': 'the use of the State to redistribute wealth, and to maintain full employment'.[100] On the latter, Brittan had already undergone his 'second thoughts' as he had incorporated Friedman's natural rate theory into his analysis of how

85

the pursuit of full employment beyond the natural rate of unemployment had generated inflation.[101] On the former, Brittan had for some time been preoccupied with how British political elites, and the majority of the intellectual classes, had since the Second World War subscribed to a particular vision of Britain as an unequal society, and a programme of remedy that had 'done immense harm to my country'.[102] Importantly, such issues of equity and ethics would preoccupy him for the next thirty years and more.[103]

The ECD paper is of additional interest for what it reveals of Brittan as an innovator and as a propagator of the more technical, largely but not exclusively American, political science literatures which were to be so successful in undermining the foundations of the ideal of benign government. The public choice literature first made a serious entrance in Brittan's *Capitalism and the Permissive Society* (1973), although in ECD Hayek and Schumpeter feature more than Buchanan, Tulloch or Downs. Nonetheless, the presence of public choice logic is evident in the pessimism of Brittan's conjecture, deriving as it does from an explicit analysis that there were insufficient incentives in a competitive political marketplace for political elites to behave responsibly to maximise societal long-term interests, and that this was also the case for the group self-interests he had identified as the second of the tensions of liberal democracy (ECD, p. 145):

> The basic difficulty is that the benefits from restraint in the use of group market power are 'public goods'. They consist of things such as price stability, fuller employment or faster economic growth, which are thinly diffused among the whole population, while the costs are incurred by the group which exercises restraint.

This part of the argument was couched in terms of the trade unions but, of course, is capable of generalisation on the theme that Britain then, as now, enjoyed no constitutional mechanism to prevent politicians raising expectations beyond the feasible level. Public choice theory, especially what we now label constitutional economics, was then being developed by Buchanan and Tulloch, with much of it reported in IEA publications from the mid-1970s onwards.[104] In ECD, Brittan appealed principally to an older authority, Joseph Schumpeter, whose conception of democracy was, here put pithily by Beetham, in terms of the liberal anxiety of 'too much politics is bad for society, and too many people demanding things is bad for politics'.[105] That said, Brittan's was not the position of pessimism about the human condition that motivated the neo-conservatives, as he has shown from subsequent work which has explored economics and ethics in a post-industrial landscape.

Finally, from a longer-term perspective the 'overload' research programme of which ECD is part was extremely productive as political science: one can trace a clear lineage from these concerns of ungovernability in the 1970s through the hollowing-out literature of the late 1980s and 1990s and onward to the Economic and Social Research Council's Whitehall project and beyond.[106] ECD's particular contribution cannot be fathomed as such, but what can be said with some confidence is that while in the short term it may well have added to the noise of crisis, in the longer term it was helpful for those seeking to distinguish between the demand side and the supply side of overload: between the problems of excess demand on resources (and how these might be contained) and the supply side of government and its institutions being incentivised to supply less. Within such territory lay the possibility of remedies.

Conclusion

If citations be the 'coinage of reward in academia', as would be claimed by economists (of social scientists, the quickest to embrace bibliometrics),[107] and the size and status of one's address book be a proxy for influence in the Whitehall village, then, as a journalist, Brittan must be without equal in postwar Britain. He was no academic *manqué*. From a different standpoint, academic historians have often been rather dismissive of journalism and its practitioners, typically wrapping their condescension in the phrase that while journalists write the first draft of history it is left to the professionals to complete the job, and on weak foundations. The accusation against journalists is further confounded by the claim that, for the 1970s, it was social scientists, typically political scientists, who wrote the second draft of the history of that decade in Britain, and that, born of their parochialism, it was largely negative and ahistorical by professional standards. Again it would be difficult to implicate Brittan (or Jay) in such a charge: the British sickness as specified was avowedly a broader sickness of Western liberal democracy. Britain might well be first but others would surely follow, this a clear message of both the essays we have studied closely here. In an age in which journalists are held in low repute, and rightly so in the round, it is salutary to be reminded that Brittan was part of an exceptional generation of British journalists who contributed not just to the rise of the *Financial Times* as a global force but who had a wholly disproportionate influence on British political life.

Of course, Brittan's ECD predictions for British liberal democracy proved unduly pessimistic; conversely, his optimism of HBBS, that macroeconomic problems were temporary and 'unlikely to be repeated in so blatant a form' (HBBS, p. 268), proved ill-founded, though his careful, historical analysis of relative economic decline has proved durable. On the former, as he acknowledged in ECDR, 'Democracy has survived better than I feared', but this was because it had abandoned the full-employment commitment, which was 'hardly a satisfactory, desirable or even sustainable basis of survival'. Even more fundamentally, the problem of unconstrained majority rule ('elective dictatorship') was, if anything, magnified by the time he came to write ECDR, as, with the then apparent Thatcherite hegemony, the right was now not interested in constitutional (including electoral) reform to improve British government and politics (ECDR, pp. 199, 202–3). However, since Brittan's ECD paper, successive British governments have responded to overload by moderating their economic policy goals, including trying to depoliticise monetary policy by granting operational independence to the central bank on the setting of interest rates. One suspects that few of the political elite, perhaps rather more of the official policy-making community, knew they were dancing to a Schumpeterian tune in so doing.

To an immeasurable extent Brittan's ECD paper helped shape opinion that more constitutional safeguards were necessary for good or at least better government. Certainly, nearly forty years after its publication, Brittan, in chapter 4 of the present volume, judges the methodological advances of ECD as more important than the headline prediction about the fate of liberal democracy. With his enduring interest in the role of government, Brittan rightly belongs in the pantheon of neo-liberal public intellectuals, but his disdain for partisanship and his insistence that government is 'a device rather than a totem'[108] means that he was never more than a resource for the New Right. Brittan's ECD was not a prescriptive paper, and it is axiomatic that by the standards of constitutional political economics there remains enormous scope in Britain as elsewhere to adjust incentives and penalties for politicians so as to further improve economic policy. The potential of the Hayekian agenda thus remains largely untapped. Similarly, debating the health of British politics remains a hardy perennial, with voter disengagement now a particular worry. The erosion of legitimacy is the leading edge of many other problems of contemporary British politics. It is the quantitative indicator of distrust of politicians, scepticism about democratic institutions and disillusionment with the democratic process. As Rose noted in his major overload study, 'indifference cripples political authority without causing it to collapse'.[109] In modern polities, and particularly in Britain, where the media have produced corrosive cynicism among consumerist citizens,[110] voter disengagement is very dangerous in terms of the natural response that political elites make in an intensely competitive political marketplace. In ECD Brittan fretted about ultra-competitive politicians generating unrealisable expectations of voters who, lacking budget constraints, subscribed to a mirage of social justice. *Plus ça change, plus c'est la même chose.*

Notes

1 I thank Sir Samuel Brittan for extended conversations on this and related projects; also Roger Backhouse, Ben Jackson, George Peden, Hugh Pemberton, Neil Rollings and James Thompson. All remaining errors remain exclusively my responsibility. This chapter is a companion piece to my article 'Brittan on Britain: "The economic contradictions of democracy" redux', *Historical Journal*, 54:4 (2011), pp. 1141–68, and book *Inside the Department of Economic Affairs: Samuel Brittan, The Diary of an 'Irregular', 1964–6* (Oxford: Oxford University Press, 2012), the latter an edition of part of his diary which forms important longer-term background to the present chapter and the companion paper.

2 S. Brittan, 'How British is the British sickness?', *Journal of Law and Economics*, 21:2 (1978), pp. 245–68, at p. 268.

3 S. Brittan, 'The changing economic role of government', in J. D. Hirst (ed.), *The Challenge of Change: Fifty Years of Business Economics* (London: Profile Books, 2003), pp. 70–4.

4 Brittan, 'How British is the British sickness?', p. 245.

5 S. Brittan, 'The economic contradictions of democracy', *British Journal of Political Science*, 5:2 (1975), pp. 129–59, at p. 129.

6 J. D. Tomlinson, *The Politics of Decline: Understanding Post-war Britain* (London: Longman, 2000), pp. 89, 96.

7 B. Brivati and R. Cockett (eds), *Anatomy of Decline: The Political Journalism of Peter Jenkins* (London: Phoenix, 1996), p. 91, quote taken from one of a series of articles on the 'English sickness' in 1978.

8 I. Budge, 'Relative decline as a political issue: ideological motivations of the politico-economic debate in post-war Britain', *Contemporary Record*, 7:1 (1993), pp. 1–23; B. E. Supple, 'Fear of failing: economic history and the decline of Britain', *Economic History Review*, 47:3 (1994), pp. 441–58; Tomlinson, *The Politics of Decline*; J. Tomlinson, 'Thrice denied: "declinism" as a recurrent theme in British history in the long twentieth century', *Twentieth Century British History*, 20:2 (2009), pp. 227–51; R. English and M. Kenny (eds), *Rethinking British Decline* (London: Macmillan, 2000); D. E. H. Edgerton, 'Science and the nation: towards new histories of twentieth-century Britain', *Historical Research*, 78:199 (2005), pp. 96–112; and R. Middleton, 'The political economy of decline', *Journal of Contemporary History*, 41:3 (2006), pp. 573–86.

9 Edgerton, 'Science and the nation', p. 98.

10 Middleton, 'The political economy of decline', p. 577.

11 N. F. R. Crafts, 'Britain's relative economic decline revisited', *CEPR Discussion Paper*, 8384 (2011), provides an update on his classic account of postwar under-performance and policy failure.

12 B. Jackson, 'At the origins of neo-liberalism: the free economy and the strong state, 1930–1947', *Historical Journal*, 53:1 (2010), pp. 129–51; Middleton, 'Brittan on Britain'; and B. Jackson and R. Saunders (eds), *Making Thatcher's Britain: Essays on the History of Thatcherism* (Cambridge: Cambridge University Press, 2012).

13 Tomlinson, *The Politics of Decline*, p. 89.

14 S. Brittan, '"The economic contradictions of democracy" revisited', *Political Quarterly*, 60:2 (1989), pp. 190–203.

15 M. J. Wiener, *English Culture and the Decline of the Industrial Spirit, 1850–1980* (Cambridge: Cambridge University Press, 1981) and C. Barnett, *The Audit of War: The Illusion and Reality of Britain as a Great Nation* (London: Macmillan, 1986). These are rightly especial targets of Tomlinson, *The Politics of Decline*,

esp. pp. 58–61, and feature prominently in English and Kenny (eds), *Rethinking British Decline*, chs 2–3.

16 Some thoughts on solutions are proffered in S. Brittan, *The Economic Consequences of Democracy* (London: Temple Smith, 1977).

17 A. Maddison, 'Phases of capitalist development', *Banca Nazionale del Lavoro Quarterly Review*, September 1977, 103–37; the full version comes with his *Phases of Capitalist Development* (Oxford: Oxford University Press, 1982).

18 HBBS, p. 266, cites M. Olson, *The Logic of Collective Action* (Cambridge, MA: Harvard University Press, 1965) and a 1978 mimeo of what would become 'The political economy of comparative growth rates', in D. C. Mueller (ed.), *The Political Economy of Growth* (New Haven, CT: Yale University Press, 1983), pp. 7–52; see also M. Olson, *The Rise and Decline of Nations: Economic Growth, Stagflation and Social Rigidities* (London: Yale University Press, 1982).

19 R. Cockett, *Thinking the Unthinkable: Think-Tanks and the Economic Counter-revolution, 1931–1983* (London: Harper Collins, 1994).

20 C. Robinson (ed.), *Arthur Seldon: A Life for Liberty* (London: Profile Books, 2009), esp. part II, is an important supplement to Cockett, *Thinking the Unthinkable*, on the IEA.

21 A. Seldon, *Capitalism* (Oxford: Basil Blackwell, 1990), p. 74.

22 D. W. Parsons, *The Power of the Financial Press: Journalism and Economic Opinion in Britain and America* (Aldershot: Edward Elgar, 1989), p. 100, has both Brittan and Lawson as members of the 'Newton generation', appointed by Gordon Newton (editor of the *Financial Times* 1949–72) and having common cohort characteristics: 'a scholarly grasp of economics; an interest in ideas; and a desire to influence policy'; see also D. Kynaston, *The Financial Times: A Centenary History* (London: Viking, 1988), esp. pp. 222–3, 240, 251. Lawson (b.1932) was with the *Financial Times* 1956–60 and Brittan (b.1933) 1955–61, and 1966 to present, with 1961–64 at the *Observer* and 1964–66 as a civil service 'irregular' in the Department of Economic Affairs (see Middleton, *Inside the Department of Economic Affairs*, table 1).

23 N. Lawson, 'Britain and Europe', *Prospect*, 37 (January 1999).

24 Cockett, *Thinking the Unthinkable*, p. 325.

25 N. Bosanquet, 'Sir Keith's reading list', *Political Quarterly*, 52:3 (1981), p. 324. The two items were *Government and the Market Economy: An Appraisal of Economic Policy Since the 1970 General Election* (London: IEA, 1971) and *Second Thoughts on Full Employment Policy* (London: Centre for Policy Studies, 1975).

26 For example, A. M. Gamble, 'The free economy and the strong state', in R. Miliband and J. Saville (eds), *Socialist Register* (London: Merlin Press, 1979), pp. 1–25, at p. 2; N. Thompson, 'Economic ideas and the development of economic opinion', in R. Coopey and N. W. C. Woodward (eds), *Britain in the 1970s: The Troubled Economy* (London: UCL Press, 1996), pp. 64–5; and Tomlinson, *The Politics of Decline*, p. 89.

27 For example, D. S. King, *The New Right: Politics, Markets and Citizenship* (London: Macmillan, 1987), p. 82; and C. Pierson, *Beyond the Welfare State? The New Political Economy of Welfare* (Cambridge: Polity Press, 2nd edition, 1998), pp. 143–4.

28 M. Prasad, *The Politics of Free Markets: The Rise of Neoliberal Economic Policies in Britain, France, Germany and the United States* (Chicago, IL: University of Chicago Press, 2006), p. 117.

29 J. Peck, *Constructions of Neoliberal Reason* (Oxford: Oxford University Press, 2010), p. 83.

30 D. Marquand, *Britain Since 1918: The Strange Career of British Democracy* (London: Weidenfeld & Nicolson, 2008), p. 260.

31 M. Cowling, 'The sources of the New Right: irony, geniality and malice', *Encounter*, 73 (November 1989), pp. 3–13.

32 Cockett, *Thinking the Unthinkable*, p. 214.

33 R. Desai, 'Second-hand dealers in ideas: think-tanks and Thatcherite hegemony', *New Left Review*, 203 (January/February 1994), p. 53. A. Denham and M. Garnett, *Keith Joseph* (Teddington: Acumen, 2001), p. 255, have the speech as mainly the work of Alfred Sherman, with Brittan and Alan Walters assisting.

34 G. T. Pepper, *Inside Thatcher's Monetarist Revolution* (London: Macmillan, 1998), p. 22.

35 See M. J. Oliver, *Whatever Happened to Monetarism: Economic Policy-Making and Social Learning in the United Kingdom Since 1979* (Aldershot: Ashgate, 1997), pp. 52–3.

36 S. Brittan, *How To End the 'Monetarist' Controversy: A Journalist's Reflections on Output, Jobs, Prices and Money* (London: IEA, 1981).

37 S. R. Letwin, *The Anatomy of Thatcherism* (London: Fontana, 1992), pp. 155, 290; and Cockett, *Thinking the Unthinkable*, p. 215.

38 *Financial Times*, 12 March 1981, cited in J. Campbell, *Margaret Thatcher*, Vol. II: *The Iron Lady* (London: Jonathan Cape, 2003), p. 112.

39 P. Booth (ed.), *Were 364 Economists All Wrong? A Discussion of the Impact and Legacy of the 1981 Budget* (London: IEA, 2006). But see G. K. Fry, '"A bottomless pit of political surprise"? The political "mystery" of the Thatcher era', *Twentieth Century British History*, 21:4 (2010), p. 552, for this *not* being some sort of Stalingrad.

40 Brittan, *Government and the Market Economy*, p. 19.

41 D. R. Harvey, *A Brief History of Neoliberalism* (Oxford: Oxford University Press, 2005), pp. 79–80.

42 See S. Brittan, 'Hayek, the New Right and the crisis of social democracy', *Encounter*, 54 (January 1980), pp. 31–46, reprinted in S. Brittan, *The Role and Limits of Government: Essays in Political Economy* (London: Temple Smith, 1983), p. 50n, on an incident in 1976 which 'convinced me after earlier hesitations that the Conservative Party was decidedly not where I wished to be'.

43 S. Brittan, *Against the Flow: Reflections of an Individualist* (London: Atlantic Books, 2005), p. xi.

44 English and Kenny (eds), *Rethinking British Decline*, p. 92.

45 *Ibid.*, p. 100. Famously, of course, Brittan wrote in July 1990 that Thatcher was not a Thatcherite: see J. Ranelagh, *Thatcher's People: An Insider's Account of the Politics, the Power and the Personalities* (London: Fontana, 1991), p. 22n, for the full context.

46 One recognised in 1971 with the accolade of financial journalist of the year: 'Top award for Mr Samuel Brittan', *The Times*, 26 April 1971, p. 17.

47 The phrase originates from Alan Ryan in 1984, cited in Parsons, *The Power of the Financial Press*, p. 180.

48 P. A. Hall, 'Policy paradigms, experts and the state: the case of macroeconomic policy-making in Britain', in S. Brooks and A. G. Gagnon (eds), *Social Scientists, Policy and the State* (Westport, CT: Praeger, 1990), pp. 53–78; P. A. Hall, 'The movement from Keynesianism to monetarism: institutional analysis and British economic policy in the 1970s', in S. Steinmo, K. Thelen and F. H. Longstreth (eds), *Structuring Politics: Historical Institutionalism in Comparative Analysis* (Cambridge: Cambridge University Press, 1992), pp. 90–113; and P. A. Hall, 'Policy paradigms, social learning and the state: the case of economic policy-making in Britain', *Comparative Politics*, 25:3 (1993), pp. 275–96.

49 Hall, 'Policy paradigms, experts and the state', p. 66.

50 Hall, 'Policy paradigms, social learning and the state', p. 287.
51 P. Jay, 'On being an economic journalist', *Listener*, 88 (24 August 1972), p. 239; see also Parsons, *The Power of the Financial Press*, p. 183.
52 A. Shonfield, *British Economic Policy Since the War* (Harmondsworth: Penguin, 1958).
53 G. C. Peden, 'Economic knowledge and the state in modern Britain', in S. J. D. Green and R. C. Whiting (eds), *The Boundaries of the State in Modern Britain* (Cambridge: Cambridge University Press, 1996), pp. 171–2.
54 R. Roberts, '"A special place in contemporary economic literature": the rise and fall of the British bank review, 1914–93', *Financial History Review*, 2:1 (1995), 41–60.
55 For example, S. Brittan, *Participation Without Politics: An Analysis of the Nature and Role of Markets* (London: IEA, 1975), part 2 of which comprised extensive extracts from *Capitalism and the Permissive Society* (London: Macmillan, 1973) and *Is There an Economic Consensus? An Attitude Survey* (London: Macmillan, 1973).
56 Notably, for a US audience, a reworked version of HBBS and an assessment of the first Thatcher government, respectively, 'How English is the English sickness?', *Washington Quarterly*, 3 (1980), pp. 151–66, and 'The Thatcher experiment', *Washington Quarterly*, 6 (1983), pp. 99–110.
57 The fixed exchange rate was finally abandoned in June 1971. In print, Brittan first supported floating in September 1970, in *The Price of Economic Freedom: A Guide to Flexible Exchange Rates* (London: Macmillan, 1970), although in the second 'intermediate' edition of the Treasury book, *Steering the Economy: The Role of the Treasury* (London: Secker & Warburg, 1969), p. 295, he made clear that a 'floating exchange rate is at the heart of [his preferred] long-term strategy' (see also, though more equivocally, pp. 319–22).
58 S. Brittan, *The Treasury Under the Tories, 1951–64* (Harmondsworth: Penguin, 1964).
59 Although not listed in the book, elsewhere there is a list of the forty-six persons who gave the private interviews. Starting with William Armstrong, then joint permanent secretary at the Treasury, and including the Prime Minister and Chancellor of the Exchequer, and his predecessor, this list comprises a veritable 'who's who' of British economic policy-making at this time – see Middleton, *Inside the Department of Economic Affairs*, p. 4.
60 Brittan, 'Samuel Brittan (b. 1933)', in R. E. Backhouse and R. Middleton (eds), *Exemplary Economists* (Cheltenham: Edward Elgar, 2000), vol. II, p. 280.
61 For example, Brittan in the preface to *Capitalism and the Permissive Society*, p. xvii, and Jay in 'Left, right, left', *Financial Times Magazine*, 92 (12 February 2005), pp. 25–7.
62 P. Jay, 'Pursuit of group self-interest seen as main threat to liberal democracy', *The Times*, 4 September 1974, pp. 1, 17.
63 P. Jay, 'Historic years at the Treasury', *The Times*, 18 August 1969, p. 21; 'Revising a Treasury standard', *The Times*, 29 June 1971, p. 15.
64 M. Tracey, *In the Culture of the Eye: Ten Years of Weekend World* (London: Hutchinson, 1983), p. 64.
65 P. Jay, '1964–79', in I. McLean and C. Jennings (eds), *Applying the Dismal Science: When Economists Give Advice to Governments* (London: Palgrave, 2006), p. 39; cf. Parsons, *The Power of the Financial Press*, pp. 180–4.
66 Later, he wrote that 'After the Treasury book [*The Treasury Under the Tories*; later revised as *Steering the Economy*] it is probably my best-known work (although not among economists)' (Brittan, 'Samuel Brittan', pp. 288–9).
67 Brittan, *The Role and Limits of Government*, p. 234n.

68 A search of EconLit, the American Economic Association's *Journal of Economic Literature* (*JEL*) dataset, yields no citations for ECD but this is not surprising as the *JEL* does not include the *British Journal of Political Science* among the journals enumerated.

69 This is a minimum figure, for, as is clear from table 5.1, his 1977 essay collection is also highly cited and this contains a version of ECD. A similar proviso applies for HBBS citation counts, as a version of this essay is in the essay collection ranked fifth.

70 R. E. Goodin, 'The state of the discipline, the discipline of the state', in R. E. Goodin (ed.), *The Oxford Handbook of Political Science* (Oxford: Oxford University Press, 2009), pp. 1–57; R. E. Goodin and H.-D. Klingemann, 'Political science: the discipline', in R. E. Goodin and H.-D. Klingemann (eds), *A New Handbook of Political Science* (Oxford: Oxford University Press, 1996), pp. 23ff; and N. Masuoka, B. Grofman and S. L. Feld, 'The political science 400: a 20-year update', *Political Science and Politics*, 40:1 (2007), pp. 133–45. That the mean political science citation is still zero is confirmed by T. Plümper, 'Academic heavy-weights: the "relevance" of political science journals', *European Political Science*, 6:1 (2007), pp. 41–50.

71 M. W. Giles and J. C. Garand, 'Ranking political science journals: reputational and citational approaches', *Political Science and Politics*, 40:4 (2007), p. 749.

72 In both political science and economics the book remains a significant medium for publication, and bibliometrics methodology in the social sciences (and humanities) has begun to embrace this plurality; see A. J. Nederhof, 'Bibliometric monitoring of research performance in the socials sciences and humanities: a review', *Scientometrics*, 66:1 (2006), pp. 81–100.

73 A. King, 'Adventures in bureaucracy', *The Economist*, 14 January 1989, p. 97. Neither Jenkins nor Riddell appear in the SSCI or A&HCI with cited items.

74 M. Blaug and R. P. Sturges, *Who's Who in Economics: A Biographical Dictionary of Major Economists, 1700–1981* (Brighton: Wheatsheaf, 1983), pp. 49–50.

75 In *The Economist* Brittan scored forty-eight gross hits (twenty-eight net of book advertisements etc.) between 1960 and 2011, and Jay sixty-six gross hits (forty-two net). Searches conducted on Economist Historical Archive, 1843–2006, at www.tlemea.com/economist/home.asp, and subsequently *Economist* online edition, www.economist.com, accessed 8 June 2011.

76 A-W. K. Harzing and R. van der Wal, 'Google Scholar as a new source for citation analysis', *Ethics in Science and Environmental Politics*, 8:1 (2008), pp. 62–71.

77 Search conducted 9 June 2011 on 'Brittan economic contradictions' and 'Brittan how British is the British sickness'.

78 Developed by Harzing and available from www.harzing.com/pop.htm, accessed 9 June 2011.

79 The Research Excellence Framework (REF) exercise set for 2014 in British higher education has prompted a number of disciplinary discussions about appropriate metrics; for political science, see the symposium 'Assessing research quality', *Political Studies Review*, 7:1 (2009), pp. 1–92, and I. McLean, 'Reputational and bibliometric methods of evaluating people and journals in political science: a UK perspective', PSA conference paper, April 2010.

80 A scientist has an index h if h of his or her papers (totalling N_p in number) have at least h citations each, and the other $(N_p–h)$ papers have no more than h citations each. For once, Wikipedia is an appropriate source, at http://en.wikipedia.org/wiki/ Hirsch_number, accessed 9 June 2011; see also Masuoka, Grofman and Feld, 'The political science 400', p. 143, who reject the h-index, as it can have 'very strange properties'.

81 Tomlinson, *The Politics of Decline*, p. 89; see also p. 97 n34, which asks the reader to compare the 'apocalyptic tone' of ECD with the 'much more measured' HBBS. The works referenced are, in the first paragraph, P. Jay, *A General Hypothesis of Employment, Inflation and Politics* (London: IEA, 1976), and P. Jay, 'Englanditis', in R. E. Tyrrell (ed.), *The Future That Doesn't Work: Social Democracy's Failures in Britain* (New York: Doubleday, 1977), pp. 167–85; those in the second paragraph, N. Johnson, *In Search of the Constitution: Reflections on State and Society* (Oxford: Pergamon, 1977) and J. E. Alt, *The Politics of Economic Decline: Economic Management and Political Behaviour in Britain Since 1964* (Cambridge: Cambridge University Press, 1979).

82 A. King, 'Overload: problems of governing in the 1970s', *Political Studies*, 23:2–3 (1975), pp. 284–96.

83 I. Crewe, 'Reputation, research and reality: the publication records of UK departments of politics, 1978–1984', *Scientometrics*, 14:3–4 (1988), pp. 235–50.

84 His published work appeared in a number of the standard 'decline' collections; for example, HBBS was reproduced nearly in full in the much used (for undergraduates) D. Coates and J. Hillard (eds), *The Economic Decline of Modern Britain: The Debate Between Left and Right* (Brighton: Wheatsheaf, 1986), ch. 30; he is a staple of key declinist 'political economy' works between the late 1970s and mid-1980s, from Alt, *The Politics of Economic Decline*, to A. M. Gamble and S. A. Walkland, *The British Party System and Economic Policy, 1945–1983: Studies in Adversary Politics* (Oxford: Clarendon Press, 1984); and, among commentators, he features in the standard textbooks of the 1970s and 1980s, for example D. Kavanagh, *Thatcherism and British Politics: The End of Consensus?* (Oxford: Oxford University Press, 2nd edition, 1990), esp. pp. 124, 147, on Thatcherism, and A. M. Gamble, *Britain in Decline: Economic Policy, Political Strategy and the British State* (London: Macmillan, 4th edition, 1994), pp. 33–4, 125, 155, on Britain in decline.

85 English and Kenny (eds), *Rethinking British Decline*, p. ix.

86 R. English and M. Kenny, 'Public intellectuals and the question of British decline', *British Journal of Politics and International Relations*, 3:3 (2001), p. 277.

87 S. Collini, *Absent Minds: Intellectuals in Britain* (Oxford: Oxford University Press, 2006); see the symposium on Collini with contributions from Michael Kenny, Rodney Barker and Edmund Neill, together with Collini's response, in *Political Studies Review*, 6:1 (2006), pp. 1–41.

88 A poll of 100 public intellectuals by *Prospect* magazine (21 August 2004) had Brittan ranked seventy-first.

89 R.W. Johnson, 'Nairn and the break-up of Britain', *Political Studies*, 26:1 (1978), p. 119.

90 S. Brittan and P. Lilley, *The Delusion of Incomes Policy* (London: Temple Smith, 1977), p. 178.

91 Tomlinson, *The Politics of Decline*, pp. 105–9; for Brittan's journalism and essays, see his *Against the Flow* and www.samuelbrittan.co.uk.

92 S. Brittan, 'The Thatcher government's economic policy', in D. Kavanagh and A. Seldon (eds), *The Thatcher Effect: A Decade of Change* (Oxford: Oxford University Press, 1989), pp. 1–37, and S. Brittan, *Capitalism With a Human Face* (Aldershot: Edward Elgar, 1996), ch. 11.

93 Middleton, 'Brittan on Britain'.

94 G. Duncan, 'A crisis of social democracy?', *Parliamentary Affairs*, 38:3 (1985), pp. 267–81, at p. 278.

95 This section is a greatly compressed version of the British Academy conference paper from whence it sprung; for more of the original, see Middleton, 'Brittan on Britain'.

96 Notably, Robert Bacon and Walter Eltis in three *Sunday Times* articles (2, 9 and 16 November 1975), the first version of what will become their *Britain's Economic Problem: Too Few Producers* (London: Macmillan, 1976); and M. Friedman, 'The line we dare not cross: the fragility of freedom at "60%"', *Encounter*, 47 (November 1976), pp. 8–14. On the latter, 'Economist says Britain is close to collapse', *The Times*, 25 October 1976, p. 1, conveys the impact of Friedman's message.

97 T. Wilson, 'The economic costs of the adversary system', in S. E. Finer (ed.), *Adversary Politics and Electoral Reform* (London: Anthony Wigram, 1975), pp. 99–116; and King, 'Overload', p. 164.

98 G. Debnam, 'The adversary politics thesis revisited', *Parliamentary Affairs*, 47:3 (1994), 420–33.

99 Jay, *A General Hypothesis* and 'Englanditis'.

100 D. Beetham, 'Four theorems about the market and democracy', *European Journal of Political Research*, 23:2 (1993), p. 198.

101 Brittan, *Second Thoughts*; M. Friedman, 'The role of monetary policy', *American Economic Review*, 58:1 (1968), pp. 1–17; Cockett, *Thinking the Unthinkable*, pp. 184–5.

102 Brittan, 'The economic tensions of British democracy', in Tyrrell (ed.), *The Future That Doesn't Work*, p. 143.

103 Brittan, *Capitalism with a Human Face*; and *Essays, Moral, Political and Economic* (Edinburgh: Edinburgh University Press, 1998).

104 N. Thompson, 'Hollowing out the state: public choice theory and the critique of Keynesian social democracy', *Contemporary British History*, 22:3 (2008), p. 372. Buchanan became an IEA adviser in 1967; notable early IEA publications include G. Tulloch, *The Vote Motive* (London: IEA, 1976); IEA, *The Economics of Politics* (London: IEA, 1978); and J. M. Buchanan, J. Burton and R. E. Wagner, *The Consequences of Mr Keynes: An Analysis of the Misuse of Economic Theory for Political Profiteering With Proposals for Constitutional Disciplines* (London: IEA, 1978).

105 Beetham, 'Four theorems', p. 199.

106 C. Skelcher, 'Changing images of the state: overloaded, hollowed-out, congested', *Public Policy and Administration*, 15:3 (2000), pp. 3–19, and R. A. W. Rhodes, 'The governance narrative: key findings and lessons from the ESRC's Whitehall programme', *Public Administration*, 78:2 (2000), pp. 345–63.

107 M. Blaug and H. Vane (eds), *Who's Who in Economics* (Cheltenham: Edward Elgar, 3rd edition, 2003), p. viii n2.

108 Brittan, 'The changing economic role of government', p. 81.

109 R. Rose (ed.), *Challenge to Governance: Studies in Overloaded Polities* (London: Sage, 1980), p. 23.

110 G. Stoker, *Why Politics Matters: Making Democracy Work* (London: Macmillan, 2006), pp. 127–32.

6

Alternative European and economic strategies

Stuart Holland

As Lawrence Black and Hugh Pemberton note in their Introduction (chapter 1), one feature of the challenge posed for conventional thought by developments in the 1970s was the opening up of what Peter Hall has called a 'marketplace for ideas'. Some ideas can become *idées forces* if they are seriously analytic, grounded in realities and recognised as addressing real problems. But such recognition depends on individual and collective perceptions, on personal dispositions and on whether new ideas can penetrate the defences of a system which itself is a matrix of vested interests, prevailing modes of thought and Weberian hierarchy. Also, language itself may become a trap when its meaning misrepresents what was the case, as it did in the claim of New Labour to have renounced allegedly Old Labour policies of the 1970s.[1] For these were new in relation to previous Labour thinking on economic management and, had they been implemented, might have enabled Labour to fulfil Harold Wilson's aspiration that it should be 'the natural party of government' and avoided key errors later made by New Labour, such as salvaging banks without assuring management control.

My first involvement with Whitehall, in 1965, when still a graduate student at Oxford, was to write papers and attend meetings in the Department of Economic Affairs on European regional policy to inform the drafting of the regional chapter of the National Plan.[2] I then was an economic assistant in the Cabinet Office from January 1966 and later a political assistant in No. 10 from shortly before the November 1967 devaluation through to June 1968, when I left to take up a research fellowship at the University of Sussex.

What struck me from the start of this Whitehall experience was that Labour was in office but not in power. This distinction was well made by Norman Lamont after sterling was forced out of the European Exchange Rate Mechanism in September 1992. But it already was relevant in the 1960s. Although Labour had a majority of nearly 100 seats from March 1966, speculation against sterling caused Wilson to adopt a deflationary package in July which not only 'blew the government off course' but ended any pretension to plan rather than react to events. The problem was compounded by a civil service that too often combined arrogance with ignorance, too few ministers in both economic and foreign affairs who could challenge them and too few special advisers who could offer alternatives – as on the key question of whether Britain should make a second application to join the European Economic Community (EEC), which also was central to my relations with Wilson, not least since I managed in 1967 to gain a 'Yes' from De Gaulle to do so, which the Foreign Office had not and which scarcely knew what was happening at even a high level within the EEC.

Britain and Europe

European planning initiatives in the 1960s were central both to gaining consent from de Gaulle for the second application to join the EEC and to my case for alternative economic strategies in the UK in the 1970s. For example, in March 1966, at the same time as Labour was winning the British general election with a massive majority, the French Vice President of the European Commission, Robert Marjolin, who formerly had headed the Marshall Aid programme, had published a medium-term economic policy report from a committee of national representatives, including the heads of the French, Italian and Belgian plans, and the German under-secretary for economy, advocating both joint macro-economic planning and European industrial, social and regional policies.[3] I briefed Wilson through Thomas Balogh, his senior economic adviser, not only that this was entirely compatible with Labour's National Plan, but that joint macroeconomic policies at the European level, especially with mutual currency support, could reduce pressure on sterling. The case was then strongly reinforced by the speculation against the pound that resulted in the July 1966 deflationary package, and Wilson from then on backed it as part of a second UK application to join the EEC.[4]

Clearly the key player for any of this would be de Gaulle, who already had vetoed the first UK application in January 1963. But de Gaulle also gained another veto of major importance at Luxembourg in January 1966, which was that qualified majority voting in the EEC, due to have been adopted that year, would not obtain 'in cases of important national

97

interest'. This was a block on Jean Monnet's design for a supranational Europe, since any member state could decide which national interests were important to it. It was crucial for Labour, which, since Attlee, had been opposed to a European federalism that could override Parliament. I therefore recommended to Wilson that we support the Luxembourg veto. By contrast, a Foreign Office paper in January 1966, concerned with diplomacy but oblivious to the politics, claimed that majority voting was vital to the other EEC states to avoid dominance by either Germany or France and asserted that no second application could succeed until de Gaulle either died or resigned.

But I also had learned in Paris in January 1966 from Jean Saingeour, head of forecasting at the French Ministry of Economy and Finance, that France could not readily afford the range of advanced technology projects to which de Gaulle was committed, such the TGV high-speed rail network, the national computer programme *Plan Calcul*, energy self-sufficiency through nuclear power generation, supersonic military aircraft, its Diamant space launcher and a second-generation Concorde. When I asked Saingeour what he foresaw, he replied 'grave social tensions', since the cost of these projects would conflict with the expansion of higher education, new universities and major programmes for regional development and urban regeneration. He did not say he foresaw the events at the Sorbonne of May 1968, but got the dilemma for France, and the outcome, entirely right.

Faced with the parallel dilemma of seeking to maintain the sterling exchange rate while also expanding higher education (including funding new universities), financing regional development and regenerating urban areas, the incoming 1964 Labour government had cancelled the development of three military planes in favour of US aircraft already in production, wanted to scrap the 1962 treaty with France to develop Concorde and was cutting back its commitment to the European Launcher Development Organisation (ELDO), for which the French Diamant launcher was crucial. Yet it was clear to me from the meeting with Saingeour that, on a shared cost basis, with Britain in the EEC, France and other member states could sustain a range of advanced technology projects not only in defence but also in civil technologies such as high-speed rail, computers and other electronics and, over the longer term, a cleaner, quieter, larger and more commercially viable Concorde 2. This could be done through a European Technology Community, whose decision-making would be consensual rather than Monnet's supranational qualified majority voting.

Understandably, Wilson liked this combination of proposals. Within three weeks of the 1966 July measures he appointed me a member of a deputy-secretary-level inter-departmental working party to consider a second British application to join the EEC. By the time the study was complete, the *Sunday Times* commented that Wilson's mind was evidently completely made up, though it was surprised to find that someone who thought 'a week is a long time in politics' could appear to be so convinced. But he was so, on the triple basis of accepting de Gaulle's veto on majority voting as the safeguard of parliamentary sovereignty, backing Marjolin's planning initiative as Labour's National Plan writ Europe-wide and building on his own 1964 election pledge to harness 'the white heat of technology' through a European Technology Community that would allow member states jointly to finance advanced technology projects which individually they could not readily afford.

The proposal for a Technology Community surfaced in various statements between September and December 1966. But the second application then stalled, both internally within Whitehall and because the message was not clear to de Gaulle. One reason not only was that the Foreign Office was opposed to de Gaulle's veto but that the ambassador in Paris had not disguised this, with the outcome that de Gaulle had cut relations with the embassy. Nor did the Foreign Office know anything about Marjolin's report for European planning, nor much care about the degree to which this could relaunch Labour's National Plan.

When Harold raised Marjolin's report in cabinet and asked George Brown, by then Foreign Secretary, for his response to it, Brown stormed back to the Foreign Office and demanded why he had not been briefed on this 'damn alleged whatever' European planning project. In Weberian manner, his permanent secretary, Sir Paul Gore-Booth, turned to the deputy secretary, Sir Con O'Neill, who passed the request down to the under-secretary for European affairs, who passed it to his assistant secretary, who passed it to his principal, who then passed it to his assistant principal, who was charged to look into it. The assistant principal then asked the permanent delegation of the Foreign Office in Brussels to brief him. But it neither had ever heard of Marjolin's report nor even could find a copy of it. He asked how I had learned of it, to which I referred to two and a half pages of coverage of it in *Le Monde*. He then asked how I had found a copy, to which I said from the Information Office of the EEC in London. When he found that it was the only one they had, he asked me to copy it to him, which I did. He then suggested lunch and admitted that it was hard to understand since it was in French, which he had not studied since O-level, was about European planning and economics, of which he knew nothing, and would I kindly copy him my memo to the Prime Minister on it.

I declined, saying that it was better that the Foreign Office made its own independent valuation, but went straight from this to a meeting of the official cabinet sub-committee considering the case for pursuing a second application to join the EEC. When its chair, Derek Mitchell, formerly Wilson's principal private secretary, asked Sir Con O'Neill, the senior official in the first failed application, what he thought of my claim that Marjolin's report could enable joint planning at a European level, O'Neill lied, claiming that 'the Office' had fully considered the question and that I had no grounds for the claim. Derek, to whom I had just told the outcome of the lunch, then invited me to put some questions to O'Neill, which I did and which confirmed that he had no grounds for his claim.[5]

Getting through to de Gaulle

But thereafter the would-be second application stalled, not least since the Foreign Office could not get through to de Gaulle. Balogh then got diverted by the case for a North American Free Trade Area, rather than a second application to join the EEC, which did not suit Wilson since the pressure from the right within the cabinet was threatening a split if he did not make one. Then, early in May 1967, he found me in my office and suggested a one-to-one meeting at No. 10 after an evening vote in the House. He asked how I thought Germany would respond to my proposal of a European Technology Community, which might be on an Anglo-French axis since, although Germany during the war had pioneered key technologies such as jet aircraft and ballistic missiles, it had, on US insistence, renounced these. I answered that we should propose that the German Democratic Republic be granted associate status and that it therefore would be able to participate in joint ventures in civil technology.

Liking this, and commenting that Willy Brandt would welcome it, Wilson then said: 'If only I could get this through to de Gaulle'. It was when I asked why he could not that I learned that de Gaulle had cut relations with the Paris embassy. I then asked if he wanted me to get through to de Gaulle. He laughed, said that if I could it deserved a malt, poured me one and asked in return, if I would not mind, how I would do so. I then told him that I knew Pierre Joxe, the son of Louis Joxe, de Gaulle's interior minister, and probably could put the case to Louis. On 10 May 1967, within hours of Pierre confirming that Louis would see me the next Friday, Wilson formally applied for membership. Yet the odds on success looked poor, since de Gaulle then reiterated six reasons, at his press conference the same week, why Britain could not join the Community.

At my meeting with Joxe in the Ministry of the Interior on the Friday I addressed each of these. I indicated that Britain would accept the Luxembourg veto on qualified majority voting within the EEC, which was new since Foreign Office officials had made so many statements deprecating it, plus offer mutual support of the sterling area and the franc zone against currency speculation. I then submitted that the proposal of a European Technology Community could mean joint Franco-British finance for a range of the advanced technology projects that Saingeour already had indicated to me could not be readily afforded by France alone.

Joxe affirmed that explicit support for the Luxembourg veto would be vital in confirming a wider confederal construction of Europe, and volunteered that the proposal for a Franco-British axis for a Technology Community was of far more interest than what they had understood from Wilson's public announcement of it. However, he then said that an explicit renunciation of the special relationship with the USA was imperative, and would be a precondition for acceptance of a second application.

The issue already was public knowledge, but I had not anticipated that he would underline this with the words: 'The logic must be explicit'. Words rarely come when one needs them, rather than after the event. But in this case I found myself responding that 'in politics, as in love, it denies logic to renounce a relationship before it is clear that another and better is probable', at which he smiled. I also submitted that the logic of a new Technology Community would be clear to Washington, not least in the context of Jean-Jacques Servan-Schreiber's at the time highly publicised *The American Challenge*.[6] Besides which, the Prime Minister had already stated to Parliament that the UK and Europe were risking an 'industrial helotry' to the USA. The new 'special relationship' would not be with the USA, but with Europe, through France.

I expected Joxe to thank me, and state that he was sure that the President of the Republic would consider the case carefully and no doubt report back in due course. But he volunteered that de Gaulle was waiting for a report from him in the Elysée and that he would himself report back to me the next morning. He did so. De Gaulle had agreed to a second UK application on such a basis but with one proviso. This was *not* that there should be a declaration that the special relationship with the USA was over, but that the technology cooperation projects between the UK and France within a European Technology Community should be agreed, at least in outline, in advance. I rang Marcia Williams, Harold's political secretary, to say that the answer was yes to a second application and then debriefed him in London. He immediately got an outflanked Foreign Office to set about planning the round of the capitals of the Six with George Brown which followed.

The missed opportunity

However, Wilson's subsequent failure to indicate even outline programmes for joint technology ensured de Gaulle's rejection of the application after he and George Brown visited Paris. He used the opening to de Gaulle on a short-term tactical basis to avoid conflicts within both the cabinet and the Parliamentary Labour Party (PLP) at a time when the right was pressuring him to apply for EEC membership but at least some of the left could have opposed him had the application succeeded. Regrettably, this confirms the 'successful failure' hypothesis advanced by Oliver Daddow and others who asked 'what networks of contact and methods of persuasion were used in Downing Street, Whitehall and abroad to secure support for a second attempt to join the Community?' even if they could not at the time answer it.[7]

By contrast, I was convinced that Harold could have succeeded in the second application without splitting the PLP, rather than some abstentions or minority votes against. The left's concerns about Monnet-style supranationalism had been blocked by the Luxembourg veto of January 1966. European planning as a relaunch of the National Plan in a more credible international framework, plus mutual currency support, would have appealed to many members of the PLP who had been dismayed that the National Plan had been abandoned under pressure from financial markets. A European Technology Community could have transformed a Common Market with a federalist neo-liberal agenda into a different, more forward-looking confederal Europe. It also would have been consistent with Wilson's earlier stress on 'the white heat of technology' and introduction of a Ministry of Technology at a time when the major criticism of his leadership was inconsistency. Besides which, the government's majority on a motion to approve a successful second application would not be threatened, since the bulk of the Tories and the Liberals, who had supported the first application, would support the second.

Moreover, for a wider public, whether or not Britain should be 'in Europe' was not at the time a divide on left–right lines. Acheson's acerbic quip that Britain had lost an empire but not yet found a role had a wider resonance. Many of those who had experienced the Second World War (and possibly the First) recognised the case for a framework for European cooperation. Some of them were deeply concerned that this should not deny the sovereignty of Parliament, but acceptance in the Luxembourg Accord of de Gaulle's veto had safeguarded this.[8]

Wilson's failure to follow through on the principle of mutual currency support also was an historic missed opportunity, not only for Britain, as evidenced by its later being forced out of the Exchange Rate Mechanism by the Bundesbank unilaterally increasing interest rates, but also for Europe, as made dramatically clear from 2010 in the refusal of Germany to support other member states against speculation on bond markets which threatened the disintegration of the Eurozone. For a priority concern of Germany in the 1960s was that the UK, with its long-standing democratic tradition, should be a member of the EEC.

A common presumption at the time, echoed by Balogh, was that the Bundesbank was wholly independent and that this would frustrate any common monetary policies. Yet the constitution of the Bundesbank explicitly stressed that, without prejudice to its prime responsibility to assure price stability, it also had to support 'the general economic policies of the government', of which mutual currency support could be one in a Treaty of Accession both for the UK and for the countries of the European Free Trade Area (EFTA), which it was known at the time would follow its lead – if it led – and join with it. This still is relevant at the time of writing in relation to the Eurozone crisis, since the provision that the Bundesbank was obliged to support the general economic policies of the Bundesrepublik was translated to the constitution of the European Central Bank, which has to 'support the general economic policies' of the European Union, even if it routinely – but wrongly – claims that it is 'wholly independent'.

Back to analysis: 'the missing middle' in Keynes

At a personal level, Wilson's failure to think and act strategically both on Europe and on other issues, such as not relaunching the National Plan on the basis of European models of planning through leading firms, influenced my decision to resign from No. 10 even though this meant vacating a first-floor office in No. 10 for a Portakabin on a mud slope at Sussex. But, from the mid-1960s, it was clear to me that if there were to be any success for more strategic thinking on economic policy this needed an analytic challenge to the then dominant but shallow Keynesian orthodoxy that full employment and welfare could be achieved by 'appropriate' fiscal, monetary and exchange rate policies.

Evidence of how shallow this was came after the first of the oil price increases implemented by the Organization of the Petroleum Exporting Countries (OPEC), in September 1973, when those in Whitehall who until then, like Nixon in 1971, had assumed that 'we are all Keynesians now' found within months that they were not. But challenging this could not readily be achieved by day-to-day running of a policy unit, even if from inside No. 10, not least when the most progressive economists as advisers to the government had failed either to move beyond Keynes or to recognise the need to do so. For most Keynesians by the 1960s had presumed, as Keynes had in his Concluding Notes in *The General Theory*, that, provided the state intervened to manage the level of demand at the macro level, the micro supply side of the economy could be left to the mechanisms of perfect or imperfect competition.[9] In the latter, Keynes had been influenced by Joan Robinson.[10] Yet imperfect competition was not only an issue of whether a firm with strong brand attachment could charge more for a product, as had been claimed by Robinson, but whether the oligopoly dominance of markets by a handful of firms could collectively prove monopolistic, as had been claimed by Edward Chamberlin.[11]

Keynes also assumed that trade was between different companies in different countries, and that changes in the exchange rate would adjust trade imbalances and assure full employment.[12] But in this he had failed to recognise that capital in the 1930s already was multinational rather than only national.[13] Postwar Keynesians displaced the degree to which the increased domination by multinational companies of the supply side of the UK economy had divorced the Keynesian macro–micro synthesis. Such domination meant they had price-making power rather than taking prices from allegedly sovereign consumers. By the later 1960s their foreign production already was double that of their exports, which meant that they would not deliver the increased exports at lower prices that Keynesians assumed should flow from a devaluation of sterling, since to do so would be to compete against themselves abroad.[14]

This was to be confirmed during the 1970s by two studies, including one covering the 220 companies which at the time constituted two-thirds of UK visible exports, by Peter Holmes, who found that none of them had reduced prices in foreign markets because of the 1967 devaluation rather than for other reasons.[15] Holmes was surprised that this seemed to deny the cardinal assumption of profit maximisation in microeconomic theory, whereas it fulfilled it – if in a different, multinational context – in the sense that to have followed through the devaluation by lower prices in markets where they already were producing would have lowered their profits in them. In the following chapter Wickham-Jones asserts that my stress on the role of multinationals seemed overstated, since other economies seemed to be flourishing with them. But the UK was at this time the second most multinational economy in the world after the USA and four times more so in terms of foreign production relative to exports than Germany and Japan. This was a key reason why the UK, like the USA, was subject to structural trade deficits, whereas Germany and Japan generated major trade surpluses.

Mesoeconomics

By 1972–73 I had begun to conceptualise 'the missing middle' in macro–micro syntheses – both Keynesian and monetarist – as mesoeconomic, as in the Greek *mesos*, meaning intermediate or middle, in that multinational big business dominated both macroeconomic outcomes and smaller national microeconomic firms.[16] The conceptual framework was not inconsistent with Keynes' stress on the importance of effective demand, but was influenced by theorists of oligopoly such as Kalecki, Perroux and Sylos-Labini.[17] There also was evidence on the increased role of oligopoly in British industry. I had seen findings in advance of their publication, by S. J. Prais of the National Institute of Economic and Social Research, that the share of the top 100 companies in UK manufacturing output had increased from 20 per cent in 1950 to 40 per cent in 1970.[18] The analysis was influenced also by Robin Murray,[19] who had drawn my attention to the work of Stephen Hymer.[20]

In 1965, when I had written papers for the Department of Economic Affairs on European regional planning for the draft of the National Plan, I was much influenced by the key role given to leading firms in French regional policy, which had been drawn from the work of François Perroux,[21] but did not gain a follow-through on this in the National Plan itself. Later regional policy was still in a macro framework influenced by the claim of Nicholas Kaldor, an affable and generous leading Keynesian, that a wage subsidy or employment premium for firms in the regions would give them the equivalent of an 'internal devaluation'. Yet this assumed that there were normal profits among 'price-taking' rather than 'price-making' firms, and that they would pass on the £1.50 weekly Regional Employment Premium (authored by Kaldor and introduced in 1967) in lower prices, becoming as competitive as firms in more developed regions, or more so. The same micro–macro rationale obtained for the 40 per cent investment grants at the time being offered to firms to locate in the regions. None was as effective as had been anticipated, since British multinational companies already were being attracted to Asia and Latin America by labour costs which were a minor fraction of those anywhere in the UK.

Planning through leading firms

By 1966 I also had come to realise that the need to align the oligopoly power of leading firms to national planning objectives had become central to all French planning. For example, shortly before joining Thomas Balogh in the Cabinet Office in January 1966, I had learned from Jean Saingeour not only that France could not readily afford the advanced technology projects to which de Gaulle was committed (see under 'Britain and Europe', at the start of the chapter), but that the French Ministry of Economy and Finance in 1964 – the year Labour had come into government – had required leading French firms to enter into *contrats de stabilité* (stability agreements). By these the firms could change any prices they wished for any product, which gave them flexibility, provided that their overall output–price ratio was consistent with the national target for inflation – at the time some 3 per cent, to encourage Keynesian 'animal spirits' by a constant increase in cash flow. The aim was a macro policy outcome, that is, if the price leaders kept to the target, the national inflation target was likely to be met, since smaller micro firms would be uncompetitive if they exceeded it.

Yet by 1966 the Ministry of Economy and Finance realised that it had no proper knowledge of the basis on which firms were declaring costs, not least through internal and international transfer pricing. In other words, leading firms allowed their subsidiaries to charge prices to other subsidiaries or the parent company which inflated their nominal costs and understated real profits. To respond to this, Saingeour told me, it was about to introduce *contrats de programme* (planning agreements). By these, French multinational companies had to submit information on the whole range of their costs and pricing framework on their national and international operations. The ministry also decided to use *contrats de programme* to leverage other outcomes from leading firms in both the private and public sectors, including more investment in less developed regions and greater commitment to innovation and long-term investment projects.

The scale of such operations within the French Ministry of Economy and Finance from 1966 was striking. Half of its senior staff were engaged in planning agreements with leading firms, at a time when the British Treasury was still focusing on Keynesian stabilisation policy and relying on short-term changes in indirect taxes and interest rates. Such planning agreements were not compulsory. But they were obligatory for any major company that wished to gain public grants or public purchasing, which, of course, near to all of them did when de Gaulle was sustaining very long-term public investment projects with macro-scale budgets. The Belgian planners knew of this both directly and through Marjolin's Medium Term Economic Policy Committee and paralleled it with *contrats de progrès* (progress agreements) for research and innovation, as well as *contrats prototypes* to translate technical progress into prototypes. The Italians at the same time were introducing *contrattazione programmata* (planning agreements) with leading firms with the main aim of getting them to commit investment in the Mezzogiorno in return for public purchase contracts.

Alternative economic strategies

When I left No. 10 in 1968, I had no idea that I would shortly thereafter be able to convince the National Executive Committee (NEC) of the Labour Party of the case for any economic strategy, let alone one involving planning agreements, nor that Wilson would so vehemently oppose these, given that he had shown interest in them and recommended them to Peter Shore at the Department of Economic Affairs, even though neither he nor Peter followed through on them as a basis for relaunching the National Plan. Nor that the case for them and for selective holdings in leading firms would initially gain consensus from the right of the Labour Party, and only then support from the left.

But some of this merits attention to the meaning of words in context, since the term 'Alternative Economic Strategy' was not used by anyone until the Labour government had abandoned the commitments to the economic strategy based on planning agreements and selective holdings in leading firms in Labour's programmes of 1972 and 1973.[22] Also, there were several economic strategies in the 1970s, including the following:

(1) The strategy of the NEC, in which the key initial and proactive players were Ian Mikardo and Judith Hart. I influenced and also drafted many of its economic statements from 1972 to 1983, though early drafts were amended by the NEC and later drafts also in the deletion by Tony Benn of any reference to continental European or Japanese examples of planning through leading firms.

(2) Roy Jenkins' strategy in his *What Matters Now*, for which I drafted the key opening chapter, 'The needs of the regions', which was both a national and regional strategy for a major state holding company and which Roy later claimed was an alternative to the NEC's proposals, although the only the key difference was that it referred to holdings being taken in twenty to twenty-five sectors, rather than in twenty to twenty-five firms.[23]

(3) Tony Crosland's alternative, amounting essentially to the claim that there was nothing wrong with the National Plan of 1965 other than the failure to devalue early enough after the 1964 general election, and with only a limited role for what he earlier, in *The Future of Socialism* (1956), had accepted as the case for competitive public enterprise.

(4) The Labour government's alleged strategy in the form of the Industry Act 1975, with a diminished and mainly salvage version of a National Enterprise Board and abandonment of planning agreements with leading firms as the condition for public money in the private sector.[24]

(5) An Alternative Economic Strategy in the sense of the term used by Tony Benn and Francis Cripps after Tony had been shifted from Industry to Energy, which was for import controls and, in Tony's case, against Europe, rather than working with it.[25]

(6) My own restatements of the case that had been endorsed by the NEC and the party conferences of 1972 and 1973, as set out in *The Socialist Challenge* of 1975, which was in favour of Euro-Keynesianism in terms of joint demand management and European meso-level accountability of multinational companies.[26]

Industrial strategy and the NEC

In my first paper to the NEC Industrial Policy Sub-committee, 'Planning and policy coordination', in 1972,[27] I drew on European examples of how, if big business wanted either public grants or public purchasing contracts, it should be obliged to enter into negotiation of a planning agreement with government and to reveal what it was doing on transfer pricing, as the French had done since 1966. The paper also recommended that one of the options for planning was to convert the Treasury into a Ministry of Economy and Finance on the French model. But a parallel case in my early and later papers for the NEC was for a state holding company, modelled on the Italian Istituto per la Ricostruzione Industriale (Industrial Reconstruction Institute, IRI). Reference to this in Labour's programme of 1972 passed almost without notice at the time.

The party already was committed in principle to the case for a state holding company. I had submitted a paper on this with Richard Pryke which was informed by a project I had led (on resigning from No. 10) on the IRI and other European state holdings.[28] Its opening chapter summarised the case that both the private sector and Keynesian macro-economic policies needed to be matched by selective public holdings in leading firms to ensure a broad wave of long-term investment in industry and to offset negative externalities such as regional imbalance and transfer pricing by multinational companies.[29] I combined this with the case that such a state holding company or companies could counter globalisation and the attraction of multinational companies to countries with lower labour costs by offsetting low labour costs by higher-value-added innovation and, through its own operations, gain information on the degree to which multinational companies were transfer pricing and evading profits through tax havens.[30]

Building support

Initial support in the Labour Party for the idea of state holding companies came from the centre right, through Bill Rodgers. At his suggestion, I wrote a paper on the case for them and for planning agreements for a conference organised by the *Socialist Commentary* journal, which stressed the case for a *multi-sectoral* holding company, rather than nationalisation of individual sectors, on the grounds that, as Pryke and I put it in the paper for the NEC, 'its operating companies in different manufacturing sectors can contribute to a "broad wave" of investment throughout manufacturing rather than investment increases in isolated sectors'.[31]

Bill then invited me to become an adviser to the Trade and Industry Sub-committee of the House of Commons Expenditure Committee, of which he was chair, and which I persuaded to visit Italy to assess the validity of my claims for the IRI. In 1972 it published a unanimous cross-party report recommending the establishment of a major British state holding company.[32] The committee then took my recommendation that it should take evidence from leading companies on the effectiveness of regional development grants and the 1960s Labour governments' regional employment premium, which, I argued, on Italian precedents, was unlikely to have influenced the companies in locating in less developed regions when they already could gain lower-cost labour through globalisation. The evidence confirmed this.[33]

One of the next politicians to show interest in the case for a state holding company was Roy Jenkins, when I drafted his lead chapter, 'The needs of the regions', in a Fontana paperback, *What Matters Now*.[34] I knew this was his personal manifesto for leadership of the Labour Party but was not concerned, since I both wanted to gain as broad support in the party as possible for the case that a wide-ranging state holding company could both promote a broad wave of innovating investment in British manufacturing and offer a Labour government a means to countervail multinational companies.

It was only then, after cross-party support in the Commons, and from Bill Rodgers and Roy Jenkins on the centre right of the Labour Party, that I was invited to make the same case to the NEC, and wrote a paper for it on planning and policy coordination.[35] As a result, the NEC set up two committees to examine the case, one on public ownership and the other on planning. Out of these came a new Labour Party economic strategy in its 1972 and 1973 programmes. From 1971 through to the summer of 1973 there was therefore a consensus across the Labour Party on the case for a new and major state holding company in industry, and for planning agreements.

The collapse of consensus

The chapter I drafted for Roy Jenkins made the same case as I had made in my paper for *Socialist Commentary*, in which I had proposed that the state should have a shareholding in at least one leading firm in all the main twenty plus sectors of manufacturing, and also in banking, mortgage finance and insurance. Simple arithmetic meant that this implied twenty to twenty-five firms. Yet when the NEC – now left controlled for the first time since the Second World War – published its opposition green paper on the case for a National Enterprise Board in April 1973, and stated explicitly that this meant a controlling public holding in twenty to twenty-five firms, Jenkins denounced the proposals as 'outdated nationalisation'. Likewise, the media near unanimously referred to a proposal to 'nationalise the top twenty-five companies' rather than to the taking of a controlling shareholding in twenty to twenty-five of the top 100 companies. Nor was there any recognition that these companies had now come to command the heights of British industry, were not responding to exchange rate changes, were investing abroad rather than in the UK at an accelerating rate, and that such foreign investment tended to substitute for exports.[36]

The case gained useful support both from John Kenneth Galbraith and from another leading Harvard economist, John Dunning.[37] But denunciation by Jenkins, and such headlines as 'the top twenty-five' companies, caricatured it as dogmatic regress to old-style nationalisation. This then was abetted by Tony Benn pronouncing that there would be 'compulsory planning agreements with the top 100 companies'. My earlier papers on planning had raised the question of whether there was a case for making planning agreements compulsory rather than voluntary, but only in that if leading firms wanted public grants or contracts they would be obliged to negotiate a planning agreement on how they used them.[38]

Again, the meaning of words is in their use and their use is understood or misunderstood in terms of how they are perceived by whom and in which context. I remonstrated with Tony at the next – and last – of the regular meetings that he had convened in Holland Park[39] that his use of the term 'compulsory planning agreements' made the policy sound like *Gosplan*, and was entirely wrong, since what we were offering was not a totally planned economy but a means of harnessing oligopoly power on the lines of European planning models, thus gaining better value for public money in the private sector, and direct leverage on outcomes. But Tony kept using the phrase 'compulsory planning agreements with the top 100 companies', which duly was denounced by influential sections of the press.

Misperception of the case also was compounded by default. Judith Hart and I had offered to brief Harold Wilson on the case for planning agreements and a state holding company. He did not decline, but Marcia Williams responded that this would have to be sometime in the future, given his other commitments, which happened to include his completing his memoirs of the 1964–70 governments. But this proved near fatal. He therefore had not been able to gain a briefing on the 1973 NEC green paper on a National Enterprise Board before choosing to announce that he would 'veto' it, on reading press headlines that Labour wanted to 'grab the top twenty-five companies'.[40] Though in a press conference ten days later he then asked journalists whether they actually had read the green paper and when near to none said yes, advised them 'It's not as bad as you think'.

When it was pointed out to him by the then chair of the party, Bill Simpson, that he could not veto an NEC proposal before it was considered by the forthcoming 1973 party conference, he then offered the press another headline by pronouncing that he would resign if the conference endorsed it (which it did, though he did not). He thereby aided the perception that the industrial strategy was a throwback to 'old-style nationalisation' rather than a recognition that multinational capital in an already global era needed countervailance in the public interest by such a strategy if Britain were to reinforce and sustain its industrial base rather than succumb to de-industrialisation.

The 1974–79 Labour governments

When Labour came into government on a minority basis after the election of February 1974, Judith Hart appointed me as her special adviser on overseas development. Tony Benn, now Secretary of State for Industry, then co-opted me onto the drafting committee for a new Industry Bill chaired by Eric Heffer and including Michael Meacher and Tony's economic adviser, Francis Cripps. To 'stop Benn', the Treasury transferred a deputy secretary from the Inland Revenue, Alan Lord, to the Department of Industry.[41] Lord congratulated Eric on the degree to which the industrial strategy proposals were detailed but then tried to derail them by claiming that, 'in the experience of the department', I had overstated the case that big business did not face locational costs by investing in the regions. If Lord had won on this he could have undermined the whole case for a National Enterprise Board, since support for its promoting investment in the regions had ranged from Roy Jenkins and Bill Rodgers and moderate trades unionists through to the left of the party. He must have known this, but not that, in claiming so, and with no knowledge himself of industrial policy, he had been misadvised.

At the initial meeting of the working group to draft the Industry Bill Eric Heffer asked me whether Alan Lord's view was right. I replied that if it were so it would be interesting to see the evidence. In classic Weberian manner, as in the Foreign Office on Marjolin's European planning framework, Lord then went 'down the line', asking the under-secretary on the working group, who asked the assistant secretary, who asked the principal, who asked the assistant principal, who then asked the economic adviser. The response then was passed back 'up the line' that there was such evidence. Yet I knew that the economic adviser in question had undertaken a study, for the department, which indicated that, of the top 100 companies in the UK, only two ever even had made a cost analysis of alternative locations in the regions and that this had been after they had decided already to locate there rather than abroad.

There was thus no basis for Lord's claim. It therefore was not surprising that he failed to respond to requests from Eric Heffer actually to proffer any such evidence. Then, when confronted by Eric on the report by the economic adviser, he admitted that there was none, that for the first time in his experience as a civil servant he had been misled, and offered an abject apology, thereby undermining any further resistance to the proposals for either the National Enterprise Board (NEB) or the planning agreements. The draft for the Industry Bill as then submitted for approval to Tony Benn fully reflected Labour policy.

But whereas the draft for the bill had begun with an analysis of the multinational character of British big business, and then made the case for planning agreements to gain better value for public money in the private sector, Tony Benn then reversed this when he redrafted it as the government white paper *The Regeneration of British Industry* – opening with the case for public shareholdings in twenty to twenty-five leading firms.[42] This fell into the stereotypical view of 'Bennery' as nationalisation. The problem was compounded by Tony also still constantly referring to 'compulsory planning agreements' with the 'top 100' companies, despite my submitting to him that one could not have a 'compulsory agreement' and that such agreements would have to be negotiated individually with firms with different priorities in different sectors. This had been central to the opening section I had drafted for the Industry Bill but he deleted it as well as reference to European examples of planning agreements.[43]

The outcome

In 1975, I resigned as an economic adviser when it became plain that the Industry Act would make both public shareholdings in leading firms and planning agreements 'voluntary'. I had warned Tony Benn at the last meeting at his home, after the 1973 Labour Party conference, attended also by Tony Banks and Margaret Beckett (then Margaret Jackson), that if he followed through his claim that Labour's programme was 'fundamentally incompatible with membership of the Common Market' and called for a referendum on this basis, he not only would be wrong, since we had premised the programme on continental European models, but that in doing so he would risk losing both the referendum and thereby the industrial strategy which had just been endorsed by the conference. Tony did not want the advice, led the call for a referendum on such grounds, lost it and enabled Wilson overnight to replace him as Secretary of State at the Department of Industry by Eric Varley. The latter then assiduously assured British and other multinational companies in Britain that the government welcomed their contribution to the British economy and had no intention of insisting on planning agreements, but therefore also had no intention of requiring any accountability for public money in the private sector.

Nonetheless, the Labour governments from 1974 introduced two major state holding companies. The first, modelled on the Italian IRI was the NEB. The other was the British National Oil Corporation (BNOC), modelled on the Italian state hydrocarbons corporation, Ente Nazionale Idrocarburi (ENI). By 1979, before being abolished by Margaret Thatcher, the NEB was directly or indirectly employing a million people in British manufacturing. However, unlike either the IRI or ENI, Wilson persuaded a cabinet already dysfunctionally split on the case for an industrial strategy that neither the NEB nor the BNOC should be able to buy into leading firms on a market basis, even though European state holding companies did so. He also gained cabinet support against the case that it should be obligatory for big business gaining public subsidies or public purchasing to negotiate planning agreements, thereby denying the means by which Britain might emulate French success in promoting 'national champions' and opening the way for Eric Varley to give such an assurance when replacing Tony Benn.

In practice, apart from directly or indirectly safeguarding up to a million jobs in manufacturing, most of which thereafter were lost, there were foregone potential gains. The BNOC's own operations made it possible to identify transfer pricing by major private sector oil companies in the North Sea. But, as Chancellor, Denis Healey never followed through on this, taking at face value the oil majors' claim that if taxed they would pull up their rigs and locate elsewhere, which, with the North Sea oil bonanza already in flow, was implausible. The cost of pulling up a rig rather than gaining oil from it contradicted common sense and economic logic, since it literally was what economists metaphorically deemed a 'sunk cost'. Denis thereby left the gains from North Sea oil to Margaret Thatcher, who was able to use the revenues from it to reduce personal and corporate taxation.

Moreover, the potential of the NEB was never fully realised, for it was handicapped by taking over British Leyland, which at the time amounted to most of the British motor industry, whereas I had advocated that this be brought into a reintroduced Industrial Reorganisation Corporation, since the NEB itself should have been reinforcing and promoting success rather than subsidising and underwriting earlier failure. It did, however, still manage to invest in innovative companies such as Ferranti, rescued by the NEB in 1975 from a cash-flow crisis. Likewise, the NEB provided initial funding for Inmos, a semiconductor company which, in addition to a site in the USA, set up a UK design centre in Bristol, which worked on a ground-breaking new microprocessor, and a UK factory in Newport. The Inmos shareholding was disposed of by the Conservatives after the 1979 election, though the company was ultimately to leave a lasting legacy of advanced computing technology skills in Bristol.

What then emerged as the Alternative Economic Strategy was a hybrid of my initial recommendations of state holding companies in manufacturing and finance, plus planning agreements with major companies, plus import controls. This was under the influence of Francis Cripps, Tony Benn's economic adviser at the Department of Industry. My relations were good with Francis then, had been before and were to be so thereafter. He and Terry Ward readily worked with me and others on econometrics for the *Out of Crisis* project for an Alternative European Strategy, backed when he was French finance minister by Jacques Delors, and then later on the econometrics for the 1993 report for Delors for new financial instruments to fund convergence and cohesion in a single-currency area, including European Union bonds, which hit the headlines in 2011 as a means of safeguarding the Eurozone.[44] There therefore was no conflict of personalities. But I strongly disagreed with the case for import controls argued by Francis and Terry in the early 1970s, not least because, by raising the price of imports, they also would have created inflationary pressures when the UK had hardly recovered from the oil shock of 1973.

Need it have gone wrong?

Given what 'went wrong' with divisions in the Labour Party and government in the 1970s and early 1980s and then the long march to neo-liberalism under Thatcher, Blair and Brown, I have been bound to question whether, with such a close relationship with Wilson in the 1960s, and had I accepted his offer to become the head of a policy unit at No. 10 in 1967, there might have been a chance of ensuring that policies which gained resonance in the Labour Party in the early 1970s also could have gained his support.

There is no easy answer. Had I stayed close to him I could have explained the case in detail, as I had that for a European Technology Community. Yet he might no more have endorsed such policies as an economic strategy than he had the potential for an alternative Europe through such a Community. When I told him I intended to resign, and when he had asked me whether I understood that I had been of more use to him on Europe than the whole of the Foreign Office, I said 'Yes, but you did not follow through', adding, and meaning it, that 'Your heart's in the right place but we regard it as a major victory if we roll back an initiative by one or more departments which are totally opposed to party policy. There is no strategy for relaunching the National Plan and none on Europe. We are constantly reacting to events.'

The dilemma of relying on support from Wilson was later evidenced when, in October 1974, within days of Labour winning the second election that year with a small majority, he declared that the manifesto commitment to a National Enterprise Board as a state holding company would be dropped and substituted by a National Investment Bank, on which he had been advised by Harold Lever. But the case for the NEB had gained support throughout the Labour movement on the grounds that bank credit would do nothing to recover confidence in investment in an economy which had just been hit by the first of the OPEC oil price rises and which faced recession, and that what was required was a broad wave of long-term innovating investment led by a state holding company in industry.

On the day that the press reported that the NEB would be dropped in favour of an investment bank, Judith Hart suggested that I draft a letter for the Tribune group meeting that afternoon, to be signed by them and press released, to the effect that they would not support legislation for such a bank rather than a National Enterprise Board. Since the government had a majority of only four, this had political force, since abstention by even a handful of the seventy-member Tribune group would have defeated it. Harold dryly commented that he was surprised the Tribune group had reacted so fast.[45] But, as a result, the Investment Bank proposal was dropped, and the outcome was a National Enterprise Board, though differing in practice from its design.

What followed

From 1975 the case that I was arguing for an alternative European strategy attracted attention in particular from Jacques Delors, who also had resigned as an adviser to a prime minister – Jacques Chaban-Delmas – and who at the time was merely a temporary professor at the University of Paris Dauphine. Neither of us anticipated that he later would be a President of the European Commission with such a high profile that most people, encouraged by the *Sun*, presumed that he was President of Europe. We met on a committee of the Commission which had been remitted to consider structural factors in inflation and our report was an early statement of the case for economic and social cohesion. Ineptly, the Commission sought to repress it, calling back whatever copies it could and pulping them, which, when Delors leaked this to the press, ensured the 'banned' report major coverage. But we formed a network of left economists, including a young Dominique Strauss-Kahn, which, when Delors became finance minister in 1981, produced the *Out of Crisis* report which elaborated the case for a social Europe.[46] This influenced both Andreas Papandreou and François Mitterrand in calling for a new Messina conference at the Athens and Paris European Councils of 1983 and 1984, which led to the first

115

revision of the Rome Treaty in the Single European Act of 1986, and its commitment to cohesion, with the internal market, as the 'twin pillars' of European union.[47]

In 1979 I was elected Member of Parliament for Vauxhall, whereon my influence over any outcome in the UK was less than it had been when not a Member. But when Neil Kinnock was elected Labour leader by the 1983 party conference he invited me to become shadow Minister for Development Cooperation. Neil was strongly influenced by the 1983 *Out of Crisis* report, which Charles Clarke had drawn to his attention, and supported a far more positive approach to European confederal cooperation. He also was the first leader of the party explicitly to support and advocate the case for state holdings and planning agreements with leading firms.[48] Whether his more positive attitude to Europe would have happened anyway, as Mark Wickham-Jones suggests in this volume, is open to question. It had been a challenge which Harold Wilson flunked and Tony Benn failed, yet in which Neil showed real leadership quality.[49]

Alternatives and the financial crisis

Does this mean that alternative economic strategies for the UK are buried in the ashes of Labour's defeat in 1979 and the ritual thereafter of heralding the phoenix of 'New Labour'? Not necessarily if in reassessing the 1970s it is recognised that the case for selective shareholdings in leading companies and accountability for public money in the private sector still has relevance, not least following the financial crisis of 2008. Such ownership and control had been integral to Labour's programmes from 1973 to 1983, prompting the brilliant comment by Alistair Darling in 2008, when Labour salvaged Northern Rock, the Royal Bank of Scotland and other banks, that the government's programme now *was* Labour's programme of 1983. Yet, while he may have aspired to this, it was not to be. Gordon Brown made it clear that the government would salvage the banks but neither manage them nor hold them to account for how they used the public money which had saved them from their own folly. This was a lamentable error but not only of current judgement. Gordon had founded the case for 'New Labour' on not resorting to 'Old Labour' public ownership and control.

If there is to be public money in the private sector, it should be on the basis of accountability for how it is used.[50] Otherwise, and this was one of the few cases where Margaret Thatcher was right, it is simply throwing money at a problem and creating others. Naturally Gordon Brown did not admit this in the *exculpa mea* of his *Beyond the Crash*.[51] Yet the outcome was both a denial of common sense and entirely dysfunctional. The banks took public money without the accountability which was integral to the case for planning agreements with big business and used it to recapitalise themselves rather than passing it onto cash-starved small and medium-sized firms. Likewise, they also deterred consumer spending by charging excessive interest rates in order to recapitalise themselves. Rather than saving individual deposits, which would have been thoroughly justifiable, shareholders' capital was saved, which denied the basic market principle that shareholders are entitled to higher than average returns if they can gain them because they also face and are liable for risk.

This was a catastrophically more negative outcome than the so-called 'winter of discontent' of 1978–79, which was held to have discredited 'Old Labour' but which was in fact a discredit to Harold Wilson, Denis Healey and Jim Callaghan in neglecting the Social Contract that was closely identified with it. For the Social Contract as I had conceived it, argued successfully for it in the Industrial Policy Sub-committee of the NEC against Tony Crosland, and elaborated in *The Socialist Challenge*, had been designed to allow for real income increases in return for productivity gains provided that, as in French planning agreements, the overall output–price ratio of leading meso firms was consistent with a national target for inflation. Instead, it had been exploited as a rebranding of an inflexible macro incomes policy which restrained wages while doing nothing to tax and redistribute meso profits. As an outcome, many skilled workers whose natural disposition was not to vote Tory abandoned Labour in 1979 to vote for Margaret Thatcher.

And whatever happened to meso?

The meso concept aimed to fill the missing middle in the alleged Keynesian macro–micro synthesis. At the time it gained next to no traction as most Keynesians deplored its challenge to what they had thought and taught on fiscal, monetary and exchange rate policy since Keynes' *General Theory*. When I stated it in *The Socialist Challenge* in 1975 it was regarded as polemical at best. When elaborated in two volumes by 1987, it gained positive responses in the national press as well as in the academic literature. In the *Economic Journal*, Hans Singer, whom I knew and who himself had known Keynes well, claimed that he was my 'hero', which he was not since, although heroic, he also failed to recognise the degree to which oligopoly and multinational capital, already evident in the 1930s, had undermined his assumption that if governments managed demand they could leave supply to perfect and imperfect competition.

There also was a remarkable endorsement of the meso concept and the manner in which it had divorced both the Keynesian and monetarist macro–micro syntheses in a lead review in the American Economic Association's *Journal of Economic Literature*, which commented that 'In scope, comprehensiveness, accessibility and insight, these books have no equal. Economists, especially teachers of economics, are in his debt.'[52] Yet they were not paradigm shifting, perhaps reflecting Max Planck's view that a new paradigm 'does not triumph by convincing its opponents and making them see the light, but rather because its opponents eventually die off, and a new generation grows up that is familiar with it'.[53] Notably, for years there was no reference to the meso concept in the now four-volume Palgrave *History of Economic Thought*, inspired and for years edited by Neil Kinnock's former economic adviser, Lord Eatwell, a Keynesian.

This echoes the degree to which mainstream Keynesians in the 1970s and thereafter strenuously resisted the need to 'descend' from macro monetary and fiscal policies to recognise the central role of leading firms. Yet the relevance of meso in the sense of a few firms dominating macroeconomic outcomes – if without reference to the concept – came to dominate the agenda of the Western world after the sub-prime crisis of 2007, in the decision that some banks so dominated macro finance that they were 'too big to fail' and that, had they been allowed to do so, the entire financial system of the West could have collapsed. Whereas China, with state control of its banking system, and a focus on investment rather than speculative finance, such as I had stressed in *The Socialist Challenge* in 1975, not only emerged relatively unscathed but its three main banks then became the leading three in the world.

The meso concept also is relevant to currently unresolved issues of global governance, since the G20 is itself a meso institution. Its twenty governments represent more than 85 per cent of the global economy, with some 150 smaller economies constituting the rest. This merits reference to the chances that were missed in the 1960s in Europe in relation to enabling decision-making rather than qualified majority voting. Neither China nor the USA would accept a framework for global governance that could minoritise them by a majority decision, whereas they might well accept a confederal global framework in which, as in the proposal for a European Technology Community, or Marjolin's Medium Term Economic Policy Committee, they could join with others in initiatives on which they mutually agreed, such as an orderly recycling of global surpluses.[54]

There is further current relevance of the meso concept in the declared but as yet unfulfilled ambition of the G20 to make global banks more accountable. For when so few of them dominate national or global finance – only some six in the USA and the UK and only twenty-nine big cross-border banks among 6,200 in the European Union[55] – gaining transparency on their operations becomes feasible without needing similar scrutiny of all banks.[56] This to some degree already had been recognised by 2011 in the 'stress tests' demanded of the major banks by the European Union and new transparency requirements in the USA. Such accountability of the major global banks – less than 1 per cent of the total – could achieve such transparency while leaving thousands of smaller banks subject only to general regulation. Whether achieving it would need to wait for a further financial crisis if the Eurozone disintegrates because rating agencies rule rather than governments govern, and thereby pull down the dollar and much of the Western world, remains to be seen.

Notes

1 Ludwig Wittgenstein was right in these regards, both on perception of the same things differently, as in the *Gestalt* psychology of Jastrow on which he drew, and on the risk of being trapped by language. L. Wittgenstein, *Philosophical Investigations* (Oxford: Blackwell, 1953).

2 Department of Economic Affairs, *The National Plan* (London: HMSO, 1965).

3 European Commission, *Avant Projet de Premier Programme de Politique Économique à Moyen Terme* (Brussels: European Commission, 1966).

4 To clarify the use of the terms, disinflation is the reverse of inflation, while deflation is reducing demand either by tax increases or by public expenditure cuts, or both.

5 Not that this was without cost. When Harold Wilson later wanted me to be the first economic adviser to the Foreign Office both O'Neill and Sir Paul Gore-Booth threatened to resign if I were appointed, and Harold backed down.

6 J-J. Servan-Schreiber, *Le Défi Américain* (Paris: Denoël, 2008).

7 O. J. Daddow (ed.), *Harold Wilson and European Integration: Britain's Second Application to Join the EEC* (London: Cass, 2002), p. 17.

8 It also has been widely overlooked that no decision since the Luxembourg Accord has been taken in the European Council of heads of state and government by qualified majority rather than unanimity, and rarely so in other key councils. A motion by qualified majority was moved once in the Ecofin Council of finance ministers against 'excess' French and German budget deficits, in 2004, but failed.

9 J. M. Keynes, *The General Theory of Employment, Interest and Money* (London: Macmillan, 1936).

10 J. Robinson, *The Economics of Imperfect Competition* (London: Macmillan, 1933).

11 E. Chamberlin, *The Theory of Monopolistic Competition* (Cambridge, MA: Harvard University Press, 8th edition, 1962). For Chamberlin the dynamics of competition included the effort of big business to increase its monopoly powers.

12 These dimensions of Keynes had been central to the case that had been argued by Tony Crosland in his *The Future of Socialism* (London: Jonathan Cape, 1956) for rejecting further nationalisation of entire sectors of industry, even though Crosland accepted the case for competitive public enterprise to countervail monopolistic dominance of a sector. They were central also to Crosland's claim on a key committee of the Labour Party National Executive Committee that there was nothing wrong with the National Plan other than that the government had not devalued sterling in July 1966 rather than November 1967.

13 Such as Ford already producing in the UK, General Motors doing so through Opel in Germany and Vauxhall in the UK, ICI and Anglo-Dutch Unilever throughout the British Empire, Siemens, Krupp and IG Farben throughout Europe and the global 'seven sisters' in oil. Following the November 1967 devaluation, General Motors not only did not allow Vauxhall to lower prices in Germany, it already had forbidden it to export to Germany.

14 D. E. Hague, W. E. Oakeshott and A. A. Strain, *Devaluation and Pricing Decisions* (London: Allen & Unwin, 1974); P. Holmes, *Industrial Pricing Behaviour and Devaluation* (London: Macmillan, 1978).

15 Such as lowering prices to gain entry to a market, or to eliminate a smaller competitor. See further S. Holland, *The Socialist Challenge* (London: Quartet Books, 1975), translated as *O Desafio Socialista*, 2 vols (Lisbon: Iniciativas Editorais, 1976) and as *La Sfida Socialista: Movimento Operaio e Potere in Europa* (Bari: De Donato, 1979), and also translated into Greek (Athens: Papazzisis Publishers, 1978).

16 S. Holland, *The State as Entrepreneur. New Dimensions for Public Enterprise: The IRI State Shareholding Formula* (London: Weidenfeld & Nicolson, 1972); S. Holland, 'Mesoeconomics, new public enterprise and economic planning', *Annals of Public and Cooperative Economics*, 45:2 (1974), pp. 147–60, translated as 'Mesoéconomie, enterprise publique e planification', *Annales de l'Economie Publique, Sociale et Cooperative*, 45:2 (1974), and as 'Mesoeconomia e nuova impresa pubblica', *Economia Pubblica*, 11–12 (1975).

17 M. Kalecki, *Theory of Economic Dynamics: An Essay in Cyclical and Long-Run Changes in Capitalist Economy* (London: Allen & Unwin, 1954); F. Perroux, *L'Économie du XXième Siècle* (Paris: Presses Universitaures de France, 2nd edition, 1964); P. Sylos-Labini, *Oligopoly and Technical Progress* (published originally in 1962, revised and republished Cambridge, MA: Harvard University Press, 1969).

18 S. J. Prais, 'A new look at industrial concentration', *Oxford Economic Papers*, 26:2 (1974), pp. 273–88.

19 R. Murray, *Multinational Companies and Nation States: Two Essays* (Nottingham: Spokesman Press, 1971).

20 S. Hymer, 'The multinational corporation and the law of uneven development', in J. Bhagwati (ed.), *Economics and the World Order* (New York: Macmillan, 1972), pp. 113–40.

21 See, for example, the centrality of leading firms to regional development in F. Perroux, 'La firme motrice et la region motrice', in *L'Economie du XXieme Siecle* (Paris: Presses Universitaires de France, 2nd edition, 1964), pp. 192–241.

22 *Labour's Programme for Britain* (London: Labour Party, 1972); *Labour's Programme 1973* (London: Labour Party, 1973); *Labour's Programme 1976* (London: Labour Party, 1976); and *Labour's Programme, 1982* (London: Labour Party, 1982). This is a simple point, but one which has been mistaken by J. Callaghan, 'Rise and fall of the Alternative Economic Strategy: from internationalisation of capital to "globalisation"', *Contemporary British History*, 14:3 (2000), pp. 105–30.

23 See R. Jenkins, 'The needs of the regions', in R. Jenkins, *What Matters Now* (London: Fontana, 1972), pp. 23–37; and the opposition green paper *The National Enterprise Board* (London: Labour Party, 1973).

24 For example, in Wilson's decision to make planning agreements with the top 100 companies voluntary rather than obligatory. The term 'the top 100 companies' actually was taken by me from the National Board for Prices and Incomes' designation of 'Category 1' firms and is a classic example of something considered innocuous in one context becoming lethal in another, especially when combined

with Tony Benn's constant referring to 'compulsory planning agreements with the top 100 companies', against which I remonstrated.

25 In chapter 7 of the present volume, Mark Wickham-Jones writes that I seem to have accepted the former. In fact, I had opposed it strenuously at an earlier meeting of the Planning Working Group, on the grounds that multinational companies dominating two-thirds of British trade would evade import controls either by transfer pricing or by relocating production abroad.

26 Holland, *The Socialist Challenge.*

27 S. Holland, 'Planning and policy coordination', Labour Party Archive, Research Department 315, March 1972.

28 S. Holland and R. Pryke, 'The state holding company', Labour Party Archive, Research Department 271, February 1972.

29 Holland, *The State as Entrepreneur.*

30 W. Kennet, L. Whitty and S. Holland, *Sovereignty and Multinational Companies* (London: Fabian Society, 1971).

31 S. Holland, 'Extending public ownership: towards a state holding company', *Socialist Commentary*, December 1971, pp. 11–12.

32 House of Commons, *Public Money in the Private Sector*, sixth report from the Trade and Industry Sub-committee of the Expenditure Committee (London: HMSO, 1972).

33 House of Commons, *Regional Development Incentives: Minutes of Evidence to the Trade and Industry Sub-committee of the Expenditure Committee* (London: HMSO, 1972).

34 Jenkins, *What Matters Now.*

35 Holland, 'Planning and policy coordination'.

36 Some of the press were more nuanced and avoided headlines suggesting that the National Enterprise Board would take over 'the top twenty-five' companies. For example: 'Labour group plan to take control of major companies', *Financial Times*, 19 April 1973; 'Labour executive approves plan for state control of 25 companies', *The Times*, 31 May 1973.

37 J. K. Galbraith, 'Labour's new programme', *New Statesman*, 22 June 1973; R. Vernon, *Big Business and the State: Changing Relations in Western Europe* (London: Macmillan, 1974).

38 Holland, 'Planning and policy coordination'.

39 Well covered by M. Hatfield, *The House the Left Built: Inside Labour Policy-Making, 1970–75* (London: Gollancz, 1978).

40 '"I'll quit" Wilson warns Benn boys', *Evening News*, 31 May 1973.

41 M. Hatfield, 'Treasury started Benn campaign', *The Times*, 17 June 1974.

42 Department of Industry, *The Regeneration of British Industry* (London: HMSO, August 1974).

43 It gained an *ex post* justification since it transpired that such calling forward of longer-term investment projects by the Japanese Ministry of Trade and Industry at the time had been the means whereby it transformed Japan from a producer mainly of heavy engineering goods into a global pacemaker in computers and other electronics. See D. Okimoto, *Between MITI and the Market: Japanese Industrial Policy for High Technology* (Palo Alto, CA: Stanford University Press, 1990).

44 S. Holland (ed.), *Out of Crisis: A Project for European Recovery* (Nottingham: Spokesman Press, 1983); S. Holland, *The European Imperative: Economic and Social Cohesion in the 1990s. A Report to the Commission of the European Communities* (Nottingham: Spokesman Press, 1993).

45 I. Aitken, 'Left wing purrs as Lever loses cream', *Guardian*, 30 October 1974.

46 Holland, *Out of Crisis.* The project highlighted the meso case for accountability

of multinational companies which was supported both by Dominique Strauss-Khan and by Jacques Delors but not successfully followed through. Delors backed and recommended this to the then head of Eurostat when he later was President of the European Commission but the individual concerned took early retirement and the initiative failed to revise Eurostat accounting to include a meso dimension.

47 The original 1955 Messina conference had committed the then six member states of the Coal and Steel Community to establish a European Economic Community.

48 N. Kinnock, 'A new deal for Europe', *New Socialist*, February–March 1983; N. Kinnock, *Making Our Way: Investing in Britain's Future* (Oxford: Basil Blackwell, 1986). Open minded, in marked contrast to Wilson in opposition from 1970, Neil asked for help in drafting both the book and the article, to which, of course, I agreed.

49 In 1989 I resigned from Parliament for several reasons, including an appeal from Jacques Delors to design financial instruments to seek to make a reality of the commitment of the 1986 Single European Act to economic and social cohesion. Neil Kinnock responded with remarkable good grace, saying that 'If anyone else offered me a by-election in the only Labour safe seat on the Thames I would throw them out. But, in your case, and working with Delors, go with my blessing.' Again, these were at the time underestimated leadership qualities.

50 That there should be accountability for public money in the private sector was argued by the Expenditure Committee of the Commons in 1972 and 1973 on a cross-party basis, both informing and reinforcing Labour's programmes from 1973 through to 1983.

51 G. Brown, *Beyond the Crash: Overcoming the First Crisis of Globalisation* (New York: Simon & Schuster, 2010).

52 J. E. Elliot, 'Book reviews: *The Market Economy: From Micro to Mesoeconomics; The Global Economy: From Meso to Macroeconomics*', *Journal of Economic Literature*, 28:1 (1990), pp. 66–8.

53 M. Planck, *Scientific Autobiography and Other Papers* (New York: Philosophical Library, 1949), cited by T. Kuhn, *The Structure of Scientific Revolutions* (Chicago, IL: University of Chicago Press, 1996), p. 151.

54 S. Holland, 'The United Nations, the G20 and the case for a World Development Organisation', *Revista Temas de Integração*, 27–8 (2009), pp. 25–41.

55 F. Moss, 'The financial crisis and its fallout for the ECB's monetary policy conduct', contribution to The Sovereign Debt Crisis: Towards Fiscal Union in Europe?, Economic and Social Committee, Brussels, 7 June 2012.

56 For an analytic exposition of meso accounting and its micro and macro implications, see S. Holland, *The Market Economy* (London: Weidenfeld & Nicolson, 1987), ch. 9.4, 'Accounting and accountability'.

7

The challenge of Stuart Holland: the Labour Party's economic strategy during the 1970s

Mark Wickham-Jones

In July 1975, Quartet Books, an eclectic British publisher, brought out a 400-page book by a young academic at the University of Sussex.[1] Stuart Holland had been one of the principal architects of the Labour Party's industrial policies, measures that dominated the programme put forward by the party in opposition after 1970. His volume *The Socialist Challenge* generated considerable debate in scholarly journals and in the national media. Attention was divided: some commentators praised Holland's vision and the breadth of his analysis about the state of the British economy; others were brutally dismissive. In *The Times*, Peter Hennessy described Holland's book as one of the 'healthier and more striking blooms' on the political left.[2] *The Economist* labelled Holland 'the new socialist orthodoxy', while Robert Skidelsky stated, 'it is arguably the most important book from the British left since Anthony Crosland's *The Future of Socialism*, whose central thesis it explicitly sets out to disprove'.[3] By contrast, Brian Walden was scathing: 'the most important thing about Stuart Holland's theories is that they are, in the main, irrelevant to what is happening now'.[4] Noting the utter abandonment by the Labour government of the kind of policies advocated in the volume, Peter Jenkins decided that 'the publication of Mr Holland's book could not be more untimely'.[5] Jenkins complained that it was 'infinitely depressing' and offered a 'narrow and mechanical and dispiriting vision of socialism'.

The Socialist Challenge was published at a time when considerable economic and political uncertainties confronted the UK. In it, Stuart

Holland outlined an ambitious interventionist industrial strategy based around far-reaching measures of public ownership and planning. He articulated a series of coruscating criticisms of the 1970–74 Heath administration and of its Labour successor. He directly repudiated the existing orthodoxy that had dominated his party's platform for the better part of twenty years, the relatively moderate social democracy articulated by Anthony Crosland.[6] Until just before *The Socialist Challenge*'s publication, Holland had been a political adviser, working for Judith Hart at the Ministry of Overseas Development. His resignation probably reflected an anticipation of the publicity his book would attract.[7]

Today, many of the book's proposals seem far reaching in their radical intent and certainly they are far removed from the prevailing orthodoxies of contemporary economic policy. Manifestly, much has changed in the intervening thirty-five years or so. However, the attention generated by *The Socialist Challenge* is an indication of just how important Holland's ideas were perceived to be at a time of acute economic crisis and considerable political uncertainty. The existing parameters that had shaped economic policy in the UK had, arguably, shattered, creating the policy space in which the initiatives mapped out in *The Socialist Challenge* were discussed. To be sure, the Labour government elected twice in 1974 appeared to have jettisoned the core features of Holland's approach; by contrast, however, the Labour Party tenaciously and assiduously continued to advocate them, against the better judgement of its parliamentary leadership. The publicity given to Holland was on a par with that offered in 1956 to Crosland's seminal *The Future of Socialism*: I can think of no other books on the British left that have generated such attention on publication and I believe it would be very unlikely to happen again.[8] Holland's ideas about economic policy dominated discussion on the left of British politics for more than a decade between the early 1970s and 1983.

In this chapter, I provide an account of Holland's contribution to Labour Party politics during the 1970s. My principal aims are: to offer an evaluation of Holland's impact on Labour's economic strategy; to evaluate what influences he drew upon in the proposals that he developed for the party; and to consider what tensions might exist in his work. How important a figure was Holland in shaping the measures that Labour adopted? Upon what sources did he draw? How original were his proposals? How feasible an economic strategy did he come up with? Of course, much has been written on these issues in the intervening decades. However, the current remoteness of the debates of the 1970s makes this an appropriate point to revisit such matters. Moreover, there is a wealth of archival material, somewhat unsystematically stored, about Labour politics upon which to inform any discussion. In his contribution to this volume and elsewhere, Holland has offered an engaging and fascinating insider's account of the party's policy-making process in this period.[9] A couple of caveats should be noted. I make no attempt to evaluate Holland's considerable academic corpus. His work has an obvious importance in terms of pioneering debates about the inter-nationalisation of the economy and anticipating many contemporary concerns with globalisation. I do not discuss his work in the 1980s or 1990s. I do not assess the arguments that took place within the Labour government between March 1974 and June 1975 as the industrial strategy upon which the party was elected was initiated and then dis-carded. I take it as axiomatic that the Labour government did forsake these measures, though, given the release of archival material on these matters, I am sure there is much more to be written about them. My focus is on Stuart Holland's involvement in party policy-making and on the ideas that he articulated in such an engagement.

The chapter proceeds as follows. In the next section I offer an account of policy-making within the Labour Party after 1970. The following two sections address, in turn, how important Holland was to Labour and what inspired his work. I then address some tensions within his argu-ments and consider his legacies, before drawing together the material in my conclusion.

Policy-making in the Labour Party after 1970

Following its June 1970 general election defeat, Labour had begun a re-evaluation of the party's programme pretty much immediately.[10] Many figures were disappointed with the established thinking that had guided Labour in office between 1964 and 1970, in terms of either Croslandite revisionism or the rhetorical modifications to it that Harold Wilson had offered. But the old nostrums of the party's left seemed equally prob-lematic, in the form of an emotional and under-theorised commitment to sweeping nationalisation. There was much internal dissatisfaction with Labour's record in office: widespread perceptions of economic decline created something of a 'moral panic' in the party – a sense that the outgoing administration had not achieved the goals it had set itself. In such a conjecture, there was considerable space to debate ideas and to develop policy. Labour's ruling National Executive Committee (NEC) decided to restructure the organisation of the party's internal policy-making committees. Six were to be located directly within the formal process of policy formation, reporting to the Home Policy Sub-committee, which in turn fed into the NEC. In particular, a new committee was established, the Industrial Policy Sub-committee. There was also another committee dealing with the economy, the Finance and Economic Affairs Sub-committee, and the party resorted to a myriad of working groups in this period, dealing with specific issues such as the banking sector and the possibilities of capital sharing schemes. However, it was the Industrial Policy Sub-committee which came to dominate the process of policy formation. Enjoying a wide remit, it quickly took the initiative in terms of drafting discussion papers and reviewing them at regular meetings. An early party statement was agreed at the 1971 conference.

Following that conference, the Industrial Policy Sub-committee decided to set up a working group to deal with the public sector. Stuart Holland, who had experience working in Whitehall for the Labour government before joining the University of Sussex, was invited to join the new group. Together with Richard Pryke, another economist sympathetic to the Labour Party, he drafted a paper outlining the case for a state holding company.[11] The Industrial Policy Sub-committee held a weekend meeting in February 1972 at which this was discussed alongside papers on price controls, manpower policy and industrial democracy. A month later, Geoff Bish, the party official who served as secretary to the Industrial Policy Sub-committee, suggested that it examine another paper by Holland on planning.[12] Soon afterwards he was co-opted onto the Industrial Planning Sub-committee. The committee was dominated by the left of the party, although not to the total exclusion of the right – Anthony Crosland was a member, if infrequent in attendance. It was also serviced by a radicalised Labour Party Research Department.

Holland's background was unusual in comparison with some on Labour's left in that he had worked with figures associated with the right of the party such as Roy Jenkins and William Rodgers. As he recounts in chapter 6, through Rodgers he had advised the Trade and Industry Sub-committee of the House of Commons. He had helped Jenkins to draft the discussion concerning industrial policy in the latter's volume *What Matters Now*.[13] I think it is probably indicative both of Holland's eclecticism and of the technocratic strand to his thought that, at this stage, he worked with both sides of Labour's ideological divide.

Holland offered proposals for both a state holding company and for programme contracts to be concluded between governments and big firms to agree the latter's strategic objectives. In April 1972, both were included, albeit briefly, in the Sub-committee's draft of *Labour's Programme for Britain*.[14] The Industrial Policy Sub-committee, however, decided to tone down some of the language of the draft since the proposals were still at a tentative stage.[15] The reference to programme contracts was dropped, given 'the need to be fairly modest in our claims for any new planning system'.[16] That to the state holding company (SHC) was revised 'to delete the various references which tended to pin down too closely the role of the proposed SHC', given the incomplete stage the work was at.[17] In the autumn of 1972, the Industrial Policy Sub-committee returned with a more radical draft of the measures. In a paper for the sub-committee, Holland produced a more theoretical grounding for the policies, based on the notion that the economy was characterised by a growing tendency to monopolisation in each sector, which had eroded competitive market pressures. Such a concentration of capital could be tackled only by public ownership of profitable manufacturing firms, alongside interventionist planning: 'A socialist government can harness the market power of its own companies as an instrument for the planned transformation of the economy, both making internal company profits and promoting external social and regional benefits'.[18] The public ownership of twenty such firms would have a major impact on the economy. In another paper, Holland claimed,

> The direct contribution of the NEB [National Enterprise Board – as the state holding company was labelled] companies also will be matched by a pull effect on private companies of a kind which previous indicative planning and financial handouts did not promote – both because many private companies will be compelled to follow the NEB companies' lead or lose market shares and profits, and because many private companies will secure new orders for equipment and supplies from the investing NEB companies.[19]

Alongside such public enterprises, programme contracts offered an interventionist tool by which governments could exert pressure on companies. Holland suggested that the top 100 companies should probably be required to enter into such an arrangement.[20]

In tandem with these developments, the Public Sector Group, established as a spin-off from the Industrial Policy Sub-committee, drafted an opposition green paper on the NEB, published in April 1973.[21] The NEB represented a development of Pryke and Holland's original paper on a state holding company. The proposal had been around in Labour policy documents since the late 1960s, but Holland's conception represented a dramatic escalation in its interventionary scope. In particular, the green paper contained a proposal that Labour should take over one profitable private company per sector of the economy, between twenty and twenty-five in all, in order that a government could exercise leverage over it, regain power and control, and so combat the tendency to monopolisation.[22] No such number had been offered a year earlier in *Labour's Programme for Britain*.[23] However, the principle of controlling firms in each sector was mentioned in passing in the February 1972 Holland and Pryke paper, though without an explicit figure.[24] In 'Planning strategy, tactics and techniques', Holland suggested two dozen such nationalisations.[25] The proposals of the two internal committees fed directly into the draft of *Labour's Programme 1973*, published in May that year. The contents of this document had been vociferously opposed by senior figures within the Parliamentary Labour Party as well as some on the NEC, many of whom were aghast at the scale of intervention involved and at the apparent threat to the private sector. Perhaps unsurprisingly, attention focused on the dramatic proposed extension of public enterprise. After a bitter meeting of the NEC, however, the proposal to take over 'some twenty-five of our largest manufacturers' was retained and the document was published with it in.[26] In effect, the Alternative Economic Strategy had been born.

Figures on Labour's right were horrified at the proposals the party had published. Initially, those who opposed the plans had been rather disengaged from the process. Many former ministers were poor attendees at the party's internal policy-making committees. Arguably, they appeared to regard internal party debate as a low priority alongside their other activities. They did marshal a number of critical responses, albeit in a rather fragmented fashion. In the 'marketplace for ideas' within Labour, their analysis had little impact. Their views were discredited by the perceived failures of the 1964–70 governments, a weakness made all the more significant by the fact that they appeared to hold on to many of the policies that had been so disappointing in these years. Members of Labour's right seemed to suggest that if only ministers had been tougher (presumably a euphemism for devalued earlier?) outcomes would have been much better. In short, they failed either to articulate an alternative set of measures to those mapped out by Holland or to justify the retention of existing commitments. But Labour's marketplace for ideas did not just reflect the inherent quality of the material mobilised by its participants. The struggle over Labour policy was heavily shaped by political and institutional factors. Many on the right failed to engage in terms of mobilising support for their position. By contrast, Holland's ideas enjoyed considerable backing from the party's left, whose position, as I noted above, was structurally stronger than in the past. Labour's institutional configuration in the early 1970s facilitated the 'triumph' of these ideas. I think it is also important to note that structuring policy-making in this way, along with the prevalent culture and rhetoric of the party, meant that debate became increasingly polarised, Holland's links to Jenkins and Rodgers notwithstanding.

Subsequent Labour documents, especially the complete programmes published in 1976 and 1982, confirmed much of the detail of the policies sketched out in 1973. Some additions were made to the economic strategy contained within them: import controls were added in 1975 and confirmed in the 1976 version. In his work, Holland placed little emphasis on protection. However, he does not seem to have objected to import controls: when the Industrial Policy

Sub-committee endorsed the use of 'selective import controls either by quotas or surcharges as the particular situation demanded' only one member of the committee, the MP Eric Deakins, dissented.[27] Holland did not. Writing later, Holland noted 'I am not wholly persuaded about the import controls case, which is always isolated by the press, but it may be necessary'.[28] Another addition concerned industrial democracy. Although it had been present in the 1973 version, by the early 1980s Labour made much more of its commitment to workers' participation in decision-making.

In chapter 6, Holland rightly notes the diversity over economic strategy that existed on the left. Manifestly many different positions were articulated over the next decade or so, both inside and outside the Labour Party, especially when the definition of the alternative strategy is cast as widely as it is by Holland. Particular groups put very different emphases on aspects of the programme. The diversity of these factions is an indication of the overall strength of Labour's Alternative Economic Strategy and the domination it achieved. I am less persuaded that there are fundamental variants at the core of the approach articulated by Labour from 1973 onwards. Stripped of rhetoric and the contextual circumstances of the period, my view is that for the decade after 1973, Labour's economic strategy was remarkably consistent.

It is worth considering what this strategy amounted to. Since the early 1950s, Labour's economic approach had been dominated in one form or another by a prevailing Keynesian orthodoxy. *Labour's Programme 1973* thus marked a significant departure for the party. With its commitment to the extension of public ownership to profitable companies to counter the monopolisation of the economy, Holland's approach owed as much to Marx as to Keynes. To be sure, Labour had advocated nationalisation before, not least in the sweeping commitment of clause IV of the party's constitution. But previously it had neither offered detail about what future public ownership might involve nor outlined a theoretical underpinning. Nor, since 1945, had the party placed nationalisation and planning at the centre of its economic programme. Edward Heath's administration may have been the first to break with the postwar consensus; Labour had acted equally decisively in jettisoning past commitments. Another way of conceptualising the change that had taken place would be to consider it in terms of Peter Hall's model of change: with the publication of *Labour's Programme 1973*, the party had changed not only the settings of its policy instruments and the tools that it deployed (first- and second-order change).[29] It had, effectively, shifted the hierarchy of goals to which policy was aligned. The document therefore marked a pivotal moment in the polarisation of British politics.

Holland's contribution

How important was Stuart Holland's contribution to *Labour's Programme 1973*? Commentators and scholars alike have identified him as a central figure in the development of Labour's economic strategy during the early 1970s. In numerous accounts, together with a few politicians such as Tony Benn and Judith Hart as well as party officials such Geoff Bish, Holland is identified as being central. But whereas the politicians gave rhetorical support to the shift leftwards and party officials are presented as facilitators to the process of policy formation, Holland is taken to be the architect of the ideas. Certainly, officials manipulated the process, drafted documents and dominated the formalities of the network of Labour's policy-making committees and working groups. However, the overall contents and the fine detail of what was agreed owed much to Holland. Contemporary accounts emphasise these points. Noting the hostility of the Labour leadership to the party's policy, Nora Beloff wrote in the *Observer* in 1973, 'In their view the party is unduly in the grip of paid officials at Transport House'.[30] In a long, well informed account written in the summer of 1975 Mike Hartley Brewer concluded, 'Stuart Holland had virtually single-handedly committed a great party to his particular view in the vital industrial policy field'.[31]

Such emphasis on the ideas of a single expert academic is at odds with conventional social science, which places more weight upon explanations based on material factors and popular preferences. Political scientists are uncomfortable with the notion that ideas might be important determinants of policy outcomes, pointing to the severe methodological difficulties in assessing such a claim. In the case of the Alternative Economic Strategy, however, such analytical problems can, for the most part, be overcome, given the wealth of data and archival evidence that is available concerning the Labour Party's policy-making process. From a process-tracing perspective, it is fairly straightforward to map the evolution of Labour's policies during the early 1970s. Textual analysis comparing the papers written by Holland with those subsequently agreed as Labour Party policy documents offers confirmatory evidence. Holland was a seemingly tireless member of policy-making committees, drafting around two dozen briefing papers for the party, including in 1972 four major expositions of the new policies. The contents of those, written before the publication of draft proposals by Labour, outlined in some detail the Alternative Economic Strategy. In chronological terms, Holland joined the Industrial Policy Sub-committee and outlined proposals for planning agreements and the NEB which were then taken up forcefully by Labour. I have already noted the policy space that existed for the party after 1970: in supplying detailed ideas, Holland's analysis made a major contribution to filling that vacuum.

A comparison of two Labour documents – one produced before Holland's involvement in policy-making and one published after his participation – confirms this account. In 1971 *Economic Strategy, Growth and Unemployment* opened with detailed attacks on Conservative economic policies, placed considerable weight on expanded retraining programmes, emphasised the regional dimension to policy and indicated that the party needed to develop its philosophy of public enterprise.[32] By contrast, *Labour's Programme 1973* placed planning agreements and the NEB at the centre of its approach, a manifest reorientation of the party's strategic outlook. The interim *Labour's Programme for Britain* and the discussion over its draft, noted above, give a sense of how that realignment took place under Holland's influence. Confirmation of the strategic direction given to the work of the Industrial Policy Sub-committee by Holland is to be found in the material discussed before he joined it in 1972. Benn submitted two papers in 1971. One, 'Mintech 1970/75', a review of the Ministry of Technology written in 1970, demanded close contact between government and firms so that they would become 'better acquainted with actual problems of manufacturing, and industrial management will be kept informed of government thinking'.[33] The second was tentative and exploratory, proposing government share purchases, balloting workers about directors, a shorter working year and income ratios in firms.[34] Neither mapped out a coherent agenda for industrial policy.

Moreover, it is striking that Holland's agenda was profoundly at odds with the existing attitude of many on Labour's left for whom a commitment to public ownership was a defining feature of their ideological identity and who were sweeping in their hostility to private ownership and market mechanisms. They demanded sectoral nationalisations across whole industries. Holland's advocacy of individual public firms working within the market was far removed from such a position and initially many were suspicious of his ideas, regarding them as 'rather right wing'.[35] Remember, Holland had been associated in the early 1970s with the right of the Labour Party. At one meeting of the Industrial Policy Sub-committee 'both Mr Dickens and Mr Mikardo suggested that there were advantages in extending public ownership on an industry by industry basis'.[36] Geoff Bish concluded, 'There was just enough planning in it to buy off the left'.[37] In his diaries, Tony Benn records being briefed in March 1973 by Holland, along with Geoff Bish and Margaret Jackson, a party official, about the new policies, measures that he was then to take up with enthusiasm.[38] Most left-wingers came round, with gusto, to endorse Holland's position. The left's initial attitude to Holland confirms the point that the adoption of his ideas was not just due to reasoned argument within the marketplace for ideas but reflected political and structural factors as well. There may have been a tactical dimension to this alignment. Holland may have put more emphasis on the radical and theoretical dimension of his ideas in the autumn of 1972 in order to ensure support from the party's left, albeit at a cost of alienating the right and polarising debate. In so doing, he may have downplayed the empirical and European dimension, one that he now places more weight upon.

It is also apparent that, once they had been agreed, Holland's core ideas, about planning agreements and the NEB, exercised a considerable grip on discussions of the Industrial Policy Sub-committee. Dissatisfied figures – such as Antony Crosland and Edmund Dell – did on occasion seek to challenge his claims. But they did so largely on a rhetorical basis at meetings of the committee during the latter months of 1973. No internal party papers of any substance were produced to confront Holland's arguments. Nor, for that matter, were any written to support them (though occasionally individuals did suggest minor additions to the approach).

Such was the hegemony established by Holland over the Industrial Policy Sub-committee by 1974 that when any other proposals came to it for discussion, they were evaluated on the basis of their compatibility with the agenda that he had established. Proposals would be tabled and assessed through the prism of Holland's analysis before a decision was made as to whether they might be added to Labour's battery of economic measures. As such, all substantive discussions of economic strategy within the committee took place on the basis of Holland's outlook. For example, in 1975, a paper by the party's Research Department on training policy emphasised that 'unless Labour Party industrial policies are carried out and the demand for labour sufficiently and selectively stimulated, the policies detailed below for dealing predominantly with supply aspects will be ineffective'.[39] When the paper came to the Industrial Policy Sub-committee, 'Mr Holland said that the NEB and planning agreements would have a role to play in job creation which could be tied to the ending of resistance to change. There was general agreement that retraining had to be tied to job creation and job placement.'[40]

Later in 1975, John Hughes, a Ruskin College academic and left-wing economist, put two papers before the Industrial Policy Sub-committee advocating an institution to channel investment and the establishment of a Swedish-style investment fund in the UK.[41] The committee appeared distinctly unimpressed, noting that 'the idea of a general increase in investment with no central plan was thought to be contrary to current trends in Labour Party policy'.[42] Holland 'expressed a concern that a scheme to channel institutional funds into industrial investment might end up as a cyclical instrument. Schemes for using institutional funds had to be in the context of the NEB and planning agreements so that there was control over the demand for investment funds as well as the supply.'[43] Hughes tried to point out the impracticality of waiting for planning agreements in the present climate, given the hostility of the Labour government. The committee was unmoved: plans had to be 'within the context of our other policies on the NEB and planning agreements'. Labour briefly flirted with the idea of investment funds but soon dropped them. When the committee discussed finance for industry, it was emphasised that any funds must not undermine planning agreements.[44] In early 1976 the committee looked at productivity and reached the conclusion that it 'had to be seen in the context of the party's overall industrial strategy, and that it was crucially related to levels of investment, planning agreements and industrial democracy'.[45] Holland's arguments not only shaped the contents of *Labour's Programme 1973*, they dominated subsequent discussion of economic and industrial issues.[46] The emphasis placed by Holland chapter 6 on the existence of different strategies underestimates his contribution. From the left's perspective, in the marketplace for ideas, he exercised, for a time at any rate, a near monopolistic domination.

Holland's influences

In designing the Alternative Economic Strategy, Holland drew on numerous influences. The most surprising that he alludes to is probably Tony Crosland, Labour's revisionist theorist. In his detailed 2004 account of the emergence of Labour's programme during the early 1970s, Holland offers an insight into his personal relationship with Crosland. Repeating suggestions that he has made elsewhere, he indicates that Crosland could have taken credit for the ideas associated with the NEB, given their similarity to the case made in *The Future of Socialism* for competitive public enterprise.[47] On the face of it there were some similarities between such a concept and the proposals Holland put forward. In a footnote, Holland writes, 'I thoroughly agreed with his [Crosland's] case. I never advocated more "nationalisation" in any of the papers I wrote in the early 1970s for the NEC, nor in any of my books or articles published thereafter.'[48]

However, Holland's claim about the similarities is unpersuasive. The scale of each is very different. Crosland envisaged competitive public enterprise as an occasional tool, one to be used to improve the efficiency of a particular firm. Holland's approach was more sweeping in intent, one designed to change the way that all firms operated within the economy. It was intended as the basis for a transformation of society and the attitude that it projected towards the private sector was essentially hostile. Directly (through public enterprise) or indirectly (through planning agreements) it wanted to control all private firms. Moreover, the NEB and planning agreements were at the centre of the strategy: for Crosland competitive public enterprise was a minor aspect of an economic policy that remained dominated by orthodox Keynesian demand management.

A close comparison of Crosland's text with Holland's argument gives an indication of the differences. Competitive public enterprise is mentioned in four places in *The Future of Socialism*. Three are one-page references; the other is an eight-page section.[49] The first three were inconsequential: in one he noted the lack of available talent to operate such a system. In the eight-page section he sketched out what such a form of public ownership might involve. He conceived of public enterprises as having 'the maximum degree of freedom and independence in their day-to-day affairs', making their own decisions about investment and prices.[50] Crosland was concerned by how such companies would be chosen for public ownership and how they would operate: 'To say that we shall compulsorily nationalise one chemical firm rather than another, or this aircraft firm rather than that, will be attacked as unfair, arbitrary, and dictated by political and not economic motives'.[51] Crosland proposed a state investment trust, 'provided with public funds but independent of the Government, with instructions simply to make a profit by buying, establishing or selling productive concerns'.[52] By contrast, Holland envisaged the NEB making compulsory acquisitions of firms – one per sector of the economy – according to some set of clear criteria. Such firms would not be independent of the planning apparatus but would be located within it: the government would be able to set strategic objectives. Their operations would not be guided by a simple attempt to make profits but by other objectives as well. In making the case for a state holding company with Richard Pryke, Holland indicated that compulsory acquisition had advantages. In 'Planning and policy coordination', one of his first papers for the Labour Party, Holland concluded that 'it could well be necessary to introduce compulsory purchase'.[53]

In any case, in the discussions of the Industrial Policy Sub-committee, Holland was bitterly critical of the revisionist approach. He told it at one meeting that 'the analysis of capitalism put forward by Anthony Crosland in the 1950s was no longer valid – not least because of the sharp growth in the degree of concentration in manufacturing'.[54] With Pryke, he was critical: 'It seems to have been imagined by those who first thought about competitive public enterprise that they could be brought into existence through the State establishing new factories on green field sites', a possibility they rejected outright.[55] Alan Budd, later to become a senior civil servant at the Treasury, commented, 'if the intention was to convert the revisionists, the tone is far too hostile; it appears instead to be written for the left'.[56] *The Socialist Challenge* is littered with a plethora of criticisms of Crosland: reading and re-reading it, I am always struck by the extent to which it is a direct response to and critique of the revisionist model. If Holland wanted to locate his approach within Crosland's framework, he adopted a curiously aggressive approach to so doing. I sense some regret in his 2004 piece that the two sides had been so hostile to each other in 1973: 'another chance for consensus had been lost'.[57] At the time, however, each grouping seems to have relished the ideological conflict.

It is apparent that Holland was much influenced by Marxist theory. The ideas contained within *The Socialist Challenge* drew heavily on important strands from Marxist economic debates, notably Holland's emphasis on monopolisation and on the role of multinationals. His analysis of the power of capital was underpinned by notions of class and of class conflict. It is of little surprise that commentators were quick to see Holland's approach as being inspired by Marxism. Brian Walden was contemptuous in the *Observer*, characterising it as 'the New Marxism – or the old kind of mascara'.[58]

It would be mistaken to take Holland to be a dogmatic or even a particularly coherent Marxist. It would certainly be wrong to conclude that Holland's influences were confined to debates among Marxist economists. Extremely well informed from a scholarly point of view, he drew from general discussions of postwar political economy. On one occasion, for example, a paper had to be summarised in less technical form and Andrew Shonfield's *Modern Capitalism*, the seminal text on comparative European political economy, a book that heavily influenced later Labour Party economists, was frequently cited. A favourite quotation was Shonfield's claim that French planners were able to be 'part industrial consultant, part banker and part plain bully'.[59]

In fact, Holland's work exhibited a strong empirical strand. His papers for the Labour Party as well as *The Socialist Challenge* were strongly influenced by the existing arrangements of a host of European countries. The basis for planning agreements was taken from the French system of *contrats de programme*.[60] The basis for the NEB was the Italian regional agency, the Italian Istituto per la Ricostruzione Industriale (Industrial Reconstruction Institute, IRI). Holland's work is littered throughout with references to other countries and what might be learnt from them. In defending Labour's plans in the *Guardian* in May 1973 he wrote, 'This system has proved its potential in countries with a background of more state intervention than Britain, such as France and Italy.'[61] In 'Planning and policy coordination', Holland was forthright that Labour could plan successfully only if it was prepared to learn from 'national planning abroad, particularly the continental Western European economies'.[62]

Indeed, there is an ambiguity about Holland's attitude towards Europe in his work. Not only did he draw on the experience of particular European polities, at times he advocated inter-governmental cooperation across Europe and, unlike many of his colleagues, occasionally he exhibited a positive attitude towards the European Economic Community (EEC). During the debate over British entry into the Common Market, Holland had taken issue with some of the critics about the impact that membership might have. Describing opponents as 'alarmist', he argued that France and Italy had interventionist industrial policies within the EEC and claimed that harmonisation across countries might challenge multinational power.[63] By the late 1970s, he placed much more emphasis on the benefits of cooperation, whether on the basis of the EEC or some other international arrangement.[64] In doing so, Holland argued that he was 'against purely national strategies and advocate[ing] a much greater degree of coordination between socialist forces'. In his words, he offered 'a challenge to parochial modes of thought and strategies all too widespread in the Left in Britain'.[65]

These features of his work mark a pronounced contrast between Holland and many other advocates of the Alternative Economic Strategy. They tended to see the approach in national terms and were much less inclined to take note of how the UK might learn from other polities. Equally, they were uninterested in working within the Common Market, believing that nationally based action was feasible and desirable. On one occasion when Holland pointed out the success of strong regional authorities in West Germany, his colleagues were unappreciative: 'some members of the committee felt that W. Germany and Italy were not properly analogous to the UK'.[66] On another occasion, discussing a document from the Swedish social democrats that advocated coordinated action across borders, 'the committee agreed that the emphasis should be on national action that could be taken by a Labour government rather than international action either by trade unions or by national groupings'.[67]

There is a marked contrast between the divergent influences that shaped Holland's *Socialist Challenge* and, for example, the nationally based strategy advocated by Tony Benn in his 1979 volume *Arguments for Socialism*. Something like one-quarter of *The Socialist Challenge* is taken up with discussion of the social democratic experience elsewhere. In his collection, Benn makes only occasional, passing reference to other countries. There is no sustained analysis as to what might be learnt from such cases. Quite the contrary: he is at pains to emphasise the historical and peculiarly British character of Labour's trajectory. In making the case for planning agreements and the NEB, he does not discuss their foreign provenance. Benn thus articulates Holland's strategy but not its empirical foundations.[68] Interestingly, writing in the *Workers' Control Bulletin*, Holland highlighted this distinction: 'The advocacy of workers' control by Tony Benn in the seventies has owed more to his experience of the limits of technocracy and the example of the Upper

Clyde Shipbuilders than to any foreign model'.[69] Benn's approach was 'specifically, if not idiosyncratically, British'. More recently, Holland has been blunter: 'Immediately it [the strategy] was nearly wrecked in practice by the nationalism of Tony Benn'.[70]

In terms of policy documents, nevertheless, it was the nationally based strategy that came to dominate Labour's approach. The frequent references to European countries that cropped up in Holland's papers for the party were watered down and effectively dropped from official publications. *Labour's Programme 1973* had a very brief reference to planning agreements being deployed in France, Belgium and Italy and only a glancing mention of Swedish manpower planning.[71] *Labour's Programme 1976* referred to Swedish training and experiments in employee control. It also noted the difficulties of worker directors elsewhere in Europe.[72] In September 1981, Tony Benn complained about references to Japanese and French planning in a draft party document; in the event, a proposed appendix on arrangements abroad was dropped and the publication made only brief reference to foreign experience, without naming either country by name.[73] Arguably, such a dilution was problematic: some of the subtleties and pragmatism of Holland's account were lost in the construction of a nationally grounded strategy. It was surely harder to make a case among the wider electorate for a strategy that looked dogmatic and untried than it would have been for one that worked elsewhere. Labour might have been able to stomach Holland's Marxism; his Europeanism was beyond the pale.

Then and now: criticisms of the Alternative Economic Strategy

As with *Labour's Programme 1973*, the attention generated by *The Socialist Challenge* was not uncritical. A wide range of points were raised in debate about both publications. Space precludes a full discussion of these, many of which were rebuffed by Holland and others on Labour's left. In the *Observer*, Walden rebuked Holland scornfully for his jargon and his lack of originality, writing, 'The use of obscure terms is almost obligatory in propagating analytically futile theories' and 'This conclusion [about the power of multinational companies] is so obvious I wondered what all the fuss was about'.[74] Here I examine a number of tensions within Holland's contribution to Labour's policy.

The first concerns whether mechanisms of national planning could be made compatible with a firm commitment to industrial democracy. The emphasis placed on planning agreements and the NEB indicated that a government would set targets across the economy for a range of indicators. But such targets might easily be at odds with those objectives desired by workers acting within individual firms. The aspirations of workers within individual firms might conflict with the requirements of a national plan. Yet proponents of the Alternative Economic Strategy demanded both interventionist planning and considerable autonomy on the shop floor. Certainly Holland addressed the question of industrial democracy in his work, not least in several chapters of *The Socialist Challenge*. But there is a sense in which he seems to have assumed that major conflicts of interest would not occur: workers and governments would pretty much painlessly reach agreements as to what goals should be adopted. He also indicated that tactics could be left to workers, while governments would take responsibility for strategic issues, a position that assumed workers would be satisfied with such an arrangement and that there would be no conflict between the goals adopted and the means proposed to secure them.[75] Critics of Holland on the left tended to place far more emphasis on workers' control and much less on the institutions of national planning.

A second tension concerned the economic climate in which the strategy was designed. The basis of Holland's account of monopolisation indicated that price-setting firms were securing abnormal profits. In the dire economic conditions of the mid-1970s, such a claim appeared by no means obvious. Holland suggested that firms under-reported profits and transfer-priced their surpluses to more favourable tax regimes. Accordingly any evidence of an apparent profits crisis was unreliable.[76] In the atmosphere of the mid-1970s, with rising unemployment and increasing bankruptcies, the assertion seemed counterintuitive. Such circumstances raised the question of loss-making companies: what support should be given to firms in economic trouble? At times, the strategy appeared to indicate that there should be support for any firm in difficulty, a position seemingly at odds with the need to accept structural change in the economy. A discussion of the Industrial Policy Sub-committee in 1975 concluded, in a rather confused fashion, 'In principle all lame ducks should be helped, but we had to have clear criteria to decide which should not'.[77] Robert Skidelsky suggested that any link between multinational power and economic decline, as asserted by Holland, was tenuous: other countries had also experienced growing concentrations of capital without experiencing such profound economic difficulties.[78]

A third tension, already noted, concerned the extent to which national-level action was feasible at all. In retrospect, it appears that the whole strategy put an immense faith in the capacities of the state. Arguing that existing public interventions had been undermined by the power of multinational firms, Holland argued that the state could exert control through planning agreements and competitive public enterprise. Such a position made assumptions about the capability of the state in terms of being able to impose itself on the private sector through the new tools, and about the skills of state personnel to manage public enterprises. In outlining the NEB, Holland claimed that 'the initial extension should be painful enough for those concerned "to encourage the others" not to go continent hopping'.[79] Recall his quotation from Shonfield about the need for the state to be part bully. For the most part, Holland's outlook was underwritten by a determined optimism: he 'felt that by using planning agreements to reactivate investment projects which companies had postponed, an increase in investment could be achieved in less time than generally believed and at a lesser cost in resource terms'.[80] Critics were quick to latch onto this optimism about the state. Peter Hennessy asked, 'Even if sufficient public capital were available for their creation, where is the untapped pool of entrepreneurial talent [in public enterprises]?'[81] Peter Jenkins complained that 'Mr Holland seems to think that somehow all the problems of industrial society and all the problems of democracy … will evaporate in the process of what he calls "socialist transformation"'.[82] Victor Keegan asked what difference sweeping nationalisation might make to economic performance: 'It would do nothing to create extra markets.… And it is not as if the existing public enterprises have worked out a viable way in which they and the Government can be involved in macro-planning.'[83] Many concluded that the potential benefits of such far-reaching interventionism had been wildly exaggerated. In the sweeping promises that it offered and in the overall grip that it exerted generally on Labour's outlook, arguably the strategy delayed by some time the adoption by the party of a more realistic approach to economic policy.

A fourth tension concerns the nature of the proposed interventions. In 1978, writing with Tony Banks, a union official who had also been involved in Labour's policy-making process, Holland drew a distinction between outright nationalisation and a controlling shareholding.[84] They claimed that the contrast between the two positions was not just semantic but an indication that the NEB had been conceived on a more modest scale. They had proposed that it build up shareholding gradually over one parliament. Later, Holland retained the contrast between nationalisation and public shareholding: he had suggested, he claimed, that 'the State's holdings in individual companies could be much less [than 100 per cent] and even in a minority'.[85] He continued, 'Thus a 15 per cent or 20 per cent shareholding could be on condition that the company located new plants in the regions'.

An examination of Holland's papers for the Industrial Policy Subcommittee and Labour Party policy documents confirms neither the specific distinction between nationalisation and shareholding nor this general analysis. In the four major papers that Holland wrote for the Labour Party during 1972, I can find no detailed advocacy of selective purchases of equity to exercise control over firms. The thrust of Holland's argument was that the government should take over firms outright and manage them through the NEB.

The only exception to this is that, with Pryke, he noted that taking over insurance companies would give the state holding company equity shares in a myriad of firms reflecting the shareholding of the insurance firms.[86] Elsewhere Holland indicated that the NEB should increase its shareholdings in those companies that were already partly publicly owned.[87] Labour's policy documents are a shade more qualified in this respect. In its brief reference to a state holding company, *Labour's Programme for Britain* of 1972 spoke of 'majority and complete shareholdings'.[88] The green paper on the NEB quoted that passage from the 1972 document and went on to talk of a 'controlling interest in firms in the growth sectors of industry'.[89] It stated, 'If the public sector is to play its full part in overall planning for investment, pricing and full employment, it is essential that wherever the NEB takes over a company by acquiring shares in it, those shares must either be a total holding, or at least a controlling interest'.[90] *Labour's Programme 1973* was a little less strong on this matter: the NEB 'would always take a controlling interest in its participating firms'.[91] None of these papers or documents envisaged the NEB as intervening on the basis of equity stakes of 15 or 20 per cent; all were more ambitious in their scope.

In his work from 1972–73, Stuart Holland was manifestly committed to 'a major extension of public ownership in manufacturing industry'.[92] In 'Planning strategy, tactics and techniques', he argued, 'A socialist government can harness the market power of its own companies as an instrument for the planned transformation of the economy, both making internal company profits and promoting external social and regional benefits'.[93] He continued,

> There is a case for nationalising two dozen really top companies.... Taking twenty of the leading companies into public ownership, plus one of the big three banks and two or three of the leading insurance companies ... would give us the kind of direct instruments we need for both 'push' and 'pull' effects, plus the impact effect on a public wanting to see that we mean business.[94]

After the February 1974 general election, Holland defended nationalisation: 'Labour's public ownership proposals', he argued, 'were not irrelevant luxuries.... The public ownership of twenty-five companies in these conditions would be a real lever for radical change.'[95] In their original conception of a state holding company, Holland and Pryke had advocated swift action: 'what must be recognised is that the holding company is likely to be still born unless some way is found of enabling it to acquire a number of private firms at an early date'.[96]

Holland projected that the public ownership of twenty firms would give the government 38 per cent of net profits and 33 per cent of net turnover of the top 100 manufacturing firms.[97] Similar figures were repeated in the green paper.[98] In chapter 6, Holland censures the media for their reporting of the commitment to nationalise twenty-five companies. My conclusion is that it was a radical proposal, albeit an understandable one in the circumstances of the 1970s.

In 2004, Holland complained about 'Tony Benn's eccentric and unwarranted use of the term "compulsory planning agreements with the top 100 companies"'.[99] He echoes this point in his contribution to this volume. It is hard, however, to distinguish the view he attributes to Benn from his own proposal from 1972 that 'There also would be a strong case for making the contracts obligatory for leading manufacturing companies, including at least the main companies within the top hundred firms'. It is manifest that Holland envisaged 'a compulsory operation of the system'.[100] Overall, Holland offered a strategy and projected a discourse in which nationalisation was a central part.

A last tension concerns how much popular support, either within the party or with the wider electorate, Holland's ideas ever enjoyed. In party political terms, the initiative for *Labour's Programme 1973* came neither from conference resolutions nor from wider debates within the party nor from existing policy legacies but from the policy-making committees. Some left-wingers, as noted, did not fully recognise the nature of the measures. Even after their publication and subsequent adoption (in formal terms such endorsement came at the 1976 conference), it is arguable whether the measures were fully understood. An earlier discussion had noted, 'It was agreed that there was no point in having an economic statement of academic interest only … a means had to be found of communicating our strategy to the grassroots'.[101] Later, Holland recalled, 'You could with hindsight say that the way in which the policies were initially debated and fought for within the party was inadequate'.[102]

In terms of the wider electorate there is little evidence of popular endorsement. Walden claimed, 'He does not seem dimly aware that Labour voters are unprepared for his nostrums'.[103] Holland's response to such equivocation, in effect that a determined government could push the measures through and generate support, looks naïve and might be taken as another indication of over-optimism. He claimed that Labour could secure popular support: 'Provided the lessons of continental state companies can be presented with sufficient glamour (Renault and Alfa Romeo are known as good cars and can now be shown to be good regional employment promoters), we can give a new political glamour to the case for both state leadership and the Programme Contracts system'.[104] Later in the same paper, he argued that such measures could be successful electorally and the managing directors of existing firms could be, effectively, presented with a *fait accompli*: 'There would be a hullabaloo which would last at least four weeks' but opinion would be won over.[105] Victor Keegan suggested that there would be 'total and fearsome opposition from industry'.[106] Holland's judgement, which seems somewhat optimistic, was that with a popular campaign against big business there was the prospect of a 'four-term success' for the Labour Party.

Holland's legacies

The Alternative Economic Strategy dominated Labour's official pro-gramme until 1983. In office between 1974 and 1979, of course, the party leadership found it remarkably easy to sideline the key features of the approach. Between 1974 and 1975 most of its central components were watered down or explicitly rejected by the Labour administration as its advocates found themselves marginalised (and in many cases excluded from government). Such rejection reflected some of the tensions within the strategy discussed above as well as the institutional configuration of the party and the polarisation of its politics. Ideas were debated and argued over but the organisational structure of the party alongside the nature of the Westminster system of government made it remarkably easy for a leadership to abandon a strategy to which it had never been reconciled. (Of course, the administration's trajectory had profound consequences for the internal politics of the party after 1979: space precludes a discussion of these here.)

Following Labour's crushing defeat in the 1983 general election, the policies were pretty much abandoned over the next four years. Certainly by the time of the 1987 general election, little remained of the measures once promised by Labour. Such development in party policy is un-surprising: whatever the feasibilities of the measures themselves, their intimate association with the June 1983 defeat meant that they had to be jettisoned in order that Labour rebuild itself in electoral terms. In effect, the circumstances of 1983 created another policy vacuum concerning the party's economic strategy.

The main exception to this abandonment of the Alternative Economic Strategy concerns its orientation in the wider world, the element of Holland's thinking that the party had downplayed most during the 1970s. After 1983, Labour exhibited a growing and positive Europeanism, one that was redolent of some of Holland's earlier work. The party came to terms with British membership of the European Union and advocated coordinated international action. Developing close and friendly relationships with social democrats elsewhere, Labour looked explicitly to European arrangements in developing new economic policies and especially to the measures advocated by reformist parties. Such policies were far removed from the analysis of monopolisation proffered by Holland: instead, they argued that market failures, in terms of poorly coordinated investment and research and development alongside an unskilled workforce, were at the heart of Britain's economic difficulties. Moreover, the emphasis on Europe would almost certainly have been present without any contribution from Holland, who remained a Labour MP and, for some of this period, was an opposition Treasury spokesperson. Nevertheless, Holland continued to advocate European cooperation over economic issues and his arguments helped to shape Neil Kinnock's reorientation of Labour in that direction. In 1989, he resigned as an MP to become professor of economics in Florence.

Conclusion

In this chapter, I have sought to offer a concise account of Stuart Holland's contribution to the development of Labour's economic policy during the 1970s. I have located that contribution within the difficult economic circumstances and volatile political atmosphere of the period. In the context of the party's formal policy-making committees, I have emphasised the importance of Holland's ideas in shaping the commitments offered by Labour. I have detailed the myriad influences on Holland and charted some of the criticisms that were made of his work – at the time as well as since then. If some of my observations have seemed critical, I hope such an assessment can be taken as a reflection of the importance of Holland's work, in terms of its contribution both to Labour's economic programme as well as to more general debates about the character of British social democracy. The ideas he put forward were especially significant at what was a pivotal period in the development of postwar British politics, one which had a decisive impact on subsequent developments. Holland's involvement in these developments should not be underestimated. My interpretation of his work is clearly different from his in important respects. In part, such contrast may reflect distinct understandings of what is meant by 'nationalisation'. But I am curious also about his conclusion, noted above, that his work should be located within the revisionism of Anthony Crosland. Such a judgement seems to me to underestimate profoundly the originality of *The Socialist Challenge*. Indeed, in my judgement the theoretical significance of *The Future of Socialism* has been overestimated.[107] It did not offer an especially original input to debates about reformism. Rather, synthesising existing accounts, its importance is as an empirical account of the practical aspirations of British socialists in the decades immediately after 1945. Moreover, for all the feeble protestations about its interest in Swedish social democracy, it did not break with the insularity that has shaped the trajectory of socialism in the UK during the last 100 years or so. By contrast, though *The Socialist Challenge* offered less analysis of cultural and social issues than did *The Future of Socialism*, it did establish clear theoretical foundations for the claims that it made and it did attempt to open up the social democratic project within the UK to external influences. That few socialists were able either to engage meaningfully with the book's theoretical propositions or to connect with its European aspirations is one of the lost opportunities of postwar social democracy.

The years in which Stuart Holland's ideas dominated Labour's economic policy proved to be extremely difficult ones for the party. Successive electoral defeats were accompanied by bitter disputes within the party, disagreements which spilled over into a vicious and fratricidal civil war during the early 1980s. Indeed, it is probable that there is a clear causal link between that civil war and the party's poor electoral performance: disillusioned voters ceased to perceive Labour to be a credible electoral force and turned away from it. I do not wish, of course, to suggest that Stuart Holland is to blame for this outcome. The policies of *Labour's Programme 1973* and the hostile reaction of the party leadership fuelled the demands for constitutional reform that in turn led directly to the violence of intra-party debates during the late 1970s and 1980s.

In conclusion, I think three points arise from this discussion. First, ideas mattered within Labour's debates about economic policy in this period. Holland's proposals did much to shape the party's approach. His contribution is all the more remarkable in that his work appears, as he notes in this volume, to have had relatively little impact in academic circles of professional economists. But Holland's capacity to influence Labour, in turn, reflected the institutional configuration of the party and political alignments within it. The triumph of his ideas reflected Labour's structures as well as the prevailing economic crisis.

Second, should more have been done to try to unite the party around an agreed economic programme? To left-wingers, Holland offered a persuasive account of monopolisation and of the kind of action that might correct it, so furthering socialist objectives. Could Labour's right have supported this strategy in any form? Holland had worked with members of the party's right, such as Roy Jenkins and Bill Rodgers. Why did the left insist on such a far-reaching programme? I perceived some regret, noted earlier, on this matter. Participants in Labour's policy debates during the 1970s must ask themselves in retrospect why they found it impossible to reach agreement. Was the promise to take over twenty-five companies worth the conflicts, disunity and distrust that it generated? I am sure the aggressive, male-dominated culture of the party had something to do with this state of affairs. The fractured character of British labourism, with its antipathy to state interventionism in wage setting, intensified by the experiences of the 1960s, heightened the difficult circumstances. It precluded the development of a more moderate, European-inspired programme that might have been coordinated with the industrial policy. But it remains an open question, all the more puzzling given Holland's recent interpretation of his approach, as to why some sort of compromise could not have been reached.

Finally, would Labour have been better to have taken an alternative trajectory? Holland resurrected public ownership from the ritualistic and rhetorical demands made at party conference after party conference for more nationalisation and offered it a theoretical justification it had hitherto lacked. But in so doing, other elements of the party's programme were lost. Going into opposition in 1970, Labour had placed considerable emphasis on manpower planning. In the mid-1970s, the party also looked briefly to Swedish-style investment funds. Neither these nor other policies were developed while planning agreements and the NEB dominated the party's programme. Nor did Labour's attempt to negotiate some sort of arrangement with the trade unions amount to much: the Social Contract, poorly specified in opposition, quickly gave way to desperate attempts to control inflation. The domination of the party's programme by interventionist planning may have limited the party's capacity to draw on other European reformist experiences in the development of a modest, credible strategy.

Notes

1   S. Holland, *The Socialist Challenge* (London: Quartet Books, 1975). For a background discussion of some of the themes raised in this chapter see: M. Wickham-Jones, *Economic Strategy and the Labour Party* (Basingstoke: Macmillan, 1996); and M. Wickham-Jones, 'The new left', in R. Plant, M. Beech and K. Hickson (eds), *The Struggle for Labour's Soul* (London: Routledge, 2004), pp. 24–46. Papers and publications on these themes from the 1970s, especially from within the Labour Party, demonstrate an enthusiastic and at times inconsistent capitalisation. In this chapter I have standardised capitalisation, with an emphasis on lower case. I am indebted to Stuart Holland and Hugh Pemberton for shaping my ideas on these issues.
2   P. Hennessy, 'Seen from the left', *The Times*, 24 July 1975, p. 7.
3   *The Economist*, 2 August 1975, p. 104; R. Skidelsky, 'A call to arms', *Spectator*, 9 August 1975, pp. 187–8, at p. 187.
4   B. Walden, 'The new Marxism – or the old kind in mascara', *Observer*, 3 August 1975, p. 6.
5   P. Jenkins, 'Critique of pure socialism', *Guardian*, 25 July 1975, p. 10.
6   C. A. R. Crosland, *The Future of Socialism* (London: Jonathan Cape, 1956).
7   He had published an equally critical pamphlet for the left-wing publishing house Spokesman. See 'Government adviser quits over economic policy', *The Times*, 22 May 1975, p. 2.
8   See M. Wickham-Jones, '*The Future of Socialism* and New Labour: an appraisal', *Political Quarterly*, 78:2 (2007), pp. 224–40.

9 S. Holland, 'Ownership, planning and markets', in R. Plant, M. Beech and K. Hickson (eds), *The Struggle for Labour's Soul: Understanding Labour's Political Thought Since 1945* (London: Routledge, 2004), pp. 163–86; and S. Holland, 'Demythologising "Old Labour"', *Spokesman*, 110 (2010), pp. 17–29.

10 See M. Hatfield, *The House the Left Built* (London: Gollancz, 1978).

11 S. Holland and R. Pryke, 'The state holding company', Labour Party Archive (hereafter 'LPA'), Research Department (hereafter 'RD', later coded 'RE') 271, February 1972.

12 S. Holland, 'Planning and policy coordination', LPA, RD 315, March 1972.

13 R. Jenkins, *What Matters Now* (London: Fontana, 1972).

14 'The contribution to the green paper', LPA, RD 336, April 1972, pp. 9, 17 and 19: 'Leading companies are "invited" to submit advance programmes to the Government covering key aspects of their strategic activity', p. 19.

15 LPA, Industrial Policy Sub-committee minutes, 18 April 1972, p. 1, and 25 April 1972, pp. 2–3.

16 LPA, Industrial Policy Sub-committee minutes, 25 April 1972, p. 2.

17 *Ibid.*, p. 3.

18 Stuart Holland, 'Planning strategy, tactics and techniques', LPA, RD 442, October 1972, p. 6. See also S. Holland, 'The new economic imperatives', LPA, RD 473, November 1972.

19 S. Holland, 'Coping with multinational companies', LPA, RD 437, October 1972, p. 5.

20 Holland, 'Planning strategy, tactics and techniques', p. 11.

21 Labour Party, *The National Enterprise Board*, opposition green paper (London: Labour Party, 1973).

22 *Ibid.*, p. 21.

23 Labour Party, *Labour's Programme for Britain* (London: Labour Party, 1972), p. 29.

24 'Within particular sectors, it need not control more than one or two leading companies'; Holland and Pryke, 'The state holding company', p. 11.

25 Holland, 'Planning strategy, tactics and techniques', p. 28.

26 Labour Party, *Labour's Programme 1973* (London: Labour Party, 1973), p. 34.

27 LPA, Industrial Policy Sub-committee minutes, 27 June 1975, p. 1.

28 S. Holland, 'An alternative economic strategy', *Spokesman*, 34 (winter 1977–78), pp. 133–6, at p. 136.

29 P. A. Hall, 'Policy paradigms, social learning, and the state', *Comparative Politics*, 25:3 (1993), pp. 275–96.

30 N. Beloff, 'Labour's half-baked plan, by Crosland', *Observer*, 10 June 1973, p. 1.

31 M. Hartley Brewer, 'Scaled down version', *Guardian*, 3 November 1975, p. 14.

32 Labour Party, *Economic Strategy, Growth and Unemployment* (London: Labour Party, 1971).

33 T. Benn, 'Mintech 1970/75', LPA, RD 123, June 1971, p. 1.

34 T. Benn, 'Towards a socialist industrial strategy', LPA, RD 125, June 1975.

35 Hartley Brewer, 'Scaled down version', p. 14. Tony Benn had 'initially given them a cool reception'.

36 LPA, Industrial Policy Sub-committee and Public Sector Working Group minutes, 28 November 1972, p. 2.

37 Quoted by Hartley Brewer, 'Scaled down version', p. 14.

38 T. Benn, *Against the Tide* (London: Hutchinson, 1989), pp. 8 and 11.

39 'Manpower policy', LPA, RE 45, February 1975, p. 15.

40 LPA, Industrial Policy Sub-committee minutes, 11 March 1975, p. 2.

41 J. Hughes, 'The "Institutions", risk capital and UK real investment', LPA, RE 90, March 1975; and J. Hughes, 'A possible application of the Swedish

"investment funds" system in the context of planning agreements and the NEB', LPA, RE 91, March 1975.

42 LPA, Industrial Policy Sub-committee minutes, 25 March 1975, p. 1.
43 *Ibid.*, p. 2.
44 LPA, Industrial Policy Sub-committee minutes, 27 June 1975, p. 2.
45 LPA, Industrial Policy Sub-committee minutes, 28 January 1976, p. 1.
46 A qualification can be made regarding Holland's Europeanism: I discuss this below.
47 Holland, 'Ownership, planning and markets'.
48 *Ibid.*, p. 185.
49 Crosland, *The Future of Socialism*, pp. 358, 476, 482 and 487–95.
50 *Ibid.*, p. 488.
51 *Ibid.*, p. 492.
52 *Ibid.*
53 Holland, 'Planning and policy coordination', p. 19.
54 LPA, Industrial Policy Sub-committee minutes, 31 October 1972, p. 1.
55 Holland and Pryke, 'The state holding company', pp. 16–17.
56 A. Budd, *The Politics of Economic Planning* (Glasgow: Fontana, 1978), p. 125.
57 Holland, 'Ownership, planning and markets', p. 176.
58 Walden, 'The new Marxism or the old kind in mascara'.
59 See, for example, Holland, 'Planning and policy coordination'.
60 See, in particular, S. Holland, 'Inflation and price control: a note on the French programme contracts', LPA, RD 605, February 1973; see also chapter 6.
61 S. Holland, 'Labour's chosen task', *Guardian*, 24 May 1973, p. 18.
62 Holland, 'Planning and policy coordination', p. 1.
63 S. Holland, 'Regions are no worse off inside EEC', *Guardian*, 16 July 1971, p. 14.
64 Culminating in S. Holland (ed.), *Out of Crisis* (Nottingham: Spokesman Press, 1983).
65 S. Holland, 'Power in the community: a critique of federalism', LPA, RE 1118, no date but 1977. See also S. Holland, 'Competition and the containment of the meso-economic (multinational) firm', LPA, RE 1115, no date but 1977.
66 LPA, Industrial Policy Sub-committee minutes, 29 July 1975, p. 1.
67 LPA, Industrial Policy Sub-committee minutes, 11 November 1975, p. 2.
68 See T. Benn, *Arguments for Socialism* (London: Jonathan Cape, 1979).
69 S. Holland, 'Wither Labour now?', *Workers' Control Bulletin*, 5 (1978), pp. 2–4, at p. 3.
70 Holland, 'Ownership, planning and markets', p. 180.
71 Labour Party, *Labour's Programme 1973*, pp. 17 and 22.
72 Labour Party, *Labour's Programme 1976* (London: Labour Party, 1976), pp. 32, 34 and 35.
73 See Wickham-Jones, *Economic Strategy and the Labour Party*, p. 177.
74 Walden, 'The New Marxism or the old kind in mascara'.
75 S. Holland, 'Industrial democracy', LPA, RD 930, November 1973, p. 1.
76 See Wickham-Jones, *Economic Strategy and the Labour Party*, p. 148.
77 LPA, Industrial Policy Sub-committee minutes, 21 June 1975, p. 4.
78 Skidelsky, 'A call to arms', p. 187.
79 S. Holland, 'A note on the revision of Labour's Programme', LPA, RD 644, February 1973, p. 5.
80 LPA, Industrial Policy Sub-committee minutes, 21 June 1975, p. 2.
81 Hennessy, 'Seen from the left', p. 7.
82 Jenkins, 'Critique of pure socialism', p. 10.
83 V. Keegan, 'Taking the Holland road', *Guardian*, 27 November 1978, p. 21.

84 T. Banks and S. Holland, 'Founding the NEB', letters, *The Times*, 22 September 1978, p. 15.
85 Holland, 'Ownership, planning and markets', p. 164.
86 Holland and Pryke, 'The state holding company', p. 28.
87 Holland, 'The new economic imperatives', p. 7.
88 Labour Party, *Labour's Programme for Britain*, p. 29.
89 Labour Party, *National Enterprise Board*, p. 12.
90 *Ibid.*, p. 12.
91 Labour Party, *Labour's Programme 1973*, p. 34.
92 Holland, 'Labour's chosen task'.
93 Holland, 'Planning strategy, tactics and techniques', p. 6.
94 *Ibid.*, p. 28.
95 'Report on Birmingham conference', *Spokesman*, 29 (winter 1974–75), p. 98.
96 Holland and Pryke, 'The state holding company', p. 29. They also appeared to be hostile to cooperation with the private sector: 'What must also be avoided is the adoption of some non-solution such as joint ventures in partnership with private enterprises', pp. 29–30.
97 Holland, 'Planning strategy, tactics and techniques, p. 31.
98 Labour Party, *National Enterprise Board*, p. 21.
99 Holland, 'Ownership, planning and markets', p. 179.
100 Holland, 'Planning strategy, tactics and techniques', p. 11. Elsewhere Holland wrote of 'introducing obligatory investment, employment, pricing, trade and location contracts for both the new publicly owned companies and the other companies in the top hundred'. See 'The new economic imperatives', p. 3.
101 LPA, Industrial Policy Sub-committee minutes, 21 June 1975, p. 2.
102 M. Prior, 'Problems in Labour politics:, interviews with Stuart Holland, Frank Field, and Michael Meacher', in D. Adlam (ed.), *Politics and Power 2: Problems in Labour Politics* (London: Routledge & Kegan Paul, 1980), pp. 5–36, at p. 20.
103 Walden, 'The new Marxism or the old kind in mascara'.
104 Holland, 'Planning strategy, tactics and techniques', p. 8.
105 *Ibid.*, p. 29.
106 Keegan, 'Taking the Holland road', p. 21.
107 See Wickham-Jones, *'The Future of Socialism* and New Labour'.

8

Jam today: feminist impacts and transformations in the 1970s

Lynne Segal

The close of the 1970s was a confusing time for many feminists in Britain, with intensifying divisions within the Women's Liberation Movement that had flowered spectacularly throughout much of the previous decade. Yet 1979 was an exciting year for me and my closest friends and political allies. During the run-up to the general election that would usher in the momentous upheavals of Margaret Thatcher and nearly two decades of the Conservatives in power, Sheila Rowbotham, Hilary Wainwright and I embarked upon what briefly proved a surprisingly influential project, attempting to build on what we saw as the strengths of the autonomous, loosely networked women's movement of the 1970s to unite the various factions of the left and Labour movement through grass-roots solidarity and activism. With Rowbotham as its leading author, our slim pamphlet *Beyond the Fragments: Feminism and the Making of Socialism* was published later that year.[1] The interest it triggered led to an expanded version being republished and appearing in several editions in the following two years, selling internationally and translated into several languages, including Turkish, Portuguese, Italian and German. It also gave rise to a noisy conference of 3,000 people in Leeds in August 1980. Over the years we have heard from feminist groups and trade union activists in India, Turkey and the Brazilian Workers Party, to name a few, emphasising the significance of that book in informing their ways of working, while even today, working on this chapter in September 2011, I see on the web Pam Currie, a leading member of the Scottish Socialist Party, citing *Beyond the Fragments* for its emphasis on tackling sexism in political parties.[2] Looking back, I think we were right to point to feminism and its key priorities, working locally and linking personal life and political issues, as one of the key political developments of the 1970s, although we were more than optimistic in imagining that people with similar but far from identical political goals and ways of organising could work together and agree on common action.[3] One of the most interesting questions for those reflecting upon the 1970s today, however, is surely what had given three women the confidence to imagine we could embark upon such an ambitious project in the first place.

Women had been drawn into the thick of left politics from the close of the sixties, making the seventies, in a sense, our delayed sixties. The huge optimism energising feminists in the seventies was the most notable feature of the landscape I inhabited then, reaching out to embrace hundreds of thousands of other women, near and far. Feminist hopes were gigantic, and our victories lasting, or some of them. Moreover, for many years feminists remained among the most committed political activists and even, to our own surprise, increasingly competent and confident players in the public domain that took us into the new and soon very different political landscape of the 1980s. From the margins, where some remained, to the centre, where more professional women were increasingly found, feminist thought had begun shifting epistemological outlooks across the social sciences and humanities, affecting state policies, union practices and transforming cultural spaces generally.

As this book exemplifies, there is now a consistent trend when studying the contemporary to view the world through decades. It is certainly how I view my own life, which seems to unfold in complete accord with what is recalled as the key notes, the distinctive themes, of each new decade after 1945: born into the postwar bulge, growing up in the conservative, conformist, acquisitive fifties; entering adulthood in the youth-oriented, risk-taking, hedonistic, swinging sixties; becoming a single mother, feminist, militant woman in the seventies; fighting against the rise of the right in the eighties; retreating into the more reflective mode of academic life in the more quiescent nineties, with its distinct internal struggles, including over the meaning of politics, and the politics of meaning. Neat, too neat, of course. This decadal harmony must be partly deceptive, a mnemonic device, assisting transcription, with other details of a life fading out in the process.[4] Moreover, it was precisely my seventies, full of the most intense excitement, hope and rising confidence, which on reflection deviated most from the keynotes others provide for that decade. I recall the 1970s as a time of endlessly varied immersion in left community activism, an era when our borough councils retained significant autonomy and local politics meant contact with a multiplicity of resource centres, housing cooperatives, tenants' associations, alternative presses, union branches linked to trade councils, socialist clubs, anti-racist campaigns, and so much more, all making the notion of 'community' back then a significant attachment for many of us dwelling in the supposedly anonymous metropolis. Yet many survey this decade in quite the opposite way, not as a time of rising excitement, hope and confidence but as a period of growing tedium, gloom and despair, especially after 1976. This sense of decline, generating fears of crisis and decay, is at least what Andy Beckett reports in his interesting assessment, *When the Lights Went Out*.[5]

As many have noticed, this illustrates that even people who occupy very similar locations experience the very same eras in vastly different ways. There are further hurdles to be surmounted in any assessment of the role of second-wave feminism in the shaping of, and the legacies from, the 1970s. They begin with that decadal demarcation itself and extend, in ever more heated debate, into contests over the precise impact of feminist thought and activism. Are women's liberationists best seen today as significant agents of change, responsible, in the confident words of the American poet Adrienne Rich, in 1973, for a women's renaissance 'far more extraordinary and influential' in shifting perspectives than the earlier European Renaissance from theology to humanism'?[6] Or, are seventies feminists better viewed as merely the passive vehicles of historical processes, barely a blip in the relentless march of economic neo-liberalism, with its diverse impact on women's lives? Thus, some see those strident women of yesterday as largely irrelevant to, or else hopelessly enmeshed within, the surging tides of economic forces, perhaps even assisting capitalism, as Juliet Mitchell would later suggest, in pushing women 'into the future first', to become exemplary low-paid, flexible workers.[7] In the footsteps of Marx, I too am swayed by those who notice that it is capitalism itself, in its shifting formations, which has to date proved the most 'revolutionary' force of all. Wherever given free rein, it is always at work destabilising the old to create new patterns of production and consumption in its restless search for cheap labour, new markets and maximum profit for those with their hands on its fiscal motors. However, given the complexity of all human affairs, it is surely unwise to imagine any single, linear thrust when mapping historical change.

Women's 'sixties' renaissance

Decades are best viewed with shifting borders. The story of women in the seventies, for instance, begins firmly within the crucible of the sixties, though this rarely emerges within the fiercely contested accounts of that decade. The sixties is the decade either celebrated or impugned for the

rise of interest in individual freedom, civil rights and personal life generally, yet it is hardly ever women who are visible in reflections on those
years. Whether historians are mapping what they term the 'long sixties',
like Gerd-Rainer Horn recently surveying the twenty years of popular
protest movements stretching from the rise of the New Left in 1956 to
the beginning of the decline of such movements in 1976, or isolating its
iconic flashpoint, France, May '68, there is one cluster that routinely falls
beneath the radar of analysis, whatever direction it points.[8] The most
familiar historical accounting, the memorabilia, of the sixties, and even
more so of May 1968, all place men definitively, men exclusively, at the
centre of both the decade and its defining year. We learn nothing about
the women who appeared, in almost equal numbers, alongside the angry
and rebellious young men whose names routinely appear in the scholarly
and popular restaging of those years. Yet women's presence in the sixties
was already mutating into much more than their provocative depiction as
the masturbatory aids for male bonding adorning so much of the underground press and outlaw manifestos of those years. Indeed, before the
decade was out, many male militants were already worrying that their
revolution was over, just as scores of women were finding their voice.

The Women's Liberation Movement had its origins fully within the
political and cultural currents of the 1960s, at least within all of those
that overflowed into the 1970s. It was in 1965 that Mary King and Casey
Hayden wrote a widely circulated document on the status of women
in the Student Non-violence Co-ordinating Committee (SNCC) to
register black voters in the USA. One of their number, Barbara Epstein,
would later recall the strength white women gained from supporting
black women, who offered them a different model of 'strong' womanhood, when they lived with them and worked in voter-registration
campaigns in the southern states in the mid-sixties.[9] Women guerrilla
fighters in Vietnam provided other images of strong women for budding
feminists then, as lifelong anti-war activist, Leslie Cagan, also from the
USA, recalls when describing the electrifying impact of meeting some of
them in Bulgaria in the spring of 1968.[10] Strength was certainly necessary for many a sixties woman if and when she dared to rise to speak
at radical meetings, as women later reported from a host of different
countries about their experiences during that decade. In the UK, Sheila
Rowbotham recalled her intense humiliation, finding herself an 'object
of derision', when speaking at a British student rally in 1968, wearing
a mini-skirt.[11] In New York, in early 1969, the journalist Ellen Willis
reported similar jeers and derision greeting women who dared to speak:
'The men go crazy. "Take it off! Take it off the stage and fuck her".'[12]

Jeered and rejected or not, however, it was women who in the end
would emerge as the most decisive victors of the 1960s. The spirit of
resistance, in combination with that increasingly accessible contraceptive

pill from the mid-1960s, was giving women a new-found energy. It was the dreams of the sixties some women took with them into the seventies, as they marched by then ever more confidently along the very same pathways they had trod during the previous decade, although with several critical swerves, even while mouthing many of the same words. 'She's leaving home', the Beatles chorused in 1967 and, indeed, she was; young women were on the verge of a mass exit. Over the next few years, ever more single young women fought every obstacle to establish that it was possible, if still certainly often perilous, to leave home, have sex and much else besides (though not yet to obtain a mortgage or other forms of basic financial backing) free from dependence on some man who had authority over them. Moreover, as I have suggested above, women working alongside or within the various civil rights, anti-racist, anti-imperialist and, eventually most importantly of all, the anti-Vietnam War movements of the sixties had also been learning how to organise, work politically and to bond with each other – if at first rather hesitantly. In the UK, this is just what Sheila Rowbotham's superb memoir of the decade, *Promise of a Dream*, captures.[13]

Thus, while it is correct to see the goals of women's liberation as significantly breaking away from aspects of sixties politics, since women were always at the heart of its agenda, it is useful to look for continuities. Those political currents and theories of the sixties, in Britain filtering down from ex-Communist Party members, such as Raymond Williams, E. P. Thompson, Raphael Samuel, alongside other voices from the New Left, especially Stuart Hall, all impacted on second-wave feminism, with their emphasis on the role of culture in politics, on the significance of cross-class alliances and above all on the need to respond to calls for direct action and the building of networks of solidarity rather than forms of party building. These were precisely the political perspectives and strategies favoured by feminists as they began to differentiate themselves, to a degree, from the revolutionary stances of their Old Left comrades. Moreover, behind the braggadocio of certain male radicals, some sixties men themselves were early on rather receptive to the feminists soon in their midst. Men were certainly being challenged, but it was some men, alongside women, at least for a while, who followed feminists in trying to work to unify anti-war, anti-racist and left politics with women's liberation. The chauvinist male bonding and blatant sexism of sixties radical men had indeed created women's collective militancy, though it would take them many years, as some would later reflect, to overcome their timidity, if and when confronting mixed left gatherings. Nevertheless, it was precisely within those sixties publications that women announced that the time had come for them to fight their battles on their own. This was what Juliet Mitchell announced when she was the sole woman on the editorial board of *New Left Review*, in which she published the influential essay 'Women: the longest revolution', in 1966.[14] Soon, Sheila Rowbotham, as the lone woman on the board of the radical left magazine *Black Dwarf*, headed up by Britain's best-known student radical, Tariq Ali, was soliciting and penning articles for an issue of that magazine heralding 'The year of the militant woman', which appeared in 1969. Rowbotham was reading Doris Lessing and Simone de Beauvoir, eagerly searching for ideas on how to bring women's personal issues to politics, while at the same time interviewing women sewing machinists on strike at Ford factories, and other militant working-class women who, alongside those female fighters in Vietnam, provided the early role models for the Women's Liberation Movement.[15]

1969 was the year the arresting young Australian in Britain, Germaine Greer (then working with the quintessentially sixties radical porn magazine *SUCK*), was busy writing *The Female Eunuch*, which became an instant bestseller in mainstream culture. It was also when the first Women's Liberation groups appeared in the UK, a year after they became visible in the USA. Just for a change, as Rowbotham later wryly noted, the assertive predictions of a left paper 'had been vindicated by history'.[16] The year 1969 really was the turning point in the rebirth of 'militant woman' in Britain, just as 1968 had proved its decisive moment in the USA. Like it or loathe it, despite and because of all its hitherto unexamined male chauvinism, the sixties was the decade that nurtured women's liberation.

The heyday of women's liberation

The Women's Liberation Movement of the 1970s emerged in critical dialogue with a broader left movement fighting for an anti-racist, anti-imperialist, peaceful and, above all, more egalitarian world. Even in the USA, where more conventionally liberal movements (such as the National Organization of Women) were far stronger than in Britain, one prominent wing of the movement was militantly leftist and radical. In the decades since this resurgence of feminism, we can loosely discern the successive dominance of three distinct styles and perspectives, although earlier outlooks continued to contest their replacements. During the foundation and spread of the British Women's Liberation Movement, 1969–76, there was an emphasis on women's shared needs, alongside struggles to end gender inequalities and cultural subordination. This turned into a dual and contradictory prioritising of women's 'difference' – and differences between women – in the 1980s, accompanying the deepening of divisions within feminism itself and greater detachment from the left. Subsequently, there has been a shift towards discursive analyses of the instability of all identities, as feminist theory settled into the post-structuralist academy of the 1990s. However, looking back at feminism in the seventies one can detect more contention than this overview suggests, both at the time and, most significantly, since.

In the 1970s, feminism grew rapidly as a remarkably influential social movement in much of the Western world, peaking in the mid-seventies, before dissolving as any coherent organisation, at least one capable of staging annual conferences, by the end of that decade. The last annual women's liberation conference in the UK took place, with much fractious controversy, in Birmingham in 1978. However, testifying to its lasting impact, it was from 1977 that the United Nations General Assembly formally marked International Women's Day as a time for celebrating women's rights around the world, as Jocelyn Olcott discusses in a recent article on women's representation internationally.[17] Nevertheless, although it affected the lives of millions of women, over thirty years later the scholarship analysing the distinctiveness of this upsurge of grass-roots feminist activism remains sparse. As I suggested in *Why Feminism?*, the struggles of that period largely disappear in the many academic texts coming from its more contemporary progeny, which are often dismissive of what is seen as the theoretically unsophisticated, totalising outlook of seventies feminism.[18] Indeed, in the 1990s, when a few middle-aged feminist historians in the USA, including Rosalyn Baxandall, Linda Gordon and Patricia Romney, began trying to recapture the diversity of the movement in which they participated, they announced that they could not recognise themselves in what they viewed as the distorting accounts of women's liberation then circulating in academic or more popular forums.[19]

This dearth of thoughtful reflections prompted two other veteran US feminists, Rachel Blau DuPlessis and Ann Snitow, to embark upon their own memoir anthology, attentive to ambiguities, ambivalences and possible evasions as early women's liberationists recall their engagement in its past. Later assessing the diverse and largely forgotten material they finally assemble, DuPlessis and Snitow reflect upon the caricature and forgetting that haunt all political actions, including women's, suggesting: 'amnesia about political movements is not only an innocent effect of general forgetfulness, but is socially produced, packaged, promulgated, and perpetuated'.[20] In a theme that we see repeated in the UK, what emerges in their text is above all accounts of lives that were shaped by their optimistic belief that collective action could (and, for a while, did) transform everything, from personal lives to workplace conditions, social policy, the law and, indeed, would impact upon almost every aspect of culture. It is a useful reminder, if only to ponder how strange such optimistic rhetoric and sensibilities appear in the current political climate; the words not so much of another generation, with less sophisticated ideas, as of different creatures.

Certainly, that is an impression often expressed by old feminists re-calling their youthful activism. From New York, the journalist and writer Meredith Tax mourns: 'I feel like one of the last surviving members of a nearly extinct species – the committed left-wing feminist'.[21] Although still working successfully to promote women's writing and struggles through the international forum Women's WORLD (Women's World Organization for Rights, Literature and Development), which she helped to found in the 1990s, Tax feels she can no longer make her own voice heard at home, in the USA. It is a salient reminder of changing times, for those aware that it was she who published one of the earliest underground classics of women's liberation, *Woman and Her Mind: The Story of Everyday Life*, which sold 150,000 copies in pamphlet form around the world in the early 1970s. In the UK, when I myself began soliciting older feminists' recollections as background for my reflections in *Making Trouble*, I encountered, and reported, identical sentiments: 'I feel like a survivor of a lost world, a pre-Jurassic relic', the poet and scholar Denise Riley wrote.[22]

Context is crucial here. The early seventies were still relatively affluent times for my generation of women, whatever our class, and horizons could easily expand along with the increasing possibilities for jobs, across the social spectrum. With new opportunities opening up for women, high expectations came easily to many of us. One after another, older feminists today express the rising spirit of confidence they shared back in the seventies, many of them today mourning its passing. Thus the social researcher and peace activist Cynthia Cockburn wrote to me to suggest 'it seemed that things could only go forward, these changes are irreversible', or as another feminist scholar, Ursula Huws, expressed the same thought: 'it felt as if the boundary between understanding the world and changing it was dissolved'.[23] These particular feminists are still active as older women today, in peace movements and organisa-tions for global justice, but they emphasise that both their mood, and the zeitgeist itself, has reversed. Pessimism resonates most immediately with the global contemporary climate, whether ideologically, politically or economically.

The seventies were different, and especially for women. When women began meeting autonomously, networking and joining broader campaigns, local, national and international, collective agency and confidence grew surprisingly rapidly. It would end up changing the style, language, outcome and even the meaning of 'politics'. It is hard to encompass the extent of the personal and social transformation that feminists began to envisage. Some campaigns began on the home front, for nurseries, reproductive rights, shared housework or against domestic violence and sexual abuse. Others extended outwards, to embrace demands for better education, training and employment rights for women, with more women joining trade unions and tackling discrimination and 'harassment' at work. Looking further afield, feminists were soon active combating militarism worldwide, fighting racism and the legacies of imperialism or supporting Third World development projects; founding women's health movements or working generally for global peace and against ethnic strife. Changing political practices was an integral part of much of this work, with feminists not simply researching women's lives in altogether new ways, but determined to challenge existing ways of seeing, speaking and writing about gender and sexual difference.

Thus, whether creating new living spaces, sharing childcare in collective households, or establishing cooperative workplaces, many feminists, myself included, shared the radiant hopes that sustained daily political energies and engagements. As I describe in *Making Trouble*, every aspect of women's personal, cultural, economic and political lives were now reassessed through a feminist lens, with attempts to combine the personal and the political the overarching agenda.[24] The creative outburst flowing from this mindful refiguring of any and all hitherto demeaned descriptions of womanhood was soon evident everywhere: whether splashed as slogans on banners and badges, distilled in ponderous pamphlets, indeed, in every genre of literary and aesthetic endeavour. Quickly impacting upon the mainstream media, evolving feminist representations of the complex nature of womanhood, seen (after de Beauvoir) as a product of the shifting situation of women in an enduringly androcentric world, soon looped back to reshape popular accounts of reality and the possibilities for political action within it.

The practice and rhetoric of textual deconstruction entering certain realms of French philosophy in the 1970s was apparently far removed from the feminist activism of the 1970s, and would begin to be articulated in feminist thought only once feminist scholarship was settled inside academic institutions, well over a decade later. Nevertheless, there was considerable attention given to the situational specificity of women, although it was a multiplicity attributed not so much to the discursive positioning of women as to their structural belongings in relation to class, race, employment, housework and, before long, sexual orientation. At least, these political differences between women were registered early on, in what was the most influential socialist feminist writing in Britain in the 1970s, with some awareness of their accompanying symbolic resonance. Here is Sheila Rowbotham, one the most widely read and translated British feminists of the seventies, pondering differences between women in 1972: 'Our own indications are only tentative and incomplete.... Women's liberation is too narrow in social composition to comprehend the differences between middle class and working class, black and white, young and old, married and unmarried, country and townswomen.' Moreover, she adds, prophetically, 'it is clear that most of the isolated gains we can make can be twisted against women and that many partial gains are often a means of silencing one group at the expense of another'.[25] Imbibing Gramsci and de Beauvoir, Rowbotham emphasised the role of language as one of the crucial instruments of domination:

> As soon as we learn words we find ourselves outside them.... The underground language of people who have no power to define and determine themselves in the world develops its own density and precision.... But it restricts them by affirming their own dependence upon the words of the powerful.... There is a long inchoate period during which the struggle between the language of experience and the language of theory becomes a kind of agony.[26]

Academic feminism, let alone the reign of post-structuralism within it in the 1990s, had yet to dawn, yet Rowbotham, writing these words at this time, in her mid-twenties, was hardly ignorant of the issues it would address in its suspicion of identity claims and subject positions. Moreover, in my view, her nuanced words were not so exceptional; I recall them as endlessly debated in my milieu. Feminists certainly asserted that, as women, we were strong, proud, beautiful, whatever took our fancy at the moment, and yet, at the very same time, many women were becoming feminists partly because of our uncertainties about what on earth it meant to claim to be a 'woman'. Though seventies feminism would later be severely chastised for its essentialism, the category 'woman' was rarely seen as unitary, despite the oversimplifications that inevitably tend to accompany calls for collective action, or the divisive growth of a more fundamentalist feminism in the years to come.

Another seventies practice that would be criticised in later theoretical reflections was the appeal to women's shared experiences, seen as key to the 'consciousness raising' groups that often drew seventies women into feminism. Yet here, too, there was already some awareness of the limitations of such commonalities. Again, Rowbotham early on recorded the problems of relying on direct experience, seeing it as both a strength and a weakness of feminist thought, while suggesting that: 'Analysis is not enough alone, for we enter the beings and worlds of other people through imagination, and it is through imagination that we glimpse how these might change'.[27] In memoirs or personal communications, seventies feminists have often mentioned that imaginative leap that would turn them, seemingly for the first time, into paying attention to other women, with an energy that for a while generated a passionate desire for solidarity with just those women they had often hitherto barely registered, from night-cleaners to sex workers or women in prison.

In contrast to subsequent reiterations about the feminism of these times, it was this promiscuous embrace that made the early years of the Women's Liberation Movement not so much defined by its hostility to men as by its positive affirmation of new relationships between women, its search for 'sisterhood'. Although insisting on their own political autonomy, in many of their collective battles for change most seventies feminists also joined forces with other radical groups with shared goals. In Islington, for instance, feminists helped to launch an 'anti-cuts campaign' when Harold Wilson (who narrowly defeated Edward Heath as Prime Minister in February 1974) embarked on spending cuts, a campaign which was relaunched under James Callaghan, as monetary controls led to his Labour government threatening further cuts in education and health spending.

The collapse of a vision

How to reform state structures and policies, both local and national, was a priority in some feminist analyses in the 1970s, especially for socialist feminists such as Elizabeth Wilson, Mary McIntosh and Annette Kuhn. They argued that the state was not itself inherently 'patriarchal', but served generally to control and sometimes to restructure the often contradictory and conflicting needs of the existing male-dominated capitalist economy, as well as to support the then still officially endorsed patriarchal formation of family life.[28] From here, the call for increased social provision and community resources for those caring for dependent people at home accompanied attempts to redefine notions of domestic work as 'work', essential to economic growth and involving labour which should not be seen as intrinsically confined to women.

Strategic priorities were fiercely debated, whether seeking support for the self-help resources that feminists set up and ran, including the battered women's refuges and rape crisis centres, or making demands on the state or seeking trade union support for fostering communities and workplaces more compatible with maximum choice and flexibility for both women and men.[29] The impact of this strand of women's liberation would result in the Equal Pay Act of 1970 being extended into several key pieces of legislation in 1975 (although it would be another eight years before the Equal Value Amendment Regulations enabled women to claim equal pay for work of equal value). In 1975, the Sex Discrimination Act made all discrimination against women in education, recruitment and advertising illegal, and the Employment Protection Act introduced statutory maternity provision and made it illegal to dismiss a woman because she was pregnant. That year also child benefit (paid directly to mothers) replaced the former family allowance, paid to men. The following year the Domestic Violence Act gave women legal rights to eject violent husbands or partners. This campaigning strand of feminism, concerned with legislative and social change generally, remained an enduring source of ideas and tactics for promoting women's interests, with feminists working in diverse radical and reformist coalitions alongside other progressive forces.[30]

The strengths of the outlook, ways of working and many achievements of the Women's Liberation Movement in the 1970s had inevitable limitations. The shared energy and close friendships built up in the small groups most feminists preferred, with their principled rejection of any structures of leadership, could leave some women feeling distanced from such informality, hence suspicious of the imagined joys of 'sisterhood'.[31] The dedication to ideals of equality, where everyone was encouraged to develop every range of skills, could obviously prove inefficient, while also evoking resentment against those seen as too authoritative, ambitious or successful. Meanwhile, the accompanying disavowal of envy and competitiveness between women made its inevitable concealed expression all the more embittered, as some New York feminists, such as Muriel Dimen, would later discuss, citing problems of 'feminist rectitude'.[32] The resulting prescriptiveness is clearly a danger within movements apparently relying upon consensus, which usually entailed disregarding the incongruous or divisive as in some way not 'feminist'. Most strident in the USA, but soon spreading elsewhere, this fed into the fiercest contestations over feminist sexual politics, pornography and debates over the role of power in erotic fantasy and sexual practices, as a more fundamentalist feminism determined to make men's sexual violence against women its overriding agenda became more widespread from the close of the seventies.[33]

This was indeed the issue that came to a head in the very last annual women's liberation conference (in Birmingham in 1978). The final plenary at that conference descended into utter chaos as the participants attempted to debate the motion of a small but determined group of revolutionary feminists aiming to name men's sexual violence against women as *the* fundamental cause of women's oppression. The acrimony this generated brought to an end any further attempts to hold national conferences of the whole of the women's movement.[34] From the USA, Joan Nestle, among others, would later describe some of the similar debates over sexuality tearing feminism apart in her milieu from the close of the 1970s.[35]

Bringing all these divisions around sexuality, race, class and heterosexism into the open destroyed any notion of women's cosy unity. Race would soon prove an even more explosive issue than class and sexual orientation, whether in the USA or the UK, for although poverty and racism were constant preoccupations of women's liberation, both in theory and in practice, feminist groups remained overwhelmingly white, and predominantly middle class. Thus, by the close of the seventies division was more apparent than unity in many feminist gatherings, as newly empowered groups of women expressed their sense of marginalisation within the movement itself. In Britain, the first black women's conference was held in 1979 and here, as in the USA, the most painful clashes over race would occur in the second decade of resurgent feminism, with black women challenging the priorities of white feminist analysis over the previous decade for privileging sexism over racism, and ignoring the particularities of ethnic difference. Thus, Valerie Amos and Pratibha Parmar would argue in the early 1980s that 'the gains made by white women have been and still are at the expense of Black women'.[36] Nevertheless, the feminism Amos critiqued would before long help to launch her, at least, on a stellar career in British government and the United Nations, where she now resides with the global elite of the most powerful women in the world.

There were of course race- and class-bound limitations in the diverse perspectives and practices of women's liberation, rubbing against other inevitable power dynamics, moralising and self-policing. Nevertheless, it was not primarily internal power dynamics that would destroy the early energies of grass-roots movements, feminist or otherwise, but instead the more ruthless and unyielding forces soon confronting activists of any progressive stripe in Thatcher's Britain. The internal conflict and divisions within feminism were real enough at the close of the 1970s, but while new voices could constantly be heard within feminist spaces, what was disappearing was any forward motion towards the more egalitarian or caring world they all required. As economic survival became more problematic for more people, the social networks sustaining progressive thought and practice withered, while the public mood shifted, gradually becoming more aligned with Thatcher's increasingly hegemonic anti-welfare, market-driven culture.

Seventies feminism in historical perspective

How significant were seventies feminists in forging political change in Britain? As I said in my opening, the answer is contentious. Feminist writing and campaigning challenged the legitimacy of many of the old patterns of culture, politics, domesticity and working lives. Liberation rhetoric inspired an explosion of creative work from women, in theatre, music, fiction, film, fashion, publishing and higher education, as the vicissitudes of women's lives and histories spiralled outwards from the early, fiercely critical, yet soon unexpectedly confident, platforms of women's liberation into more popular arenas. In 1972, Marsha Rowe, with Rosie Boycott, launched the most successful magazine of women's liberation, *Spare Rib*. Over thirty years later, she wonders how women today can understand the spirit of that time, with its anger, joy and exhilaration, as women fought all notions of female inferiority, including their own: 'daily life took on a new sublimity, as our potential was released on all fronts. One was flying. Eventually we had to land. That came with a bump.... But reality itself had changed. We had changed the world, we were changed ourselves, and that dialectic is still going on, to my great fascination, giving me optimism and courage.'[37]

Yet, as a few feminists soon realised, some of this readiness to listen to women's words would rather quickly enable them to be reworked for mainstream incorporation, although some feminist aspirations for countering discrimination and injustices would prove easier to integrate than others. For capitalism itself was increasingly attending to difference, diversity and the promotion of self-help agendas, although in ways newly individualised and gutted of their former collective and confrontational mode. This encouraged and at least partially satisfied many women's aspirations to lead richer and more varied lives. However, other feminist demands, especially those for improved welfare provision, shorter working hours in paid work, or other ways of making jobs more compatible with domestic responsibilities, would grow further removed from the cultural mainstream.

Thus, both despite and because of feminism, women's lives continued to change and become ever more diverse from the 1970s. As some women moved upwards in their professional lives, others became, relatively, more disadvantaged in the harsher economic climate from the close of the decade. The triple whammy of trade unions in retreat, limits on public spending and greater economic insecurity took its toll, with Britain becoming overall an increasingly more unequal society than it had been in the seventies.[38] With the expansion in the managerial and service sector there were further occupational openings for women (although they moved more slowly into the upper echelons of the rapidly burgeoning financial sector, from which they remain still largely absent), even as industrial production declined, undermining men's employment prospects. What feminists did not control, though did sometimes continue to try to confront, was the growing acceptance of intensifying inequalities accompanying the new fiscal regimes, both nationally and globally. However, the socialist feminism I had inhabited in the seventies was no longer at the cutting edge of feminist scholarship, as it embedded itself more securely into the latest theoretical turns in academic life in the 1980s and, especially, the 1990s.[39] The broader political and cultural conjunctures framing intellectual work encouraged moves away from commitments to economic analysis and structural constraints for ever more abstract analysis of subjectivity, semiotics and textual analysis, at the very time when material inequality was deepening around the globe.[40]

Nevertheless, feminists who remained attentive to the dangers of the incorporation of aspects of feminist thought into mainstream capitalist agendas included Gayatri Spivak, the most eminent 'post-colonial' feminist critic, who spent much of the 1990s criticising the failure of Western academics to prioritise institutional sites of cultural agency. She argued that the reduction of cultural knowledge to respect for the recognition of cultural diversity and difference was now itself doing the work of promoting US-led, corporate capitalist interests in the new 'financialisation' of the world. Instead, she suggested: 'There is space for a reconstellation of the Marxist project here, one which analyses the neo-colonial situation as one where systematic economic restructuring, international sub-contracting and new forms of super-exploitation of women are thwarting any hopes for justice under capitalism in an intensified North–South divide'.[41] The feminist critical theorist Nancy Fraser also spent much of that decade deploying Axel Honneth's reformulations of Habermas and the second Frankfurt School to insist on the need for an analytic separation between struggles for recognition for the culturally marginalised and campaigns for redistribution for the economically disadvantaged, however intertwined subordination and exploitation usually became.[42]

These thoughts tell us much about the diverging legacies of seventies feminism. As I argued in *Making Trouble*, just a few women have clambered up the corporate ladder, occasionally reaching the pinnacle of world power. At the very bottom are the many Third World women, on the move horizontally, leaving their own families behind to reach richer countries where they are increasingly needed to perform caring work and domestic chores, as well as sexual servicing. These divergences can be confronted today only from within a more genuinely global perspective than we possessed in the seventies, but that is another story. Yet, since I suggested decades have moveable borders, it is also a story that contains elements of the past, as traditional images of women as second class and vulnerable are reinforced today by those post-colonial labour flows from poorer to wealthier nations, even as professional armies, primarily male, move from richer to poorer countries, flexing old imperial muscles.[43] There is much more to discuss here, including some Islamic women taking to wearing of the veil in what they see as a defiant and empowering personal choice, especially in spaces where they are free to reject it. Difficult as it may seem to translate, these women can perhaps be seen as returning to a very particular way of claiming difference as an empowering identity, not so unlike seventies women, in order to challenge Westernised notions of modernity in the context of current global confrontations.[44] It was the 'seventies' which most vociferously introduced terms like 'personal politics' and 'cultural politics' to encompass the significance of just such shifts in identity, bringing marginalised groups into alliance with others in the political arena. Observing how political allegiance derives from the ways in which collective consciousness is constituted through culture and interpersonal relations at any particular historical moment might surely be seen as one of the most important legacies of the politics of social movements. It is why rethinking and refining the imaginative challenge of 'seventies' feminism remains of interest today.

Notes

1 See S. Rowbotham, H. Wainwright and L. Segal, *Beyond the Fragments: Feminism and the Making of Socialism* (London: Merlin Press, 1980). (Originally published as a pamphlet by Islington Community Press, 1979.)
2 P. Currie, 'Reaching beyond the fragments: women and a new Marxist platform in the SSP', *International Viewpoint*, online magazine, IV440 (September 2011), at www.internationalviewpoint.org/spip.php?article820, accessed 7 November 2011.
3 For a critique of the libertarian politics of the 1970s informing *Beyond the Fragments* see: E. Wilson, 'Beyond the ghetto: thoughts on *Beyond the Fragments: Feminism and the Making of Socialism* by Hilary Wainwright, Sheila Rowbotham and Lynne Segal', *Feminist Review*, 4 (1980), pp. 28–44; M. Farrar, 'The libertarian movement of the 1970s: what can we learn?', *Edinburgh Review*, 82 (winter 1989), pp. 58–74.
4 See L. Segal, *Making Trouble: Life and Politics* (London: Serpent's Tail, 2007). Many of the arguments in this chapter were first aired in that book.
5 A. Beckett, *When the Lights Went Out* (London: Faber & Faber, 2009).
6 A. Rich, 'Towards a woman-centered university', in A. Rich, *Lies, Secrets and Silences: Selected Prose, 1966–1978* (New York: W. W. Norton, 1979), p. 126 (originally written in 1973).
7 J. Mitchell, 'Reflections on twenty years of feminism', in J. Mitchell and A. Oakley (eds), *What Is Feminism?* (Oxford: Blackwell, 1986), pp. 34–48.
8 G.-R. Horn, *The Spirit of '68: Rebellion in Western Europe and North America, 1956–1976* (Oxford: Oxford University Press, 2007).
9 B. Epstein, 'On the origins of the Women's Liberation Movement from a strictly personal perspective', in R. Blau DuPlessis and A. Snitow (eds), *The Feminist Memoir Project: Voices from Women's Liberation* (New York: Three Rivers Press, 1998), p. 175.
10 L. Cagan, 'Something new emerges', in D. Cluster (ed.), *They Should Have Served That Cup of Coffee* (Boston, MA: South End Press, 1979), p. 237.
11 S. Rowbotham, *Promise of a Dream* (London: Penguin, 2000), p. 188.
12 Ellen Willis, reported in A. Popkin, 'The personal is political', in Cluster, *They Should Have Served*, p. 198.
13 Rowbotham, *Promise of a Dream*.
14 J. Mitchell, 'Women: the longest revolution', *New Left Review*, 40 (December 1966), pp. 11–37.
15 Rowbotham, *Promise of a Dream*, p. 209.

16 *Ibid.*, p. 252.
17 J. Olcott, 'Globalizing sisterhood: International Women's Year and the limits of identity politics', in N. Ferguson, C. S. Maier, E. Manela and D. J. Sargent (eds), *The Shock of the Global: The 1970s in Perspective* (Cambridge, MA: Belknap Press/Harvard University Press, 2010), pp. 281–93.
18 L. Segal, *Why Feminism? Gender, Psychology, Politics* (Oxford: Polity Press, 1999).
19 P. Romney, unpublished notes prepared for roundtable discussion, 'Writing about a visionary movement in the "get real" world of the '90s: the history of women's liberation in the United States', 10th Berkshire Women's Conference, North Carolina, June 1996.
20 R. Blau DuPlessis and A. Snitow, 'A feminist memoir project', in DuPlessis and Snitow (eds), *The Feminist Memoir Project*, p. 23. See also K. King, *Theory in Its Feminist Travels: Conversations in U.S. Women's Movements* (Bloomington, IN: Indiana University Press, 1994).
21 M. Tax, 'For the people hear us singing, "Bread and Roses! Bread and Roses"', in DuPlessis and Snitow (eds), *The Feminist Memoir Project*, p. 321.
22 Denise Riley, reply to my circular, 2005, in Segal, *Making Trouble*, p. 133.
23 Cynthia Cockburn, Ursula Huws, both quoted in Segal, *Making Trouble*, pp. 136–7.
24 See my chapter, 'Hearing voices', in Segal, *Making Trouble*, pp. 56–90.
25 S. Rowbotham, *Dreams and Dilemmas* (London: Virago, 1983), pp. 59, 75.
26 *Ibid.*, pp. 32–3.
27 *Ibid.*, p. 218.
28 E. Wilson, *Women and the Welfare State* (London: Tavistock, 1977); M. McIntosh, 'The state and the oppression of women', in A. Kuhn and A. Wolpe (eds), *Feminism and Materialism: Women and Modes of Production* (London: Routledge & Kegan Paul, 1978), pp. 254–89.
29 M. Barrett and M. McIntosh, *The Anti-Social Family* (London: Verso, 1982).
30 See S. Rowbotham, *The Past Is Before Us: Feminism in Action Since the 1960s* (London: Pandora, 1989).
31 Jo Freeman argued this, early on, from her own personal experience in the USA, in her widely read and frequently anthologised 'The tyranny of structurelessness', *Second Wave*, 2:1 (1972), pp. 20–42.
32 M. Dimen, 'In the zone of ambivalence: a journal of competition', in S. Weisser and J. Fleishner (eds), *Feminist Nightmares: Women at Odds* (New York: New York University Press, 1994), p. 362.
33 See C. MacKinnon, *Feminism Unmodified: Discourses on Life and Law* (Cambridge, MA: Harvard University Press, 1987).
34 J. Rees, 'A look back at anger: the Women's Liberation Movement in 1978', *Women's History Review*, 19:3 (2010), pp. 337–56.
35 J. Nestle, 'A fems' feminist history', in DuPlessis and Snitow (eds), *Feminist Memoir Project*, p. 345.
36 V. Amos and P. Parmar, 'Challenging imperial feminism', *Feminist Review*, 17 (*Many Voices, One Chant: Black Feminist Perspectives*) (autumn 1984), p. 5.
37 Quoted in L. Segal, *Making Trouble*, pp. 119–20 (original communication from Marsha Rowe, 23 November 2005).
38 See Beckett, *When the Lights Went Out*, pp. 409–10.
39 As summarised in the introduction to M. Barrett and A. Phillips, *Destabilizing Theory: Contemporary Feminist Debates* (Cambridge: Polity Press, 1992).
40 Segal, *Why Feminism?*
41 Gayatri Chakravorty Spivak, interviewed by Peter Osborne for *Radical Philosophy* in 1994, published as 'Setting to work: transnational cultural studies', in P. Osborne (ed.), *A Critical Sense* (London: Routledge, 1996), p. 166.

42 N. Fraser, 'From redistribution to recognition? Dilemmas of justice in a "post-socialist" age', *New Left Review*, 212 (1995), pp. 68–93.
43 See C. Venn, *The Postcolonial Challenge: Towards Alternative Worlds* (London: Sage, 2006), pp. 157–8.
44 See N. Göle, 'Islam in public: new visibilities and new imaginaries', *Public Culture*, 14:1 (2002), pp. 173–90.

9

Women and the 1970s: towards liberation?

Pat Thane

Real life is not sliced neatly into decades, and the 'sixties' of popular imagination – the riot of cultural change and political activism – did not begin until around 1965/66 and continued to the mid-1970s. Nor did the major cultural changes evident from the later sixties spring from nowhere. They had roots in gradually accumulating change, even through the supposedly dull, conservative 1950s. And the 'seventies' remembered by some, but not all, with gloom, began in the middle of the decade with the 'oil shock' and the international economic crisis and continued through inflation, unemployment and strikes to the election of Margaret Thatcher. This change was reinforced for the left in Britain and elsewhere by the great hope arising from Allende's victory in Chile in 1970, then the misery of the bloody defeat in 1973 and the subsequent international rise of the political right.

At this time, however we slice it chronologically, there were profound cultural and social changes in Britain and other higher-income countries, though their exact dimensions and their origins are still only dimly understood. These included important shifts in women's roles and in gender relations. The Women's Liberation Movement (WLM), of which Lynne Segal evokes her personal experience so vividly in chapter 8, and other movements of the time were both products of and contributors to wider cultural, political and economic shifts.

The pre-history of women's liberation

We begin with Lynne Segal's challenge that we still lack a scholarly analysis of the distinctiveness of the 'surge' of feminism that, as she rightly says, started in the 1960s and continued into the 1970s, and to attempt to historicise it. How did it come about? How and why did it differ from previous British women's movements? What did it lead to?

Women's movements in Britain have a long history, more continuous and more complex than the familiar imagery of a 'first wave' culminating in the partial concession of the vote in 1918, followed by a surprising quiescence until the 'second wave' from around 1968. There was a great deal of activism by women demanding gender equality in the 1920s and 1930s which had largely been forgotten by 1968 and is barely understood today. After 1918, women carried on campaigning, though less colourfully than the pre-First World War suffragettes. There were marches and demonstrations but women did not chain themselves to railings, set fire to post boxes or engage in other spectacular, memorable actions. They felt that the first step of achieving the vote for women aged thirty and above gave them the legitimacy to lobby and to work politically, by quieter constitutional means, but with determination. They fought for equal voting rights with men, that is, at age twenty-one (achieved in 1928); for changes in the law, especially in family law, to gain at last, among other things, equal divorce rights, equal rights to custody of their children and improved support for unmarried mothers and their children, which were achieved between the wars; for improvements in the appalling conditions of housing, health and welfare, thereby contributing to the emergence of the post-Second World War welfare state; and they fought strongly for equal pay and equal opportunities in the workplace, which have still not been achieved, though we have gradually come rather closer. Working-class as well as middle-class women were active, the former especially on welfare and workplace issues concerning women working inside and outside the home.[1] From 1919, women served as magistrates and jurors, and some became lawyers, for the first time, so that women no longer faced isolation in wholly male courtrooms as they had throughout history.[2]

It is likely that there were more women active, on a greater variety of issues, from a wider range of social backgrounds between the wars than before 1918. They were no longer held together by the big overarching campaign for the vote, but this had not been the only issue before 1918. Rather, the vote was seen as the essential first step towards the wider equalities that were needed and so it united many women. Once it was partially achieved, it was time for further steps forward on a range of fronts. There was no single uniting issue, especially after the equal franchise was achieved in 1928, but members of single-issue groups worked and marched together, supported by organisations with a wider remit, such as the National Union of Societies for Equal Citizenship (NUSEC, successor to the National Union of Women's Suffrage Societies) and the National Council of Women (NCW).[3] They campaigned and participated at central- and local-government levels.

Women between the wars put forward ideas that the WLM was later to reproduce, unknowingly it seems: the strong belief, for example, particularly of working-class women in the Labour Party and the large Co-operative Women's Guild, that domestic work in the home was *work*, and as vital to society and the economy as paid employment, not least because it enabled men to work and children to grow up as future workers and contributors to society. They demanded improved workplaces for women, that is, modern, well equipped homes and an eight-hour working day (with eight hours of sleep and eight hours of leisure) – just what men were demanding – as well as improved child-care and social services to relieve women of some of their labour.[4] The 'wages for housework' and nursery campaigns of the 1970s had more in common with interwar demands than later feminists realised.

The 'second wave' women showed no evident awareness of the history of these interwar influences and parallels, though it would be interesting to know to what extent some of them absorbed them and other ambitions, unconsciously, from their mothers, grandmothers and other older women who had been active in, or remembered, earlier movements. This possibly hidden process of transmission between generations would be difficult but interesting to explore. But, in general, the memory of the women's movement of the interwar years and after was lost, or dismissed as liberal, middle-class 'reformist' compromise with a capitalist political system which had served only to reinforce that system. Sheila Rowbotham's influential, invaluable *Hidden From History*, her path-breaking retrieval of hundreds of years of women's history, published in 1973, acknowledged that they 'did use the vote to change the laws; they even, despite the economic conditions of the 1920s and 1930s, accomplished some welfare reforms', that 'their achievement, in their own terms' was not 'negligible'.[5] But they did not, she believed, continue the pre-1918 feminists' 'attack on male-dominated culture as a whole ... no longer in opposition to the structure and culture of capitalist male-dominated society' and 'confined feminism to a series of isolated goals', losing a previous unified vision.[6]

Rowbotham overestimated how widely this 'attack' was shared among pre-1918 feminists and underestimated the vision and the unity of the diverse women's groups of the interwar years. She also underestimated the urgency of the need for better welfare in a period of mass unemployment, severe poverty, malnutrition, bad housing and high death rates, and of legal issues at a time when women did not have equal divorce or custody rights to men. Whatever their political inclinations, it is perhaps understandable that, against this background, women aimed for 'reformist' remedies that seemed (and often were) within their grasp rather than reaching for the more elusive goal of revolution. Ironically, Rowbotham's own writings, including *Hidden From History*, were dismissed as 'reformist' by socialists who regarded feminism itself as a diversion from the road to revolution.[7]

Rowbotham's interpretation was consistent with the politics of leading post-1968 activists: hostile to formal party politics, hostile to reform rather than revolution against both capitalism and male domination, and optimistic that these could, foreseeably, be overthrown. A big difference between the 1960s and the 1920s and '30s was that such revolutionary language could safely be uttered in public, as it could not so soon after the Russian revolution of 1917 without risk of exclusion from public life or even imprisonment. Feminists of the sixties and seventies perhaps did not always appreciate their freedoms compared with their predecessors, and the extent to which these were built on the successful campaigns of their liberal foremothers.

Historians are now more aware than in the 1960s and '70s of the continuing struggle of British women after as well as before 1918 and of what the 'second wave' owed to them. Yet the belief continues that, after the Second World War, the struggle did die out until the late 1960s. Martin Pugh, in an influential textbook, asked whether the 1950s were 'the nadir of feminism?', and he saw feminism as reviving somewhat later in the decade.[8] It has taken historians even longer to get around to serious research on women's movements in the later 1940s, '50s and early '60s than those of the interwar years, or to question the image of the 1950s as just 'conservative, conformist, acquisitive' as Segal describes that decade in the previous chapter in the present volume.

A different picture is beginning to emerge, of continuing activism after the war, though probably on a smaller scale than before. A very active cross-party equal pay campaign, following on from women's strikes for equal pay during the war, led to the introduction of equal pay in the public sector from 1955.[9] A government survey in 1964 found over 100 active women's organisations, including feminist and political groups, professional associations, trade unions, religious bodies and philanthropic organisations, again, as in the 1920s and 1930s, often working together to promote women's causes as well as campaigning individually on their own special issues. The survey concluded that 'they exercise an undoubted influence upon the trend of domestic affairs'.[10] Large women's organisations like the Townswomen's Guilds (200,000 members in 1964) and the Women's Institutes (founded in 1915 by suffragists, reaching a peak of membership, 500,000, in the 1950s[11]) continued to campaign and to lobby government as they had between the wars (when these organisations were more radical than is generally appreciated), among other aims, to provide more and better housing, in view of the postwar housing shortage. They supported the increasing numbers of married women who combined family and paid work by demanding improved childcare, equal pay and equal opportunities in education, training and work, for example in the sciences, where gender inequality was extreme at all levels.[12] They were also concerned with issues arising from the new postwar welfare legislation, pointing out the inequalities women experienced in pension rights, tax allowances and widows' pensions, as well as when divorced or separated, and expressed concern about women's health care and access to birth control information.

Older feminist organisations active between the wars, including the Fawcett Society, the Six Point Group, the Women's Freedom League, the Suffrage Fellowship and the Status of Women Group were still active in the 1960s. From 1966 the Six Point Group and the Fawcett Society initiated alliances between these women's rights groups and others, such as the National Council of Married Women, the National Council for Civil Liberties and women's professional and employment organisations, including the British Federation of Business and Professional Women, the British Federation of University Women, the Association of Headmistresses, the Women's Employment Federation and the Trades Union Congress (TUC) Women's Advisory Committee. Their main aims were equal opportunities in education and work, equal pay, equal taxation and better treatment for unmarried mothers. These liberal feminists encouraged women to join trade unions, supported women's strikes, such as that of women machinists at Ford's Dagenham works in 1968, and joined the Labour movement rally in Trafalgar Square in 1969 organised by the National Joint Action Committee for Women's Rights. They and many others supported the militant campaign by women in Hull from 1968 for better safety standards for men on fishing trawlers following a disaster in which three Hull trawlers sank and fifty-eight men died. This led to the formation of equal rights groups in Hull and elsewhere.[13]

Through the 1960s women became increasingly active along a number of pathways in demanding a public voice and promoting gender equality. Many of the demands were 'reformist' and liberal, but they were necessary and they kept women's public presence and demands for equality alive. The campaigns of the 1950s and the early and mid-1960s seem often to have involved older women, many of them survivors of prewar campaigns, and to have had difficulty in attracting younger women. This was perhaps partly because this was a period of unusually high marriage rates, earlier ages at marriage and rising birth rates, and many younger women were otherwise occupied. But these movements have been little studied.[14] Not all of them survived. The Women's Freedom League closed in 1971, the Open Door Council in 1967 and the National Women's Citizens' Association in 1974.

The 'permissive' sixties

Nor, surprisingly, has there been much study of the background to the unusual spate of liberal legislation passed by Parliament under Harold Wilson's premiership between 1965 and 1970. These included changes as important to women as the Abortion Act 1967, which at last legalised abortion. It followed a long campaign by members of the Abortion Law Reform Association (founded 1934). It worked closely with parliamentarians to manoeuvre the law through Parliament, using methods successfully employed by women's organisations between the wars.[15] Also path breaking was the ruling in the same year that, for the first time, local authorities could provide birth control advice to anyone who requested it (and not only to the respectably married or about to be married, as before) and could provide supplies, such as the newly available birth control pill, free of charge. In 1969 'no fault' divorce was introduced, enabling incompatible couples to end their marriages without undertaking the charade of pretending that one had committed adultery, as had been necessitated by the previous law; and couples gained equal rights to household assets. Thereafter, the proportion of petitions for divorce that were brought by women increased from 58 per cent in 1961–65 to 72 per cent in 1976–80.[16]

The Equal Pay Act 1970 owed much to the continuation of campaigns of the 1950s and before by women in trade unions and the Labour Party, together with feminists in older groups and in the new WLM. From 1967 the Fawcett Society took the lead in coordinating a disparate lobby.[17] The campaign gained from the government's aspiration to join what is now the European Union, which was committed to equal pay and other equalities, following campaigns by women in Europe.[18] It also owed much to the determination of a woman Secretary of State for Employment, Barbara Castle, who introduced the Bill and guided it through the Commons. It gave individuals the right to the same pay and benefits as persons of the opposite sex where both performed 'like work', work 'rated as equivalent under an analytical job evaluation survey' or 'work that is proved to be of equal value'. Claims were to be brought through an employment tribunal and awards for claims upheld could result in back pay of up to two years. The Act was imperfect and compliance by employers was voluntary until 1975. It was drawn up in a hurry and rushed through Parliament before the election of 1970, which Labour lost, and its impact was limited.[19] On one level, it seemed to endorse socialist feminist castigation of the limits of reformism; on another, it suggested the potential for successful collaboration between the disparate strands of feminism.

The changes of the late sixties that benefited women were part of a remarkable, larger wave of liberal legislation which included: the abolition of capital punishment, temporarily in 1965 and permanently in 1969; in 1967, decriminalisation of homosexual relations between partners aged over twenty-one; stricter sanctions against racism introduced in the Race Relations Act 1965; and the Chronically Sick and Disabled Persons Act 1970, which improved provision and removed some of the pervasive discrimination against disabled people. These changes owed something to the emergence of new radical movements from the mid-1960s. For instance, the Campaign Against Racial Discrimination was founded in 1964 and the Disablement Income Group in 1965. The Gay Liberation Movement was not founded until 1970, though the more conventionally campaigning Homosexual Law Reform Association was formed in 1958.[20] The WLM was formed in 1969.

The legal changes and the various campaigns and movements of the time are perhaps best seen as products of profound cultural changes as Britain, along with other higher-income countries, most of which experienced similar changes around the same time, adjusted to an unprecedented postwar experience of sustained prosperity and stability. The precise causes of all the changes remain elusive, but are likely to have been associated with the emergence into maturity of a generation who had grown up since the war, with higher living standards, taking for granted health services and other state welfare provision, better educated, with higher expectations, assuming continuing prosperity and full employment, less deferential than older generations, and whose ideas were promoted by an also less deferential, more populist press.

Out of this background came a variety of new organisations, challenging the status quo, including the Vietnam Solidarity Campaign, the International Marxist Group, intellectual organisations such as the New Left and older, still active groups such as the Campaign for Nuclear Disarmament (CND, founded 1958). More conventionally, but no less significant, new non-governmental organisations emerged, pushing the state to repair the holes in a welfare state which was being shown not to have eliminated poverty. This was especially so after the election of a Labour government in 1964, which it was hoped would continue the development of the welfare state begun by its predecessors between 1945 and 1951. These new activist organisations included: the Child Poverty Action Group (CPAG, founded 1966), demanding improved child benefit (achieved in 1975); Shelter (founded 1966), campaigning for the homeless; and the Disablement Income Group (1965), set up by a woman suffering from multiple sclerosis who discovered that married women not in paid employment had no entitlement to disability benefits. These organisations were generally staffed and supported by a younger, more assertive, media-savvy generation, often graduates in the newly developing social sciences, along with older radicals.[21]

Together, these legal and cultural changes and new organisations and movements set the tone for the seventies, ushering in a culture of more diverse, outspoken political radicalism than Britain had seen for some time, evident, as we will see, in the WLM, among others. It was also a culture more liberal and tolerant of cultural diversity and differing lifestyles, at least on an official level, and increasingly in reality through much of society. There emerged a more diverse and, above all, more open sexual culture in which relationships between people of the same sex or unmarried people of different sexes, and the children of unmarried parents need no longer be hidden, shameful secrets as before. From the early 1970s, divorce rates rose sharply, marriage rates fell, the average age at marriage rose and birth rates declined, while open cohabitation by unmarried couples increased. By 1975, an unprecedented 49 per cent of births were registered by unmarried parents, most of them co-habiting; by 1983 the percentage had risen to 61.3.[22]

None of this sprang up wholly new in the 1960s. It had roots in gradual changes through the 1950s and before, though the coming of the contraceptive pill in the 1960s was an important trigger.[23] The cultural shift was stark and startling to many, though at least as striking was the extent of everyday tolerance of practices deemed deviant and shameful not long before. Of course, the changes sparked moral panics, but the public moralists did not speak for everyone. These changes offered particular freedoms to women, previously the more socially constrained sex. They created a cultural climate that was new in the 1970s but which has lasted to the present.

The women's movement in the seventies

These reflections on previous history are intended to contextualise the post-1968 women's movement and certainly not to diminish its importance and its innovations. The post-1968 'second wave' was different from earlier women's movements, though similar to other radical movements of the day, in its forms of organisation, political affiliations, tactics, many of its objectives and the backgrounds of its activists.

As Lynne Segal describes in chapter 8, its organisation was consciously non-hierarchical, without clearly defined leaders, committees and the formality of many previous organisations. Politically, as she also makes clear, it was aligned strongly with the left, whereas previous women's movements, particularly between the wars, had tended to avoid open political affiliation for fear of arousing opposition to their causes. The post-1968 women were often reacting against the way that women were treated by men on the left, and they identified with international radical movements of the period, though internationalism had always characterised women's movements.[24]

Tactically, they preferred direct action to lobbying and patient negotiation to achieve gender equality through change in the law, which had characterised much previous women's activism, though not of course the militant suffragettes, who were seen as a model. Like other movements of the day, they were critical of, or hostile to, political parties rather than feeling a need to work with them, though more so at national than local level, as Lynne Segal has described in relation to her own local activism.[25]

Their objective was to 'make the personal political', more centrally and explicitly than for their predecessors, and a public issue was made particularly of physical and sexual violence against women. They sought mainly to support poor and excluded women, rather than, as many previous activists had done, both supporting poorer women and seeking property and other legal rights and better education, which more immediately benefited more privileged women. Women of the WLM of course had gained much from the successes of these earlier campaigns, which gave them a more secure background from which they could demand more equalities.

Women activists in the past had also campaigned against domestic violence and physical abuse of women and children. In the late nineteenth century, Frances Power Cobbe and others campaigned against domestic violence – 'wife torture' as Cobbe called it. They achieved less than they hoped but they did influence the Matrimonial Causes Act 1878, which allowed a woman for the first time to separate legally from an abusive husband and to oblige him to pay maintenance to herself and her children – provided that she was not guilty of adultery.[26] Between the wars also there were very active campaigns against physical and sexual abuse, but in those days it was considered improper to discuss sexual matters in public and they were referred to in such coded language that it is easy to overlook the nature of the activism and the passions which inspired it. One way that these activists hoped to bring about change was by the appointment of women to the police force for the first time, so that abused women could take their problems to, hopefully sympathetic, policewomen.[27] They succeeded in getting women appointed to the police, but in small numbers, and the problems of domestic violence and rape did not disappear or, so far as we can tell, diminish.

A real and lasting achievement of the 'second wave' was to give rape and domestic violence public names, to put the reality of these issues on the public agenda, from which they have never since disappeared – though nor unfortunately have these crimes against women disappeared.

They created new means to support women victims by setting up refuges for victims of domestic violence and rape crisis centres. They were able to do these things partly because of the shift in the cultural climate towards greater openness and less secrecy about sexual matters, so that they could be discussed in public and the press would print them without fear of prosecution for obscenity. And they had the support of left-wing politicians, especially at local level, in some places at least, who funded refuges and rape crisis centres. In the 1970s, local government still had some power and independence from central government and, as Lynne Segal has described, feminists and other radicals could work with some local authorities on this and other issues, including improving housing provision. This local autonomy was to be severely eroded by the Thatcher governments of the 1980s, not least in retribution for some of them supporting radical causes in the 1970s, notably the Greater London Council, which was disbanded in 1986.

In supporting poorer women in the workplace, such as night-cleaners, the 'second wave' women were less different from their predecessors, many of them working women themselves, who were active from the late nineteenth century in promoting women's trade unionism and seeking improvements in the working conditions of low-paid women.

The backgrounds of many women activists of the 'second wave' were different from those of their predecessors, partly in that they came out of a very different cultural climate and a different economic situation. They were mostly younger women who had grown up in the relative prosperity of Britain since the end of the war. Like their predecessors, they seem to have been mainly, though not exclusively, middle class in origin, and white, with fewer coming from the aristocratic elite – or if they did, they kept quiet about it in left-wing feminist circles in the seventies. They were likely to be better educated than earlier activists, more likely to have gone to university – though we should not overstress this, for in the mid-1970s only around 7 per cent of those aged eighteen to twenty-one went to university in the UK and only about 30 per cent of these were female.[28] Hence the continuing campaigns for equal educational opportunities.

The women of WLM perhaps felt less need to campaign on some of the issues that preoccupied earlier generations because many of these seemed to have been resolved, now that there was a welfare state and, at least in principle, better access to education for women; inequalities in property and family law, including divorce and custody law, had been removed, birth control was available free of charge from local clinics and abortion was legal. They were free to take up new causes, with new tactics.

How did the WLM come into being? It had many sources. One route was that followed by some historians who were active in establishing the founding Women's Liberation workshop in 1970. Lynne Segal took a complementary route, more focused upon contemporary issues, for example local government and housing, in which, of course, the historians were also involved. Historians were prominent in the early days of the British WLM perhaps because of the existence already of a strong left-wing strand among British historians, with which the women identified, though increasingly critically. E. P. Thompson, Eric Hobsbawm and Christopher Hill were already prominent in the late 1960s, though they were not always sympathetic to feminism. More sympathetic was History Workshop, a movement of left-wing historians which sought to include a broad range of people outside as well as inside the academy, which began in 1966 at Ruskin College, Oxford, led by Raphael Samuel.

History Workshop led directly to the formation of the British WLM. Historians, particularly Sheila Rowbotham, Anna Davin and Sally Alexander, who became leading figures in the WLM, were very active in History Workshop. Anna Davin has described how, as a mature student of history at the University of Warwick, 1965–69, she became active in the university women's group, which was closely affiliated to the socialist group. She was also active in History Workshop. Women increasingly wanted to discuss women's history at History Workshop meetings, which caused some tensions. These came to a head at the 1969 meeting, at the end of which Sheila Rowbotham suggested that women who wanted to discuss women's history should hold a meeting of their own. Some men laughed! Anna Davin reproached them and some apologised. The women held their meeting, out of which came the first Women's Liberation workshop, also held at Ruskin College, in 1970. According to Davin, there were tensions around that also, between those who wanted to focus on women's history and those concerned with more contemporary issues. In the end, the first workshop combined the two. It was a major success – the organisers expected 300 women and 600 turned up.[29]

Again, this built on previous action. By 1969 there were already seventy local women's liberation groups in London,[30] and others followed in towns and cities throughout Britain, some inspired by similar movements in the USA and Europe.[31] The national workshop met annually from 1970, reaching an attendance of 3,000 in 1977. But as it grew, so did the diversity of interests represented and tensions resulted, especially between socialist feminists, who believed that capitalism was the enemy to be defeated, and radical feminists, who regarded male dominance as the main threat. The last national workshop was in 1978. It ended in some acrimony, but feminists of different persuasions continued to work together on specific issues.

Many of the women historians active in WLM, including Sally Alexander, Anna Davin and Sheila Rowbotham, had careers as historians, though not for a long time in universities (and Davin never on a permanent basis); rather, at first they taught mainly in evening classes and colleges of further education. This was partly politically motivated, by the desire to speak to a wider, less privileged, audience, but also at that time women were a beleaguered minority in university posts, with very few in senior positions and it was not easy to get university jobs. It is a sign of progress that many of the women activists ended their careers as university professors (though Sheila Rowbotham in sociology, not history), entering university posts relatively late in life, in the late 1980s and '90s, when universities became more receptive, though often, initially at least, in less prestigious universities.

Such professional advances for women were an important longer-run outcome of the 'second wave' movement and the wider feminist currents of the time. Also, as Lynne Segal suggests, women and the study of women and gender became, gradually, accepted in universities. The 1980s saw a wave of publications on the past and present of women and gender relations, much of it the outcome of work that had developed through the seventies. They were much assisted by the feminist publishing company Virago Press, established by women in 1973. Its first publication was *Fenwomen*, by historian Mary Chamberlain. It went on to publish invaluable source material in women's history, such as letters detailing the lives of working women, collected by the Co-operative Women's Guild in 1915,[32] as well as lost women's novels, new feminist writing and such works as the autobiography of the working-class suffragette and Manchester councillor Hannah Mitchell.[33] Published as low-cost paperbacks, these helped to spread the feminist message, increased appreciation of women's contribution to literature and to history, and greatly assisted the teaching of women's and gender studies at all levels.

Feminists played an important part in the continuing campaigns for equal pay, against sexual and domestic violence and against discrimination generally. Though some may have disliked parliamentary processes, many of them joined the pressure which led to the Sex Discrimination Act 1975. Few women of any strand of feminism were satisfied with the 1970 Equal Pay Act. Some employers found inventive ways to evade it, such as re-grading male workers who did the same work as women (for example, shop assistants) so that their status apparently changed although their work and pay (and that of the women) did not. But it was not wholly ineffective. An Office of Manpower study in 1971 found that in about 20 per cent of national agreements and Wages Council orders covering manual workers, discrimination had been removed or was on track for removal by 1973, in most cases by levelling women's pay up.[34] Ten years later, a team from the London School of Economics found that women's relative pay had increased by about 15 per cent (compared with the 46 per cent gender gap in 1969) across all sectors and industries.[35] There were some real improvements in the seventies, though they fell far short of feminist aspirations.

Between 1970 and 1972 liberal feminist groups worked with parliamentarians to introduce wider-ranging anti-discrimination legislation, leading to some unsuccessful parliamentary bills. When Labour returned to government in 1974 feminists of all strands, along with trade unionists and the National Council for Civil Liberties, worked with and lobbied Labour to devise effective legislation. Again, the influence of the European Economic Community, which Britain had joined in 1973, made a difference.[36]

The outcome was the Sex Discrimination Act 1975. This outlawed discrimination on the basis of sex in employment, education and advertising and in the provision of housing, goods, services or facilities. At last, married women no longer needed their husband's agreement to sign a hire purchase or any other financial agreement, even when they had independent earnings. The Act established the Equal Opportunities Commission to oversee implementation and with powers of investigation.

The new law was soon criticised, especially by left-wing feminists, for not going far enough and the Commission was criticised for not being active enough. It certainly took a while to get into its stride. It became more effective in the eighties, successfully supporting women who took equal pay cases to the European courts, having failed in the British judicial system, investigating claimed abuses and helping to bring about amendments to the legislation which strengthened sanctions against discrimination.[37] Among other things, the Sex Discrimination Act brought real improvements in women's opportunities in education and in certain professions. It successfully put pressure on Oxford and Cambridge colleges at last to give in to co-education, like all other British universities, though it did not oblige them to do so.[38] The strict gender quotas which restricted women's entry to medical schools and the less formal but severe barriers to equality in the legal profession were dismantled. In 1971 women were just 4 per cent of all lawyers, by 1990 27 per cent. In medical schools the proportion of women grew from a small minority to over 50 per cent by the 1990s.[39] As we have seen, there was slow progress for women in university posts, though it was still barely discernible in the 1970s, and progress was still slower at higher levels of management in business and finance. But at least there were signs of change.

There were still fewer improvements for women in lower-paid, lower-skilled work, in particular due to the economic crisis and growing unemployment of the mid-1970s. This caused problems especially for the growing numbers of lone mothers, resulting from the spread of divorce, separation and the choice by some women to raise children alone. The proportion of lone parents (overwhelmingly mothers) rose from 7.5 per cent of all families with dependent children in 1971, to 10.7 per cent in 1981, to 17.5 per cent in 1991.[40] The downside of the freedoms created by the pill, the legislation of the late 1960s and the wider cultural shifts of which they were part was that women generally had significantly lower incomes than men following a partnership break-up[41] and were far more likely to be caring for children on their own, sometimes without financial support from the father.

The growing number of lone mothers led to increased pressure on the Labour government to improve provision for them, from organisations such as the Child Poverty Action Group and the older One Parent Families (founded by feminists in 1918 as the National Council for the Unmarried Mother and her Child and working ever since to support this stigmatised group)[42] supported by women from the various strands of feminism. The outcome was that from 1975 child benefit was raised for all children, with an additional benefit for lone-parent families. The rules on supplementary benefit for lone parents were relaxed to enable them to earn more in addition to benefit. From 1977, unmarried mothers could at last qualify for council housing (leading to their being accused of becoming pregnant in order to qualify). All mothers gained from the introduction of statutory maternity leave in 1975, giving a right to eleven weeks' leave before birth and twenty-nine weeks after at 90 per cent of their pay for six weeks and statutory sick pay for the remainder, subject to their having worked for specified period.[43] At the same time, it became illegal to dismiss a woman because she was pregnant. These, along with improved pensions and other changes, were all features of real improvements in the welfare system under the 1974–79 Labour governments, despite the economic crisis, though many of them were not long to survive the change of government in 1979. Despite scepticism about reform, feminists and other radical groups engaged with the state to achieve further improvements, including encouraging innovative movements such as claimants' unions, to assist welfare claimants to gain and defend their rights.

Another change in the law which benefited many women was the Domestic Violence and Matrimonial Proceedings Act 1976. This for the first time enabled a wife to obtain a court injunction against a violent husband. This was decidedly an outcome of pressure from feminists. The first refuge for 'battered wives', as they were often called at the time, was established in Chiswick in 1972 by Erin Pizzey, who gained much media attention. There was a great deal of local action on the issue. By 1975, a total of 111 local groups were campaigning and by 1980 about 200 women's refuges were in operation. The National Women's Aid Federation (NWAF) was established to coordinate activity, with branches throughout Britain, based on the principles of local autonomy, open-door policies at all refuges (no woman would be turned away) and the rights of women residents to self-determination. The NWAF gave expert evidence to the House of Commons Select Committee which laid the groundwork for the 1976 Act.[44]

Campaigns against physical and sexual violence against women continued after the law was changed. The first rape crisis centre opened in London also in 1976. In 1977 came the first 'Reclaim the Night' march, asserting the right of women to move around safely at all times. Such campaigning was much needed. The violence did not go away. Still in 2008–10, on average 167 women were raped every day in the UK and only one in five attacks was reported to the police; one woman in four was likely to experience domestic violence at some point in her life; and two women were murdered every week by a partner or ex-partner.[45]

Above all, the WLM made feminism public again, partly through flamboyant events like the dramatic disruption of the televised Miss World event at the Albert Hall in 1970. The public sexual objectification of women was another target of the movement. The wider effects in raising women's (and men's) consciousness of gender inequalities, outside WLM's own consciousness-raising groups, is hard to judge, but there were signs of growing public activism among women of all backgrounds, whether or not they called themselves feminist, and of somewhat more widespread sensitivity to gender issues. Among other manifestations, working women resisted continuing poor treatment. In 1974, some 600 Asian workers, mainly female, went on strike at the Imperial Typewriter Company in Leicester against low pay and poor conditions of work, but white workers at the factory and their union refused to support them.[46] There were signs of progress by 1976, when more than 130 mainly Asian female staff of the Grunwick photo-processing firm in Willesden, north London, came out on strike, again over pay and conditions, including forced overtime, and the refusal of the owner to allow them to join a union. This time they were supported by the Trades Union Congress, by white workers, including in other occupations, by feminists of all persuasions and by Labour politicians. As the 1970s went on, trade unions became more supportive of gender and race protests in the workplace. The strike was widely publicised but, after two years, it failed. The militantly right-wing owner, supported by right-wing political groups, was intransigent: 130 workers had been sacked, none were reinstated and no trade union was recognised.[47]

Organisation among black and Asian women increased during the 1970s in other ways. Immigration had reached a peak in the 1960s before restrictions were introduced in 1968 by the Labour government, following increasing racial tensions. This was somewhat tempered by the strengthening of race relations legislation in the same year and the establishment of the Community Relations Commission, though sanctions against discrimination remained weak. In the seventies, women of immigrant backgrounds were perhaps more confident in challenging discrimination, bad working conditions and violence against women within their own communities. This had support from white feminists, though black women complained that WLM marginalised their interests.

The Organisation of Women of Asian and African Descent (OWAAD) was formed in 1978, by female students, to bring women together nationally. Southall Black Sisters was founded in 1979 to meet the needs of Asian and Afro-Caribbean women, in particular to support them against violence. Also in the late 1970s, Brixton Black Women, Liverpool Black Sisters, the Manchester Black Women's Co-op, Baheno Women's Organisation in Leicester and other groups were established. The first national black women's conference, organised by OWAAD, was held in 1979, with 250 women attending. It led to the formation of more local groups.[48] The women of WLM, despite their good intentions, often had difficulty connecting with women of other classes and races, hence the emergence of separate organisations of black women in a society in which racial divisions were still acute.

Afterwards

In the less hospitable atmosphere of the 1980s, with the first, distinctly non-feminist, woman Prime Minister, feminism had a lower profile and the WLM fragmented. This was probably due less to internal divisions than to the difficulties of sustaining such a movement in the new political climate. But their aspirations survived. Many feminists turned to more orthodox party politics, especially at local level, judging this the most effective way forward. The Greater London Council (GLC) funded a number of women's groups and projects and set up the first Local Government Women's Committee to give women a formal voice in decision-making. In 1984 it spent almost £8 million on gender equality activities, in addition to expenditure on efforts to improve race relations in the capital. There were similar successes in Edinburgh and elsewhere, usually where there were Labour-controlled councils, but the abolition of the GLC in 1986 demonstrated the fragility of such successes. They lasted longer in Scotland, where Conservatism was weak.[49] At national level, the opposition was so seriously divided, and the government so unreceptive, through the 1980s that feminists could make little impact until the 1990s.

An important eventual outcome was the shift of the Labour Party to all-women shortlists in 1997, following campaigns by women in the party, which led at last to the election of a significant number of women to Parliament in 1997, though mainly for one party, Labour.

Also, feminists took advantage of the constitutional changes in Wales and Scotland in 1999 to ensure that the newly created electoral systems enabled the better representation of women, with the result that by 2003 Wales was the only country in the world with gender equality among its elected representatives; and women were almost 40 per cent of Members of the Scottish Parliament. Change in the Westminster Parliament was much slower. Following the 2010 election women were only 21.5 per cent of MPs, and they were still heavily concentrated in the Labour Party. There were strong continuities in personnel between the WLM and these political activists.[50]

Conclusion

Some permanent changes for the better, such as these, came out of the women's movement of the 1960s and 1970s. Because they were not immediate, they are often overlooked. From the perspective of women's opportunities and gender relations, it is hard to be seriously negative about the seventies. The hopes of many feminists for a revolution in gender relations were not realised, then or since. What did occur was closer to the expectations of more moderate feminists: continued steady, slow but somewhat accelerating, progress towards equal opportunities in work and education, equal pay and, to a lesser degree, in the home. Females grew up with higher expectations, more often encouraged by parents who were less likely to assume that marriage was the only future for a woman, not least because marriage was much less secure. Women were less often objects of taken-for-granted disparagement, though private behaviour changed less in some quarters and problems of sexual and physical violence against women hardly diminished.

The positive changes owed at least as much to the militants as to the moderate feminists. Like the militant suffragettes, they made inequalities that had for too long been brushed aside into inescapable public issues and gave support and strength to women aspiring to challenge discrimination and disadvantage. They provided a framework which enabled the tactics of liberal reformers to achieve some successes. Throughout the history of women's movements, the different strands have coexisted, operating in different spheres at different times, sometimes cooperating, sometimes not, each more active and influential at different conjunctures. In the seventies it was the turn of the militants and they did a lot more good than harm. The same might be said of the other new movements of the seventies. Homophobia and racism have by no means disappeared but they are far less pervasive, and are subject to stricter legal controls, than in earlier times, and seeds of resistance to other forms of discrimination, on the grounds of disability and age for example, were sown and have grown. Peter Hall has rightly described the 1970s as a 'marketplace for ideas', many of which did not go away even in the inhospitable atmosphere of the 1980s.

Notes

1   C. Law, *Suffrage and Power: The Women's Movement, 1918–28* (London: I. B. Tauris, 1997); J. Alberti, *Beyond Suffrage: Feminists at War and Peace, 1914–28* (London: Macmillan, 1989); P. Thane, 'What difference did the vote make?', in A. Vickery (ed.), *Women, Privilege and Power: British Politics, 1750 to the Present* (Stanford, CA: Stanford University Press, 2001), pp. 253–88; P. Thane, 'The women of the British Labour Party and feminism, 1906–1945', in H. L. Smith (ed.), *British Feminism in the Twentieth Century* (Aldershot: Elgar, 1990), pp. 124–43.

2   A. Logan, *Feminism and Criminal Justice: A Historical Perspective* (Basingstoke: Palgrave, 2009).

3   Law, *Suffrage and Power*; Thane, 'What difference'.

4   Thane, 'The women of the British Labour Party'.

5   S. Rowbotham, *Hidden From History: 300 Years of Women's Oppression and the Fight Against It* (London: Pluto, 1973), p. 161.

6   *Ibid.*, p. 162.

7   L. Segal, 'A local experience', in S. Rowbotham, L. Segal and H. Wainwright, *Beyond the Fragments: Feminism and the Making of Socialism* (London: Merlin, 1979), p. 158.

8   M. Pugh *Women and the Women's Movement in Britain* (London: Macmillan, 2nd edition, 2000), pp. 284–311.

9   H. L. Smith, 'The problem of "equal pay for equal work" in Great Britain during World War II', *Journal of Modern History*, 53:4 (1981), pp. 652–72; H. L. Smith 'The politics of Conservative reform: the equal pay for equal work issue, 1945–1955', *Historical Journal*, 35:2 (1992), pp. 401–15; P. Thane, 'Towards equal opportunities? Women in Britain since 1945', in T. Gourvish and A. O'Day (eds), *Britain Since 1945* (London: Macmillan, 1991), pp. 183–91; C. Beaumont, 'Housewives, workers and citizens: voluntary women's organisations and the campaigns for women's rights in England and Wales during the post-war period', in N. Crowson, M. Hilton and J. McKay (eds), *NGOs in Contemporary Britain: Non-State Actors in Society and Politics Since 1945* (Basingstoke: Palgrave Macmillan, 2009), pp. 67–9.

10   Beaumont, 'Housewives', p. 59.

11   M. Andrews, *The Acceptable Face of Feminism: The Women's Institute as a Social Movement* (London: Lawrence & Wishart, 1997).

12   Thane, 'Towards equal opportunities?', pp. 200–1.

13   E. Meehan, 'British feminism from the 1960s to the 1980s', in Smith (ed.), *British Feminism*, pp. 192–3.

14   But see Beaumont, 'Housewives'; J. Freeguard, 'It's time for women of the 1950s to stand up and be counted' (unpublished DPhil thesis, University of Sussex, 2004); C. Backford, 'Ideas, structures and practices of feminism, 1939–1964' (unpublished PhD thesis, University of East London, 1996).

15   M. D. Kandiah and G. Staerck (eds), *The Abortion Act 1967*, Institute for Contemporary British History Witness Seminar Programme (London: Institute for Contemporary British History, 2002) transcript of a seminar in London, 10

July 2001, at King's College London, at www.kcl.ac.uk/innovation/groups/ich/ witness/archives/PDFfiles/AbortionAct1967.pdf, accessed 10 November 2011.

16 D. Coleman 'Population and family', in A. H. Halsey and J. Webb (eds), *Twentieth Century Social Trends* (London: Macmillan, 2000), p. 62.

17 Meehan, 'British feminism', pp. 195–6.

18 J. Lovenduski, *Women and European Politics: Contemporary Feminism and Public Policy* (Brighton: Wheatsheaf, 1986).

19 A. Zabalza and Z. Tzannatos, *Women and Equal Pay: The Effects of Legislation on Female Employment and Wages in Britain* (Cambridge: Cambridge University Press, 1985).

20 A. Holden, *Makers and Manners: Politics and Morality in Post-War Britain* (London: Methuen, 2004); J. Weeks, *Sex, Politics and Society: The Regulation of Sexuality Since 1800* (Harlow: Longman, 1981); J. Weeks, *Coming Out: Homosexual Politics in Britain from the Nineteenth Century to the Present* (London: Quartet, 1990).

21 P. Thane, 'Voluntary action in Britain since Beveridge', in N. Deakin and M. Oppenheimer (eds), *Beveridge and Voluntary Action in Britain and the Wider British World* (Manchester: Manchester University Press, 2010), pp. 121–34; T. Evans, 'Stopping the poor getting poorer: the establishment and professionalization of poverty NGOs, 1945–95', in Crowson *et al.* (eds), *NGOs in Contemporary Britain*, pp. 147–63.

22 Coleman, 'Population and family', pp. 51–4; P. Thane, *Happy Families? History and Family Policy* (London: British Academy, 2010).

23 H. Cook, *The Long Sexual Revolution: English Women, Sex and Contraception, 1800–1975* (Oxford: Oxford University Press, 2004).

24 K. Offen (ed.), *Globalizing Feminisms, 1789–1945* (London: Routledge, 2010).

25 L. Segal, 'A local experience', pp. 157–210.

26 L. Williamson, *Power and Protest: Frances Power Cobbe and Victorian Society* (London: Rivers Oram Press, 2005), pp. 78–85; F. P. Cobbe, 'Wife-torture in England', *Contemporary Review*, 33 (April–July 1878), pp. 55–87.

27 L. A. Jackson, *Women Police: Gender, Welfare and Surveillance in the Twentieth Century* (Manchester: Manchester University Press, 2006).

28 C. Dyhouse, *Students: A Gendered History* (London: Routledge, 2006), p. 99.

29 A. Davin, *The Women's Liberation Network Workshop* (London: Women's Library, November 2008).

30 E. Setch, 'The Women's Liberation Movement in Britain, 1969–1979: organization, creativity and debate' (unpublished PhD thesis, Royal Holloway, University of London, 2000). Setch mainly focuses on London.

31 Meehan, 'British feminism', pp. 193–4.

32 M. Llewelyn Davies, *Maternity: Letters from Working Women* (London: Virago, 1978).

33 G. Mitchell (ed.), *The Hard Way Up: The Autobiography of Hannah Mitchell, Suffragette and Rebel* (London: Virago, 1977), 'Introduction' by Sheila Rowbotham.

34 G. L. Buckingham, *What To Do About Equal Pay For Women* (London: Gower, 1973).

35 Zabalza and Tzannatos, *Women and Equal Pay*.

36 Lovenduski, *Women and European Politics*.

37 H. McCarthy, 'Gender equality', in P. Thane (ed.), *Unequal Britain: Equalities in Britain Since 1945* (London: Continuum, 2010), pp. 112–15.

38 Dyhouse, *Students*, pp. 155–71.

39 Women and Equality Unit, *Key Indicators of Women's Position in Britain* (London: UK Government, Department of Trade and Industry, 2001), p. 83.

40 K. Kiernan, H. Land and J. Lewis, *Lone Motherhood in Twentieth Century Britain* (Oxford: Oxford University Press, 1998), p. 22.
41 *Ibid.*, pp. 138–41.
42 P. Thane, 'Unmarried motherhood in twentieth century England', *Women's History Review*, 20:1 (2011), pp. 11–31.
43 P. Thane and T. Evans, *Sinners? Scroungers? Saints? Unmarried Motherhood in Twentieth Century England* (Oxford: Oxford University Press, 2012).
44 Lovenduski, *Women and European Politics*, p. 78.
45 Statistics taken from www.womensaid.org.uk/domestic_violence, accessed 26 August 2011.
46 A. Coote, 'An unresolved strike', *Guardian*, 12 July 1974, reprinted in K. Cochrane (ed.), *Women of the Revolution: Forty Years of Feminism* (London: Guardian Books, 2010), pp. 21–5.
47 A. Wilson, 'Finding a voice: Asian women in Britain', in H. Safra Mirza (ed.), *Black British Feminism* (London: Routledge, 1997), pp. 31–5.
48 Brixton Black Women's Group, 'Black women organizing', *Feminist Review*, 17 (autumn 1984), pp. 84–8.
49 McCarthy, 'Gender equality', p. 115.
50 E. Breitenbach and P. Thane (eds), *Women and Citizenship in Britain and Ireland in the Twentieth Century: What Difference Did the Vote Make?* (London: Continuum, 2010).

10

Stanley Cohen's *Folk Devils and Moral Panics* revisited

Bill Osgerby

In December 1976 Sex Pistols guitarist Steve Jones sparked one of the decade's biggest media furores when he called presenter Bill Grundy 'a fucking rotter' on live TV. The band were appearing on *Today*, Thames Television's early-evening news show, ostensibly to promote their debut single, 'Anarchy in the UK'. However, baited by Grundy, *Today*'s cantankerous host, the Pistols sneered, swore and made themselves as disruptive as possible. The interview was barely ninety seconds long, and the band's insults were jokey, but the impact was seismic. The following morning the tabloid press frothed with outrage. A flurry of histrionic headlines ('The Filth and the Fury',[1] 'The Punk Horror Show'[2]) cast the Pistols as the leaders of a new, malevolent youth cult – punk rock – while nervous promoters cancelled their concerts, radio stations blacklisted their single and the band was unceremoniously dropped by its record company.

Many tabloid readers were, no doubt, alarmed by the ensuing coverage of punk rock and the Sex Pistols. The *Sunday People*, for example, ran a three-week feature series that presented punk as 'dangerous', 'sick' and 'sinister'; the *Sunday Mirror* called for a robust public response with its headline 'Punish the Punks'; and throughout 1977 the British media were peppered with sensationalist stories about punk music and its followers.[3] However, readers of Stanley Cohen's *Folk Devils and Moral Panics*, originally published in 1972, may have had an eerie sense of déjà vu. Cohen's book analysed an earlier episode from the annals of British youth culture, but one which seemed remarkably similar to 1970s punk in terms of the media responses it elicited. Taking as his focus the 'battles' that flared during the early 1960s between the Italian-suited mods and their leather-clad, motorcycle-riding rivals, the rockers, Cohen explored the relation between the events and their coverage in the press. Highlighting the exaggeration and distortion endemic to newspaper portrayals of mods and rockers, Cohen argued that the press outcry had generated a level of public concern that was out of all proportion to the actual threat. The overblown social alarm, Cohen contended, constituted a moment of 'moral panic' in his classic (and oft-cited) description of the phenomenon:

> Societies appear to be subject, every now and then, to periods of moral panic. A condition, episode, person or group of persons emerges to become defined as a threat to societal values and interests; its nature is presented in a stylised and stereotypical fashion by the mass media; the moral barricades are manned by editors, bishops, politicians and other right-thinking people; socially accredited experts pronounce their diagnoses and solutions; ways of coping are evolved or (more often) resorted to; the condition then disappears, submerges or deteriorates and becomes more visible. Sometimes the object of the panic is quite novel and at other times it is something which has been in existence long enough, but suddenly appears in the limelight.[4]

For Cohen, then, the concept of 'moral panic' denoted processes through which the media contributed to the escalation of social events through misrepresenting and magnifying the activities of real or imagined deviant groups – or what he referred to as 'folk devils'. In these terms, overdramatic and angst-ridden press reports fanned the sparks of an initially trivial incident, creating a self-perpetuating 'amplification spiral' which steadily escalated the social significance of the original phenomenon. Youth culture, Cohen argued, had been especially central to these outbursts of disproportionate dread. Since 1945, he contended, youth groups had 'occupied a constant position as folk devils' – Teddy boys, mods and rockers, skinheads and hippies all lining up in the 'gallery of types that society erects to show its members which roles should be avoided and which should be emulated'.[5]

As many authors have observed, the media debacle surrounding the Sex Pistols and punk rock during the late 1970s can easily be seen as an entry in the roster of Britain's moral panics.[6] Indeed, the whole decade has sometimes been seen as punctuated by a series of media-driven panics amid a pervasive sense of conflict. Most famously, Stuart Hall and his colleagues drew on Cohen's ideas in *Policing the Crisis*, their influential study of politics, policing and the media.[7] For Hall and his associates, the 1970s saw a structural shift in British social and political life as the country was wracked by economic decline and ideological confrontation. Against this backdrop, they argued, a media-orchestrated moral panic surrounding street crime operated as a symbol for an expansive sense of national crisis and decline, and served as a foundation on which popular support was recruited for a more authoritarian form of political state. As Hall and his team put it, Britain during the 1970s was 'battening itself down for "the long haul" through a crisis':

> There is light at the end of the tunnel – but not much; and it is far off. Meanwhile, the State has won the right, and indeed inherited the duty, to move swiftly, to stamp fast and hard, to listen in, discreetly survey, saturate and swamp, charge or hold without charge, act on suspicion, hustle and shoulder, to keep society on the straight and narrow. Liberalism, that last back-stop against arbitrary power, is in retreat. It is suspended. The times are exceptional. The crisis is real. We are inside the 'law-and-order' state.[8]

Subsequent shifts in the social and political landscape, alongside developments in media and cultural analysis, mean the arguments advanced in both *Folk Devils and Moral Panics* and *Policing the Crisis* have to be re-evaluated and revised. Nevertheless, their impact is incontestable. The notion of moral panic, in particular, has wielded considerable influence and has been invoked in studies of media responses to a plethora of perceived social ills, stretching from soccer violence and 'video nasties' to AIDS and child abuse. The term, moreover, has increasingly seeped out of the academy to inform journalistic discourse and public debate more generally. Following the rioting that swept through London, Manchester and other British cities in August 2011, for example, a blogger writing for the *Independent* warned that 'Victorian-style moral panic debates' were surfacing in political responses to the disturbances,[9] while the *Daily Mail* reported that Lord Macdonald, the former Director of Public Prosecutions, had 'urged judges to avoid the "moral panic" elsewhere in society when sentencing those involved in the riots and looting'.[10] Indeed, Cohen himself has estimated that the number of citations of 'moral panic' in British newspapers grew from a total of just eight between 1984 and 1991 (inclusive) to an average of 109 per year from 1994 to 2001,[11] leading him to reflect that contemporary episodes of moral panic have seen the media become more self-reflective in their coverage, so that 'the same public and media discourse that provides the raw evidence of moral panic [also] uses the concept as first-order description, reflexive comment or criticism'.[12] The concept of moral panic, then, is relevant to issues beyond the analysis of British media, politics and society during the 1960s and 1970s. It has also become central to many attempts – made not only by academics, but by growing numbers of politicians, journalists and cultural commentators – to understand the development of public opinion and social attitudes, and to interrogate the way these can be moulded and manipulated by the state, the media and moral crusaders.

'The times they are a-changin'': intellectual ferment and the National Deviancy Symposium

Although *Folk Devils and Moral Panics* was first published in 1972, according to its author the term 'moral panic' actually 'very much belongs to the distinctive voice of the late Sixties'.[13] The book itself was based on Cohen's PhD thesis, written at the London School of Economics in 1967–69, and was constituent in a broad wellspring of new theoretical perspectives that took shape during the late 1960s, reaching fruition in the following decade. As Cohen's close colleague Jock Young explains, these developments were embedded in their historical context. 'The sudden outburst of intellectual output occurring in the period 1968–75', he argues, was not so much a series of abstract theoretical debates as a set of 'strident signals of the change into modernity occurring in the world surrounding the academy'.[14] The period was characterised by political, social and cultural convulsions as the escalation of the Vietnam War, the rise of student protest and new counter-cultural movements, together with the emergence of a strident second-wave feminism all raised sharp questions about the status quo. And, as Young emphasises, the rising generation of British sociologists was profoundly shaped by this milieu. 'We were all', he remembers, 'moved by the times: the possibility of change, the worlds of diversity that the new bohemia promised, the youthful colonisation of leisure and the rejection of austerity and discipline in a world seemingly in fast-forward, all of which made the choice of being on the side of progress well-nigh inevitable'.[15] This was a cohort of young academics, then, who were fierce critics of conservatism, the establishment and the forces of social control. Instead, they allied themselves with radical political activism and the emerging subcultures of youth. As David Garland puts it:

> This was the outlook of the hip, deviance-appreciating, participant observer who was often culturally closer to deviants than to their controllers, and who saw criminal law as a misplaced form of repression, at least as it applied to the soft deviance of drug taking and sub-cultural style. In the face of what they regarded as uninformed, intolerant and unnecessarily repressive reactions to deviance by conservative authorities, these sociologists developed a standard critical response, a critique with which to counter oppressive social reaction.[16]

It was a critique that found focus with the formation of the National Deviancy Symposium (soon renamed the National Deviancy Conference, NDC) in July 1968. The NDC was formed as a radical breakaway from the Third National Conference of Teaching and Research on Criminology at the University of Cambridge. Infused by the rebellious spirit of the era, seven Young Turks of British sociology – Kit Carson,

Stanley Cohen, David Downes, Mary McIntosh, Paul Rock, Ian Taylor and Jock Young – renounced the mainstream criminological research then dominated by the Home Office and the Institute of Criminology, based at Cambridge. For the NDC gunslingers, this criminological establishment was pervaded by positivist and empirically fixated assumptions which effectively bolstered existing mechanisms of social control. In place of this orthodoxy, the NDC looked towards more challenging accounts of the social world.

Sir Leon Radzinowicz – founding director of the Institute of Criminology – later recollected that the formation of the NDC reminded him 'a little of naughty schoolboys, playing a nasty game on their stern headmaster'.[17] Nevertheless, the NDC quickly developed in size and stature, and wielded considerable influence over the development of British criminology, sociology and communication studies throughout the 1970s. At its first conference, in York, the membership grew from seven to around twenty, as the original founders were joined by figures such as Phil Cohen and Laurie Taylor. By the seventh conference, in October 1970, the number had risen to 130, growing to 230 in 1971 as collaboration was secured with social workers, radical activists and other groups beyond the academic world. The intellectual output of the NDC was also rich and prolific. No less than thirteen conferences were organised by the NDC between 1968 and 1973, the sixty-three British speakers producing nearly 100 books on crime, deviance and social control. But the impact of the NDC extended well beyond the study of crime and deviance.[18] Early contributions to gender studies were also presented (from, for example, Mary McIntosh and Ken Plummer), while the first flourishes of what was to become cultural studies were also a significant feature (with contributions from the likes of Mike Featherstone, Stuart Hall, Dick Hebdige and Paul Willis).

As Stanley Cohen has recalled, significant differences and incipient tensions always existed between the ideas of the original NDC members. But they shared a common hostility to the orthodox criminological paradigms and their positivist underpinnings, and all found more value in 'the sceptical, labelling, and social reaction perspectives' that had emerged in America.[19] Key influences were Albert Cohen and Howard Becker, whose work had transformed the American sociology of deviance during the 1950s and 1960s. The former's study of juvenile gangs had challenged conventional accounts of 'criminality' by emphasising the meanings gangs held for their young, working-class members, whose disadvantaged background precluded mainstream avenues to status and success.[20] Instead, Albert Cohen argued, the gang subculture offered an alternative source of prestige by replacing the core values of the 'straight' world – sobriety, ambition, conformity – with an alternative value system that celebrated defiance of authority and illicit thrills. Becker's work also challenged criminological assumptions by arguing that 'deviance' was not a quality inherent to particular forms of behaviour, but was a socially constructed category, a pejorative label applied to the actions of certain individuals who then come to identify with the negative categorisation.[21] In this way, Becker argued, the application of a 'deviant' label becomes a self-fulfilling prophecy, as people thus designated come to see themselves in terms of the way they have been classified and stereotyped.

The concepts of labelling and interactionism were a major influence on the work of the NDC. Drawing on these ideas, its members argued that 'crime' should be seen as a socially constructed and historically dynamic category, their analyses focusing on societal reactions to 'crime' and 'deviance', and the role of the law, social control agencies and the media in shaping their very nature and constitution. As a consequence, Young explains, the object of study was effectively reversed:

> The focus of the problematic shifted; where meaning was taken from the deviant, it was returned appreciated, and whereas the powerful had somehow magically been seen as existing outside the world of explanation, their activities and the impact – often self-fulfilling – of their activities became the centre of attention.[22]

'We will fight them on the beaches': mods, rockers and moral panics

Folk Devils and Moral Panics, then, was part of a broad set of intellectual shifts during the late 1960s and early 1970s. It was constituent in the 'new deviance' theories associated with the NDC and its attempts to recover the 'meanings' in human behaviour which were seen as denied (or reduced to clinical imperatives) in the positivism of the administrative criminology then dominated by the Home Office. But the study was also indicative of a burgeoning interest in the social impact of the mass media. Indeed, Cohen suggests that both he and Young drew inspiration for the concept of moral panics from the work of American media theorist Marshall McLuhan.[23] In his influential analysis of the consequences of the shift from print to electronic media, McLuhan argued that the real message of the media lay not so much in their textual content as in their formal characteristics – or, as he famously put it, 'the media is the message'.[24] For McLuhan, the form and structure of print media had encouraged a 'linear', rational and decidedly individualist sense of the world, but in the 1960s the dawn of electronic media had intensified visual sensations and engendered a more collective set of cultural experiences.

This 'implosive' dimension to the modern media was a key concern for both Cohen and Young. 'The media', they explained, were 'the major and at times the sole source of information about a whole range of phenomena', and modern societies faced 'a continual bombardment by images of phenomenon [*sic*] that otherwise could be conveniently forgotten'.[25] Within the media's flow of information and images, however, certain issues receive greater exposure than others and, they argued, while some phenomena 'are not selected for attention at all, others are given continual exposure ... while yet others are suddenly thrust into the public consciousness'.[26] Invariably, crime and deviance figure prominently in the media bombardment, but abrupt bursts of focused coverage lead to moments of heightened public anxiety. As Young explained, through 'the *implosion* of the mass media, we are greatly aware of the existence of deviants, and because the criterion of inclusion in the media is newsworthiness it is possible for moral panics over a particular type of deviancy to be created by the *sudden* dissemination of information about it' (original emphasis).[27]

Young, in fact, is credited by Cohen with the first published use of the term 'moral panic'.[28] Published in 1971, Young's work had paralleled Cohen's own and, similarly, was informed by theories of labelling and social interactionism. His research focused on social reactions to drug use in the Notting Hill area of London, then a district of high deprivation and a hub of bohemian hippiedom. A wave of media concern about drug crime in the area, Young argued, had a reinforcing or 'snowballing' effect. A 'great panic over drug abuse', he contended, had resulted in the setting up of specialised police squads to target drug crime, which, in turn, produced an increase in drug-related arrests.[29] In these terms, the surge in statistical indices of drug crime did not point to a genuine leap in the scale of illicit drug use, but was an outcome of media concerns and consequent shifts in law enforcement practice. Perceptions of a growing 'drug problem', therefore, were misplaced. Instead, there was a 'mythical' quality to the 'great panic'. It was a 'fantasy crime wave' generated through the interaction of the media, public opinion and the authorities.

Nevertheless, while Young may have first coined the term 'moral panic', it was Cohen who most systematically enunciated and popularised the concept in his study of the 1960s mods and rockers feuds. Many of the ideas at the heart of *Folk Devils and Moral Panics*, however, had been rehearsed in an earlier (lesser known) study Cohen had co-authored with Paul Rock.[30] This had focused on the figure of the 1950s Teddy boy and the media anxieties that had crystallised around him. The Teddy boy's style of long, drape jackets and drainpipe trousers was partly an appropriation of an upmarket, Savile Row fashion inspired by the rakish chic of the Edwardian gent (hence the sobriquet 'Teddy' boy).[31] But the Ted's 'look' was also a variant of the American-influenced styles that had become popular among many working-class youngsters in Britain during the 1940s – a trend inspired by the iconography of the Chicago gangster and the zootsuit styles imported with the arrival of GIs during wartime. First identified by the media in the working-class neighbourhoods of south London in 1954, the Teddy boy was soon being presented as a violent delinquent stalking streets and dancehalls all over the country. The negative imagery surrounding the Ted was further compounded in the sensational press coverage of cinema 'riots' that followed screenings of *The Blackboard Jungle* (1955), *Rock Around the Clock* (1956) and other films with rock'n'roll associations. As Rock and Cohen observed, these sporadic disturbances were actually quite insignificant in terms of their scale, but they attracted a welter of over-wrought publicity in which the Teddy boy was painted as a new and uncontrollable social menace.

A similar picture emerged in media responses to a spate of urban disorders in Nottingham and Notting Hill in 1958. Dubbed 'race riots' by the press, the incidents were actually a series of racist street attacks by white mobs. Media coverage and political responses, however, ignored issues of racism. Instead, the events were presented as the consequence of an 'alien' presence in British cities and tighter immigration controls were suggested as the logical remedy. But the tacit racism of this analysis was also accompanied by a rhetoric of concern about youth and delinquency. Drawing attention to the numbers of Teddy boys involved in the disorders, *The Times* speculated that the events could be partly explained as 'the latest manifestation of that youthful ruffianism, long endemic in both areas, which has variously expressed itself in raids on post offices, the wrecking of cinemas and cafés, and gang clashes and stabbings'.[32] By exploiting the familiar themes of violence and criminality that had settled around the Teddy boy, therefore, Rock and Cohen argued that the media had effectively drawn a veil over the institutional dimensions to racism and discrimination and, instead, a small group of working-class youngsters became 'a scapegoat for respectable British society to cover up its own failures and prejudices in dealing with its immigrant population'.[33]

Media coverage of the Teddy boy, however, was not simply an exercise in scapegoating. Crucially, Rock and Cohen argued that the sensationalised press stories also gave greater form and substance to the Ted as a distinct subcultural identity. Drawing on Becker's concept of 'labelling', the two authors argued that the sensationalist media reports of the 1950s introduced the Teddy boy not only to the public but also to himself:

> He learned that, because he wore Edwardian suits, he must be a certain type of person. His suit led to differential treatment. He could not pretend that he was a member of 'normal' society because people did not treat him

as one. He was rejected from more and more public places; in some areas only the cafés and the streets were open to him. He thus became even more conspicuous and menacing. Above all, he learned that he shared common enemies and common allies with those who dressed like him.[34]

By the early 1960s, the drape suit and brothel-creeper shoes of the Teddy boy had been largely displaced by the chic, Italian-inspired styles associated with the mod subculture. Media responses to mod style, however, often reproduced the fearful and overblown treatment given to the earlier Teds. Like the Teds before them, the mods' appearance was often presented by the media as a symbol of national decline – an approach that coalesced in press responses to the seaside 'battles' that flared between the mods and their leather-jacketed nemesis, the rockers.

In Cohen's famous study of the events, reports of the first recorded mod/rocker clash set the scene for, and gave shape to, those that followed. The opening skirmish took place at the Essex resort of Clacton in March 1964. Working-class youngsters had traditionally visited seaside resorts at holiday times, but that Easter was cold and wet, and Clacton's facilities for young people were limited. With little to do, minor scuffles broke out between local lads and the visiting Londoners, a few beach huts were vandalised and some windows broken. But, in the absence of other newsworthy material, reporters from national newspapers seized upon the relatively innocuous events and created headlines and feature articles suggesting there had been a wholesale breakdown of public order. As Cohen described:

> On the Monday morning following the initial incidents at Clacton, every national newspaper, with the exception of *The Times* (fifth lead on main news page) carried a leading report on the subject. The headlines are self-descriptive: 'Day of Terror By Scooter Groups' (*Daily Telegraph*), 'Youngsters Beat Up Town – 97 Leather Jacket Arrests' (*Daily Express*), 'Wild Ones Invade Seaside – 97 Arrests' (*Daily Mirror*). The next lot of incidents received similar coverage on the Tuesday and editorials began to appear, together with reports that the Home Secretary was being 'urged' (it was not usually specified exactly by *whom*) to hold an enquiry or to take firm action.[35]

Cohen's chief criticism of the media's account of the episode, then, was that it exaggerated and distorted what took place. Newspaper text was peppered with phrases such as 'riot', 'siege', 'orgy' and 'screaming mob'; and this, combined with wild exaggerations of the numbers involved, resulted in the perception that events were considerably more violent than had actually been the case. As a consequence of the news coverage, police, journalists and young people all expected trouble at

Whitsun, the next bank holiday. And, again, a series of minor incidents at a number of seaside resorts – including Brighton, Margate and Eastbourne – prompted larger-than-life press stories, while police forces coordinated massive operations to turn back youths as they arrived at seaside towns and arrested those who resisted.

In his analysis of the incidents, Cohen argued that the media were especially important in shaping the early ('inventory') stage of social reaction because they produced 'processed or coded images' of deviance and deviants.[36] In the social reaction and moral panic that followed, Cohen suggested, three key processes stood out. The first, *exaggeration and distortion*, saw the seriousness of events inflated, together with the numbers involved, the extent of the violence and the damage to property. The second, *prediction*, saw the media forecast that such events would be repeated, while in the third process, *symbolisation through language*, 'images were made much sharper than reality', so that terms like 'mod' came to stand for youth style and its deviant connotations.[37] For Cohen, then, the press coverage of the 'seaside invasions' had not been a neutral 'window' on events, but had actually been a crucial factor in their creation. The 'mods and rockers' had initially been fairly ill-defined youth styles, but were given greater form and substance in the sensational news stories. And the two subcultures steadily polarised as youngsters throughout Britain began to identify themselves as members of either camp – the mods or the rockers. Media reports also influenced the agencies of social control. Sensitised by the press stories, police forces began cracking down on the slightest hint of 'mods and rockers' trouble. As a consequence, arrest rates soared and magistrates (keen to show they were 'getting tough' with the tearaways) imposed harsher penalties. Media attention and exaggerated press reports, therefore, fanned the sparks of an initially trivial incident, creating a self-perpetuating 'amplification spiral' which steadily escalated the social significance of the events. Indeed, unbeknown to Cohen, even the British government was worried by the episode. Using newly released Home Office documents unavailable to Cohen in 1972, Richard Grayson has shown that the reports of seaside 'invasions' so perturbed ministers that consideration was given to the introduction of more punitive legislation to resolve the mods and rockers 'problem'.[38]

Folk Devils and Moral Panics may have dealt specifically with the 1960s mod/rocker episode, but its particular focus was, in many respects, unimportant. Indeed, even in the first (1972) edition of the book, Cohen asked, 'who on earth is still worried about the Mods and Rockers?',[39] while in an extended introduction to the second (1980) edition he observed that the book had been '"out of date" even when it originally appeared'.[40] More important than its account of the mod/rocker affair were the study's wider implications. The book's crucial contribution was the way it illustrated the processes a moral panic passes through as a threat takes shape, is disseminated and caricatured by the media, is seized upon by moral crusaders and experts, and is eventually resolved through the adoption of special measures.

'Crisis? What crisis?' Panic, hegemony and the 1970s

Cohen's analysis neatly highlighted the media's role in creating social phenomena and escalating their impact. Yet it had less to say about the character and meaning of these social phenomena themselves, or their place in a wider social and political context. Indeed, Cohen himself was well aware of some of these omissions, acknowledging that the focus of his research was more on moral panics than on folk devils. In his study of the 1960s seaside 'battles', he explained, '...the Mods and Rockers are hardly going to appear as "real, live people" at all. They will be seen through the eyes of societal reaction and in this reaction they tend to appear as disembodied objects, Rors[c]hach blots onto which reactions are projected.'[41] Closer attention to both the 'Rorschach blots' and their historical context came from authors associated with the Centre for Contemporary Cultural Studies (CCCS), based at the University of Birmingham.

Originally founded in 1964 by Richard Hoggart, under the directorship of Stuart Hall (who succeeded Hoggart in 1968) the collective research of the CCCS was – like that of Cohen, Young and the NDC trailblazers – central to the 'sudden outburst of intellectual output' that characterised the late 1960s and 1970s. Drawing on a battery of American and European sociological, political, philosophical and semiotic theories, the work of the CCCS spanned a formidable array of themes and issues – including the form and meaning of media texts,[42] the structures of working-class culture,[43] power and gender relations,[44] and the political dimensions of racism.[45] The nature and significance of youth culture was also a key concern, and was explored in the CCCS anthology *Resistance Through Rituals*, published in 1976.[46] Mapping out a history of postwar British youth styles, the CCCS approach synthesised the ideas of cultural theorists such as Raymond Williams, radical Marxists such as Antonio Gramsci and European semioticians such as Roland Barthes. According to this approach, youth movements such as Teddy boys, mods, rockers and skinheads could be understood as a succession of cultural – or *sub*cultural – responses by working-class youngsters to changing patterns of social and economic relations. From this perspective, working-class youths were seen as creating new identities, ones pertinent to their changing life experiences, by fusing together elements of their 'parent' culture (for example, working-class argot, neighbourhood ties and particular notions of masculinity and femininity) with elements derived from other cultural sources – in particular the commercial world of pop music and fashion.[47] Crucially, however, this approach was underpinned by Marxist notions of class-based conflict and struggle. For the CCCS, Britain's postwar subcultures were 'concrete, identifiable social formations constructed as a collective response to the material and situated experience of their class'.[48] Seen primarily as rebellious attempts to '*win space* for the young' (original emphasis),[49] subcultures were interpreted as a form of symbolic or 'ritualistic' resistance against ruling-class ideas and power structures. The effect of this approach was to turn subcultural styles into texts, the CCCS authors deploying strategies of semiotic analysis in their attempts to 'read' the subversive meanings ingrained in the mod's chrome-festooned scooter or the skinhead's boots and braces.[50] Hebdige, for example, interpreted 1970s punk style as a form of 'semiotic guerrilla warfare'[51] that shared the same 'radical aesthetic practices' as Dada and surrealism:

Like Duchamp's 'ready mades' – manufactured objects which qualified as art because he chose to call them such, the most unremarkable and inappropriate items – a pin, a plastic clothes peg, a television component, a razor blade, a tampon – could be brought within the province of punk (un)fashion.... Objects borrowed from the most sordid of contexts found a place in punks' ensembles; lavatory chains were draped in graceful arcs across chests in plastic bin liners. Safety pins were taken out of their domestic 'utility' context and worn as gruesome ornaments through the cheek, ear or lip ... fragments of school uniform (white bri-nylon shirts, school ties) were symbolically defiled (the shirts covered in graffiti, or fake blood; the ties left undone) and juxtaposed against leather drains or shocking pink mohair tops.[52]

The concept of moral panic elaborated by Cohen was also a significant influence on the work of the CCCS.[53] Compared with Cohen, however, the CCCS deployed the idea of moral panic in a much broader historical and political framework. As CCCS author Tony Jefferson later recalled, the main interest of Cohen had been 'the "what" and the "how" of a moral panic' and he had '(mostly) neglected the "why" question: why the panic happened when it did'.[54] For the CCCS theorists, the sociological ideas of labelling and interactionism that underpinned Cohen's work certainly had much to offer, but they had a limited and ahistorical view of politics and power. So, while the CCCS team certainly drew on the notion of moral panic, they integrated the concept within a broader analysis of shifts in British social, economic and political life since 1945 – a project initiated in *Resistance Through Rituals* (1976) and developed more rigorously in *Policing the Crisis* (published two years later).

The CCCS thesis drew on a fusion of sophisticated Marxist theories in which Gramsci's notion of hegemony – or the moral, cultural, intellectual (and thereby political) leadership of society – was pivotal. For the CCCS, Gramsci's concept offered a way of understanding 'the moment when a ruling class is able, not only to *coerce* a subordinate class to conform to its interests, but to exert a "hegemony" or "total authority" over subordinate classes'. 'This', the CCCS authors explained, 'involves the exercise of a special kind of power – the power to frame alternatives and contain opportunities, *to win and shape consent*, so that the granting of legitimacy to the dominant classes appears not only "spontaneous" but natural and normal' (original emphasis).[55] According to this model, Britain during the 1950s represented a period of 'true "hegemonic domination"'.[56] It was time when a 'high wage, mass-production domestic-consumer-orientated modern economy' laid the basis for a profound unity between rulers and ruled.[57] Modernisation, economic growth and consumer affluence provided the bedrock for ideologies that could successfully 'dismantle working-class resistance and deliver the "spontaneous consent" of the class to the authority of the dominant classes'.[58] But the basis upon which this consent was won was intrinsically unstable. It depended, the CCCS team argued, on continued economic growth, for which Britain was ill-equipped. The international strength of the British economy was inherently weak, investment remained low, and towards the end of the 1950s inflation began to eat into both wages and profit margins. Britain's reduced share of world trade caused pressure on the balance of payments and led to a series of 'stop–go' budgets and a compulsory 'pay pause' in 1961. By the early 1960s, then, the moment of spontaneous consent and 'expansive hegemony' was disintegrating and, during the late 1960s and 1970s, it collapsed irrevocably amid a deepening world recession, growing inflation and a steady sharpening of industrial conflict. Against this backdrop, the CCCS authors argued, the 'repertoire' of control was 'progressively challenged, weakened, exhausted' and gave way to 'a *crisis* in the hegemony of the ruling class' (original emphasis).[59]

According to the CCCS team, therefore, the 1970s marked a profound transformation in Britain's social and political structures as the postwar consensus gave way to a more coercive form of relations. Politically, they argued, this shift was embodied in the figure of Conservative Prime Minister, Edward Heath, whose election in 1970 signalled the collapse of attempts to rule on the basis of popular consent:

> The birth of Mr Heath's government in the disguise of 'the trade union of the nation' is a moment of profound crisis in the exercise of hegemony. The dominant group has nearly exhausted its function to unite and reconcile conflicting interests within the framework of its ideological canopy; its *repertoire* of responses are close to exhaustion; the mechanisms of consent have been decisively undermined. There is precious little left except a vigorous imposition of class interests, a struggle to the death, the turn to repression and control.[60]

One clear manifestation of this 'crisis in hegemony' during the 1970s was, the CCCS team contended, a sustained moral panic about street robbery. Of course, street crime was hardly new. But in the 1970s, the CCCS authors argued, street robbery – or 'mugging' as it was increasingly dubbed by the press – was configured by politicians and the media as a virulent 'new strain of crime' associated principally with young, black perpetrators. For the CCCS theorists, the hysteria about 'mugging' was a classic moral panic, where the magnitude and intensity of the reaction was 'at odds with the scale of the threat to which it was a response'.[61] The 'racial' symbolism central to the panic, moreover, leant it particular resonance by setting in motion 'the demons which haunt the collective subconscious of a "superior race"', triggering 'images of sex, rape, primitivism, violence'. But *Policing the Crisis* gave a more 'panoramic' and politically inflected account of a moral panic than that originally offered by Cohen. The CCCS team carefully unpicked the way the relatively autonomous institutions of the state – the police, the judiciary and the media – contributed to the panic independently, while at the same time coalescing to reproduce the ideas of the ruling elite and legitimise a shift towards authoritarianism. They drew particular attention to the way the routine structures of news production led to a close correlation between the views of the state and those of the media. The practical pressures of constantly working against the clock and the professional demands of impartiality and objectivity, the CCCS authors argued, combined to produce 'a systematically structured over-accessing to the media of those in powerful and privileged institutional positions'.[62] The media thus tended to reproduce symbolically the views of these 'primary definers', a process that effectively reinforced dominant viewpoints and bolstered existing power structures.

Overall, then, *Policing the Crisis* argued that the 1970s saw the media condense the themes of race, crime and youth in a protracted moral panic about mugging. Drawing together broader notions of crisis and national decline, this helped orchestrate popular acceptance of a political order increasingly willing to rule through force and compulsion rather than consent. In place of the 'consensus politics' that had characterised the 1950s, therefore, a new 'control culture' began to consolidate itself, a more coercive form of political state that reached fruition in the New Right policies of Margaret Thatcher's Conservative governments of the 1980s.[63]

Policing the Crisis was undoubtedly an ambitious and wide-reaching study. For some, it represents a landmark in Marxist theorising about crime, the media, law and order and the state.[64] But it has also attracted its fair share of criticism. Detractors have seen it, for example, as a superficial examination of criminal statistics and police practices,[65] an over-politicised and excessively deterministic model of 'moral panic',[66] and an oversimplification of the processes of news production.[67] The thesis elaborated in *Policing the Crisis* may also rely rather too heavily on its appraisal of the shifting political strategies of the Labour and Conservative parties during the late 1960s and 1970s. These shifts certainly marked significant changes in electoral tactics, but whether they added up to an organic 'crisis' in hegemonic relations of the kind envisioned by Gramsci is moot. Before one can speak confidently of a 1970s hegemonic 'crisis', a profound shift between rulers and ruled would have to be demonstrated across *all* areas of social, economic and cultural life, rather than simply in the realm of political strategy. And, even here, some contemporary commentators saw the 1970s as being characterised by continuity rather than 'crisis'. Donald Sassoon, for example, argued that the postwar political consensus provided the basis for a hegemony that lasted, whichever party was in power, until the late 1970s.[68]

Nevertheless, Britain was undoubtedly confronted by significant problems during the 1970s: rising unemployment, spiralling inflation, a global recession, a terrorist bombing campaign, industrial conflict and budding urban disorder. Moreover, an atmosphere of confrontation and a melodramatic rhetoric of 'Britain on the brink' also figured in areas of cultural life. Joe Moran, for example, shows how shrill warnings of insurgency by a leftist 'enemy within' spread from marginal pressure groups such as Aims of Industry and the Economic League into mainstream media like *The Times* and *The Economist*, while in 1976 even viewers of the TV talent show *Opportunity Knocks* were enjoined by host Hughie Green to 'Stand up and be counted!' at a time when, Green solemnly pronounced, 'Britain [was] old and worn, on the brink of ruin, bankrupt in all but heritage and hope'.[69] Moral panics about cultural decline and a rising tide of 'permissiveness' also punctuated the period. Symptomatic was the uproarious response to punk rock. Indeed, with some justification, Jon Savage sees the 1976 release of 'Anarchy in the UK', the Sex Pistols' first single, as a pivotal event. The song's 'ringing phrases', Savage argues, 'were powerful enough to insert the idea of anarchy, like a homoeopathic remedy, into a society that was already becoming polarised'.[70] Punk, however, was more than just a constituent of this polarisation. As Hebdige notes, punk did not simply respond to its historical moment but, crucially, it also dramatised 'what had come to be called "Britain's decline"'. 'The punks', Hebdige argues, 'appropriated the rhetoric of crisis which had filled the airwaves and the editorials throughout the period and translated it into tangible (and visible) terms'.[71]

At the same time, however, Moran observes that much of the 1970s 'crisis talk' now seems overstated. Though serious, he notes, Britain's economic problems 'did not threaten the survival of the nation in the same way as the Battle of Britain'. Daily events also remained essentially banal, with a survey of newspapers and TV at the end of 1976 suggesting that 'ordinary life in Britain was more resilient than the talk of imminent chaos implied'.[72] For Moran, this demonstrates the complexities and contradictions that pervaded the 1970s and challenges the 'narrative-driven decadology' – dominant in popular memory and political mythology – that casts the period as 'a unified entity with a distinctive character'.[73] Moreover, from this perspective, punks were not the only ones who had 'dramatised' the 1970s rhetoric of crisis. According to Moran there was also a marked dimension of theatricality to the decade's angst-ridden media panics and tub-thumping political campaigns which – like punk – traded on media images of conflict. Rather than simply reacting to an existing condition of tension and anxiety, therefore, these responses can be seen as strategies that actively sought to bring about such a condition, deliberately heightening a sense of apprehension as a means of garnering attention and support.[74]

Colin Hay also highlights the way a narrative of crisis was actively constructed during the 1970s.[75] Focusing specifically on the economic and political conflicts of the winter of 1978–79 – dubbed the 'winter of discontent' by tabloid newspapers such as the *Sun* – Hay holds that the industrial disputes of the period should not be trivialised and nor should the severity of the economic problems then facing the country be underestimated. However, he contends, there was nothing inherent in the events that made it inevitable that they be understood in terms of a 'crisis'. Indeed, such conditions were by no means unprecedented and, arguably, Britain's economic situation had actually been considerably worse earlier in the decade. According to Hay, therefore, the 'winter of discontent' was in many respects 'a manufactured crisis – lived, experienced and responded to through a particular construction of the events'.[76] For Hay, the winter of 1978–79 saw the tabloid media and New Right politicians deploy particular rhetorical strategies and linguistic devices to orchestrate a *notion* of 'crisis' in which the beleaguered state was presented as being 'under siege' from 'militant trade unionists' and their 'extremist' leaders. In these terms, the New Right and its media allies effectively framed the terms in which the 'winter of discontent' was represented and understood, 'reading and interpreting each and every episode, event and policy failing … as a symptom of a more general crisis which required a decisive and systematic response'.[77]

According to Hay, therefore, the 'winter of discontent' *was* a watershed that marked the passing of Keynesianism, corporatism and the postwar consensus. Crucially, however, it did so *not* because – as the New Right and the tabloids insisted – the events were precipitated by excessive union power and the failings of Keynesian economics. Instead, the winter of 1978–79 was a moment of transition because the New Right successfully *framed* events in those terms, effectively presenting the period's economic and industrial conflicts as amounting to a 'crisis of an overextended, overloaded and ungovernable state in which the trade unions were "holding the country to ransom"'.[78] A 'crisis', Hay, argues, is not an objective, ontological condition, but is a subjective perception 'brought into existence through narrative and discourse'.[79] And, during the 'winter of discontent', a compelling narrative of 'crisis' was constructed through political bombast and tabloid headlines, so that this construction 'came to have a life of its own – in that actors oriented themselves towards what they perceived to be occurring in and through the understanding of the unfolding drama that it provided'.[80] From this perspective, then, the 1970s 'crisis' can be seen, at least in part, as a symbolic myth peddled by forces whose interests lay in generating a mood of fear and confrontation.

'Carry on screaming': moral panics in contemporary society

Since the 1970s the concept of 'moral panic' has retained influence, with many authors building upon Cohen's original thesis. Here, the work of Erich Goode and Nachman Ben-Yehuda is especially noteworthy. In *Moral Panics: The Social Construction of Deviance* (a book dedicated to Cohen) Goode and Ben-Yehuda begin by differentiating moral panics from social problems and moral crusades. Social problems, they argue, differ from moral panics because they lack folk devils or wild fluctuations of concern, while moral crusades are distinct campaigns initiated by particular interest groups or moral entrepreneurs. For Goode and Ben-Yehuda, moral panics are specifically defined by five clear criteria. Concern, hostility, consensus and volatility are all important attributes but, they suggest, a dimension of *disproportionality* is especially crucial – moral panics are, by definition, disproportionate reactions to perceived threats.[81] As such, 'moral panic' should be understood as a concept rather than a theory. As Goode explains:

> There is no moral panics 'theory'. The moral panic is a sociological phenomenon, an analytical concept much like stratification, interaction, deviance and social movements. Examining the moral panic no more makes one the advocate of moral panics 'theory' than studying gender makes one the advocate of gender 'theory'. Among students of the moral panic, there are advocates of a diversity of 'theories'. And all sociological concepts are social constructs. The important thing is, do they have real-world referents? And do those referents manifest interesting and revealing patterns in social life?[82]

As Chas Critcher observes, therefore, moral panics can be theorised according to almost any sociological framework. And, while Cohen's original book was based on symbolic interactionist theories, subsequently 'a whole range of social scientists have been willing to insert the moral panic concept into their own theoretical perspectives'.[83]

For some writers, however, the notion of moral panic is problematic. Ian Taylor, for example, has warned that dismissing fears of crime and violence as spurious 'moral panics' not only devalues 'ordinary' people's experiences of these phenomena, but also creates a political vacuum open to exploitation by a reactionary 'law and order' lobby.[84] Similarly, John Springhall voices reservations about attempts to 'debunk' sensational crime stories by stressing historical precedent along the lines of 'there's nothing really new about all this'. Such responses, he argues, risk sliding into an academic condescension that shows insufficient regard for genuinely held fears and concerns.[85] While sensitive to these issues, Cohen argues that highlighting the way a social problem is constructed by the media does not necessarily question its existence; nor does it dismiss issues of causation, prevention and control. Rather, he argues, it reveals the way media discourse gives particular meanings to the problem and 'draws attention to a meta debate about what sort of acknowledgement the problem receives and merits'.[86]

Other authors suggest the notion of moral panic suffers from significant conceptual problems. Critics such as P. A. J. Waddington, for example, argue that moral panic theorists use notions of 'disproportionality' in a highly selective way.[87] From this position there is room to question the basis on which societal reaction to an event or condition is judged to be 'disproportionate'. For his part, Cohen concedes that issues of proportion and appropriateness are always important, but he also points out the need to recognise how processes of 'measurement' are, themselves, socially constructed:

> The problem is that the nature of the condition – 'what actually happened' – is not a matter of just how many Mods wrecked how many deck-chairs with what cost, nor how many 14-year-old girls became ill after taking which number of ecstasy tablets in what night club. Questions of symbolism, emotion and representation cannot be translated into comparable sets of statistics. Qualitative terms like 'appropriateness' convey the nuances of moral judgement more accurately than the (implied) quantitative measure of 'disproportionate' – but the more they do so, the more obviously they are socially constructed.[88]

Kenneth Thompson, meanwhile, suggests that moral panics should not be seen as isolated, sporadic incidents, but as part of a wider, more integrated social and political condition.[89] Drawing on Ulrich Beck's notion of the 'risk society',[90] Thompson suggests that the discrete and sudden 'eruptions' of moral panic of the kind originally identified by Cohen have steadily given way to a state of more pervasive and sustained anxiety. In a similar vein, Angela McRobbie and Sarah Thornton have argued that, far from occurring from 'time to time', moral panics have now become:

> a standard response, a familiar, sometimes weary, even ridiculous rhetoric rather than an exceptional emergency intervention. Used by politicians to orchestrate consent, by business to promote sales in certain niche markets, and by the media to make home and social affairs newsworthy, moral panics are constructed on a daily basis.[91]

In response, Cohen argues that such points can still be incorporated within a moral panics framework. By definition, he contends, a 'panic' is a temporary and spasmodic 'splutter', but a sequence of distinctive panics may resonate together, nourished by the same political morality and sense of cultural unease. 'The fragmentary and the integrated', Cohen explains, 'belong together: moral panics have their own internal trajectory – a microphysics of outrage – which, however, is initiated and sustained by wider social and political forces'.[92] And this model, introduced in Cohen's analysis of the 1960s mods and rockers 'menace', could easily be applied to the ceaseless demonology of subcultural terrors that followed – from skinheads and lager louts, to New Age travellers and acid house ravers. Cohen's study neatly showed how such phenomena are given shape and definition by histrionic media coverage. Such attention, Cohen demonstrated, does not simply represent but actively participates in the creation and development of sensational folk devils.

Indeed, this was certainly so in the case of punk rock during the 1970s. Paradoxically, rather than prematurely aborting the Sex Pistols' career, the outcry prompted by their 1976 TV appearance threw the band into a media spotlight that sustained not only their notoriety but also their commercial success. Subsequently signed to Virgin Records by an enterprising Richard Branson, the Pistols' second single, the caustic 'God save the Queen', fuelled further uproar in 1977. Indeed, the record attracted particular censure given that its release was deliberately timed to coincide with the Queen's Silver Jubilee celebrations. But, despite being banned by the BBC (indeed, partly *because* it was banned by the BBC), the song shot to Number Two in the official UK chart;[93] and punk rock spread worldwide. And the Pistols' TV storm was, itself, enshrined as an important cultural moment – the *Guardian* publishing a transcript of the band's insolent exchange with Grundy as part of its 2007 booklet series honouring the 'Great interviews of the 20th century'.[94]

Since the 1970s, however, shifts in the structure and operation of the media have led some theorists to suggest Cohen's original moral panics framework requires revision. Both Angela McRobbie[95] and Sarah Thornton,[96] for example, argue that the classic moral panics model operated with an excessively monolithic view of society and the media. In their analyses of responses to the rave and 'acid house' scenes of the late 1980s both authors contend that studies of contemporary media culture need to take account of 'a plurality of reactions, each with their different constituencies, effectivities and modes of discourse'.[97] Compared with the 1960s and 1970s, they argue, the modern media are more diverse and fragmented, composed of a 'multiplicity of voices, which compete and contest the meaning of the issues subject to "moral panic"'.[98] Stressing the array of different media responses to the rave scene, McRobbie and Thornton contend that the 'classic' notion of moral panic not only fails to distinguish between different kinds of mainstream media, but also ignores the alternative accounts offered in the 'micro' and 'niche' media that mushroomed within the youth cultures of the 1980s and 1990s. In response to mass media scare-mongering about the rave scene, they contend, the subcultural press (for example, magazines such as *i-D*, *The Face* and *New Musical Express*) 'tracked the tabloids' every move, reprinted whole front pages, analysed their copy and decried the *misrepresentation* of Acid House'.[99] In these terms, therefore, the 'folk devils' have become more savvy and are better able to engage with (and contest) the media's distorted representations. Moreover, a greater range of agencies, experts and pressure groups now step forward to challenge the media's 'folk devil' stereotypes. In the late 1980s, for instance, groups such as the Freedom to Party Campaign were effectively a mouthpiece for acid house entrepreneurs, but they still succeeded in mobilising opposition to anti-rave legislation – in 1990 a Freedom to Party rally in Trafalgar Square attracted a crowd of over 10,000 supporters.

The contemporary media landscape, then, is more complex and multifaceted than that of the 1960s and 1970s. Social reality is now constituted through *competing* media representations and decoded in a *variety* of ways by sophisticated audiences. And, as a consequence, moral panics have become more complex and conflicted. Yet, for many theorists, the concept of moral panic remains deeply pertinent to an analysis of media representations of the social world and, in particular, their portrayal of crime and deviance. As Chas Critcher observes, despite the cacophony of different voices heard in the contemporary media, some voices remain considerably more powerful than others, and '[w]hen the police, the tabloid press and the governing party conjoin in the concerted campaign, the weak power base of the alternative media is revealed'.[100] For Critcher, then, account must certainly be given to the specific character of any one moral panic, to the contradictory nature of media coverage and to the complexity of social and political responses but, in attempts to understand the media's construction of social reality and its active role in shaping events, the essential features of the moral panic model 'remain an indispensable account of the basic processes at work'.[101]

Nevertheless, Critcher does detect a shift in the targets of contemporary moral panics. Although the power of 'niche' media is relatively limited, he suggests that during the 1980s and 1990s attempts to portray youth as a threatening social danger had become harder to sustain in the face of arguments to the contrary from young people themselves, their allies and expert opinion. Instead, Critcher suggests, media constructions of youth as folk devils have been increasingly displaced by representations of *children* as *the victims* of folk devils. With an eye to the mounting anxieties about paedophilia during the 1990s, Critcher speculates that the army of claim-making crusaders has now 'retreat[ed] to safer ground where its moral concerns are unlikely to be challenged'.[102]

Yet moral panics about youth, crime and public order still make regular appearances centre-stage. In 2008, for instance, lurid press accounts painted a picture of 'broken Britain' falling prey to 'a new generation of teenage thugs',[103] while 'feral gangs of hooded youths' were portrayed as 'forcing law-abiding communities into a state of siege'.[104] And, responding to the riots of 2011, Prime Minister David Cameron blamed a new 'gang' culture which, he claimed, 'was a major criminal disease that has infected streets and estates across our country'.[105] Such phrases were eerily redolent of those used to describe the mods and rockers' seaside 'battles' of 1964, and gave poignant confirmation to Cohen's 1972 prediction:

> More moral panics will be generated and other, as yet nameless, folk devils will be created. This is not because such developments have an inexorable inner logic, but because our society as present[ly] structured will continue to generate problems for some of its members ... and then condemn whatever solution these groups find.[106]

Notes

1 *Daily Mirror*, 2 December 1976.
2 *Daily Mail*, 2 December 1976.
3 For an overview of coverage of punk rock in the British media during the 1970s, see M. Cloonan, 'Exclusive! The British press and popular music: the story so far', in S. Jones (ed.), *Pop Music and the Press* (Philadelphia, PA: Temple University Press, 2002), pp. 114–33.
4 S. Cohen, *Folk Devils and Moral Panics: The Creation of the Mods and Rockers* (London: Routledge, 3rd edition, 2002), p. 1.
5 *Ibid.*, pp. 1–2.
6 See, for example, D. Hebdige, *Subculture: The Meaning of Style* (London: Methuen, 1979), pp. 96–7; and D. Laing, *One Chord Wonders: Power and Meaning in Punk Rock* (Milton Keynes: Open University Press, 1985), p. 35.
7 S. Hall, C. Critcher, T. Jefferson, J. Clarke and B. Roberts, *Policing the Crisis: Mugging, the State and Law and Order* (London: Macmillan, 1978).

8 *Ibid.*, p. 323.
9 P. Vernon, 'Riots reveal "retro racism" resurgence", *Independent*, 9 September 2011, at http://blogs.independent.co.uk/2011/09/09/riots-reveal-retro-racism-resurgence, accessed 11 September 2011.
10 *Daily Mail*, 18 August 2011.
11 Cohen, *Folk Devils*, p. xxxv, n.2.
12 *Ibid.*, p. vii. See also D. Altheide, 'Moral panic: from sociological concept to public discourse', *Crime, Media, Culture*, 5:1 (2009), pp. 79–99.
13 Cohen, *Folk Devils*, p. vii.
14 J. Young, 'Breaking windows: situating the new criminology', in P. Walton and J. Young (eds), *The New Criminology Revisited* (Basingstoke: Palgrave Macmillan, 1998), p. 15.
15 J. Young, 'Moral panic: its origins in resistance, ressentiment and the translation of fantasy into reality', *British Journal of Criminology*, 49:1 (2009), pp. 4–16, at p. 8.
16 D. Garland, 'On the concept of moral panic', *Crime Media Culture*, 4:1 (2008), pp. 9–30, at p. 19.
17 L. Radzinowicz, *Adventures in Criminology* (London: Routledge, 1999), pp. 229–30.
18 Young, 'Breaking windows', p. 16.
19 S. Cohen, 'Footprints on the sand: a further report on criminology and the sociology of deviance in Britain', in G. McLennan and J. Pawson (eds), *Crime and Society: Readings in History and Theory* (London: Routledge & Kegan Paul, 1981), p. 221.
20 A. Cohen, *Delinquent Boys: The Culture of the Gang* (Glencoe, IL: Glencoe Free Press, 1955).
21 H. Becker, *Outsiders: Studies in the Sociology of Deviance* (New York: Free Press, 1963).
22 Young, 'Moral panic', p. 8.
23 Cohen, *Folk Devils*, p. xxxv.
24 M. McLuhan, *Understanding Media: The Extensions of Man* (New York: McGraw Hill, 1964).
25 S. Cohen and J. Young, 'Effects and consequences', in S. Cohen and J. Young (eds), *The Manufacture of News: Deviance, Social Problems and the Mass Media* (London: Constable, 1973), p. 340.
26 Cohen and Young, 'Effects and consequences', p. 340.
27 J. Young, 'The role of the police as amplifiers of deviancy, negotiators of reality and translators of fantasy: some consequences of our present system of drug control as seen in Notting Hill', in S. Cohen (ed.), *Images of Deviance* (Harmondsworth: Penguin, 1971), pp. 27–61, at p. 38.
28 Cohen, *Folk Devils*, p. xxxv.
29 Young, 'The role of the police', p. 37. See also J. Young, *The Drugtakers: The Social Meaning of Drug Use* (London: MacGibbon & Kee, 1971).
30 P. Rock and S. Cohen, 'The Teddy boy', in V. Bogdanor and R. Skidelsky (eds), *The Age of Affluence, 1951–1964* (London: Macmillan, 1970), pp. 288–318.
31 See C. Breward, 'Style and subversion: post-war poses and the neo-Edwardian suit in mid-twentieth century Britain', *Gender and History*, 14:3 (2002), pp. 560–83.
32 *The Times*, 3 September 1958.
33 Rock and Cohen, 'The Teddy boy', p. 314.
34 *Ibid.*, p. 302.
35 Cohen, *Folk Devils*, pp. 18–19.
36 *Ibid.*, p. 18.
37 *Ibid.*, p. 30.

38 R. Grayson, 'Mods, rockers and juvenile delinquency in 1964: the government response', *Contemporary British History*, 12:1 (1998), pp. 19–47.

39 Cohen, *Folk Devils*, p. xlv.

40 *Ibid.*, p. xlvii.

41 *Ibid.*, p. 15.

42 S. Hall, D. Hobson, A. Lowe and P. Willis (eds), *Culture, Media, Language* (London: Hutchinson, 1980).

43 J. Clarke, C. Critcher and R. Johnson (eds), *Working Class Culture: Studies in History and Theory* (London: Hutchinson, 1979).

44 Women's Studies Group Centre for Contemporary Cultural Studies, *Women Take Issue: Aspects of Women's Subordination* (London: Hutchinson, 1978).

45 Centre for Contemporary Cultural Studies, *The Empire Strikes Back: Race and Racism in 1970s Britain* (London: Hutchinson, 1982).

46 S. Hall and T. Jefferson (eds), *Resistance Through Rituals: Youth Subcultures in Post-War Britain* (London: Hutchinson, 1976).

47 Here, the CCCS was influenced by Phil Cohen's survey of the development of postwar British subcultures. See P. Cohen, *Subcultural Conflict and the Working Class Community*, Working Papers in Cultural Studies, 2 (Birmingham: University of Birmingham, 1972).

48 J. Clarke, S. Hall, T. Jefferson and B. Roberts, 'Subcultures, cultures and class: a theoretical overview', in Hall and Jefferson (eds), *Resistance Through Rituals*, pp. 3–59, at p. 47.

49 *Ibid.*, p. 45.

50 Subsequently, the CCCS account of subcultural style and resistance was subject to considerable criticism and reconfiguration. In 'Symbols of trouble', the introduction to the second (1980) edition of *Folk Devils and Moral Panics*, Cohen presented his own, insightful critique of the CCCS approach. A thorough-going survey of shifts in the theoretical analysis of youth style can be found in P. Hodkinson, 'Youth cultures: a critical outline of key debates', in P. Hodkinson and W. Deicke (eds), *Youth Cultures: Scenes, Subcultures and Tribes* (London: Routledge, 2007), pp. 1–22.

51 Hebdige, *Subculture*, p. 105.

52 *Ibid.*, p. 106–12.

53 Stuart Hall fulsomely acknowledged the debt at a British Academy panel discussion held in 2007. An audio recording of the event, 'Moral Panics: Then and Now', can be accessed online at www.britac.ac.uk/events/2007/moral-panic/index.cfm.

54 T. Jefferson, 'Policing the crisis revisited: the state, masculinity, fear of crime and racism', *Crime Media Culture*, 4:1 (2008), pp. 113–21, at p. 114.

55 Clarke *et al.*, 'Subcultures, cultures and class', p. 38.

56 *Ibid.*, p. 40.

57 Hall *et al.*, *Policing the Crisis*, p. 299.

58 Clarke *et al.*, 'Subcultures, cultures and class', p. 40.

59 *Ibid.*

60 Hall *et al.*, *Policing the Crisis*, p. 262.

61 *Ibid.*, p. 17.

62 *Ibid.*, p. 58.

63 See S. Hall and M. Jacques (eds), *The Politics of Thatcherism* (London: Lawrence & Wishart, 1983).

64 See E. McLaughlin, 'Hitting the panic button: policing/"mugging"/media/crisis', *Crime Media Culture*, 4:1 (2008), pp. 145–54.

65 P. A. J. Waddington, 'Mugging as a moral panic: a question of proportion', *British Journal of Sociology*, 37:2 (1986), pp. 245–59.

66 M. Barker, 'Stuart Hall: *Policing the Crisis*', in M. Barker and A. Beezer (eds), *Reading Into Cultural Studies* (London: Routledge, 1992), pp. 81–99.

67 P. Schlesinger, H. Tumbler and G. Murdock, 'The media politics of crime and criminal justice', *British Journal of Sociology*, 42:3 (1991), pp. 397–420.

68 D. Sassoon, 'The silences of *New Left Review*', *Politics and Power*, 3 (1981), pp. 249–51.

69 J. Moran, '"Stand up and be counted": Hughie Green, the 1970s and popular memory', *History Workshop Journal*, 70:1 (2010), pp. 172–98, at p. 173.

70 J. Savage, *England's Dreaming: Sex Pistols and Punk Rock* (London: Faber & Faber, 1991), p. 205. See also G. Marcus, *Lipstick Traces: A Secret History of the Twentieth Century* (Cambridge, MA: Martin Secker & Warburg, 1989), p. 441.

71 Hebdige, *Subculture*, p. 87. An apposite illustration of Hebdige's point is the way punk band the Clash assumed their name after their bassist noticed how often the word 'clash' recurred in the titles and subtitles of articles in the *Evening Standard*. See M. Gray, *Last Gang in Town: The Story and Myth of the Clash* (London: Fourth Estate, 1995), p. 167.

72 Moran, '"Stand up and be counted"', p. 189.

73 *Ibid.*, p. 194.

74 *Ibid.*, p. 188. See also J. Tomlinson, *The Politics of Decline: Understanding Post-War Britain* (Harlow: Longman, 2000), p. 1.

75 C. Hay, 'Narrating crisis: the discursive construction of the "winter of discontent"', *Sociology*, 30:2 (1996), pp. 253–77; C. Hay, 'Chronicles of a death foretold: the winter of discontent and construction of the crisis of British Keynesianism', *Parliamentary Affairs*, 63:3 (2010), pp. 446–70.

76 Hay, 'Chronicles of a death foretold', p. 447.

77 *Ibid.*, p. 465.

78 Hay, 'Narrating crisis', p. 255.

79 *Ibid.*, p. 255.

80 Hay, 'Chronicles of a death foretold', p. 456.

81 E. Goode and N. Ben-Yehuda, *Moral Panics: The Social Construction of Deviance* (Oxford: Blackwell, 1994).

82 E. Goode, 'No need to panic? A bumper crop of books on moral panics', *Sociological Forum*, 15:3 (2000), pp. 543–52, at p. 551.

83 C. Critcher, 'Introduction: more questions than answers', in C. Critcher (ed.), *Critical Readings: Moral Panics and the Media* (Maidenhead: Open University Press, 2006), p. 2.

84 I. Taylor, *Law and Order: Arguments for Socialism* (London: Macmillan, 1981).

85 J. Springhall, *Youth, Popular Culture and Moral Panics: Penny Gaffs to Gangsta-Rap, 1830–1996* (Basingstoke: Macmillan, 1998), p. 8.

86 Cohen, *Folk Devils*, p. xxxiv.

87 Waddington, 'Mugging as a moral panic'.

88 Cohen, *Folk Devils*, p. xxix.

89 K. Thompson, *Moral Panics* (London: Routledge, 1998).

90 U. Beck, *Risk Society: Towards a New Modernity* (London: Sage, 1992).

91 A. McRobbie and S. Thornton, 'Rethinking "moral panic" for multi-mediated social worlds', *British Journal of Sociology*, 46:4 (1995), pp. 559–74, at p. 560.

92 Cohen, *Folk Devils*, p. xxxi.

93 At the time, many observers suspected the official chart compilation had been rigged to prevent embarrassment during the Queen's Jubilee celebrations. See Savage, *England's Dreaming*, pp. 364–5.

94 *Guardian, Great Interviews of the 20th Century: Sex Pistols – Bill Grundy, 1976* (London: Guardian Books, 2007).

95 A. McRobbie, 'The moral panic in the age of the postmodern mass media', in A. McRobbie, *Postmodernism and Popular Culture* (London: Routledge, 1994), pp. 198–219.

96 S. Thornton, 'Moral panic, the media and British rave culture', in A. Ross and T. Rose (eds), *Microphone Fiends: Youth Music and Youth Culture* (London: Routledge, 1994), pp. 176–92; S. Thornton, *Club Cultures: Music, Media and Subcultural Capital* (London: Polity, 1995).

97 McRobbie and Thornton, 'Rethinking "moral panic"', p. 564.

98 *Ibid.*, p. 560.

99 *Ibid.*, p. 568.

100 C. Critcher, '"Still raving": social reaction to ecstasy', *Leisure Studies*, 19:3 (2000), pp. 145–62, at p. 154.

101 *Ibid.*

102 Critcher (ed.), *Critical Readings*, p. 162. For a variety of studies of contemporary moral panics related to children and youth, many of which are predicated on the perception that children have become vulnerable to a 'new' wave of predatory child abusers, see C. Krinsky (ed.), *Moral Panics Over Contemporary Children and Youth* (Aldershot: Ashgate, 2008).

103 *Daily Mail*, 17 July 2008.

104 *Sunday Express*, 30 March 2008.

105 *Guardian*, 16 August 2011.

106 Cohen, *Folk Devils*, p. 172.

11

Penguin Books in the long 1970s: a company, not a sacred institution

Peter Mayer

In 1978 I was appointed Chief Executive Officer of Penguin Books by the publishing conglomerate Pearson, which had bought the firm in 1970 following the death of Allen Lane, its founder.[1] So let me begin by considering both the strengths of the company I was brought in to transform in 1978, and the reasons its authors, the media, its owners and even much of the staff felt it was failing.

Most of the books published in the 1970s after the death of Allen Lane in 1970 had been commissioned by Penguin editors earlier, in some cases years earlier. Continuing demand kept many of those books in print for at least another decade. But through most of the 1970s, Penguin faced but did not deal with a rapidly changing publishing environment and, at the same time, it was forced to operate in a highly polarised and stressful political context. These two aspects partly shaped the reconstruction that took place, but they also are not the whole story.

In the 1960s, the introduction of the Penguin Education list (designed to capitalise on the expansion of primary and secondary education and, particularly, the reorganisation of the latter on comprehensive lines) and the relaunch of the Penguin Specials series (which addressed topical current affairs issues) had been significant if nonetheless never central Penguin initiatives. Both, in different ways, involved a move to develop a publishing model for non-fiction that was based on the creation of a new kind of teaching tool for a new society – one that would help to foster a new approach to education and learning. That model reflected the activism of the period – the counter-cultural, anti-establishment movements of the late 1960s and '70s. Implicitly and explicitly, Penguin sought to be in the forefront of social change. The media and many readers and perhaps especially much of the staff saw Penguin as a unique, almost mythical institution with a position of cultural centrality. But that Penguin was rather at odds with Penguin's origins.

The Penguin Education initiative not only sought to appeal to the young, but to take a leading role in changing the world. The world, however, was not changing in the direction Penguin and many others had imagined. It was not Margaret Thatcher, who became leader of the Conservatives in 1975 and the Prime Minister in 1979, who decided on her own to turn the tanker of her party (and the country) sharply to the right: her policies to a great extent reflected what had been happening for years outside Westminster.

Unfortunately for Penguin, at least from a business standpoint, the efforts of its management, and the controversial stances taken by certain authors, such as Paul Goodman, Anthony Crosland, Ivan Illich and Jerome Bruner, diverted Penguin from the course set by Allen Lane.[2] Tony Godwin, a brilliant editorial head between 1960 and 1967, with a background in bookselling, had tried and often succeeded in navigating the perilous straits between publishing what was popular and what was socially progressive – neither direction ever meant to be exclusionary. (And for his seven years as Penguin's chief editor, he had Allen Lane himself – a very large presence and opinionated owner – to contend with.)

Penguin's original brief, established by Allen Lane at its outset, was to offer a broad range of choices to a broad reading public. It did not have the kind of definitive 'creed' that developed in the 1970s. Lane, however, had taken an early stand, continued through the war years, against the rise of fascism in Germany, Italy, Spain and Japan, and he understood what it meant for both Britain's democratic traditions and its very survival. But no one (except, perhaps, a fascist sympathiser) could have characterised his sympathies as particularly left wing.

Only towards the end of the 1960s did Penguin's list acquire a more sharply defined view – a shift to the left despite the presence, in its senior management, of conservative figures like C. M. Woodhouse and Edward Boyle. This shift reflected increasing dismay at Britain's postwar political conflicts, buttressed by an ideological labour union movement that grew in electoral importance. Shabby political compromises and socio-economic arrangements with no clear outcome produced malaise and tension in a Britain that clearly was not going to recover its prewar place in the world.

From the early 1960s, Godwin was a lightning rod for the changes taking place – not only at Penguin but in British publishing in general. His seven years at the company were an exciting time, at least to judge by his list. Penguin's non-fiction reflected the new cultural openness embodied by the youth culture of the decade. It was leftish, and it definitely appealed to new generational ideals of personal freedom and social awareness. While perhaps shocking to the generation that had endured the Depression and fought the war, it was not doctrinaire.

It was only after Godwin's involuntary departure in 1967 (the culmination of a growing difference of opinion with Lane about Penguin's publishing, marketing and distribution strategy) that Penguin's list became a virtual political platform. There was much distinguished publishing in this period: 'The Marx Library', for example, published under the Pelican imprint, became a standard work on student bookshelves. But sales dropped off markedly in the seventies as the Callaghan period ceded to the age of Thatcher. Put simply, there were not in the general reading public enough committed left-wing intellectuals or trade unionists buying books, disproving the theory of many on the Penguin staff – that small formats and low prices for ideologically worthy texts would lead to the enlightenment of working people and a rise in class consciousness. But political non-fiction in small rack-sized 'A'-format books, moreover, had never sold well in W. H. Smith or in small newsagents and kiosks, where the larger public shopped. Newsagents stocked what their independent owners thought would sell.

Godwin's unprescriptive progressivism led, however, to an increasing tendency to focus on books about emerging minorities, students, immigrants, civil rights, the environment and conditions in the workplace. One might have described the trend as 'constituency publishing' and, in some respects, it was in tune with the times – a period of fervent self-definition by individuals and interest groups. But these constituencies, even aggregated, were rather too small to maintain Penguin, given the issue of backlist reversions to be noted later.

The transformation of the focus of Penguin's non-fiction output can be seen, for example, in the Pelican list. Pelicans in the years that preceded my arrival were a major part of Britain's postwar culture, in the UK of course but probably also in the Commonwealth where there was little local publishing. The provenance of most books read was British. Pelican, connected indelibly with the Workers' Educational Association and related educational endeavours, was part and parcel of that Britain that in 1945 threw out the Conservatives, ushering in a long period in which conscious and sub rosa efforts were made to lessen the enduring and quite rigid class stratification of British life. The war itself, with so many people from different countries and backgrounds thrown together both in war theatres and on the home front, had much to do with this shift because access to educational structures was still largely privileged and exclusionary. The Pelican part of Penguin took up much of this slack, not only on social issues but also on subjects as wide ranging as jazz, animal husbandry and basic economics – in many cases, they were not especially polemical handbooks. As the years went on, from a quite generalist base, Pelican was transformed – if never totally – to topical and issue-oriented publishing. Just as Penguin Specials were moved off their perch by the BBC's television documentaries, this was often the case as well with much of Pelican. With exceptions, of course, these books sold less well than their predecessors but again, as in the case of Penguin Specials, they achieved even less purchase in the Commonwealth and the USA.

The received wisdom is that Penguin's politics changed markedly after my arrival in October 1978. The truth is a bit more complex. The man Pearson had hired – me – was a left-leaning centrist publisher with an editorial background, a British-born American with a central European parentage, who had made his career in the cut and thrust of the marketplace. It was a marketplace Penguin had deserted – not by declared intent, of course, but by virtue of its editorial choices. I certainly sought to arrest the decline of Penguin's profile and fortunes, and I certainly would have had more sympathy with Penguin's political publishing if readers had been buying its books in sufficient numbers. But I and my new management team had no interest in promoting right-wing books, nor did we. The goal was to publish a list both of fiction and of non-fiction that readers wanted to read, thus generating the capital that would underwrite Penguin's ongoing centrality and integrity as a viable, self-sustaining cultural institution.

This shift provoked many attacks from the prescriptive left, some aimed at Penguin and some directly at me. But none of our critics ever offered any economic alternative to Penguin's re-embrace of a market-based publishing model. They seemed to have no concern for the viability of the company, except for those parts that represented their own political interests. Prior to my arrival, the only treatment for the mortal wounds to Penguin's economic health that various managements had employed were cuts in staffing and title production (although, curiously, in some years the management actually published *more* books, as though more titles that did not sell would magically add up to more revenue at appropriate margins). What really happened post-1978 was not that Penguin veered to the right, but that it avoided publishing books *merely* on the basis of a hope that they would raise class consciousness. From 1980 on, there ceased to be an editorial 'we' in the political sense. 'We' did not espouse a political position. And while I do not have the statistics before me, I am quite sure that the overwhelming majority of books remained left of centre, if not prescriptively toeing any specific line.

This represented a return to an earlier period when Penguin had a wider political vision, a vision typified, for example, by the appointment of the former Conservative cabinet minister Edward Boyle to the company board in 1965. I came to know Boyle after his Penguin years, and I can be quite certain that while his personal views were conservative, he was a man of the publishing centre with considerable respect for well argued books of both the left and right. If there was a fault in this thinking, it may have been his acceptance of perfectly good books by credentialed authors that did not have a sufficient market to warrant their costs, and to prefer those books to others – equally 'good' in their own genres – for which there was a real demand. And here we come to an essential issue, which is one of definition. Had Boyle and others with major executive roles conceived of Penguin as Allen Lane had conceived of it – as a company and not as a sacred institution – many of Penguin's problems in the post-founder period would not have come to the fore, forcing change in 1978 that seemed to many outside and inside as a radical overhaul.

I also do not want to sound disingenuous. In macroeconomic and political terms, the shift to a market economy within Penguin represented a shift to the right. That shift, however, took place because, prior to 1978, so much of the company's publishing had been politically one sided and had displaced books of general interest that were marketed properly. While Britain, after the 1979 general election, moved far to the right, Penguin did *not*, and tried only to publish a non-fiction list appealing to a contemporary readership. It should also be said that Penguin's left-wing non-fiction *did* have a reading public – but one that was insufficient for a company of Penguin's size and importance. Penguin had come to rest outside the mainstream of British publishing, whereas it had once dominated and determined that mainstream. One of Penguin's wisest advisers and critics was the author and political scientist Bernard Crick, who noted that Penguin's list was preaching to the choir. But the voice did not carry to the majority of the congregants in the cathedral.

One of the profound misunderstandings about the shift that took place on my watch is that it is difficult to be as large a company as Penguin was, even then, and run, even on our part of its lists, on a monorail. Constituency publishing – narrowly focused specialised publishing that defines a house – works only for small, dedicated and usually privately owned houses. As so many British publishing companies (in fact virtually every large one) have since been acquired by a foreign conglomerate (Australian, American, German or French), it is worth considering the fact that and the reasons why Penguin remains in British hands; Pearson, with Penguin again self-sustaining, had little incentive to end its proprietorship. Some have argued that Penguin, in the 1970s, was a utopian model of focused publishing in respect of its politics. Well that may be, but its sterling image was that it had insufficient armour against competitors, like Collins, that were unwilling to sacrifice their profitability – indeed their ability to survive – for any articulated principles.

Larger and smaller companies *not* running on a monorail of identity all gained ground at Penguin's expense.

A publishing company has to pay its way, or be privately subsidised. It is remarkable that Penguin, given its worldwide reach, its backlist and admired brand and logo, was failing to do so year after year. I also believe that book publishing, and perhaps even journalism, is not as formative of a nation's politics and destiny as some of us in publishing like to think. There can be no doubt that *individual* books and authors – here I could append a long list, but readers will have their own – have been crucial in changing attitudes and consciousness. But the in-house politics of a publisher? Some modesty is in order.

It is fair to conclude that Penguin became increasingly specialised through the 1960s and 1970s, too often eschewing books from which both the general public and even a sophisticated readership of fiction and narrative history might have derived profit and enjoyment. Clearly, in a company of Penguin's size, there were many exceptions. Penguin still meant 'paperback' to British and Commonwealth readers. And even if the company was declining, there were successful initiatives, like the new 'Allen Lane The Penguin Press' imprint – a less restrictive offshoot of Penguin's mostly non-fiction publishing and Penguin Education. Many of its authors, such as Jules Feiffer, Erich Fromm, John Berger, Marshall McLuhan, Octavio Paz, Studs Terkel, Gunnar Myrdal, Hunter S. Thompson, Hannah Arendt, Claude Lévi-Strauss and Harvey Cox, among others – remained relevant for years, either on Penguin's lists or elsewhere.

Penguin Specials and Pelicans, in the late 1970s and thereafter, were initiatives that made attempts to recapture the past. They were revived in the very early 1960s and published until about 1990, and the franchise was renewed unsuccessfully several times. Penguin Specials had first made their mark during the prewar years, alerting Britain (and the Commonwealth) to the rise of fascism on the continent. But by the 1970s, Penguin Specials were being published in ever smaller numbers; without a dramatic mission to champion, they focused on dryer issues. Penguin Specials were occasionally updated and/or reissued as Pelicans, but, again, they did not have compelling subject matter for a large audience. Other media, especially the aforementioned BBC television documentaries, did their work in a more entertaining form and leeched away much of the potential readership. They also lost readers in Commonwealth countries, which were more interested in their own politics. As an increasingly post-colonial power, Britain less frequently set an intellectual agenda that could be profitably exported to its former colonies.

This fate, on a more modest scale, also befell Penguin as Penguin's Commonwealth companies, at my urging, began to become local publishers as much as importers of Penguin's UK books, thereby generating their own copyrights. Penguin Australia became truly Australian and the new Penguin India was Indian from the first. As these markets readjusted, so did the utility of Penguin's once colour-coded imprints, eroding the economies of scale in the UK home market.

Perhaps more important than any of Penguin's business and management problems in the 1970s was the loss of talent. Many famous authors, of both fiction and non-fiction, drifted away. Retailing had begun to change, influenced in part by the USA, and there were, suddenly, serious competitors in the market. The cachet of being published by Penguin was a depreciating asset in this increasingly competitive marketplace. At the same time, freshly politicised young editors straight from university arrived at Penguin in the late 1960s and 1970s to join what they saw as its engagement on the front lines of a new order. What they published suggested that they were less interested in acquiring books that might make a profit. Indeed, for many, selling and selling-out were, in their minds, much alike.

This is not to say that Penguin books did not continue to sell in large numbers. But while aggregate sales were still relatively high they were in decline; sales per title were low, eroding profitability, and other paperback publishers with mass imprints like Pan, and literary offshoots like Picador, siphoned away business. Worse still, the glorious Penguin backlist was increasingly picked over as the paperback rights reverted to their original hardback publishers, who preferred to publish them in paperback themselves, cutting out Penguin.

These problems were sometimes recognised within Penguin, and certainly within Pearson – Penguin's parent company – but the quasi-institutional nature of Penguin, and the ideology of many of its editors, made change very difficult – even as it was increasingly urgent. When I arrived, I perceived that the overhaul had to be both structural and editorial. Copyright, I understood – not size or institutional image – had to be our core priority.

The strategy from 1978 was for Penguin to become less a reprinter and more an originator of its own content. We *had* always originated books, but most of the strongest backlist titles were fiction and, as a result of a much more competitive international and domestic rights market, increasingly they were term-licensed reprints, that is, under licences with expiry dates. This increasing decimation of our backlist by reversions of paperback rights led me to a decision to boost the Allen Lane hardcover list, commission more paperback non-fiction and to build up our copyright assets by acquiring, as opportunity presented, those hardcovers firms (for example Hamish Hamilton and Michael Joseph) that controlled the main copyrights of Penguin's fiction backlist. Marketing and sales representation needed to be developed along contemporary lines. Penguin also needed to lure its best authors back into the fold. In the 1980s and '90s, quite a few did return.

With a group of colleagues who came to accept these ideas, led editorially by Peter Carson, who, alongside his profoundly serious leanings also had surprising commercial instincts, we set about making books attractive to a variety of readers at different levels. There had always been a hidden bias, even a snobbery, in the presumption of some mythical Penguin 'reader' whose elevated tastes, on the one hand, or grateful hunger for enlightenment, on the other, determined our list. Henceforth, we published books for a heterogeneous public with greatly varying appetites for reading matter, perfectly able to register their preferences at a cash register, and we adjusted the presentation of our books – covers, marketing and so forth – to account for those differences.

If Peter Carson, almost from the day I arrived from the USA, best understood what I was trying to achieve for Penguin in trying to restore its health and centrality, there were of course others who before too long accepted that a new day had to dawn. One of these was certainly Patrick Wright, who was in charge of sales during these almost twenty years and who saw to it that a more reader-oriented thrust would be manifest in bookshops, multiples and even newsagents. Although I travelled extensively and regularly, he aligned himself with these directions towards a more universal, that is, not exclusively British, Penguin. Its UK publishing became part of Penguin's overseas operations, just as Penguin's overseas companies were originating books on their own. Another was John Rolfe, who managed the backlist, our inventory and our export interrelationships with our overseas companies, given his extensive understanding of Penguin's publishing going back to Allen Lane's day. He was a major factor in the decisions of what backlist books needed reformatting and reissuing with new covers, so that they did not just appear in catalogues but actually were available everywhere for booksellers and readers. He was of immense help to Peter Carson, Patrick Wright and me in picking prices and, working with Jonathan Yglesias in production, finding a way to achieve Penguin's goals economically. There were many others of course who grasped what must have seemed a nettle at first, not the least Dotti Irving in publicity and Liz Attenborough in charge of our children's publishing after the illustrious Kaye Webb finally retired. (I was lucky indeed after my arrival that Kaye, who was Fat Puffin herself, having already retired, came back for several years to get the train on its rails again.[3])

I have not in this piece spoken about children's publishing, as the thrust of this chapter is concerned with the adult side of Penguin and especially non-fiction publishing. However, I must not leave out a proper crediting of the children's side, a most important component of Penguin for decades. Penguin's children's publishing, in those days heavily dependent on the many works of Roald Dahl and largely represented by Puffin, probably the first children's paperback line, got a massive boost when, curiously, no one but Penguin chose to bid at auction for the firm of Frederick Warne – the publishers of Beatrix Potter. I will never understand our being the lone publisher bidding, but Sally Floyer, whom I appointed to run the Potter franchise and other properties that were added to it, turned out to be the perfect appointment, producing literally millions of sales, and taking Penguin into 'special sales' (sales outside bookshops) and into book-related merchandise, from pencil tins to coffee mugs, reinforcing Potter at first, and then all of Penguin – an initiative that continues to be a factor today in Penguin's presentation of itself, making the most of both its logo and its reputation.

All these and other strands represented the shift from a publishing company that had come to rest on legitimate laurels but that had ceased to be a vibrant participant in the present and in that failing had also failed to confront an evolving future so different from what publishing had been in Allen Lane's day. Underlying these radical changes was, of course, a determination to restore Penguin's financial health. A word about Ron Blass, who was Penguin's vice chairman at that time: he was in many ways the Rock of Gibraltar, rising to his eminence from his start at Penguin as a lorry driver. It was he who probably gave me the best advice in general terms of how to deal with the non-editorial operational aspects of Penguin. Pearson, in engaging this American, probably did not know that I was not especially experienced on the non-editorial side, but Blass, operationally, with John Webster and Stephen Hall on the financial side, made a strong team at my back, helping us achieve in practical terms what the editorial shift made necessary.

The changes began in 1978, still of course in the pre-Thatcher days, a period of more ideological unions than exist now, something I had not experienced in the USA. But my view came to be that unions ultimately were made up of people who, whatever their political bent, wanted to be on a winning team. And as Penguin started to win from the early 1980s on, relationships between the unions and the management became easier to negotiate; to put it in my terms, they became normalised based on Penguin being a stronger company, asserting itself as the staff and authors wanted it to do.

These people whom I have mentioned, and others, say, in art and design, were really part of a non-ideological process and although one might think that in these major support roles the political nature of so much of Penguin's publishing in the 1960s and '70s did not engage them, it must have done so affectingly, based partly on the times in which this took place and because of the importance of Penguin in British publishing, something the staff could not have been unaware of.

Underlying these changes and shifts of emphasis was a concern for reader and author, not, as was sometimes alleged, a dumb fixation only on a bottom line. From the late 1970s the reader was respected by Penguin, the company providing not only what readers expected from it but also what readers were interested in reading. And authors were respected in the presentation of their books, which were given less of an institutional Penguin look and more of a presentation that related to the book the author had written. By appealing thereby to the likely readership, we sought to preserve the very qualities – the fundamental commitment to the best and most saleable books on a great backlist – that had made Penguin unique. Aesthetics (elegant typography – the 'Penguin page' designed by Jan Tschichold between 1945 and 1949 – upmarket cover art on books that were often not upmarket at all, colour-coded series) and some rather Maoist, *soixante-huitard* notion of moral purity had to be secondary to the books themselves – to what writers wrote and readers might choose to read.

The seeds of change planted in the late 1970s bore fruit in the 1980s and 1990s, with Penguin's return to economic health. Penguin Classics were embraced, regularly re-translated, and re-packaged; its lists were nearly four times as large by 1997 as they had been in 1978. There were inevitably numerous in-house controversies about certain works of non-fiction but the debates were bracing and did not result in censorship. Milton Friedman's *Free to Choose*, for example, quickly became Penguin's best-selling Pelican book in the economics area.[4] We published it not because Friedman's philosophy of supply-side economics particularly appealed to many of us, but because we considered it no bad thing to have British readers get from Penguin access to a book written by a Nobel Prize winner whose theories were those of Britain's elected government. I especially remember my insisting that the book be published as a Pelican, one of many efforts to bring the Pelican imprint once again to the fore. What I learned was that the book, which sold well, probably would have sold the same number of copies as either a Penguin or a Pelican. Authors and titles were becoming as much the brand as either the name of the company or the name of a series.

It could be said that Penguin's non-fiction in the 1980s changed more than its fiction – the result of reader indifference towards Penguin Education, and many worthy Pelicans and Penguin Specials, though that indifference extended even to large swathes of the 'orange' fiction list. It was also the result of an attitude adjustment among editors. While we continued to publish – and to seek out – works of high intellectual quality, alienation from or implicit contempt for the mainstream of public interest was no longer tolerated.

What therefore might have seemed like a politically inspired shift at Penguin was actually a process of redefinition. A new regime saw

Penguin less as an institution devoted to a particular educational and ideological world view, and more as a company that had to compete for readers in an increasingly crowded and diverse environment. 'Publishing' and 'public' have the same root, and Allen Lane had not founded a private club for scholars or for ideologues. Emerging from the seventies, Penguin freed itself of internal censorship and external censure. It joined a market economy and was proud to publish books of entertainment or of political and literary value from wherever they might come, and for whomever they might appeal.

Here I have to say that throughout this period of change, and despite considerable pressure from the media, Pearson, led by Michael Blakenham, never intervened in the running of Penguin, although its directors may have been troubled by individual books. In fact, Pearson was completely supportive and remained so through the publishing battles over Peter Wright's *Spycatcher*, published by Penguin in the USA, Salman Rushdie's *Satanic Verses* and the David Irving libel suit over Deborah Lipstadt's *Denying the Holocaust*.[5]

In the beginning, Penguin was, like Adam, virtually alone in the (British) garden. And perhaps it is fair to say that an Edenic grandeur, or an ideal of one, has been lost since that time. But that grandeur was ill-suited to the increasingly democratic, wired, global and heterogeneous new century already stirring in the womb by the mid- to late 1970s. And it is my own deep conviction that much more was saved – including much more of Penguin's soul – than was lost.

Notes

1 Those wishing to know more about Allen Lane, who died in 1970, can consult S. Hare (ed.), *Penguin Portrait: Allen Lane and the Penguin Editors, 1935–1970* (London: Penguin, 1995); J. Lewis, *Penguin Special: The Life and Times of Allen Lane* (London: Viking, 2005); J. E. Morpurgo, *Allen Lane: King Penguin* (London: Hutchinson, 1979); and A. McCleery, 'The return of the publisher to book history: the case of Allen Lane', *Book History*, 5:1 (2002), pp. 161–85.

2 P. Goodman, *Compulsory Mis-education* (Harmondsworth: Penguin Books, 1971); M. Kogan, *The Politics of Education: Edward Boyle and Anthony Crosland in Conversation with Maurice Kogan* (Harmondsworth: Penguin Books, 1971); I. Illich, *Deschooling Society* (Harmondsworth: Penguin Books, 1973); and J. Bruner, *The Relevance of Education* (Harmondsworth: Penguin Education, 1974).

3 'Fat puffin' was the nickname for the famous Puffin colophon, designed by Jill McDonald, but became attached by young Puffin Club members to Kaye Webb, its founder.

4 M. Friedman, *Free To Choose: A Personal Statement* (London: Penguin Books, 1980).

5 P. Wright, *Spycatcher: The Candid Autobiography of a Senior Intelligence Officer* (New York: Viking, 1987); S. Rushdie, *The Satanic Verses* (London: Penguin,

1988); D. Lipstadt, *Denying the Holocaust: The Growing Assault on Truth and Memory* (New York: Free Press, 1993). The last was reissued by Plume, an imprint of Penguin Books, in 1994 with a new introduction by the author, at which point Lipstadt and Penguin were (unsuccessfully) sued for libel by David Irving; on this, see R. J. Evans, *Lying About Hitler: History, Holocaust and the David Irving Trial* (New York: Basic Books, 2001).

12

Penguin Books and the 'marketplace for ideas'

Dean Blackburn[1]

Many writers have argued that the 1970s brought about a reconfiguration of Britain's political compass. The apparent breakdown of the Keynesian welfare policy framework that had existed since the late 1940s, it is generally agreed, came alongside an ascendency for the forces of the right.[2] The causes and extent of this realignment, however, remain highly contested.[3] The following discussion will contribute to this debate by examining the experience of Penguin Books. Understanding how such a significant organ of progressive opinion located itself within the polarised politics of the long 1970s, it will be argued, can enrich our understanding of the origins, character and outcome of the ideological contestation that took place in this period.[4]

Ostensibly, the trajectory of Penguin through the decade appears to echo the wider shifts that took place in British politics from the late 1960s. Penguin, which had maintained a centre-left political identity since its creation in 1935, seemed to reflect a period of polarised ideological dispute in this period that, in regard to its own experience, seemed to have been resolved in favour of the right. Having contributed to the intellectual resurgence of radical socialist thought throughout the 1970s, Penguin's political output seemed to make a sudden rightwards shift when Peter Mayer, an American publisher known for his work with Avon Books, was appointed as the firm's chief executive in September 1978 by Pearson Longman, which had acquired the company after Allen Lane's death in 1970. According to some on the left, Mayer's arrival brought about a betrayal of Penguin's progressive tradition. Writing in 1985, the historian Richard Gott, who had edited Penguin's Latin American Library in the early 1970s, stated that: 'Penguin today is a pretty tacky conservative publisher, owned by a large and multi-faceted public company, and run by an overly rich lowbrow American.... Its trajectory is an excellent example of the way in which serious English culture has become distorted and trivialised.'[5] Penguin, Gott believed, had fallen victim to the sort of social, cultural and economic pressures that had allowed Thatcher to gain power in 1979.

Although the following discussion will refine such an interpretation of Penguin's journey through the late 1970s and early 1980s, it none-theless provides a useful starting point from which to begin a study of Penguin's relationship with the wider political and cultural context in which it existed. Did Penguin's changing editorial direction throughout this period reflect any social, cultural and political shifts that might have determined the nature of the realignment of the late 1970s and early 1980s?

In pursuing an answer to this question, the following discussion will employ the concept of a 'marketplace for ideas' that Peter Hall has developed in his study of politics in the 1970s.[6] Hall identified a period of open political contestation surrounding economic ideas that was resolved by the 1979 general election in favour of a radical shift in the goals of public policy. This contestation, he argued, originated from a legitimation crisis of the existing Keynesian paradigm and took place within a 'marketplace for ideas' that extended far beyond the realm of parliamentary politics.

Penguin's political output suggests that such a concept may provide a useful interpretive framework for assessing the wider changes that took place in British politics over the course of the long 1970s. Having shaped and reflected the hegemony of the legitimising ideology of the postwar settlement for two decades, from the late 1960s Penguin seemed to participate in a new battle for ideas that opened up in the wake of the perceived failings of that settlement. This ideational struggle, its publications suggest, extended to almost all spheres of British life and reconfigured the terrain on which political contestation took place.

Hall's conception of the marketplace for ideas, however, might be too simplistic. In Hall's analysis the battle for ideas was essentially conceived in binary terms. Monetarist and Keynesian ideas, he argued, competed with one another for the support of policy-makers and opinion-formers. The debate over economic policy, however, was just one component of a wider ideological contest that embraced all facets of British political life. This chapter will argue that Penguin's non-fiction list of the period reflected an ideological debate that was fought in multiple arenas by an increasingly diverse set of actors. The political contestation of the long 1970s did not just reopen old debates, it also forged new ones that were rooted in the counter-cultural politics that had emerged in the 1960s. The marketplace for ideas, then, contained a wide range of ideas and political identities that were attempting to compete for influence within the polarised politics of the period. By posing a conception of ideological competition that accommodates this pluralistic character of the marketplace for ideas that emerged in the 1970s, we might be better able to understand the left's apparent retreat in this period while also recognising the constraints of the neo-liberal hegemony that seemed to be the product of this retreat. Indeed, Penguin's political publishing of the early 1980s suggests that many of the progressive ideological 'products' that emerged in the 1970s continued to play an important role in British political life long after the 1979 general election. It also suggests that the polarised politics of the period might have concealed the resilient appeal of centre-left reformist ideas and that Mayer, far from repudiating Penguin's progressive tradition, actually returned the company to its centre-left stance.

Penguin and the postwar consensus, 1945–65

Despite the substantial historiographical debate that has surrounded it, the concept of a 'postwar consensus' retains some explanatory value when describing the character of Britain's postwar politics.[7] When judged against the apparent ideological conflict and realignment of the 1970s, the two decades after 1945 appear to have witnessed a degree of political stability.[8] Although the Labour and Conservative parties disagreed significantly on a number of ideological questions, this disagreement was to some extent contained by a shared set of assumptions regarding the purpose of the state. Penguin's early history certainly suggests that some conception of consensus is useful. Not only do its publications reflect the narrowing of the parameters of mainstream political debate from the late 1940s, but the firm's publishing values and reputation seemed to evince the hegemony of a set of loosely social democratic assumptions about the objectives of political activity.

When it was founded in 1935, Penguin initiated a democratic revolution in British publishing. By inventing the cheap, quality paperback, its founder, Allen Lane, vastly expanded the audience for serious literature. To some commentators, this ongoing achievement developed into an emblem of the wartime cultural and political change that seemed to reconfigure social relationships and make a social democratic welfare settlement possible. The novelist Malcolm Bradbury noted that Penguin 'helped create a new mood of literary culture in wartime: a mood of common cause, shared experience, and the dissolution of political and cultural barriers'.[9] Richard Hoggart, who described himself as 'a graduate of Penguin University', thought that Penguin's 'paperback revolution' was so firmly connected with developments in British life that he could state, 'if we understood better the peculiar kind of "openness", the peculiar "classlessness", of Penguins we would understand better the distinctive feel of mid-twentieth-century cultural change in Britain'.[10] Echoing this sentiment, Jeremy Lewis, Lane's biographer, has described Penguin as a publisher that gave 'voice to the ideals that were made manifest by the postwar Labour government, prevailed through the "Butskellite" consensus, and were only called into doubt with the rise of Mrs Thatcher'.[11] Penguin's politically inclined 'Specials' deserve particular attention in this regard. Their themes of economic planning and social welfare reform give some sense of a leftward shift in the central gravity of political discourse that seemed to take place from the late thirties, while their tremendous sales performance also suggest that readers were coming to accommodate such ideas.[12]

In many respects these books helped reformist social democratic ideas to obtain a hegemonic status that would endure until at least the mid-1960s. Penguin's 1959 election Specials, which presented readers with the views of Quintin Hogg and Roy Jenkins in advance of polling, perhaps represent a high-water mark of this hegemony. Roy Jenkins' *The Labour Case* offered a revisionist account of socialism that saw the Keynesian mixed economy as being compatible with Labour's goals. His opposite number, Quintin Hogg, claimed Conservative parentage of the postwar welfare state and expressed a loosely social democratic belief with regard to social provision: 'the masses are entitled to demand and receive their fair share of the new goods created, a share which must increase rapidly'.[13] Substantial differences between Jenkins and Hogg certainly existed. Jenkins was primarily concerned with extending the collectivist and welfarist characteristics of the postwar settlement, while Hogg was primarily concerned with halting these changes. These differences, however, were contained by their shared faith in welfare capitalism. Both authors, it can be argued, were voicing the ideas that were dominant within their respective parties and, by selecting them as authors, Penguin was both reflecting and shaping the political culture of the postwar consensus.

Indeed, Penguin's own publishing philosophy seemed to embody a pluralist instinct that valued a constructive dialogue between different elements of moderate political opinion. Despite his socialist beliefs, W. E. Williams, Penguin's chief editor until the early 1960s, believed that the task of the publisher was to equip its readers with the tools with which they could form their own tastes, opinions and politics.[14] When Williams faded from the scene in the early 1960s, Lane sought two pillars of 'one nation' Conservatism as replacements: C. M. Woodhouse and Edward Boyle. Both were politicians as 'unsympathetic to the Monday

Club as they were to the Tribune Group'.[15] Charles Clark, editor of
Penguin Education in the years 1966–73, and a figure whose politics
lay firmly to the left, was able to remark that Boyle's influence, 'both
professionally and personally, extended in the happiest way throughout Penguin Books ... [his] greatest quality was a kind of democratic
empathy'.[16] That a left-leaning editorial policy could be presided over by
two Conservatives is itself a monument to the intellectual foundations of
the postwar consensus.[17]

The breakdown of consensus, 1966–78

According to Hall, a marketplace for ideas emerges from a legitimation
crisis of the existing policy paradigm. From the late 1960s, Penguin's
publishing began both to reflect and to shape such a crisis. The apparent
failure of the Keynesian postwar settlement to solve the social and
economic troubles of the period encouraged the development of a risk-
taking political culture in which intellectuals used its books to construct
and engage with a 'politics of emergency'.[18] The outcome was a more
polarised political discourse in which Penguin's increasingly radical
political publishing became a source of ideological contestation.

Documenting various failings of the welfare state and identifying the
relative decline of the British economy, Penguin's Specials of the early
1960s had contributed to a widespread dissatisfaction with the existing
form of the British state.[19] In a sense, however, the unifying theme of
the series in this period was a desire to repair the postwar settlement
rather than to replace it.[20] Despite the profound anxieties that were
expressed in books like Michael Shanks' *The Stagnant Society* (1961),
the most remarkable feature of the centre-left discourse about 'decline'
was the faith in welfare capitalism that it evoked.[21] The Specials of this
period may have been influential in dismantling the quiet optimism that
had fuelled the socialist revisionism of the mid-1950s, but they were
not disposed to offer radical plans for reform that departed from the
Keynesian welfare capitalist model.[22] The apparent failure of the Wilson
governments to arrest the economic and social problems that had been
highlighted by Penguin in the early 1960s, however, permitted a much
more radical discourse to enter into the Specials list.[23]

Indeed, the late 1960s saw the reformist declinism of the early part
of the decade – which had brought about some convergence of views
between the left and right on the need for economic modernisation –
being replaced by a more apocalyptic variant that encouraged a greater
degree of ideological divergence.[24] According to some accounts in
the 1970s, the whole edifice of British society seemed to be in a deep
moral decline that was institutionalised within the existing status quo.

Penguin's list became littered with texts that deployed a language of crisis and decay. In *British Capitalism: Workers and the Profits Squeeze*, for instance, economists Andrew Glyn and Bob Sutcliffe argued that an imminent crisis of capitalism would initiate a period of open class conflict that could be resolved only by 'a successful revolutionary struggle'.[25] E. P. Thompson identified a crisis in higher education stemming from its subordination to the interests and values of capitalism.[26] Urban planner Jon Rowland used his Penguin Special to proclaim the decay of communities within inner-city Britain and argued that the problem required a radical restructuring of state provision that was informed by the principles of human solidarity and justice.[27] In *Poverty: The Forgotten Englishmen*, Ken Coates and Richard Silburn suggested that the inadequacies of the Beveridgean welfare state were bringing about a 'crisis of the poor' that could be solved only by a 'structural revolution' in its operation.[28]

Moments of crisis, whether perceived or real, often serve to bolster the persuasive qualities of radical ideas, particularly if the existing dominant ideology seems incapable of explaining and solving its recognised symptoms. In the case of Penguin, the 'politics of emergency' that emerged from the mid to late 1960s encouraged it to furnish its non-fiction publishing with a more radical socialist discourse that was being constructed beyond the parliamentary arena. There is a sense of Penguin's political spirit making a generational shift from the mid-1960s. Tony Godwin, who had been appointed as Penguin's chief editor in 1960, possessed a political and cultural identity that contrasted with the open, pluralist progressivism that had been embodied by the likes of W. E. Williams and Allen Lane. Although he shared their instinctive egalitarianism, his involvement in the bohemian subculture of late-1950s London led him to take an interest in a much more radical spectrum of left opinion.[29] When the extra-parliamentary left began to relinquish their tacit support for Wilsonism in 1966, Godwin increasingly used Penguin's non-fiction lists to give voice to intellectuals who were looking beyond the parameters of the postwar settlement in their prescriptions for socialist progress.[30] Co-authored by writers associated with the 'first New Left', *May Day Manifesto* offered a 'counter-statement to the Labour government's policies and explanations' that rested on a Marxist critique of Wilson's political economy.[31] The book's underlying theme – that the Labour Party was an ineffective vehicle for socialist beliefs and that welfare capitalism had not fulfilled its promises – was repeated in numerous titles, including *Matters of Principle: Labour's Last Chance, The Labour Government, 1964–70* and *The Politics of Harold Wilson*.[32]

Although he was dismissed by Allen Lane in 1967, Godwin injected Penguin's non-fiction list with a political thrust and counter-cultural identity that would remain long after his departure. In 1969, Robert

Hutchinson, who was briefly the editor of the Specials, proposed a 'Britain in the Seventies' series that would replicate the themes of the 'Britain in the Sixties' titles that had appeared at the start of that decade. In contrast to their predecessors, however, these books were intended to serve a much more radical editorial objective. In a 'manifesto' for the series, Hutchinson wrote:

> This series of Penguin Specials will start from the recognition that it is one of the tasks of the left to battle against the mass media's bewitchment of our intelligences, and that battle initially involves a restatement of the sought after ends of political action and social change – a radical re-examination of assumptions, those prevailing in society and those prevailing in the minds of socialists ... [each] volume in the series [should show] a concern with the interlocking of the structure of our society, and the nature and necessity of structural change and how this can be effected.[33]

The directive was underlined by an analysis that evoked the Marxist themes being pursued by the New Left. In Hutchinson's view, the record of the Wilson governments had shed light on the conservatism of many state institutions, the marginal power of Parliament and the media-constructed myth of the 'affluent worker'.[34] His list of proposed authors contained several members of the non-social-democratic left, including Dorothy Wedderburn, Paul Foot, Ken Coates, Michael Barratt Brown and Trevor Park. Although the series was dropped shortly after Hutchinson left the firm in 1969, similar currents of thought were given a platform by his replacement, Neil Middleton, who remained a senior non-fiction editor until 1982.[35]

A member of the International Marxist Group and the founder of the Catholic socialist magazine *Slant*, Middleton was responsible for placing a large number of Marxist texts onto Penguin's non-fiction programme.[36] The Pelican Marx Library, which was published in association with the *New Left Review*, reproduced most of Marx's most significant works.[37] A number of Marxist-inspired critiques of late capitalism entered the Specials list and a biography of Antonio Gramsci, perhaps the leading source of ideas for the 'second New Left', was published in 1978.[38] By publishing these works in 'trade' editions that were widely distributed, Penguin played an important role in the intellectual renaissance of Marxist thought in the 1970s. Alongside these theoretical works, an effort was also made to propagate the programmatic thinking emerging within and around the Labour left. Although they did not reach publication, both Stuart Holland and Michael Meacher were contracted to write books on the subject of Labour's Alternative Economic Strategy.[39]

Within Penguin's political publishing of this period we can also identify new forms of political expression that were opening up new arenas for ideological contestation. There was a concerted attempt to give voice to the new field of cultural studies, which was utilising Marxist ideas to reach a conception of culture that recognised its relationship with the political.[40] Books about civil liberties, women's rights, student politics and ecological problems exposed counter-cultural identities and single-issue interests that could not find expression within the realm of parliamentary politics.[41] In a sense, these sections of Penguin's publishing were helping to shape new arenas of political contestation that were being occupied by an increasingly diverse set of actors. Although these new political movements tended to exhibit a discourse of personal liberation that placed an emphasis upon individual rights and democratic empowerment, their ideological identities were often distinctly ambiguous. Some were issue-based and were relatively detached from the wider ideological paradigms of the traditional left, while others were concerned with the expression of identities and interests that were in tension with the cultural identity of Labourism. The proliferation of sites of antagonism and resistance that Penguin revealed, then, provided both challenges and opportunities for the left.

From the late 1960s, therefore, Penguin's editorial policies were driven by a greater desire to lead public opinion rather than to follow it. Having once been a symbol of the social democratic spirit of the postwar consensus, its political identity became associated with a more radical discourse about the future of Britain that was deriving much of its intellectual fuel from beyond the realm of parliamentary politics.

Penguin's leftward drift was matched by an equally vigorous intellectual shift by the forces of the right. Penguin's political books provoked concerted criticism from Conservatives who were anxious to depart from the consensus politics that had endured since the late 1940s. Many of their complaints were directed towards the editorial direction of Penguin Education – a separate imprint that had been founded to expand Penguin's educational publishing. Although it was largely a product of a loose cross-party agreement over the need for an expansion of state-funded higher education, by 1970 the imprint had become the subject of fierce political contestation.[42] Politically, it identified itself with a strong egalitarian ethos and published a series of books by authors who were attempting to look beyond educational policies that were within the consensual paradigm of the early 1960s.[43] Intellectuals on the right who, by sharp contrast, were attempting to reverse many of the educational reforms that had arrived in the 1960s made direct attacks upon its published output.[44] Reviewing the Education Special *Letter to a Teacher*,[45] Conservative MP and New Right intellectual Angus Maude described it as a 'propaganda vehicle for the partisan views not of its authors but of its editors'. These editors, he argued, 'clearly do not believe that there can be any respectable alternative viewpoint to the one – "progressive", egalitarian, permissive and occasionally straight Marxist – which they themselves so glibly and consistently propound'. He even went so far as to criticise his Conservative colleague Edward Boyle, who was then overseeing Penguin's takeover by the publishing group Pearson in the aftermath of Allen Lane's death in July 1970 and whose support for comprehensive education was increasingly running counter to his party's views:

> *Letter to a Teacher* is a vintage specimen of the cult. It is guaranteed to bring a sentimental tear to the eye of every progressive egalitarian and to make almost everybody else feel faintly sick. It has been highly praised by progressive critics, and includes an enthusiastic 'afterword' by Lord Boyle, one of the rulers of the Penguin Empire.[46]

In fact, the increasing polarisation of Britain's intellectual politics can be traced through the shifting location of Edward Boyle within both Penguin and his own party. Intellectually, Boyle's instinctive centrism and distaste for blind dogmatism embodied both the ideological foundations of the postwar consensus and the ethical underpinnings of Allen Lane's model of publishing.[47] These characteristics of thinking, which had undoubtedly attracted Lane to him in the mid-1960s, increasingly alienated Boyle from the flow of his own party as it moved rightwards in the 1970s.[48] Figures like Rhodes Boyson, who attacked the progressive educational consensus, were coming to dominate the intellectual heights of the Conservative Party and clashed with Boyle on the question of Penguin's editorial policies. After Penguin had turned down Caroline Cox's *Rape of Reason*, which documented alleged attempts by left-wing groups to infiltrate London Polytechnic, Boyson proclaimed that 'Penguin's educational reputation for a narrow propagandist purpose does no credit to Penguins and has become a grave menace to the wider community'.[49] Boyle sharply disagreed and cited numerous examples of books published by Penguin that did not have a leftist perspective.[50]

Boyle did, however, have his own complaints about Penguin's non-fiction publishing. In 1977 he opposed the publication of *The Technology of Political Control*, a Marxist-inspired attack on the counter-insurgency techniques being deployed by the British state against the Irish Republican Army (IRA) and other extremists.[51] Writing to the publisher's editors, he remarked, 'I think Penguin has, with *The Technology of Political Control* reached the end of the path that one can fairly label as "international Marxist". And we shall be liable to really serious and merited criticism if we're not seen to explore other paths as well.' To repair the balance he suggested that Penguin should present the other half of the dialogue by offering the case of 'those "social-democrats" who are trying to make sense of the mixed economy'.[52] Boyle, a pillar of the postwar consensus, was no longer comfortable with the direction being pursued by either Penguin or the Conservative Party. Indeed, it was clear that the putative consensus he had embodied was being abandoned. While the policy apparatus of the postwar settlement remained intact until at least 1976, the consent that had been awarded to its legitimising ideology was being relinquished by large sections of political opinion from the beginning of the decade. The social democratic ideas that were at the core of this ideology were losing their intellectual force in the midst of a perceived crisis of the Keynesian welfare state.[53]

The outcomes of polarisation

By examining Penguin's output and identifying the reception that it received from the right, then, we can trace the declining legitimacy of the postwar settlement and the emergence of a new arena for ideological contestation in which ideas played a prominent role.[54] The resolution of this contestation has often been perceived as bringing about a decisive victory for the forces of the right. Historians of progressive political thought have often located the demise of social democratic thought in the social and economic changes of the 1970s.[55] Constructing equally declinist accounts, some cultural historians have regarded the decade as a counter-revolution against the progressive hopes that had emerged in 1968.[56] While these accounts have rightly identified the extent to which the period marked a political disjuncture, there may be some need to define the character of this disjuncture more carefully. In particular, it may be necessary, as Schulman and Zelizer have done in their study of America's rightwards shift of the 1970s, to suggest that the victory of a resurgent conservatism was far from inevitable and that its ascendency required it to make significant compromises.[57]

In devoting attention to the existence of a marketplace for ideas, we might place emphasis on the politics of uncertainty that was a precursor to its development.[58] Intellectuals and policy-makers were grappling with new ways to understand the problems that Britain was encountering and almost all elements of political life appeared to be in a state of flux. It is interesting to note the way in which Penguin's authors were unable to anticipate a right-wing ascendency. For instance, in *How to Survive the Slump* (1975), Graham Bannock stated: 'there will not be the rapid return to sound money, fuller use of the market mechanism and withdrawal of state intervention that is advocated by many distinguished economists'.[59] It might be necessary, then, to place greater emphasis on the strategic and contingent elements of the political struggle of the period – what Gramsci referred to as the 'conjunctural' terrain of the immediate struggle.[60] The swing to the right, as Stuart Hall argued in

1978, has to be understood as a response to a perceived crisis rather than as the inevitable product of the crisis itself.[61]

The disintegration of the postwar consensus unleashed a range of political forces whose identities and ideological directions were ambiguous and malleable. As we can identify within Penguin's publishing, the very definition of the political became contested and new arenas of debate opened up that could not be mapped easily onto the left–right spectrum. Although Penguin's journey through the late 1970s and early 1980s reveals a rightwards drift in Britain political discourse that helped a neo-liberal political economy to secure hegemony, it also suggests that the 1979 general election failed to bring a resolution to many of the forms of political contestation that had evolved in the previous decade.

If we place emphasis on the conjunctural components of the intellectual milieu of the 1970s, it may be useful to enquire into the operation of the forces of supply and demand that drove the marketplace for ideas. As Colin Hay has argued, the success of a hegemonic ideological project is dependent on its ability to project an ideology that is easily articulated and comprehended.[62] The left, it can be argued, largely failed to construct such a project in the 1970s. To illustrate this point it is worth making a comparison with the nature of left intellectualism in the 1940s – a period when publishers like Penguin seemed to be shaping and reflecting the ascendency of the left rather than its decline.

The parallels between these two periods are numerous. In the same way that the economic and social troubles of the interwar period fed an intellectual fervour around the idea of 'reconstruction', the perceived problems of the mid to late 1970s sparked a vigorous debate about the future of Britain in which ideas had a significant role to play.[63] In terms of the ideas that these separate crises provoked, there are also some common themes. The discourse and identity of the New Left, which provided the intellectual energy for much of the Penguin list of the late 1960s and 1970s, echoed the Popular Front politics of the late 1930s that had found its voice in the early Specials list.[64] For all these similarities, however, it is clear that there are also some substantial distinctions to be made.

The Penguin Specials list of the 1930s and 1940s reveals a number of ideological themes that were unifying the left around a gradualist programme of reform.[65] Despite the fact that many of its authors articulated very different ideological beliefs, they all tended to share a set of core beliefs about the changes needed to secure progressive goals. Full employment, a universal welfare system and a state-planned economy, they all agreed, were the foundations for progress. The vast majority of these authors were either members of the Labour and Liberal parties or were bureaucrats and journalists whose ideas found a receptive audience among policy-makers. The audience that created the demand for their ideas, although certainly diverse, seemed to have some common characteristics. In a study conducted in 1947, Mass Observation was able to identify a 'Penguin public' whose political beliefs were somewhat to the left of centre and whose cultural identity was relatively homogeneous.[66] In the long 1970s, by sharp contrast, the channels of supply and demand seemed more complex. Not only were a much wider range of ideas competing for space on the political agenda, but the audience for them seemed profoundly fragmented.

Although many of Penguin's radical books sold in large quantities, there is evidence that they were appealing to an increasingly narrow spectrum of opinion. Of the 75,000 copies that were sold of Robin Blackburn and Alexander Cockburn's *Student Power* (1969), for example, we might suspect that a large number were purchased by readers involved in higher education.[67] Charles Clark, editor of Penguin Education, admitted that the academic market was becoming a larger commercial concern for Penguin's non-fiction editors.[68] This shift in Penguin's market, it might be argued, led to a preoccupation with the intellectual trends that were coming to dominate higher-education institutions. Penguin's radical publishing may have been meeting an identifiable demand, but it was not a demand that reflected an emerging social and political consensus among substantial sections of the public.

This was precisely the argument pursued by Bernard Crick, who had been an editorial adviser to Penguin in the 1960s and whose political conscience echoed the civil progressivism of W. E. Williams and Edward Boyle. The 'old Penguin ideal' of the 'general educated reader, not the socialist', he argued, should have continued to provide the target for Penguin's editorial policies. Many of the Penguin Specials, he suggested, 'seem like a Left Wing dream of what the *Sunday Times* insight team should be doing', and the politics list contained too many books from the 'Western Marxist socialist camp', which were 'unlikely to be what most of your readers and a wider potential readership want'.[69] According to Crick, Penguin was failing to accommodate the preferences of readers who were not ideologically committed to the left: 'the centre has been neglected, both in a political and an intellectual sense'.[70] Crick also noted that the political list of the 1970s, despite exhibiting an excessive left-wing slant, was 'extraordinarily heterogeneous'.[71] Indeed, Penguin's political output in the 1970s, in stark contrast to that of the 1930s and 1940s, presented no common ideological themes around which the left were uniting.

Raymond Williams, who authored numerous titles for Penguin in this period, wrote in 1976 that Marxism, despite its profound academic resurgence, had failed to obtain an 'operative' character in Britain. *May Day Manifesto*, which had to some extent characterised Penguin's political publishing in the long 1970s, was regarded as something of a failure:

[*May Day Manifesto*] started out with a group of mainly Marxist social-ists thinking they could put together their various analyses – economic, political, international, cultural and so on – and present, however briefly, a general position. What we found, and would still find, is that they simply did not add up; in the politics, most obviously.[72]

When discussing the intellectual climate of the left, Williams remarked, 'I still prefer the productive popular formations of the Left of the thirties, and their successors today in popular and community publishing and drama, to the largely critical milieu of one kind of later Marxism'.[73] Williams' observations struck at the core of the left's dilemmas in the 1970s. The 'products' that publishers like Penguin were placing within the marketplace for ideas were diverse and competed for the attention of a readership that was becoming more difficult to describe in general terms. Criticising the fragmentation of the left, David Widgery noted in 1977, 'our bookshelves are now suitably enlarged but I'm not so sure our progress towards socialism has been that greatly advanced'.[74]

The difficulties that Penguin encountered when attempting to identify and serve an increasingly fragmented readership of its political output might be regarded as a symptom of the wider problems that the left encountered when trying to fight the battle of ideas in the 1970s. As Dennis Dworkin has noted, the identity politics that emerged with the new social movements of the late 1960s eroded the class-based con-ceptions of society that had previously allowed the left to construct a relatively analogous political strategy.[75] Penguin, in common with other agencies of leftish opinion, seemed to find difficulty pairing up socialist ideas with an increasingly diverse set of identities and interests.[76] Many of the concerns raised by Penguin's Specials of the 1970s were diffi-cult to align with a distinct left ideology. Some of the most significant counter-cultural movements of the 1970s exhibited a commercial and individualist character that was difficult to reconcile with the left's tra-ditional anti-consumerist and collectivist ethos. It is perhaps significant that Rick Rylance has identified a tension within Tony Godwin's pub-lishing philosophy: 'Godwin's two horses – one called commerce, the other called counterculture – threatened to bolt in different directions'.[77] Richard Cockett has suggested that the aspirational politics of the 'sixties generation' 'dovetailed perfectly with the older economic liberal traditions of what would become Thatcherism'.[78] The anti-authoritarian and anti-establishment sentiments of the period, he argues, were accom-modated more convincingly within the New Right critique of consensus politics. The journalist Paul Johnson, who had made a conversion from the social democratic left to the New Right over the course of the 1970s, wrote in 1978 that 'Penguin should drop its collectivist tracts and return to its earlier theme of individual liberty. That is what young people nowadays want to hear about.'[79]

The right, by contrast, seemed to communicate a response to the economic crisis that could be understood by ordinary voters and which appealed to their lived experiences.[80] When right-wing philosopher Anthony Flew attacked the progressivism of Penguin Education in 1976, *The Bookseller* suggested that his opinions might have been coming to characterise the views of an increasingly large section of the population:

> many people, positioned in the middle of the political road and with attitudes less vigorous than his, may well be influenced by his collection of essays in the philosophy of education to feel that grief at the demise of Penguin Education may now be decently contained.[81]

It also appeared that the entire vocabulary of British politics was making a subtle rightwards shift. The reception of Trevor Russel's *The Tory Party: Its Policies, Divisions and Future* (published as a Penguin Special in October 1978) – a fierce critique of the New Right made by a member of the Tory left – appears to be indicative of such a change. Although the response to the book demonstrates the extent to which the ideological direction of the Conservative Party was still heavily contested in 1978, it also exposes the way in which moderate Conservatism was becoming perceived as a force of the centre rather than a force of the right. One reviewer wrote that 'the reality of politics today is that there are three groupings – the Tory right, the Labour left and those in the centre – the progressive Tories and social democrat Labour men [sic]'.[82] The *Daily Telegraph* attacked Russel's endorsement of a Keynesian economic strategy and remarked, 'his middle way has become a left lane; no place for a Tory, only Penguin's idea of one'.[83] Echoing this view, the *New Manchester Review* called Russel a 'Blue Leftie'.[84]

It increasingly appeared that Penguin's drift to the left was causing it to lose touch with the common views upheld by a wider potential readership. It was a trend that created a growing tension between what we can loosely identify as the 'editorial' and 'managerial' wings of Penguin's senior staff.[85] While Allen Lane had been able to pair progressive publishing with commercial success, these two goals seemed to be running counter to one another in the 1970s. Chris Dolley, Penguin's managing director from 1970 to 1973, regarded Penguin's non-fiction editors as 'unworldly, donnish "red-moles", middle-class sympathisers with the 1968 student revolts who had no understanding of business and no sense of financial responsibility, and wasted valuable resources publishing Maoist tracts...'.[86]

In 1974 Dolley's replacement, Jim Rose, announced that Penguin Education was to be suspended. The decision was regarded by many on the left as a defeat for the progressive ideas that had been invested within the imprint's publishing philosophy.[87] Although the exact causes of the closure are uncertain, it is clear that the decision provoked a growing ideological tension between the two wings of Penguin's senior staff. The non-fiction programme was scaled back and senior staff expressed increasing concern about the more radical components of the list. When Penguin's publication of a Marxist critique of state repression in West Germany provoked a critical article from right-wing journalist Robert Moss, for instance, Rose expressed concern that such reviews could damage Penguin's reputation.[88] By the end of the decade editors with more moderate political inclinations began to inject the list with texts of a more centrist character. *Grunwick*, a book that was cautiously critical of the trade unions' role in the Grunwick dispute, for instance, was edited by Anthony Mott, a figure whose politics were distinctly liberal.[89]

A new consensus? Peter Mayer and Penguin Books, 1978–84

In the late 1970s, Penguin's editors, like many progressive intellectuals, were forced to reconsider the ideas and values that had guided them through much of the postwar period. Not only were economic troubles and increasing competitive pressures forcing publishers to reassess their publishing priorities in favour of commercial titles, the very way in which books were bought and sold was changing in response to social and cultural change.[90] In a sense, Penguin's vigorous left-wing publishing in the 1970s had masked the changes that had made Allen Lane's left-culturist model of publishing commercially untenable. The rise of consumer capitalism and the growing competitiveness of the increasingly globalised book trade had eroded the Lane–Hoggart idea that 'good' culture could be protected from the forces of the market.[91] This change became encapsulated by the emergence of the 'bestseller' as a major feature of the British book trade.[92] Popular fiction had, of course, always been a significant part of Britain's publishing industry, but the top-selling titles of the 1970s began to be distinguished not just by their literary qualities, which were often deemed to be of low value by critics, but also by the way in which they were produced.

By 1980 it was possible to identify a system of 'bestsellerdom' that had emerged to produce and market titles whose primary purpose was to achieve the maximum number of sales. These books were more likely to witness commercial interference in the 'ideas' stage of their development and were often marketed with the sort of expensive advertising campaigns that the likes of Allen Lane and W. E. Williams had once eschewed.[93] To some publishers, this shift in the character of British publishing represented a threat to the socio-educative function that had previously commanded a strong role in the ideological make-up of the publishing business. Speaking in 1984, Neil Middleton, who had been dismissed by Penguin in 1982, remarked: 'what has changed in British publishing, very dramatically, is that the old-style Penguin self-help, self-education sort of left-wing publishing has really gone out of fashion'.[94]

Penguin's response to the changed conditions of the mid to late 1970s was spearheaded by Peter Mayer, who was appointed as Penguin's chief executive in September 1978.[95] In some respects, Mayer's publishing philosophy appeared to mark a substantial break with that of Lane.[96] For Mayer, that a book was being read was just as important as the quality of the book itself: 'we have ... to go out and *sell* books. People must read what we publish, otherwise what is the point of doing it.'[97]

There had, of course, always been a strongly commercial instinct driving Allen Lane during his time at Penguin. Lane had always believed, however, that Penguin had a duty to make available works that were important despite the small audience that they might reach. He also believed that 'low brow' titles were a means to subsidise 'higher' forms of publishing and that Penguin's core function was an educational one. Although Mayer shared Lane's belief that publishing was ultimately about publishing books rather than increasing profits, he perhaps differed in his prescription of the publisher's role: 'Not everything has to be self-consciously noble. People read books to relax, not just to learn. All I ask is that whatever we publish should be good of its kind.'[98] This view was rooted in a belief that a good book was one which served the needs of its particular audience. Mayer was reluctant to recognise a relationship between the quality of a book and its literary sophistication: 'The distinction between up-market and down-market is not known in the US. It's a symptom of a class society. All I see are either good books or bad books.'[99]

Mayer's unwillingness to acknowledge a distinction between the 'down-market' and the 'literary' certainly represented a departure from Lane's left-culturist concern for standards and, to the likes of Richard Hoggart, was regarded as a surrender to the perils of cultural relativism.[100] But while such criticisms correctly identified significant changes in Penguin's ownership and publishing output, they overlooked the respect that Mayer held for the achievements and traditions of Penguin and his reluctance to allow business principles to overtake the social and cultural role of the publisher. In fact, his views towards political publishing were strongly reminiscent of those upheld by Lane. Like his predecessor, Mayer viewed the political role of the publisher in pluralistic terms: 'The responsibility therefore to a society we would keep free and pluralistic is finally individual, for pluralism represents our possibilities for individuality'.[101] Readers, he argued, should ultimately determine their own political views. As a result he was, as we can expect Lane might have been, rather critical of the 1970s Specials:

The received wisdom is that Penguin Specials became ever more parochial and polemical, i.e. they didn't necessarily expose an issue which the world should know about but increasingly presented a minority point of view of what *should be done* and over time lost creditability.[102]

In 1984, shortly before initiating a resurgence of the Penguin Special list, Mayer stated in an interview:

Penguin's role ought to be the continued engagement with the major issues; with unemployment; with the health service; with diet perhaps, with growth or non-growth of the British economy, with issues like proportional representation. We should be publishing on all of those issues, but perhaps not to any prescriptive pattern.[103]

Such sentiments led to the publication of a steady stream of books from the centre and the right that were at odds with the radical content of the publication programme of the 1970s. The most notable example was Milton Friedman's *Free to Choose* (published in 1980). Although Mayer expressed misgivings about the author's argument, he believed that this was an important text that Penguin should make available:

It really is an inaudible right wing document. However different in many respects I feel about it, I'm sure we should be bidding, and getting, this book. We publish for all markets and he is 'credentialed' and his views of things are part of [the] debate.... We need this book [if we] are to be contentious, alive and kicking.[104]

Neil Middleton stated in 1984 that 'the political direction of Penguin has become much more conservative than it once was'.[105] Mayer was certainly concerned that Penguin's political publishing should reconnect with a general audience. Fulfilling this task, however, did not necessitate a complete abandonment of Penguin's tradition of progressive publishing. Speaking in 1984, Mayer claimed that Penguin continued to publish 'rather more material from the left side than from the right', and although Penguin's list represented a wider section of the political spectrum from the late 1970s, there was an identifiable renewal of the firm's centre-left publishing in this period.[106] This publishing output exposes a complex picture. While it exemplifies the way in which the left was being forced to reconfigure itself in the wake of the economic and social changes that had helped to undermine the social democratic hegemony of the postwar period, it also demonstrates the way in which the 'new politics' of the 1970s had rejuvenated the centre left and equipped it with a discourse that could offer an alternative to the New Right's agenda.

In one sense, the character of Penguin's political output in the early 1980s suggests that the spectrum of ideas on the left was being drawn towards a political centre ground that had itself moved to the right. The Social Democratic Party (SDP), founded in 1981 to fill the space that it believed had been left vacant by the two main parties, provided Penguin with several authors and exerted a strong influence upon the themes that were pursued in the Specials in this period. Both David Owen and Shirley Williams had books published in Penguin's main list and there is evidence that Peter Mayer expressed personal sympathies with the party's ideological themes.[107] Reflecting the tremendous popular support that was awarded to the SDP in its early life, the books produced by both Owen and Williams sold in large quantities and received a warm reception in the press.[108]

However, the very success of such books can be partly attributed to their ability to accommodate a new set of values that had emerged after the victory of the Conservatives in 1979. In her 1981 Penguin title, Shirley Williams acknowledged that 'the balance of opinion has moved against the typical product of social democratic government.... The intellectual winds now blow from a different quarter.'[109] David Owen, perhaps more than any other leading Social Democrat, believed that social democracy had to be revised if it was to meet this intellectual challenge. His 1984 book, *A Future That Will Work*, published in Penguin's Viking imprint, represented an attempt to reconcile the traditional social democratic goal of equality with the themes of enterprise and individual responsibility that were at the core of the New Right's ideological model.[110] The economic policy that Owen advocated was termed the 'social market' – a phrase that had been introduced into British politics by Keith Joseph in 1975.[111] Although Owen's conception of the term differed substantially from that of Joseph, as an intellectual invention it certainly marked a retreat from a full-blooded social democratic political economy.

In 1981 Malcolm Wicks, who was then a member of the Fabian Society, submitted a manuscript to Penguin that offered a restatement of a traditional democratic socialist view of welfare provision. Evoking the sentiments of R. H. Tawney and Richard Titmuss, the draft was strongly criticised by Penguin's editorial adviser, Anthony Rees, for its inability to engage with the new conditions of a post-1979 world:

> The crucial point here is whether it is any longer a feasible strategy to extend the process of taking large sums of money through taxation.... It seems that very many working-class people no longer subscribe to the beliefs in question ... this draft is fatally old-fashioned.[112]

Coalescing around the journal *Marxism Today*, the intellectuals associated with the radical Penguin spirit of the 1970s embarked upon their own revisionist journey in the early 1980s. Repudiating the conceptions of class that had sustained their intellectual vibrancy in the previous decade, the 'third New Left' softened their critique of consumerism and made efforts to endorse a minimalist programme of social democratic reform that could unite all anti-Thatcher forces.[113] Over the course of 1983, Penguin gave voice to this strain of thinking by publishing a series of books in association with the Socialist Society – an organisation that attempted to forge links between the Labour Party and extra-parliamentary socialists by articulating a 'realist' socialist ideology.[114]

While these developments seem to suggest that the right had made significant progress in constructing a successful hegemonic project in the 1970s, they also suggest that we need to place emphasis on the limitations of this hegemony.[115] The election of the Thatcher govern-ment in 1979 set into motion the victory of neo-liberalism in the battle of ideas over economic policy, but there were significant arenas of in-tellectual conflict that were not resolved by the outcome of the 1979 general election. Within the policy documents of the SDP and the pages of *Marxism Today* we can identify significant components of the 'new politics' of the 1970s permeating into the 1980s.[116] To some extent the counter-cultural, single-issue politics that was spawned by the crises of the period leaked into a more centrist discourse that emerged within a body of resurgent social democratic thought. Indeed, social democratic ideas, although deprived of their ideological potency in the 1980s, con-tinued to play an important role in British political life.

Penguin's trajectory from 1978 to the mid-1980s reflects the forces that provided the terrain for a successful ascendency of the right while also exhibiting the continued vitality of the 'new' politics that had encouraged it to steer leftwards during the previous decade. While Penguin's 'commercialisation' seemed to confirm the emergence of a neo-liberal economic orthodoxy emerging from the late 1970s, it is also the case that its political output after Mayer's arrival demonstrates the new opportunities for progressive forces that had been forged by events of the previous decade.

This discourse was given an outlet by Penguin in a series of books entitled 'Know Your Rights: The Questions and the Answers'.[117] Lynne Segal, in her contribution to a book about changes in family relationships, admitted that 'Thatcherism has succeeded in mobilis-ing reactionary populist sentiments of patriotism, anti-trade unionism and anti-collectivism as the terrain of political debate has lurched defensively rightwards.' She added, however, that the New Right's traditionalist pro-family rhetoric had made little impact on women's attitudes towards their role.[118] Richard Cockett has argued that the narrow economic liberalism of Thatcherism was incapable of accom-modating the discourse of social and cultural liberation that was forged by the counter-cultural forces of the 1960s and 1970s.[119] Indeed, we can identify the roots of the New Right's decline, as well as those of its ascendency, in the politics of the 1970s.

Although the later SDP seemed to make a departure from its democratic socialist origins, it was nonetheless the vehicle for a vibrant renewal of centre-left politics that was able to harness a remarkable amount of popular support around an agenda of individual freedom that was distinct from that of the New Right. Much of its ideological character had echoes of the anti-establishment, participatory brand of middle-class dissidence that had proliferated in the 1970s. We can identify, without too much difficulty, the incorporation of substantial elements of SDP ideology in the New Labour project that would unseat the Conservatives in 1997. In Penguin's history at least, the 1970s did not represent the frustration of the radical hopes of the late 1960s but a period when new political and cultural formations were imposing themselves upon the mainstream agenda.

Thus, although Mayer's reforms of Penguin can be regarded as marking the decline of the left-culturist discourse that had once been at the core of the firm's publishing philosophy during the hegemony of the postwar consensus, it is also the case that he reconnected the publisher with the concerns of a centrist readership whose demands and needs had been significantly shaped by the social, moral and cultural agendas that had been spawned by the marketplace for ideas of the 1970s.

Conclusion

Penguin's non-fiction publishing in the long 1970s thus reveals a marketplace for ideas that was shaping and reflecting a polarisation of Britain's politics. Confronted by the perceived failings of the social democratic policy framework that had prevailed since the 1940s, intellectuals from both the political left and the right engaged with radical ideas in an attempt to provide solutions to the various crises that they observed. Penguin's published output demonstrates the uncertainty and puzzlement that dominated the intellectual climate of British politics from the late 1960s. Discourses of decline and crisis were symptoms of a 'politics of emergency' that dismantled old assumptions and identities and fostered a new receptiveness to ideas. The outcome was an intellectual climate in which almost all aspects of political life seemed to be 'up for grabs'.

These features of Penguin's publishing might suggest that we need to emphasise the ways in which the 'conjunctural' aspects of the crisis determined the outcome of the battle for ideas. The ascendency of the right was neither uncontested nor inevitable. No inevitable political trajectory, it seems, was inscribed within the conjuncture of the late

1970s.[120] Indeed, the resolution of ideational conflict seemed to be characterised by decisive intervention and contingency rather than glacial movements of opinion at either elite or popular levels. We might need to devote more attention, therefore, to what Hay has described as the 'narrativity' of the crisis.[121] The responses to the crisis were just as important as the crisis itself in determining its political outcomes.

The very nature of these outcomes might also require reassessment. Although the terrain of the political struggle provided fertile ground for the success of a neo-liberal hegemonic project, Penguin's journey from 1979 suggests that we might need to define the parameters of this hegemony more closely. While Penguin's output in the early 1980s demonstrated the emergence of neo-liberal hegemony in the sphere of political economy, it also indicates that the new 'settlement' that emerged from 1979 was incapable of neutralising the antagonisms and discontents of the previous decade. In some spheres at least, the legacy of the 1970s was an expansion, rather than a reduction, of the intellectual space in which critiques of neo-liberalism could take root. Indeed, the resurgence of Penguin's progressive publishing from the early 1980s might mean that we need to revise the declinist narratives of social democracy that have established strong currency in accounts of late-twentieth-century Britain.[122]

By helping to draw out these features of the political contestation of the 1970s, the concept of a marketplace for ideas can thus be a useful tool for reassessing the decade's location within Britain's wider postwar history. By encouraging an appreciation of the enlarged space for disagreement and conflict that appeared from the late 1960s, it conveys the sense of relative instability and flux that distinguished the intellectual climate of this period from that which had existed previously. Moreover, it can bring into focus the spaces of ideological contestation that existed beyond the formal institutions of representation and government, thus helping to identify the ideological battles that were left unresolved by the 1979 general election and the progressive intellectual inheritance that the decade donated to later periods. In several ways, then, the concept of a marketplace for ideas can be useful in the task of setting the parameters of political change in a period that was, in many respects at least, the pivot around which the history of postwar Britain turned.

Notes

1 I am grateful to the UK Arts and Humanities Research Council for funding the doctoral research on which this chapter is based.
2 D. Dutton, *British Politics Since 1945* (Oxford: Blackwell, 1991), ch. 4; D. Kavanagh, *Thatcherism and British Politics: The End of Consensus?* (Oxford: Oxford University Press, 1997); S. Hall, 'The great moving right show', *Marxism*

Today, January 1979, pp. 14–20; C. Hay, *Re-stating Social and Political Change* (Buckingham: Open University Press, 1996), ch. 7.

3 See, for instance, Hall, 'The great moving right show'; Hay, *Re-stating Social and Political Change*, pp. 128–44; H. Stephenson, *Mrs Thatcher's First Year* (London: Jill Norman, 1980); P. Kerr, 'The post-war consensus: a woozle that wasn't', in D. Marsh, J. Buller, C. Hay, J. Johnston, P. Kerr, S. McAnulla and M. Watson, *Postwar British Politics in Perspective* (Cambridge: Polity Press, 1999); D. Dolowitz, 'Thatcherism and the three "R's": radicalism, realism and rhetoric in the third term of the Thatcher government', *Parliamentary Affairs*, 49:3 (1996), pp. 455–70; B. Jessop, 'From social democracy to Thatcherism: twenty-five years of British politics', in N. Abercrombie and A. Warde (eds), *Social Change in Contemporary Britain* (Cambridge: Polity Press, 1999), pp. 14–39.

4 On the history of Penguin Books see: J. Lewis, *Penguin Special: The Life and Times of Allen Lane* (London: Viking, 2005); J. E. Morpurgo, *King Penguin: Allen Lane* (London: Hutchinson, 1979); N. Joicey, 'A paperback guide to progress: Penguin Books, 1935–1951', *Twentieth Century British History*, 4:1 (1993), pp. 25–56; A. McCleery, 'The return of the book publisher to book history: the case of Allen Lane', *Book History*, 5 (2002), 161–85.

5 R. Gott, 'Pick up a Penguin?', *Guardian*, 19 September 1985.

6 P. A. Hall, 'Policy paradigms, social learning, and the state: the case of economic policymaking in Britain', *Comparative Politics*, 5:3 (1993), pp. 275–96, at p. 286.

7 For a summary of the debate see K. Hickson, 'The post-war consensus revisited', *Political Quarterly*, 75:2 (2004), pp. 142–54.

8 Hay, *Re-stating Social and Political Change*, pp. 47–8.

9 M. Bradbury, 'Foreword', in *Fifty Penguin Years* (Harmondsworth: Penguin, 1985), p. 7.

10 R. Hoggart, *An English Temper* (London: Chatto & Windus, 1982), p. 120.

11 Lewis, *Penguin Special*, p. 402.

12 It was not uncommon for an individual Special to sell over 200,000 copies. Conservative Arthur Bryant, who spearheaded the party's attempts to counter leftish propaganda, regarded the success of Penguin's non-fiction publishing as a sign that the battle of the books was being won by the left. See E. H. H. Green, *Ideologies of Conservatism* (Oxford: Oxford University Press, 2002), pp. 141–2.

13 R. Jenkins, *The Labour Case* (Harmonsdworth: Penguin, 1959); Viscount Hailsham, *The Conservative Case* (Harmondsworth: Penguin, 1959), p. 111.

14 S. Meredeen, *The Man Who Made Penguins: The Life of Sir William Emrys Williams, Editor-in-Chief, Penguin Books 1936–1965* (Stroud: Darien-Jones, 2007), p. 245. Indeed, in the aftermath of the 1945 general election Williams believed that Penguin had 'a kind of moral commitment to give the Liberals a hearing'. Penguin Archive, Bristol University Library (hereafter 'PA'), DM 1819/22/3, Bill Williams to Allen Lane, 15 July 1949. See also Russell Edwards, 'Founder's fate', in R. Edwards and S. Hare (eds), *Pelican Books: A Sixtieth Anniversary Celebration* (Chippenham: Penguin Collectors Society, 1997), p. 16, and H. L. Beales, 'W. E. Williams', *ibid.*, pp. 21–2.

15 Morpurgo, *King Penguin*, p. 210; PA, DM 1819/22/7, Allen Lane to Edward Boyle, 1 November 1963.

16 Cited in A. Gold (ed.), *Edward Boyle* (London: Macmillan, 1991), pp. 31–2.

17 Edward's Boyle thoughts on Anthony Crosland's book *The Future of Socialism* is illuminating in this regard. See the *Guardian*, 22 March 1974.

18 L. Forster and S. Harper (eds), *British Culture and Society in the 1970s: The Lost Decade* (Newcastle: Cambridge Scholars, 2010), p. 9.

19 See, for instance, A. Hall and A. Whichelow, *What's Wrong With Parliament?* (Harmondsworth: Penguin Books, 1964); R. Malik, *What's Wrong With British*

Industry? (Harmondsworth: Penguin Books, 1964); K. Martin, *Britain in the Sixties: The Crown and the Establishment* (Harmondsworth: Penguin Books, 1963); G. Moorhouse, *Britain in the Sixties: The Other England* (Harmondsworth: Penguin Books, 1963).

20 H. Pemberton and M. J. Oliver, 'Learning and policy change in 20th century British economic policy', *Governance*, 17:3 (2003), pp. 415–41, at p. 427; A. Sinfield, *Literature, Politics and Culture in Postwar Britain* (London: Continuum, 2004), p. 281; J. Tomlinson, *The Politics of Decline* (Pearson: Harlow, 2001), pp. 88–9.

21 M. Shanks, *The Stagnant Society* (Harmondsworth: Penguin Books, 1961). For a discussion of Penguin's publications in the early 1960s see M. Grant, 'Historians, the Penguin Specials and the "state-of-the-nation" literature, 1958–64', *Contemporary British History*, 17:3 (2003), pp. 29–54.

22 See, for instance, D. Marsh, *The Future of the Welfare State* (Harmondsworth: Penguin Books, 1964) and Shanks, *The Stagnant Society*, ch. 7. In their 1964 elections Specials, neither Tim Raison (Conservative) nor Jim Northcott (Labour) expressed a desire to radically restructure the British state: see J. Northcott, *Why Labour?* (Harmondsworth: Penguin Books, 1964); and T. Raison, *Why Conservative?* (Harmondsworth: Penguin Books, 1964).

23 For an account of a Penguin author's intellectual shift from reformist to revolutionary ideas, see T. Pateman, '1968: student revolt and the making of a course-critic', *Hard Cheese*, 2 (1971), pp. 45–59.

24 Tomlinson, *The Politics of Decline*, p. 88; S. Hall, C. Critcher, T. Jefferson, J. Clarke and B. Roberts, *Policing the Crisis: Mugging, the State, and Law and Order* (London: Macmillan, 1978), p. 237.

25 A. Glyn and B. Sutcliffe, *British Capitalism: Workers and the Profits Squeeze* (Harmondsworth: Penguin Books, 1972), p. 212.

26 E. P. Thompson, *Warwick University Ltd* (Harmondsworth: Penguin Books, 1970), p. 146.

27 J. Rowland, *Community Decay* (Harmondsworth: Penguin Books, 1973), p. 147.

28 K. Coates and R. Silburn, *Poverty: The Forgotten Englishmen* (Harmondsworth: Penguin Books, 1970), pp. 234–5.

29 Godwin's London bookshop, Better Books, became a venue for subcultural expression and provided financial support for the feminist magazine *Spare Rib*. See R. Rylance, 'Reading with a mission: the public sphere of Penguin Books', *Critical Quarterly*, 47:4 (2005), pp. 57–61. In various letters to colleagues, Tony Godwin expressed personal sympathies for the ideas emerging from the New Left. In a letter from December 1966, for instance, he noted his admiration for Robin Blackburn's contribution to the 1967 Special *The Incompatibles: Trade Union Militancy and the Consensus* (Harmondsworth: Penguin Books, 1967): see PA, DM 1107/S262.

30 A. S. Sassoon, 'From Berkeley to Blair: a dialogue of the deaf?', in G. Andrews, R. Cockett, A. Hooper and M. Williams (eds), *New Left, New Right and Beyond* (London: Macmillan, 1999), p. 183. Like many on the left, Godwin had expressed enthusiasm for Wilson in 1964: see PA, DM 1107/S237, Tony Godwin to Harold Wilson, 30 June 1964.

31 R. Williams (ed.), *May Day Manifesto 1968* (Harmondsworth: Penguin, 1968), preface. Penguin also published two accounts of the events of May 1968: P. Seale and M. McConville, *French Revolution 1968* (Harmondsworth: Penguin, 1968); D. Cohn-Bendit and G. Cohn-Bendit, *Obsolete Communism: The Left-Wing Alternative* (Harmondsworth: Penguin, 1968).

32 T. Burgess (ed.), *Matters of Principle: Labour's Last Chance* (Harmondsworth: Penguin, 1968); B. Lapping, *The Labour Government, 1964–70* (Harmondsworth:

Penguin, 1970); P. Foot, *The Politics of Harold Wilson* (Harmondsworth: Penguin, 1968).

33 The 'manifesto' was quoted in correspondence with Trevor Park, a Labour MP who had been fiercely critical of Wilson's government and whom Penguin identified as a potential author for a book on parliamentary democracy. See PA, DM 1952/557, Robert Hutchinson to Trevor Park, 3 March 1969.

34 PA, DM 1952/557, R. Hutchinson to T. Park, 3 March 1969.

35 PA, DM 1294/6/2/27, BBC interview with Neil Middleton, 1984.

36 Draft of Ken Tarbuck, *Reminiscences of a Some-Time Trotskyist*, at www.revolutionaryhistory.co.uk/ken-tarbuck/autobiography-of-ken-tarbuck-to-1964.html, accessed 1 November 2011.

37 The series was published from 1973 to 1978 and contained the first English translation of *Grundrisse*.

38 See, for instance, Glyn and Sutcliffe, *British Capitalism*. The book originated as an article in the *New Left Review*. J. Joll, *Antonio Gramsci* (Harmondsworth: Penguin, 1978).

39 PA, DM 1952/Box 613, Peter Wright, memorandum, 'The politics list in the Pelican area', 1978.

40 In 1964 Allen Lane had provided funds to help establish cultural studies' main institutional apparatus, the Centre for Contemporary Cultural Studies. R. Williams, *Culture and Society* (Harmondsworth: Penguin, 1971); R. Williams, *The Long Revolution* (Harmondsworth: Penguin, 1965). Also see S. Hall and T. Jefferson (eds), *Resistance Through Rituals* (London: Hutchinson, 1976).

41 See, for instance, The Ecologist, *A Blueprint for Survival* (Harmondsworth: Penguin, 1972); A. Coote and T. Gill, *Women's Rights: A Practical Guide* (Harmondsworth: Penguin, 1974); B. Cox, *Civil Liberties in Britain* (Harmondsworth: Penguin, 1975); C. Hill, *Rights and Wrongs: Some Essays on Human Rights* (Harmondsworth: Penguin, 1969); E. Pizzey, *Scream Quietly or the Neighbours Will Hear* (Harmondsworth: Penguin, 1974); R. Bailey, *The Homeless and the Empty Houses* (Harmondsworth: Penguin, 1977); S. Rowbotham, *Women, Resistance and the Revolution* (Harmondsworth: Penguin, 1974); J. Mitchell, *Women's Estate* (Harmondsworth: Penguin, 1971); A. Oakley and J. Mitchell, *The Rights and Wrongs of Women* (Harmondsworth: Penguin, 1976).

42 M. Kogan, 'The Plowden Committee: gathering of the great and the good', *Times Education Supplement*, 24 January 1997. After the details of the Robbins report were published in October 1963, Allen Lane offered Boyle a role in expanding Penguin's educational publishing. PA, DM 1819/22/7, Allen Lane to Edward Boyle, 1 November 1963.

43 B. Jackson and D. Marsden, *Education and the Working-Class* (Harmondsworth: Penguin, 1969); D. Head, *Free Way to Learning: Educational Alternatives in Action* (Harmondsworth: Penguin, 1974). One former employee of Penguin Education wrote: 'what Penguin Education proved, I think, is that it is possible to be an educational publisher with an ideology and to make money as well'. Quotation extracted from PA, DM 1294/3/5/3, *Dis-connexions* (a magazine published by former employees of Penguin Education), spring 1976. Martin Lightfoot, the Penguin Education's chief editor, admitted that the imprint had been committed to an egalitarian ethos: 'That Penguin Education attempted to redress some balances, and that it published books which put cases for the uncertain, the unprivileged, the inarticulate and the unnoticed is of course true, and perhaps no very bad thing.' M. Lightfoot, 'Penguin Education', *Bookseller*, 14 August 1976.

44 See H. J. Eysenck, 'The rise of the mediocracy', in C. B. Cox and A. E. Dyson (eds), *Black Paper Two: The Crisis in Education* (London: Critical Quarterly Society, 1969), pp. 34–40.

45 N. Rossi and T. Cole, *Letter to a Teacher* (Harmondsworth: Penguin, 1970).
46 A. Maude, *Spectator*, 14 November 1970. Paul Johnson, who would become a speechwriter for Thatcher, wrote a similar critique of Penguin's editorial policies: P. Johnson, 'Penguin path', *Evening Standard*, 3 October 1978.
47 E. Boyle, A. Crosland and M. Kogan, *The Politics of Education* (Harmondsworth: Penguin, 1971), p. 17. Also see J. Vaizey, *In Breach of Promise. Gaitskell, Macleod, Titmuss, Crosland, Boyle: Five Men Who Shaped a Generation* (London: Weidenfeld & Nicholson, 1983).
48 W. Rees-Mogg, 'The move away from politics', in Gold (ed.), *Edward Boyle*, p. 123.
49 PA, DM 1294/17/8, Rhodes Boyson to Hans Schmoller, 13 October 1975.
50 PA, DM 1952/383, Neil Middleton to Peter Wright, Anthony Mott and Jim Rose, 8 September 1978.
51 C. Ackroyd, K. Margolis, J. Rosenhead and T. Shallice, *The Technology of Political Control* (Harmondsworth: Penguin, 1977). See Richard Moss, 'Left wing of the Penguin', *Daily Telegraph*, 12 April 1977.
52 PA, DM 1952/Box 613, Edward Boyle to Jim Rose, 26 June 1977.
53 R. E. Tyrell (ed.), *The Future That Doesn't Work: Social Democracy's Failures in Britain* (New York: Doubleday, 1977).
54 R. Lowe, *The Welfare State in Britain Since 1945* (London: Macmillan, 1993), p. 303.
55 N. Thompson, *Left in the Wilderness: The Political Economy of British Democratic Socialism Since 1979* (Chesham: Acumen, 2002); N. Ellison, *Egalitarian Thoughts and Labour Politics: Retreating Visions* (Routledge: London, 1994).
56 R. Hewison, *Culture and Consensus: England, Art and Politics Since 1940* (London: Methuen, 1995), pp. 159–208.
57 B. J. Schulman and J. E. Zelizer (eds), *Rightward Bound: Making America Conservative in the 1970s* (Cambridge, MA: Harvard University Press, 2008), pp. 1–10.
58 Hall, 'Policy paradigms', p. 289.
59 G. Bannock, *How to Survive the Slump* (Harmondsworth: Penguin, 1975), p. 25.
60 Cited by Hall, 'The great moving right show', p. 15.
61 *Ibid.*, p. 14.
62 Hay, *Re-stating Social and Political Change*, p. 149.
63 See, for instance, R. Acland, *Unser Kampf* (Harmondsworth: Penguin, 1940) and H. Laski, *Where Do We Go From Here?* (Harmondsworth: Penguin Books, 1940).
64 M. Kenny, *The First New Left: British Intellectuals After Stalin* (London: Lawrence & Wishart, 1995), pp. 12–13.
65 On the progressive unity that was forged by the Popular Front movement, see D. Blaazer, *The Popular Front and the Progressive Tradition* (Cambridge: Cambridge University Press, 1992).
66 Mass Observation Archive, University of Sussex, TC20/Box 9, 'A report on Penguin world' (1947).
67 Correspondence with Robin Blackburn, 9 October 2010; R. Blackburn and A. Cockburn, *Student Power: Problems, Diagnosis, Action* (Harmondsworth: Penguin, 1969).
68 PA, DM 1952/631, Charles Clark to Dieter Pevsner, 12 November 1970.
69 Bernard Crick, 'Political Penguins', PA, DM1952/613. Also see B. Crick, 'On bias', *Teaching Politics*, May 1972, reprinted in B. Crick, *Essays on Citizenship* (London: Continuum, 2005), pp. 35–58.
70 Crick, 'Political Penguins'.
71 *Ibid.*

72 R. Williams, 'Notes on Marxism in Britain since 1945', *New Left Review*, December 1976, p. 89.

73 *Ibid.*, p. 86.

74 D. Widgery, 'The left in Britain: a reply', *Socialist Register*, 1977, p. 57.

75 D. Dworkin, *Class Struggles* (Harlow: Longman, 2007), p. 215.

76 G. Andrews, 'The three New Lefts and their legacies', in G. Andrews, R. Cockett, A. Hooper and M. Williams (eds), *New Left, New Right and Beyond: Taking the Sixties Seriously* (Basingstoke: Palgrave, 1999), p. 77; D. Dworkin, *Cultural Marxism in Postwar Britain* (Durham, NC: Duke University Press, 1997), p. 247.

77 Rylance, 'Reading with a mission', p. 59.

78 R. Cockett, 'The New Right and the 1960s: the dialectics of liberation', in Andrews *et al.* (eds), *New Left, New Right and Beyond*, p. 92.

79 Johnson, 'Penguin's path'.

80 Hay, *Re-stating Social and Political Change*, pp. 136–9, 149.

81 *Bookseller*, 31 July 1976. *The Times* pursued a similar argument in an article that cited Penguin as an agent of Marxist ideas: 'the intellectual initiative which the left has enjoyed for years has to some extent passed to the right'. See 'The enemies of liberty', *The Times*, 21 September 1977.

82 P. Underwood, 'Will there be a left–right march to the centre?', *South Wales Express*, 31 October 1978.

83 'Turn left for middle way', *Daily Telegraph*, 22 October 1978.

84 *New Manchester Review*, 20 October 1978. Despite the considerable attention that the book received from the press, the book sold just 8,000 copies. PA, DM 1952/329, Neil Middleton to Trevor Russel, 29 January 1979.

85 Interview with Ian Savage, 9 March 2011.

86 Lewis, *Penguin Special*, p. 394.

87 An obituary published in the *Times Educational Supplement*, endorsed by a long list of names from the left, suggested that the closure was 'a worrying comment on the control of money over ideas'. 'We regret the death of Penguin Education', *Times Educational Supplement*, 1 March 1974.

88 R. Moss, 'Germany's response to terrorism', *Daily Telegraph*, 4 April 1978; PA, DM 1107/S, Neil Middleton to Peter Wright, Anthony Mott and Jim Rose, 8 September 1978; S. Cobler and F. McDonagh, *Law, Order and Politics in West Germany* (Harmondsworth: Penguin, 1978).

89 J. Rogaly, *Grunwick* (Harmondsworth: Penguin, 1977). The book was fiercely criticised by the Marxist journal *International Socialism*. See J. Rose, 'Grunwick', *International Socialism*, November 1977, pp. 27–8.

90 Penguin's total volume of sales fell from 44 million in 1974 to 39 million in 1979. E. De Bellaigue, 'The extraordinary flight of publishing's wingless bird', *Logos*, 12:3 (2001), p. 130.

91 A. Sinfield, *Literature, Politics and Culture in Postwar Britain* (London: Athlone Press, 1997), p. 331.

92 J. Sutherland, *Bestsellers: Popular Fiction of the 1970s* (London: Routledge, 1981).

93 *Ibid.*, p. 31.

94 PA, DM 1294/6/2/27, interview with Neil Middleton, September 1984.

95 'Penguin seeks remedy for flagging profits', *The Times*, 27 September 1978.

96 Sutherland, *Bestsellers*, pp. 18–28.

97 *The Times*, 27 September 1978.

98 *Ibid.*

99 Quoted in 'Can Penguin's books balance?', *Marketing*, 9 July 1980.

100 R. Hoggart, *An Imagined Life* (Oxford: Oxford University Press, 1993), p. 50.

101 P. Mayer, 'A longer view of the current account', *Bookseller*, 13 January 1979.

102 PA, DM 1294/3/6/7/3, Peter Mayer to Joy Chamberlain, Peter Carson and John Rolfe, 12 July 1984.

103 PA, DM 1294/6/2/27, BBC interview with Peter Mayer, 1984.

104 PA, DM 1952/Box238, Peter Mayer to Peter Carson, undated memo. See also R. Woffindon, 'Penguin's progress', *New Statesman*, 31 December 1982.

105 PA, DM 1294/6/2/27, BBC interview with Neil Middleton, 1984.

106 PA, DM 1294/6/2/27, BBC interview with Peter Mayer, 1984.

107 S. Williams, *Politics Is For People* (London: Allen Lane, 1981); D. Owen, *A Future That Will Work* (Harmondsworth: Penguin, 1984); S. Williams, *A Job to Live: The Impact of Tomorrow's Technology on Work and Society* (Harmondsworth: Penguin, 1985); D. Owen, *A United Kingdom* (Harmondsworth: Penguin, 1986). Owen was also approached to write a book on the National Health Service in 1984 but declined the offer due to time constraints: PA, DM 1952/148/7785, David Owen to Martin Soames, 30 August 1984.

108 PA, DM 1952/163/9348, Paul Maycock to Martin Soames, 17 February 1986. Four Gallup polls conducted for the *Daily Telegraph* in the three months following the party's launch showed support for the SDP–Liberal Alliance averaging 42.6 per cent. Cited in I. Bradley, *Breaking the Mould?* (London: Martin Robertson, 1981), p. 141. Also see A. Heath, R. Jowell and J. Curtice, 'Moderate muscle: the Alliance takes shape', *Marxism Today*, January 1989, pp. 18–21.

109 Williams, *Politics Is For People*, p. 28.

110 See D. Blackburn, 'Facing the future? David Owen and social democracy in the 1980s and beyond', *Parliamentary Affairs*, 64:4 (2011), pp. 634–51.

111 R. Cockett, *Thinking the Unthinkable: Think-Tanks and the Economic Counter-revolution, 1931–1983* (London: HarperCollins, 1994), p. 253.

112 PA, DM 1952/Box 238; M. Wicks, *A Future For All: Do We Need the Welfare State?* (Harmondsworth: Penguin, 1987).

113 E. Hobsbawn, 'Labour's lost millions', *Marxism Today*, October 1983; D. Thompson, *Pessimism of the Intellect? A History of New Left Review* (Monmouth: Merlin, 2007), pp. 121–3.

114 J. Lea and J. Young, *What Is To Be Done About Law and Order?* (Harmondsworth: Penguin, 1984); L. Segal, *What Is To Be Done About the Family?* (Harmondsworth: Penguin, 1983); Jeanette Mitchell, *What Is To Be Done About Illness and Health?* (Harmondsworth: Penguin, 1984). The books were intended to 'be for the 80s what our series "Britain in the 60s" was for that decade'. PA, DM1952/Box 132.

115 Schulman and Zelizer (eds), *Rightward Bound*, p. 3.

116 The SDP–Liberal Alliance manifesto of 1983 contained a number of policy themes that related to the extension of participatory democracy and the rights of minority groups. See *Working Together for Britain: The SDP–Liberal Alliance Programme for Government* (London: Social Democratic Party, 1983). See also S. Hall, 'Thatcher's lessons', *Marxism Today*, March 1988.

117 M. Wilson, *Immigration and Race: Know Your Rights* (Harmondsworth: Penguin, 1983); T. Gill and L. Whitty, *Women's Rights in the Workplace: Know Your Rights* (Harmondsworth: Penguin, 1983); R. Bailey, *A Guide to Your Town Hall Rights* (Harmondsworth: Penguin, 1983).

118 Segal, *What Is To Be Done About the Family?*, pp. 225–30.

119 R. Cockett, 'The New Right and the 1960s', pp. 102–4.

120 S. Hall and M. Jacques (eds), *New Times: The Changing Face of Politics in the 1990s* (London: Lawrence & Wishart, 1989), p. 18.

121 C. Hay, 'Chronicles of a death foretold: the winter of discontent and construction of the crisis of British Keynesianism', *Parliamentary Affairs*, 63:3 (2010), pp. 446–70.
122 For a challenge to this declinist thesis see J. Callaghan and S. Tunney, 'The end of social democracy?', *Politics*, 21:1 (2001), pp. 63–72.

13

Afterword. The future of the 1970s

Lawrence Black and Hugh Pemberton

Our conclusions can be only provisional and partial. The nature of this project was merely to be suggestive (not prescriptive) of ways in which the 1970s merited reassessing, and to nudge some key voices into the debate. Clearly, as many questions are begged as are answered here – or, as the familiar academic adage has it, more research is needed. In their reassessments of some of the key ideas of the 1970s our contributors illustrate the extraordinary vitality of the decade's marketplace for ideas, the way in which reactions to, albeit often difficult, events tended to be disproportionate, and the means by which a particular reading of Britain in the 1970s came to dominate the memory of that decade.

In his chapter in this volume, James Alt stands by his use of the phrase 'the politics of economic decline' when discussing British political economy in the 1970s. He concedes that in retrospect the panic over inflationary pressures was undue, or due to contingent political factors (most notably the monetarist revolution, the rise of the 'New Right' and the election of Margaret Thatcher as leader of the Conservative Party). Nonetheless, he argues that the 1970s has had an enduringly negative image precisely because, in terms of political economy, 'the decade *was* one of negatives: both economic, as conditions worsened, and political, as the comfortable policy and institutional remedies of the past failed'. In his commentary on Alt's work, Jim Tomlinson confirms that it represented a 'major contribution' to contemporary economic and political debate. But he argues for a more constructed sense of decline and crisis in the 1970s. In Tomlinson's view, the 'great fear' about the economy that gripped much of Britain's 'serious' media and its chattering classes was both excessive and out of line with the much more calm responses, for example regarding inflation, among the mass of the population, who continued to maintain their faith in the institutions of British government. Building on his work on the paradoxical panic over Britain's relative economic decline in the boom years of the 1950s and 1960s as well as in the 1970s and early 1980s,[1] Tomlinson argues that if the fifties and sixties represented an economic 'golden age', then the 1970s represents something more like a 'golden age' of declin*ism*. This was chiefly (and successfully) driven by the political New Right as it sought to lay the blame for relative decline on the putative postwar Keynesian social democratic consensus.

Three decades on, Samuel Brittan is big enough to acknowledge that, so far as his overarching concerns for democracy in the 1970s were concerned, his 'conjecture must be regarded as well and truly falsified', and he considers the various factors that made it so, noting in particular the importance of the subsequent weakening of union power. In his discussion he explains the process by which he came to write his influential analyses and is at pains to emphasise that, while he was prepared to endorse a Thatcherite analysis of union power, and of the way in which it should be reduced, he was never part of the Thatcher entourage. Roger Middleton charts Brittan's contribution to increasing perceptions in the 1970s of Britain's decline. In doing so, he explores not just the construction of the 'crisis' but also Brittan's contribution to creating the ideational political and policy space within which the New Right could develop its diagnosis of that decline as well as its proposed remedies. Middleton seeks to make his case that the contributions of journalists, most notably Brittan and Peter Jay, to the development of these ideas about both the problem and the solution, have been significantly underestimated in comparison with the influence of think-tanks.

Stuart Holland explores the roots of his ideas in European models of economic planning and the ways in which those origins, and the fact that he wished to work with rather than against capitalism, proved problematic when backing for his strategy on Labour's right (from which, ironically, support had first emerged) evaporated. He became dependent on the support of a left that was highly suspicious of Europe and tended to view 'control' of the private sector exclusively through the lens of nationalisation. In his analysis of Holland's influence, Mark Wickham-Jones concludes that Holland's contribution to Labour's economic strategy was remarkable and that his success was a function of both the prevailing economic crisis and the particular institutional configuration and internal politics of the party at the time. Equally, those forces are seen by Wickham-Jones also to explain why the Alternative Economic Strategy proved so divisive within Labour,

253

most notably because the lack of centre ground within the party meant Holland had to shape his ideas to secure support on the left, with the inevitable alienation of the right.

We get a much more positive view of the seventies from Lynne Segal. Rather than the 1960s or 1980s, she argues that it was the 1970s that marked the heyday of women's liberation, both in terms of legislation (on equal pay, sex discrimination and domestic violence, for example) and in terms of the identity and consciousness-raising elements of the movement which sought to overturn powerful prevailing norms in the 1970s. Like Holland and others in this volume, Segal offers a rich personal narrative of the 1970s, in her case in relation to metropolitan New Left feminism, entwined with the broader intellectual and political context and a less introspective and Anglo-centric approach which emphasises the importance of ideas flowing to Britain from the USA. If Segal emphasises the radical undergrowth, texts and world view of feminism as a social movement, Pat Thane situates the feminism of the 1970s in the context of its linkages, overlaps and differences with the left in general, itself revived by 1968, and with Labour in government in the 1970s. Thane argues against a tendency to emphasise the 'exceptionalism' of the Women's Liberation Movement in the decade. Instead, she stresses that this was the 'second wave' of feminism, locating it in a much longer-term battle for women's rights and emphasising the achievements of various women's organisations from the beginning of the twentieth century. Picking up the radical mantle of second-wave feminism in this way encourages a rethinking of neglected periods in women's activism. However, like Segal, Thane concludes that there is a decidedly more positive narrative to be told about the 1970s than is commonly supposed, and that historians overlook this at their peril.

In Bill Osgerby's discussion of Cohen's work on the concept of 'moral panic', we also learn much about the discipline of sociology in this decade, and the ways in which, in a rapidly expanding university sector, the discipline was shaped by a generation of young scholars (most notably those in the National Deviancy Conference and around Birmingham's Centre for Contemporary Cultural Studies) that were profoundly hostile to established orthodoxies. Osgerby argues that, in the conditions of the 1970s, the concept of moral panic proved its utility. In an exploration of the furore about punk that followed Bill Grundy's infamous interview with the Sex Pistols on prime-time television, Osgerby highlights the way in which a new set of sensational folk devils was both created and developed.

Peter Mayer sees Penguin's non-fiction output after 1970 as having followed 'fashionable' social and political trends in thinking in Britain's universities. This, argues Mayer, was a significant problem for the firm in that the intellectual roots of its output were often, and increasingly, not correlated with the interests of the general reader. Thus, for Mayer, though Penguin was plainly an important contributor to the marketplace for ideas in these years, it underperformed in the commercial marketplace as the 1970s wore on. Mayer takes on some of his critics of the time and later who saw his arrival as marking a shift in Penguin's editorial policy that was not just to the right but positively 'Thatcherite'. Rather, Mayer asserts that Penguin was merely returning to publishing books that its broader readership would actually want to buy. In his commentary on Mayer, Dean Blackburn identifies a strong sense within Penguin during the Allen Lane years that it had a mission to promote social democracy and progressive ideals and asks whether the apparent erosion of this role by the end of the 1970s tells us anything about prevailing social, cultural and political forces at a time when the social democratic settlement that Penguin helped to shape seemed to enter terminal decline. Like Mayer, Blackburn takes his analysis into the early 1980s, arguing that Penguin's 'turn to the right' was actually a return to the political centre, a concept that, while it had apparently been hollowed out in the polarising political debates of the seventies, was much more important than is generally acknowledged, and was to re-emerge politically in the early 1980s (most obviously with the creation of the Social Democratic Party in 1981). In this sense, Blackburn argues that the arrival of Mayer ensured that Penguin did not follow the left on the road to 'the longest suicide note in history' that was Labour's 1983 manifesto.

Will the real 1970s reveal themselves?

In their chapters, our contributors have engaged closely with an array of ideas that were in play in Britain during the 1970s. The decade is of considerable interest not just for the fecundity of ideas that characterised it and for the battles that were waged between contesting ideas but also because the battles that were fought were fought for very high stakes indeed. For this reason, it occupies an important, and we would argue a pivotal, place in the postwar history of Britain.

The papers are now virtually completely open. Why then is the decade so comparatively neglected by contemporary British historians? One reason may be that they are still mining possibilities presented by the sheer wealth of archival material available for earlier decades. It may also be that the 'golden age', and particularly the 1960s, provides more congenial research topics. We wonder, however, if a key issue might be the centrality of economics and political economy to the experience of the decade and a certain disconnection between this and other social science analyses. The relative neglect of the decade also means that historians have to pose fundamental questions rather than just delve deeper into established research questions and conduct research within established analytical frameworks.

The debateable extent and nature of the 1970s crisis and role of the media are among the leitmotivs in the preceding chapters and, out of them, several fundamental questions present themselves. First, how should we periodise the seventies? For political historians, the decadal periodisation has quite a powerful logic. It begins with a general election in which a Conservative government came to power apparently intending to implement a marked break with the policies of the postwar period, though within a couple of years it had executed an humiliating 'u-turn' (though both the initial shift and the u-turn were perhaps rather more constructed by political opponents, of right and left, than they were real). The decade ends in the shambles of the winter of discontent and the election of Margaret Thatcher. The magnetic narrative of the emergence of Thatcherism does tend to lure historians and commentators towards 1979 and leads to some neglect of the importance of the Heath governments. But elsewhere there is more of a case for a 'long seventies'. For economic historians, however, there are strong continuities with previous years, and the date of the putative break with 'Keynesianism' is rather less clear; indeed, one might ask whether 'evolution' rather than 'revolution' might be a better term to describe the policy shift. For social and cultural historians, likewise, continuities are as important as change – for example, and most apparently, soccer hooliganism and large-scale industrial conflict, if not punk, were still evident in Thatcher's second term.

Second, how should we deal with the issue of politicisation? A consistent theme has been that memories of the decade have, to quite a large degree, been politically constructed (and continually reinforced) by both right and left. They continue to be so. The role of the media is key here and poorly covered in current literature, but such analysis also confers considerable agency upon the forces of the New Right. The difficulty contemporary historians face is less that of objectively standing apart from such debates than explaining to what extent and how such partial representations have gained the popular currency and traction in national culture that they have.

At the time, the events of the 1970s presented an opportunity for contemporary politicians who profited from portraying the decade in negative terms. Both left and right in the 1970s shared a common sense of crisis, and of the potentialities for change that 'crisis' created. The abiding and pervasive sense of crisis (powerfully evoked in Wheen's recent study) and of political failure continued to be deployed politically in succeeding decades.[2] The enduring image of a benighted Britain in the seventies, a country in thrall to a bankrupt politics and to excessively powerful trade unions, fitted both Thatcherite and Blairite visions of a future that both projects explicitly constructed in opposition to Labour's close identification with that powerful memory, though, of course, for different reasons. As Thatcher battled the unions with a strong state and evoked 'Victorian values', so Blair distanced New Labour from the 'failings' of 'old' Labour in the 1970s, moving to a more arm's-length relationship between the party and the unions, embracing the market and adopting a more inclusive, liberal and individualistic culture. Both Blairites and Thatcherites, it should be noted, also turned their fire on the sixties, often locating in that decade the seeds of the perceived social, economic and political 'failures' of the seventies. Ironically, however, this bleak reading of the 1970s was tacitly supported by the 1960s generation – their good times giving way to bad times, long-haired hippies pursing peace and love replaced by skinheads pursing Pakistanis, introspective progressive rock replaced by the anarchism and activism of punk. It wasn't that sixties trends disappeared so much as they seemed less new, and more fragile. Thus, just as the later 1940s cemented a certain vision of the 1930s, so the 1980s and 1990s fixed a particular vision of the 1970s. This construction of the seventies, and how and why it obtained such purchase, must be grasped before historians can reconstruct a more representative 1970s.

Third, how best can we deal with the problem of economics? Economic problems, economic policies and appraisals of absolute and relative economic performance lie at the heart of the 1970s. To a large degree the political history of the decade turns on its economics, but this is also true of much of the decade's social and cultural history. Historians of all stripes must therefore engage with the decade's economic issues if they are to provide the necessary context for their research. Baldly put, virtually any study of the seventies which fails to begin with its economics will be lacking. We cannot hope to understand the decade's political, social, or cultural issues without it. Plainly, there is ample scope for sub-disciplinary cooperation with economic history. Yet the discipline of economic history is in marked decline, in contrast to more dynamic social science analyses or cultural history.

Fourth, we must confront the need for a comparative perspective. A notable feature of British debate in the 1970s was its profound insularity. One would hardly guess from many of the works published in the 1970s on Britain's economic problems, or the difficulties confronting the state, that these were global issues. Britain's crisis was not unique and 'the seventies' appear as a critical juncture in other national histories too. As several commentators hint in this volume, comparative, trans-national perspectives will also help yield a more representative history.[3] Several recent studies have suggested parallels with, for instance, US experience. The 1970s brought the USA defeat in Vietnam, the Watergate scandal, which corroded the power of the political centre, a buffeting from external bodies like the Organization of the Petroleum Exporting Countries, a bailout of New York City in 1975 and a strong sense of relative failure. If the UK's problem was 'decline', then Carter's was 'malaise' (which, like Callaghan's apocryphal 'Crisis? What crisis?', the US President never actually uttered, but which became forever associated with his infamous 1979 speech). And from the start of the decade commentators on the left no less than the emergent New Right were preoccupied with the nation's deep problems. US historians have tended to see the seventies as an 'in between' decade in which (according to the title of one book) 'It seemed like nothing happened'.[4] But it has recently been the focus of 'a dramatic revival' among historians of the USA, who have looked to mix political, economic and cultural sources, and who have come to regard it as a significant watershed. In particular, they have looked to explain why the political and social legacy of the 1960s proved to be the rise of the right and they contend that the tactics and language of the 1960s (new deal/great society liberalism, grassroots mobilisation, individual and civil rights, and identity politics) were not only assimilated by the right but were mobilised by it. Cowie's study suggests the patriotic and cultural and moral traditionalism of the New Right made effective appeals to industrial workers in the USA.[5] A case is also made for the enduring legacy of sixties radicalism being cultural, in terms of representation, rights and affirmative action, rather than socio-economic.[6]

This relates to similar developments in Britain. As Curran *et al.* have hinted, the primary political cleavages in Britain from the 1970s were cultural (a realm in which the New Right in Britain was less effective and in which one can detect the growing influence of the left and centre left) rather than socio-economic (where neo-liberalism's supplanting of Keynesianism was hegemonic).[7] For example, Thatcherite economics left a lasting legacy in a way in which a desire to reinstate 'Victorian values' did not. Thus the 1970s were not just a bridging point but simultaneously the sequel to the 1960s and the prequel to neo-liberalism, and the decade is thus distinctive and worthy of study.

Whatever the reasons behind the presently rather benighted historiography of Britain in the 1970s, we hope that this volume will encourage more scholars to research this key decade in postwar British history, rather than to continue uncritically to reproduce the hegemonic memories of the decade that continue to pervade British culture.

Notes

1 For example: J. Tomlinson, *The Politics of Decline: Understanding Post-war Britain* (Harlow: Longman, 2000); J. Tomlinson, 'Inventing "decline": the falling

behind of the British economy in the post-war years', *Economic History Review*, 49:4 (1996), pp. 731–57; J. Tomlinson, 'Thrice denied: "declinism" as a recurrent theme in British history in the long twentieth century', *Twentieth Century British History*, 20:2 (2009), pp. 227–51.

2 F. Wheen, *Strange Days Indeed: The Golden Age of Paranoia* (London: Fourth Estate, 2009).

3 See, for example, A. Wirsching (ed.), 'Forum: The 1970s and 1980s as a turning point in European history?', *Journal of Modern European History*, 9:1 (2011), pp. 8–26.

4 I. Kramnick, *Is Britain Dying? Perspectives on the Current Crisis* (Ithaca, NY: Cornell University Press, 1979), p. 45; K. Mattson, *What the Heck Are You Up To, Mr. President? Jimmy Carter, America's 'Malaise' and the Speech That Should Have Changed the Country* (London: Bloomsbury, 2009); C. Maier, '"Malaise": the crisis of capitalism in the 1970s', in N. Ferguson, C. Maier, E. Manela and D. Sargent (eds), *The Shock of the Global: The 1970s in Perspective* (Cambridge, MA: Belknap, 2010), pp. 25–48; P. N. Carroll, *It Seemed Like Nothing Happened: America in the 1970s* (New Brunswick, NJ: Rutgers University Press, 1990); T. Borstelmann, *The 1970s: A New Global History, From Civil Rights to Economic Inequality* (Princeton, NJ: Princeton University Press, 2012).

5 J. Cowie, *Stayin' Alive: The 1970s and the Last Days of the Working Class* (New York: New Press, 2010).

6 B. Schulman and J. E. Zelizer (eds), *Rightward Bound: Making America Conservative in the 1970s* (Cambridge, MA: Harvard University Press, 2008); M. Jacobs and J. E. Zelizer, 'Swinging too far to the left', *Journal of Contemporary History*, 43:4 (2008), pp. 689–93; B. Schulman, 'The empire strikes back – conservative responses to progressive social movements in the 1970s', *Journal of Contemporary History*, 43:4 (2008), pp. 695–700; S. Tuck, '"We are taking up where the movement of the 1960s left off": the proliferation and power of African American protest during the 1970s', *Journal of Contemporary History*, 43:4 (2008), pp. 637–54.

7 J. Curran, I. Gaber and J. Petley, *Culture Wars* (Edinburgh: Edinburgh University Press, 2005).

Index

Lightning Source UK Ltd.
Milton Keynes UK
UKOW04f1040090916

282600UK00010B/348/P